Considerations on Cyber Behavior and Mass Technology in Modern Society

Paolo Beneventi
Independent Researcher, Italy

A volume in the Advances in Human and Social Aspects of Technology (AHSAT) Book Series

Published in the United States of America by
IGI Global
Engineering Science Reference (an imprint of IGI Global)
701 E. Chocolate Avenue
Hershey PA, USA 17033
Tel: 717-533-8845
Fax: 717-533-8661
E-mail: cust@igi-global.com
Web site: http://www.igi-global.com

Library of Congress Cataloging-in-Publication Data

CIP Data in progress

Title: Considerations on Cyber Behavior and Mass Technology in Modern Society

ISBN: 9781668482285

This book is published in the IGI Global book series Advances in Human and Social Aspects of Technology (AHSAT) (ISSN: 2328-1316; eISSN: 2328-1324)

British Cataloguing in Publication Data
A Cataloguing in Publication record for this book is available from the British Library.

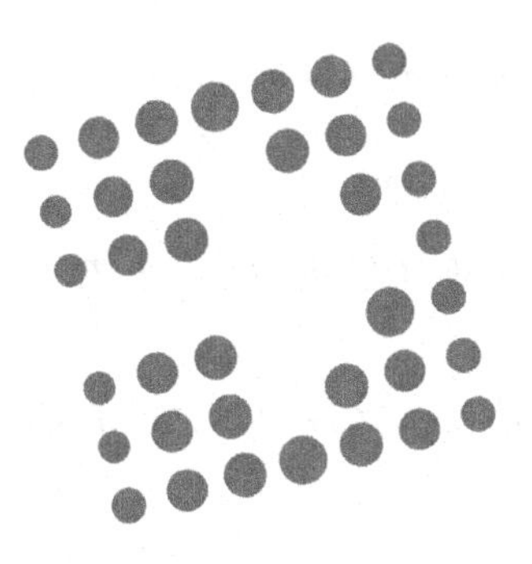

Advances in Human and Social Aspects of Technology (AHSAT) Book Series

Mehdi Khosrow-Pour, D.B.A.
Information Resources Management Association, USA

ISSN:2328-1316
EISSN:2328-1324

Mission

In recent years, the societal impact of technology has been noted as we become increasingly more connected and are presented with more digital tools and devices. With the popularity of digital devices such as cell phones and tablets, it is crucial to consider the implications of our digital dependence and the presence of technology in our everyday lives.

The **Advances in Human and Social Aspects of Technology (AHSAT) Book Series** seeks to explore the ways in which society and human beings have been affected by technology and how the technological revolution has changed the way we conduct our lives as well as our behavior. The AHSAT book series aims to publish the most cutting-edge research on human behavior and interaction with technology and the ways in which the digital age is changing society.

Coverage

- Digital Identity
- Technoself
- Information ethics
- Public Access to ICTs
- Cultural Influence of ICTs
- Technology and Freedom of Speech
- Human-Computer Interaction
- ICTs and human empowerment
- Human Rights and Digitization
- End-User Computing

IGI Global is currently accepting manuscripts for publication within this series. To submit a proposal for a volume in this series, please contact our Acquisition Editors at acquisitions@igi-global.com or visit: https://www.igi-global.com/publish/.

The Advances in Human and Social Aspects of Technology (AHSAT) Book Series (ISSN 2328-1316) is published by IGI Global, 701 E. Chocolate Avenue, Hershey, PA 17033-1240, USA, www.igi-global.com. This series is composed of titles available for purchase individually; each title is edited to be contextually exclusive from any other title within the series. For pricing and ordering information please visit https://www.igi-global.com/book-series/advances-human-social-aspects-technology/37145. Postmaster: Send all address changes to above address.

Titles in this Series

For a list of additional titles in this series, please visit: www.igi-global.com/book-series/advances-human-social-aspects-technology/37145

Adoption and Use of Technology Tools and Services by Economically Disadvantaged Communities Implications for Growth and Sustainability
Alice S. Etim (Winston-Salem State University, USA)
Information Science Reference • copyright 2024 • 383pp • H/C (ISBN: 9781668453476) • US $225.00 (our price)

Philosophy of Artificial Intelligence and Its Place in Society
Luiz Moutinho (University of Suffolk, UK) Luís Cavique (Universidade Aberta, Portugal) and Enrique Bigné (Universitat de València, Spain)
Engineering Science Reference • copyright 2023 • 439pp • H/C (ISBN: 9781668495919) • US $215.00 (our price)

Cyberfeminism and Gender Violence in Social Media
Deepanjali Mishra (KIIT University, India)
Information Science Reference • copyright 2023 • 442pp • H/C (ISBN: 9781668488935) • US $215.00 (our price)

Investigating the Impact of AI on Ethics and Spirituality
Swati Chakraborty (GLA University, India & Concordia University, Canada)
Information Science Reference • copyright 2023 • 230pp • H/C (ISBN: 9781668491966) • US $225.00 (our price)

Applied Research Approaches to Technology, Healthcare, and Business
Darrell Norman Burrell (Marymount University, USA)
Information Science Reference • copyright 2023 • 455pp • H/C (ISBN: 9798369316306) • US $285.00 (our price)

Analyzing New Forms of Social Disorders in Modern Virtual Environments
Milica Boskovic (Faculty of Diplomacy and Security, University Union Nikola Tesla, Serbia) Gordana Misev (Ministry of Mining and Energy Republic of Serbia, Serbia) and Nenad Putnik (Faculty of Security Studies, University of Belgrade, Serbia)
Information Science Reference • copyright 2023 • 284pp • H/C (ISBN: 9781668457603) • US $225.00 (our price)

Advances in Cyberology and the Advent of the Next-Gen Information Revolution
Mohd Shahid Husain (College of Applied Sciences, University of Technology and Applied Sciences, Oman) Mohammad Faisal (Integral University, Lucknow, India) Halima Sadia (Integral University, Lucknow, India) Tasneem Ahmad (Advanced Computing Research Lab, Integral University, Lucknow, India) and Saurabh Shukla (Data Science Institute, National University of Ireland, Galway, Ireland)
Information Science Reference • copyright 2023 • 271pp • H/C (ISBN: 9781668481332) • US $215.00 (our price)

701 East Chocolate Avenue, Hershey, PA 17033, USA
Tel: 717-533-8845 x100 • Fax: 717-533-8661
E-Mail: cust@igi-global.com • www.igi-global.com

Table of Contents

Preface

This book is on technology and society. Countless studies exist, as well as articles and reports in the press and mass media, conversations, and examples on social networks. But above all technology today is in everyday life of all, regardless of age, level of education, social status. It had never happened in history, as it probably had never happened that the technology was handled in majority by people who basically do not know how to use it properly.

Everyone buys and consumes technology, hardware and software, and companies that deal with virtual environments often do more business on the earth than those who produce energy, food, machines.

Faced with this contradictory situation, research addresses limited and unlinked areas, a mass education lacks adjusted to the dissemination of the media, and ultimately much of the ideas of the citizens of the global information society are based on clichés, which last changeless over the years in a world that we constantly tell ourselves is changing so rapidly.

It is not a matter of digital skills, of being able keep up with the times, of young and old generations. Since every aspect of human life is increasingly linked to the use of technology, it is a matter of human relations, politics, and economics, safeguarding the health of the planet, peace and war, life and death. And perhaps it is missing, in the time of permanent connections of everyone to everything and nothing, just the ability to connect the different elements of the extremely complex reality in which we live, so as to see also beyond the latest market trends, or the particular ideas on which groups and individuals often seem to build their own identity, in a general climate of individualism and narcissism that prevents us from practicing that natural solution to the problems of the world that could be, finally, learning to work together.

In times when we all feel very small in the face of the supranational power of finance and technological companies, we may begin to wonder how it was possible, for example, that the probably largest monopoly in history, as it was Microsoft in the 1990s, was forced to change its strategies by grassroots, non-profit, spontaneous movement, as it was the original World Wide Web. And something so had happened also to IBM, between the 1970s and 1980s, with the invention of the personal computer, upsetting the current market laws and IT development forecasts based on centralized big computer networks and terminals.

We live in the paradox of thinking about a reality that changes in a whirlwind way according to rigid and immutable rules, when the development of technology itself should suggest a wide range of possible alternatives.

What multiple viewpoints to tackle such a complex and literally global subject?

No one today can write the book of books about humans and technology. But put together a text with the intention of inserting it as a small brick inside an extremely larger building, to be built all together, that is probably what one can try to do, what many should try to do, with an overall look at the history, the real dynamics, the possible perspectives, beyond the flat description of what everyone sees from his porthole.

The starting point here are not the codified disciplines, nor the technology as proposed by the technicians, or by the market, but precisely the relationships between people, hardware and software, considering many and various examples and situations, which cannot understand and explain the whole, but may open the minds to a better comprehension of the system in which we leave, with comfort and uneasiness, opportunities and contradictions, and above all considering that, before consumers, producers, citizens more or less digital, we are human beings, with their stories, culture, basic and induced needs and desires.

The target of this book is a potentially general audience, giving the academic world the references due for a scientific point of view, but telling everybody a "story" easy to be understood and possibly interesting and useful to orient not only thought, but action, behavior. Many academic works are only for experts, in which quotations overlap content, and in general there is a huge gap between the completeness of studies and research on every topic of human knowledge that we can access in university libraries, and the littleness of the contents that are passed in the end to the public opinion, and that, however, are those which often orient the political and economic choices in the world with sometimes dramatic results, deriving from ignorance and prejudice.

Today we need not only to watch and describe reality, but to understand better how to move in it, especially in times when the global systems of billions of interactions across the Internet and social networks potentially transforms every intervention, thought, image we publish in the butterfly that flapping its wings can cause a hurricane somewhere in the planet.

Here the author tries to organize his thinking and reflections into a speech beyond the dramatic fragmentation of posts, tweets, likes, headlines with which in a nutshell we often try to synthesize a world that risks becoming increasingly unlivable, if we give up trying to understand it. And intelligence, artificial why not, but especially human intelligence, it is the mean we have to avoid being overwhelmed by stereotypes and emotions and finally act as active and conscious citizens, more responsible but in the end probably a little happier than we usually are.

"Considerations" means that it's not a systematic and finished discourse, a treaty trying to close the discussion on a matter. On the contrary, they are reflections that are still looking for their own order and that, however, in their incompleteness want to be a stimulus to action. Today's world can not only be described, because every description, every post, every tweet, even if in small part, they modify it.

Chapter 1. Technology and Uneasiness in the Globalized Planet: Wasted Widespread Power in Digital Screens

Discomfort goes through the digital age. Overdose of information, easy and automated solutions for work and leisure come from the screens, but opportunities are mainly wasted in stereotypes.

Chapter 2. Unaware Producers of Information in a World of Narrative: People and Their Lives, as It Is and As It's Told

The children and grandchildren of Television live on narratives. Dreams and nightmares of passive users that depend on the active and interactive new technologies but have not learned to handle them.

Chapter 3. The Intangible Power of New Machines in the Hands of Anyone: Expertise, Illiteracy, Control

Behind the friendly interfaces, complex and very powerful systems are distributed worldwide as market products, but since their birth they have inside and have shown the possibility to help people to go beyond the old division between producers and consumers.

Chapter 4. Senses, Thought, Connections, and Disconnections of a Divided Experience: Broken Communities in Social Networks

Non-stop connected as others decide, using devices that they know little, the inhabitants of the planet live a significant part of their existence and emotions far from their senses, in virtual worlds, and then they do not have an ESC key going back to their real lives.

Chapter 5. The Spirit of the Information Society, Technologies, and Citizens: Consumers, Hackers, the Shipwrecked of the Web

A huge misunderstanding in education. Digital systems, totally new, are taught to the masses according to the old patterns of transmitting knowledge. And people approach hi-tech environments imagining their future according to what they know from science fiction.

Chapter 6. Technique and Behaviors, Trendy, Useful, Correct: From Unified Procedures to Unified Thinking?

Resigned to a technology that they do not control, in their forced path to the future, the citizens of the information society are worried for security and rely on many small, big brothers who guide them, even in politically correct behaviors, thoughts and opinions.

Chapter 7. Children and the Clothes of the Digital Emperor: The Ball, the Doll, the Smartphone, the Animals...

When they are free to act, together, in a nurturing environment, kids can be the teachers, showing how it is possible to deal in harmony with body, nature, toys, hi-tech devices: against the fear, just playing.

Chapter 8. Body, Nature, Machines, a Feasible, Necessary Balance: Real and Virtual From Market to Experience

Going back to life is possible, from market to experience, trying to preserve bio and software diversity, in living and thinking environments.

Chapter 9. Inside and Outside Devices, the Software, and the World: Humans Can Search, Know, Invent

Not necessarily in the hands of global companies, through the immense availability of software, the way to the "digital" can be open, traced also by common people, doing things themselves, together.

Chapter 10. Active Citizens in a New Communication Society: WWW, Back to the Future! Examples to Aware Projects

A new "operating system" for human social interactions? Communities, free movements, companies, but above all aware citizens can take from technology the power to move from the information society to the communication society, facing the global challenges of the planet.

In a strongly interconnected world, academic studies, such as people's empirical observations on social networks, often stop at individual aspects of reality and what is missing is the ability to connect facts with each other, to identify the network of relationships. Which is far from easy to be traced. But we must try, also knowing that today, precisely because of the billions of interconnections chasing one another across the planet, there is no description that is not also action on reality, aware or not, and we don't know if its effect will be infinitesimal or, commented and retweeted endlessly, it will become viral.

There is nothing automatic or final in today's world, much less driven by technology, and the aim of this book is to call people to responsibility, possibly showing some possible ways, starting from knowledge and reflection on things, beyond the patina of ideology sometimes invisible but always present that surrounds them. There is a world, which without the presence of active citizens, as we today are not, is seriously jeopardizing its own future and in which the different elements cannot be separated, as if the way we consume technology was something separate from how we can't fight climate change or avoid wars.

This would like to be a book of connections and responsibilities.

They are challenging times on the earth.

As the author is writing this book, the world is not yet completely out of the crisis of Covid 19, and nobody knows how long the war in Ukraine could last. And there are perhaps a couple of decades to stop an increasingly probable climate catastrophe considering that, since the alarm was sounded several decades ago, very little has been done in the meantime to prevent it. Living in Italy and being not so young, the author saw other difficult times, as in the 70s of the last century, the red brigades and the so-called "years of lead", the bombs of neo-fascist terrorism, but today things appear possibly much sadder. To put it with a slogan: in those times people had not denied themselves hope.

Right from the seventies, after the youth revolt movements of the beat generation, hippies, 68 and feminism had tried to change things and took their course, probably having not the power to break deeply the information society, globally dominated by the fourth and fifth powers of press, radio and television, something absolutely new happened. From technological development, devices were made available that literally put information in the hands of anyone. With video recording and personal computers, the production of information was accessible to all, and then with the web and mobile devices also its distribution: not exactly a sixth power, but potentially the end of any power, the ultimate democratization of information.

It hasn't happened! Given without instructions for use to billions of people with a low literacy and high television attendance, not used to active citizenship but only to sell and buy, technology over the decades has reduced its impact on societies to doing substantially the same things as before, but in another way, without touching the previous powers, without extending participation in public life. And democracy, while we were losing this enormous opportunity to develop it, has rather lost ground on the planet, with the increasing rise of authoritarian regimes and "strong" leaders, conflicts, and wars.

Uneasiness is maybe the word that most summarizes the situation of the average inhabitants of the planet, in the present "digital" age. Perpetually connected to the rest of the world, they don't really think that they can be actors of anything and vent their anxiety crowding social networks. They upload photographs and videos, write comments on everything happens in the world, but as if at the window and resigned not to be able to take part directly. So, fight, insults against people who think otherwise, while forms of free expression also artistic, poetic, they mostly last in the short time of collecting some likes and then are destined to sink into the immense ocean of a global network that preserves everything but seems to remember nothing.

The keynote appears to be the almost absolute *uselessness* of the whole, the zero impact on the lived reality, apart from the few cases of those who become "influencers" and even manage to make money. While the success built on nothing becomes a social parameter, it is watched by many as the unlikely profession of the future. Uneasiness!

Commenting on human behavior in this world heavily marked by technology, even many people of culture are in difficulty, probably because it is not easy to understand the transition from a time of given knowledge and essentially hardware technology on which the industrial society was based until the final years of the last century, and the more and more changing knowledge and software technology of today. Moreover, their qualification is mostly based on a preparation if not temporally, conceptually preceding the change, and many categories of thinking not only humanistic but also scientific do not appear fully adequate. The result is that many seem to observe and describe reality as if it were not up to them, as if they were observing from outside. That is what this book would like not to be.

The author comes from liberal arts and educational studies and at a certain point began to work with children, not as a teacher, but as an external expert, helping educators to observe and stimulate kids' play, bodily activities, free expression, interdisciplinary and multimedia. It was the time when communication technologies became available and he started playing with them too, as well as with theatrical expression, storytelling, observation, and immersion in nature. Some "oppositions", hard for many adults to reconcile, such as that between machines and body, nature, and technology, while working with children turned out to be a total nonsense.

Regarding new technologies, being precisely *new*, there could not be rules, courses of study, certifications stating how they could apply to this or that play or activity. But there were the responses of the children who, in a proper educational environment, do not lie. They find their confidence in the relationship with adults who take care of them and listen to them, after which, due to their age, they are not still much affected by previous cultural patterns. They play freely, search, experiment as small scientists and, when they can act in group, with an educator who guarantees compliance with the rules of the game, they naturally cooperate and easily find the right solutions together, as a single child alone couldn't.

So, they can also show to the adults how to go beyond the limited horizons of codified disciplines, of stereotypical observation points, of cold laboratory procedures.

For example, what happens when children watch and comment commercials on TV *together*, or play on a PC with a sound processing software exploring and finding functions on their own, or begin to think in group about a series of macro photos of insects or even catch their pictures live, magnified by the lens of a camera? Children in group, that naturally interact, suggest and stimulate each other, sometimes find solutions that no teacher could teach, and naturally go more ahead the supposed features and limitations of the media.

Observing the same dynamics that are repeated ten, a hundred, infinite times, with the regularity of thorough scientific tests, learning from children and comparing their freshness with the babble of so much culture in front of the so-called new media, the old phrase returns tremendously topical: "Unless you change and become like little children, you will never enter the kingdom of heaven!" (Matthew 18:3).

In times when "everything changes", the old academic structures that certify, validate, establish according to the old rules what is right and what is not, cannot be the only authority anymore. Probably it is about redesigning the disciplines, or maybe even learning to build a knowledge that, at least up to a certain level, develops also outside the disciplines traditionally intended, by horizontal information, instantaneous interactions on networks, unusual possibilities of exchange, sharing, endless verification. And when and how knowledge match the reality, it is to be seen also somewhere else from traditional laboratory tests or philosophical speculations.

The "new academy" proposed by the hacker ethics can be strange in some respects, but certainly it is inside the technological revolution much more than the awkward reactions of those who cannot agree the books they have read with the television they have seen and claim to explain the "digital".

In these chapters the author starts from the uneasiness of humans struggling with new technologies and looks at behaviors induced in society by their more or less appropriate use. He tries to distinguish between technology, market, ideology, objective difficulties, attitudes, real changes, and appearances. He tries to see the problems, but also the possible solutions by thinking about them and considering various and different opinions, coming from the academic field, the information world, ordinary people, and children. The research attempts to use means and criteria appropriate to the technological change taking place, retaining the focus above all on people.

The author does not write pretending he can stay out of the fray. Trying to maintain the maximum scientific rigor, to get as close as possible to the "truth" and never to be partisan, his intent is also political: for active citizenship, democracy, freedom, social justice, against war and ignorance, against an uncontrolled development aimed only at profit, for a fair and supportive economy, respectful of humans and the planet. The world in the end is like humans want it to be.

To say it with a slogan, it is a matter of moving, as technology makes quite possible today, from the information to the communication society: communication among conscious and responsible citizens, all across the planet.

Paolo Beneventi
Independent Researcher, Italy

Chapter 1
Technology and Uneasiness in the Globalized Planet:
Wasted Widespread Power in Digital Screens

ABSTRACT

Where is the world going? On the way of the technological wonders of the "metaverse" or towards climate and environmental catastrophes, widespread wars, forced mass migrations, continuous economic crises? The same people using the latest generation of digital machines in non-stop connection with all the planet are often not at ease, worried and stressed about jobs, violence, difficulties in communicating with one another. For any big or little problems, if they don't have an app that solves it for them, they are more and more accustomed not to look for solutions but to take sides, humans against humans, divided between the virtually unlimited possibilities of the available technology and the stereotypes of a consumerism that shapes their existences according to the convenience of the market. Screens are mirrors and shields, but people maybe feel like they waste a huge amount of power in their hands, and uneasiness runs deeply through societies. This chapter explores technology and uneasiness in the globalized planet.

1. INTRODUCTION

In the early decades of the 2000s, people live immersed in technology, that makes many aspects of their lives more fun and easier, but they do not seem to be happier than before. There are many problems in the world, economy, wars, climate change, but one of the causes of widespread malaise must probably be sought precisely in an inappropriate use of technology. Often, we do not use digital media, but we are like "used" by them, that is, we adapt our behavior to certain stereotypes related to the handling of devices.

We have to deal with a technological insecurity, with a wealth of goods and commodities that – as described by Ivan Illich yet in the 80s – often results in a modern poverty, where our action is no longer free and autonomous, but plugged into market relations. The history of mass computing is marked by

DOI: 10.4018/978-1-6684-8228-5.ch001

several misunderstandings, which have not allowed for the mass of users an adequate literacy. And now science fiction scenarios open up, with artificial intelligence and metaverse, for people who have largely so far barely been able to write texts and upload photos in social networks.

Virtual reality and artificial intelligence have a long history, but today they seem to have reached such levels, that they can really enter with arrogance into our daily lives. If we are in front of an unavoidable step in technological evolution or of a commercial operation is the subject of discussion. Certainly, the simulated worlds, increasingly realistic and convincing that for decades we have been imagining in fictions and experimenting in video games, they are now for many children and adults a virtual place not only interesting and fun, but working according to precise and consistent rules that are often difficult to find in the real world. But without an adequate awareness, relying too much on artificial environments and intelligence could be a gamble.

It is not only a problem for the mental health of individuals. In the rush to continually chase the news without having understood what was before, we are wasting in fact most of the opportunities technology offers, adapting ourselves to stereotypes, and this also dangerously affect social relations and the economy, as happened around the year 2000 with the "dotcom bubble".

Little aware of the real possibilities of the devices we hold in our hands, we often use them as a shield to protect us from real or supposed external dangers and as a mirror to convert the whole world into a smug, uninterrupted selfie.

2. STRESSFUL TIMES IN THE DIGITAL ERA

We are immersed every day in an annoying background noise ... Man, in essence, has closed his eyes to his past and has lost sight of the present; he lets himself be pushed by foreign winds towards a future that is not his own and that will make him increasingly foreign to his own nature ... The institutionalized training system ... does not favor the evolutionary process of a living species, but a race to regress due to an anonymous arid bureaucratism, irresponsible and disempowering. The malaise of our time is the cry that invites us to stop occupying time and rather go back to living it. (Serafini, 2021, translated from Italian)

Certainly it is not the perception of all and it cannot be generalized, but a sense of malaise runs through our societies as probably in a few other moments of history, also for the succession of dramatic global events, that add up to a great deal of dramatic local ones and increase a general sense of insecurity: the pandemic has broken out in 2020, the war in Ukraine in 2023, the Israeli - Palestinian latest tragedy in October 2023. It is striking to hear, in an official meeting between heads of state, the President of the Italian Republic speaking to his Finnish counterpart literally saying: "The world has changed for the worse!" (Stefanoni, 2023)

They are not just the big political and economic facts. It also weighs across civil society a nagging culture of competence, performance, that puts so often people against one another, in the mass media, the social networks, the daily life of many. And some categories suffer in particular.

While adults dabble, perform on TV and on social media, play the part of influencers aiming to direct their behaviors and consumption, as young people would be nothing more than citrus fruits to squeeze, many of them, young people, get sick and die. The Istat 2021 data - reported in the two pages of Andrea

Casadio on "Domani" (8/3), title: "The La society of performance" - impress: "The boys between 14 and 19 years old who declare themselves unhappy and who claim to suffer from some psychological malaises are 220 thousand. Every day, in Italy a young man takes his own life. This phenomenon is common to almost all the countries of the world". (Folena, 2023 translated from Italian)

And on the World Day of Mental Health, the results are published of a research entitled "The Age of Discomfort" (L'era del disagio psicologico, 2023).

It may be that in countries more than in others the problem is felt in a particular way:

Here comes the bonus psychologist. An incentive to combat stress, anxiety, and depression of Italians ... 31% of the population over the age of 18 lives a situation of psychological stress. Percentage that rises to 50% under the age of 18. Hardship linked to lockdown and socio-economic impoverishment of the population. (Cottone, 2022, translated from Italian)

But the causes are certainly much more general, in all the world, and not only affect individuals:

From protective social structures and the liberalization of almost all social areas, there has been a fundamental shift in socio-structural boundaries. As a result of this structural change, the individual psychodynamics of all members of our society have changed from "What can I do?" to "What am I able to do?". This is expressed by Ehrenberg in a massive increase in depressions and borderline personality disorders as well as—in reaction—in a change of psychoanalytical theory and treatment technique. (Sandner, 2022)

Among the changes that have occurred worldwide in recent decades, one of the most important has been the rapid and massive introduction of technology into everyday life. And a question can be why, if thanks to a constant use of hardware and software, today we can do many more things, much easier and faster, this is accompanied by a greater spread of discomfort. Are we more insecure and depressed despite the technology - for a series of causes of other nature - or maybe it is the technology itself that, while it gives us so much, takes something vital from our life?

What has led to today's insecurity? The big drivers of insecurity are globalisation and technology. They have shifted low skilled jobs and now even middle income jobs offshore, created intense competition, change and uncertainty. They give great power to large corporations, while undermining the power of states and of organised labour. Crucially, they have also changed the nature of politics. (Sweeney, 2015)

Technology is not only making life easier for businesses, but it is also increasing job insecurity among employees. This has also made workers stressed out and hurt their mental health. (Ghani et al., 2022)

Technological insecurity refers to the feeling of job insecurity due to the continuous introduction of new technologies. Individuals who perceive technological insecurity are likely to suffer from lower levels of individual performance, because individuals invest their personal and job resources to keep up with the rapid technological changes, rather than to deliver high levels of individual performance. (Jungst, 2022)

Also, the mentality generated by CBSs (computer business systems), widely "promises to the population rapid, ready-made, pre-existent solutions." Many apply these solutions also to their own lives and health when they try to solve problems with "the ingestion of medication that will be immediately effective" (Bollas, 2018).

There are many aspects to the problem, and it is important not to overestimate some of them, drawing conclusions from a limited point of view, not just recording situations and behaviors, but trying to understand why they occur, what may be behind them. When individuals conform to the group, in work, friendships, real or virtual attendance, even if they feel not at ease, not by choice but because "it must" do so. When handling everyday smartphones to take bad photos and videos, many do not establish a relationship at all with the television and the movies they watch, although they have devices capable of professional quality pictures. When after several updating courses on PCs along the years, still in schools a lot of teachers need to ask someone else what they "must" do with machines and software.

Patterns are everywhere and people are accustomed not to seeing beyond them, not to seeing, in the time of all and always connected, the connections between areas even not far of the experience and knowledge. And it is probably the simplest solution, when the world around seems to change swirling in ways difficult to understand, for many to let themselves go with the stream. But in this way, it is also easy by that stream in the end to be overwhelmed.

3. TECHNOLOGY, INFORMATION, THE GROUP AND MODERN POVERTIES

Two scenes about human expectations from technology.

1983, a film, *War Games*. A boy, after connecting by modem and phone lines - nothing to do with the Web, that will start only in 1991 - with his PC to a system that does not identify itself, asks for games online like chess, backgammon, poker, and for fun writes also "Global Thermonuclear War". He doesn't know that on the other side there is secret military program that can automatically launch atomic bombs on preset targets…

2020s, a commercial on TV. A group of young people at the end of the day are gathered and they do not know what to do. One takes his smartphone and with a smart software orders a pizza...

A strange fact happens. After decades of interactive technology and mighty means for producing information in the hands of all, most people still seem to perceive technology and the future according to models born in the 50s: a centralized, authoritarian world, on the dark side, where the only hope is the help from superheroes. Or, on the optimistic side, a society where everything is automatic and humans just have to press a button to get everything they need, like in the Jetsons' cartoons.

Jetson' people have got an app for everything, so that when some problem occurs with other real people and no app can give the solution, a frequent behavior is to choose as in a market between ideas, positions, attitudes available, and take side with this or that, avoiding thinking, deepening, searching for independent elaborations. Which also becomes the way to automatically frame the others, on social networks and in daily reality, discussing sport, politics, religion, economy, environment, ways of life: from a single word, we are often labeled as right or left winged, for or against the death penalty, abortion, hunting, vaccinations.

This has always happened in the history of humanity, but it is curious how it continues to happen today, even more, in a world that we say is changing faster and faster and where an incredible amount of information could allow modern citizens not to face life only by headlines.

Figure 1. Information overload
Source: Clark (2020)

Probably it is just because the most are unable to manage the non-stop overdose of information, that so many people appear to conform their ideas and life to easy shortcuts, according to the opinion group, the work team, the community. Easy and automatic solutions are sought not only in mobile apps, but also in public life. when establishing, for example, quotas for women in elections (see ex: Rosen, 2017), or applying gender corrections to the languages (see ex: D'Achille, 2021), or stating that someone can't talk about a topic without having the right qualification, regardless of the validity of what he or she says… Technical and absolute criteria, responsibility-free choices, by people accustomed to go with the stream, whose favorite keyword seems to be *adapting*.

Even in front of important social problems that move emotional reactions, such as violence against children, or war crimes that make so much audience on TV. So, if we automatically associate "sex with minor" with the word "pedophilia", it can happen that the cases are considered in the same way of children of a few years and of teenagers of 16 or 17. And the massacres of innocent people for which we are indignant are only those committed by the opposite side. It seems as we were always behaving as in a market, supporting the favorite brand, buying that trendy shoe or mobile phone, with everything.

But, of course, these considerations themselves could be emotional and in turn be a shortcut. So, it's better to try to broaden the discourse, to look at things a little further away.

At the dawn of globalization, Ivan Illich wrote about "modern poverties", which "deprives those affected by it of their freedom and power to act autonomously, to live creatively; it confines them to survival through being plugged into market relations" (Illich, 1978).

In that time, personal computers had just been invented and the Web and smartphones were still far to come, but the situation described in a few words seems to represent well the present time. From this perspective, the core of the question is not the quality or power of the inventions, not technology, but precisely market relationships, and that would explain many things.

Technological products are symbols, are often considered for what they represent more than for what they are in fact.

You are definitely not 'cool' if you don't have the latest technology in cell phones, one or more iPads, and an e-book reader ... Even the government is pushing for the standard use of e-books instead of printed textbooks. In business and school, your status suffers if you do not have a 4G phone with Bluetooth and unlimited calling and text. (James Anthos, quoted in Modern Technology as a Status Symbol, 2016)

Confusion is increased by the fact that many devices are put on the market at such a speed that most people literally do not have the time not only to learn to use them, but often even to know of their existence. And innovations in the direction of "digital citizenship", proposed or imposed by service providers or public administration, many times they appear not to leave the people free of choosing. Change and evolution seem to be not according to real feedback from the users for whom they are intended, but to their own, distant, unknowable criteria that people must follow, in the end. And if the minds of sellers and bureaucrats are not always suited to designing efficient and rational algorithms that make the most of the possibilities offered by the new digital media, it is just because of sellers and bureaucrats, many times, not of programmers, engineers, and designers, that "technology" develop in some direction more than in another.

Bewildered by a rapid change not easy to understand, many people feel inadequate, as if it were their fault, though only in part the problem is the lack of technical expertise of the individuals, but often just the inappropriate way in which "change" is proposed.

Unease! No school has prepared the citizens of the present for all this, and they search for a haven and security in vain, in a world where the only way probably would be learning to navigate constantly in open sea. Which could also be nice and interesting.

4. THE MISUNDERSTANDING OF "BASIC" COMPETENCES ON DIGITAL DEVICES

I thought digital skills and digital literacy were the same concept until I took a course on teaching with social media. (Baptiste, 2019)

Digital skills focus on what and how. Digital literacy focuses on why, when, who, and for whom. (Bali, 2016)

A problem, during almost 50 years, it has been a general lack of understanding of the novelty of digital machines whose use, based on software rather than hardware, require a different learning and approach from all the other machines that man has used throughout history. We will see this better in the following chapters, particularly in 5, but in this introductory part we place the emphasis on a fundamental misunderstanding because of which to date, few are the users who have a sufficient basic knowledge of how these devices work. Even when we have them in hand many hours a day. Even those who have attended along the years several courses and lessons on the use of PCs that, according to a vision so to speak "evolutionary" of the necessary skills, were mostly based on the study of office software, the first to be widely used and for this considered "essential", also because in the hand of the most powerful software house in the world.

But to learn to "use the computer" from the office software is not automatic, especially if you do not work in an office! And not always the things that come first are the "basis" of what comes next.

Several years ago, for example, when it was normal to photograph in black and white, many people thought in good faith that B&W was the most "natural" way of taking pictures. But just thinking about

Figure 2. Digital literacy (developing digital literacy skills)
Source: Baptiste (2019)

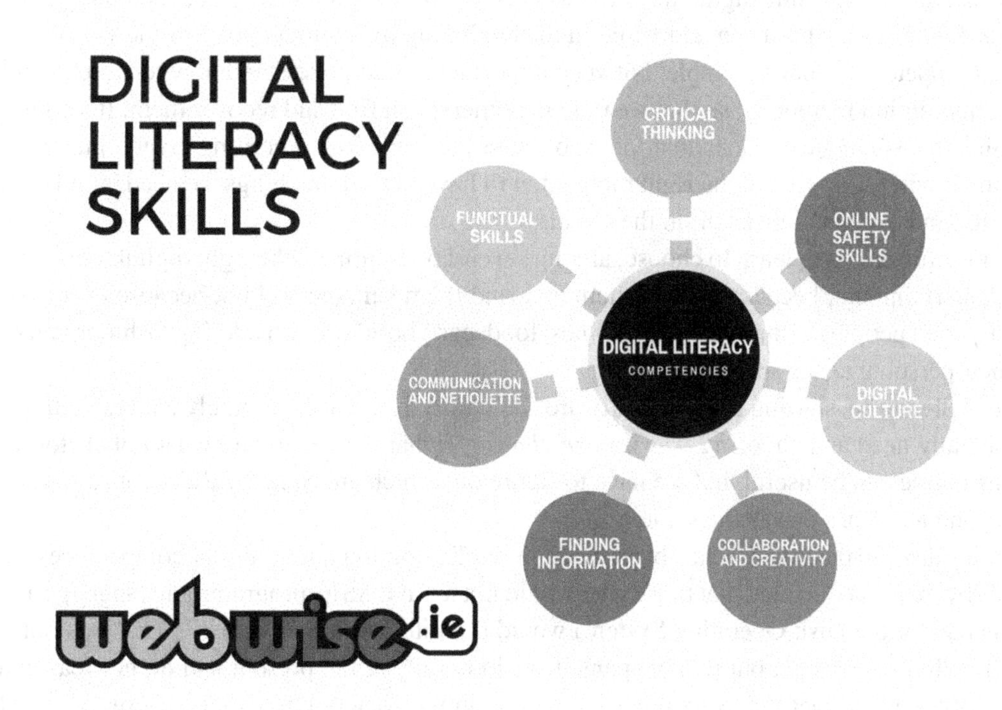

it for a moment, it is evident, since the humans see the world in color, that color photography, cinema, and television are much more natural, although for technical reasons they arrived later.

Somethings so happens with personal computers. At the beginning they were difficult, awkward, and good only for computing and office. Since computing is obviously only for mathematicians and programmers, the office software was placed at the basis of the instructions for use. But from the 1990 PCs are above all multimedia machines, so that probably their most "natural" use is for pictures and music. Why keep thinking that learning a spreadsheet or a data base is more "basic" than processing a photograph or a voice?

Basic is something that if you don't know you can't use the tool. Or something that allows you to apply to the tool very similar procedures to those you already knew before, in everyday life.

So, writing a code cannot be a basic thing. Pointing and pressing an icon with a finger, a mouse, or a paw yes, as anyone can do it and indeed does, even a cat.

If not for specific jobs when in the office, company or factory people must use just that software, asking to others what "basic" programs are to be used on computers is a nonsense, makes the tools far away and alien, prevents them from becoming an extension of our senses and abilities. That's what has happened to so many people, in all these years, who even after a lot of instruction have badly learned to read and write emails!

In order not to leave this speech in the middle, and without claiming to say a definitive word, we try here to compile a small list of skills that we consider "basic", suggested by experience and reasoning.

First, we should have clear in mind that computers and smartphones are not *to be used* in a certain way, because their uses are unlimited, depending on software and on the interests and jobs of users. It is to know that all that is inside digital devices has been put once by humans, data, and coding, and also any *Artificial Intelligence* has been addressed in the beginning by a human point of view.

A basic competence – not so simple, but very important – is to understand how to store documents of any sort into digital memories, so that we (and the others) can find and recover them. It's completely crazy to think that someone else can do it for us, because they will do it according to their intentions and not ours, and it will be us who, at the right moment, will have to find the things we need, amid terabytes of data of all kinds, on local disks or on the cloud.

Another useful skill is to learn to choose, among several possibilities, the right digital tools for work, creativity, entertainment, because we like them and find them suitable and not because everyone uses them. That's what people normally do with clothes, food, cars, holidays, considering fashions and trends, but also their personal tastes and interests.

A basic skill may be, starting from the software and hardware we use, gradually understanding better what we actually need and choosing – as *we can choose* – what to deepen and what not. Tutorials and instructions online can be useful, but we have to figure out which are right for us, because we don't all see, understand and learn things the same way.

Since the years 1980 confusion has been made in public opinion about digital competences, stating for example by many, at the time, that those who would not learn BASIC programming language and Dos (the commands for the Disk Operating System) would be illiterate in the "future"! That was nonsense, we knew it well already then, but this happens if we look only at the present and do not reason about things, or if we leave in fact the technological training, in the society but also in school, practically in the hands of the market, that obviously looks at the business of the moment.

The final (temporary final!) result is that, until today, a lot of people still don't know well what they can do with a PC or a mobile phone, don't know how to do a decent search on the Internet, and the basic "expertise" seems increasingly reduced to downloading an app for everything.

5. FROM ILLITERACY DIRECTLY TO THE METAVERSE?

To a public of users for the most part substantially not at ease with the "digital" and made increasingly illiterate by attending social networks to participate in which skills are practically not required, neither digital nor traditional, and relying on single-use apps, the most recent solutions proposed, in the year 2023, are Artificial Intelligence and "metaverse". If there were no major investments and commercial campaigns at world level, you would think it's a joke, even a mockery.

The narrative is strong:

Daniel Kwan, an American millennial film director, and his partner, Daniel Scheinert, have just won the Oscar for Best Picture for their 2022 movie 'Everything Everywhere All At Once'. In an interview last year, Kwan expressed his idea of creating a multiverse movie that delves deep into the concept of infinite universes while also having a meaningful backstory. Although the film has received three Oscar awards, the business of the metaverse is not scaling up at the same pace. (Roales, 2023)

TV commercials show us the use, productive indeed and impressive, of virtual environments for training in important jobs, such as flying an airplane or performing complex surgical operations. But what relationship can there be between this and the commercial proposals of the metaverse as the social network of the future in which, instead of exchanging verbal messages and images, we will meet as avatars that operate in a virtual universe, it is not easy to imagine.

Once a niche concept beloved of tech enthusiasts, the idea of a centralized virtual world, a "place" parallel to the physical world, has careened into the mainstream landscape this year, as epitomized by Facebook's decision in October to rebrand as Meta. Millions of people are spending hours a day in virtual social spaces like Roblox and Fortnite ... Whether in virtual reality (VR), augmented reality (AR) or simply on a screen, the promise of the metaverse is to allow a greater overlap of our digital and physical lives in wealth, socialization, productivity, shopping and entertainment ... the most exciting part of the metaverse is what it might mean for our relationships. The idea that we might be able to "feel like we're together when we're not" ... could likely lead someone to create a company on par with Facebook and Apple. (Clark, 2021)

Some authors are very optimistic about metaverse. But really people need VR and AR to feel like together, really could they feel so, after having for decades underused the web, blogs, chats, home-made CDs and DVDs? What people are we talking about? Visionaries who since the 70s of the last century were able to imagine the digital revolution starting from machines that today we would consider ridiculous? Or conformist and passive consumers who today need to find online even the phrases to quarrel with their partners, under-using machines whose power to those pioneers of the 70s would have seemed immeasurable?

It is more than 40 years that the technological elites go on imagining a future for all, but in fact, among the billion people dealing with digital devices, very few follow them, and when some certain popularizes describe the humanity's entry into fantastic worlds, in the end what the most have learned to do is writing tweets, uploading some photos, or pushing buttons that as for magic turn our faces into cartoon characters or change them from sad to smiling. Wow! But yet if asked to participate in a discussion on a blog or a videoconference to which they are not obliged, most withdraw. Why with the metaverse it should be different?

Nearly half of these expert respondents said much-more-immersive virtual settings will not have significantly broader influence in people's daily lives by 2040. Some said the buzz about extended reality (XR) is mostly what one called "typical tech hype.

Mark Nottingham, senior principal engineer at Fastly and a longtime leader in the Internet Engineering Task Force with expertise in internet and web standards, commented, "The 'metaverse' is a marketing confection with no basis in reality as of yet. Its proponents are focused on capturing a future market, not building new shared space without any single owner. There are no current efforts at interoperability, common standards, open governance or any other sign of creating what is being marketed. (Anderson & Rainie, 2022)

By the way, it's no bad to remember that Virtual Reality is a quite old thing and consumer headsets for low-cost computers are on the market since 1990.

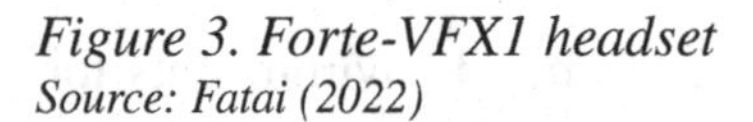

Figure 3. Forte-VFX1 headset
Source: Fatai (2022)

The 90s opened with VPL research (aka Virtual Programming Languages), the first company to sell VR goggles and gloves filing for bankruptcy. VPL research gloves were called "Data Glove'' sensed the user's finger movement and translated it into computer input ... In 1991 Sega Corporation ... announced the release of their VR headset, which they planned as an add-on peripheral, i.e. it isn't a standalone headset and would have needed to be connected to an external source, be it PC or console ... The forte VFX1 was by far one of the best consumer-level head-mounted displays of the 90s, It comprised a helmet, a handheld controller, and offered head tracking, stereoscopic 3D, and stereo audio. (Fatai, 2022)

6. ARTIFICIAL INTELLIGENCE BETWEEN CHRONICLE AND NEW MYTHOLOGY

Some of these arguments will be developed better in next chapters. But from the beginning it is important to distinguish between the current narrative on the impetuous progress of technology in recent years, the poor and trivial use that most people make of it, and the likely or bizarre ideas circulating about possible future developments.

Speaking of fields once professional and now within the reach of many if not of all, anyone experiences in everyday life how speech recognition has come a long way and now machines understand quite well people speaking, even without the need for the tone and cadence training that was needed until a few years ago. The cleanliness of the human voice extracted from the background noise in some audio recordings is impressive. Photo software works wonders in image processing programs on PCs and mobile phones. And my laptop and smartphone switch on just for me, recognizing my face, or my fingerprint, like once it used to only happen to Agent 007!

Artificial Intelligence has a quite old story, but its great popularity raised in 2023 due to what appears as a qualitative leap, in software products that are moreover freely accessible to the general public. *ChatGTP* and other software can discuss politics and economy with competence and a reasonability that sometimes nowadays we don't not find in human politicians and economists, and also it can tell stories, in which characters and narrative ingredients are skillfully mixed, according to the taste for example of a possible TV audience. So, for popular series fictions, or general analysis introducing some topics, it can really replace a good part of the work that until now had been done by human authors, who could limit themselves to a final supervision and possible corrections.

But does someone really think that a software can write articles with an *opinion* about what's happening in the world? Or a text in which it *tells* something as personal and artistic as a true novelist?

Sure, AI can write in a better English than me, that I am not native speaker (and indeed sometimes I ask it if my sentence is correct!), but it can't replace what *I think* on a subject, or *I want to tell* in a story.

The term "Artificial Intelligence" first appears in 1956, when American computer and cognitive scientist John McCarthy coined it at a summer seminar at Dartmouth College. The seminar lasts two months. In the group of participants there are cognitive scientists, computer scientists, physicists, mathematicians, engineers. There's Claude Shannon, father of information theory. There's Herbert Simon, who's going to win the Nobel Prize years later. The Dartmouth conference is considered the founding moment of artificial intelligence as a new field of study. (Testa, 2023, translated from Italian)

AI celebrated one of its first successes of public when IBM Deep Blue won a chess game against the human world champion:

Deep Blue was a chess-playing expert system run on a unique purpose-built IBM supercomputer ... It first played world champion Garry Kasparov in a six-game match in 1996, where it lost four games to two. It was upgraded in 1997 and in a six-game re-match, it defeated Kasparov by winning three games and drawing one. Deep Blue's victory is considered a milestone in the history of artificial intelligence and has been the subject of several books and films.

After his loss, Kasparov said that he sometimes saw unusual creativity in the machine's moves, suggesting that during the second game, human chess players had intervened on behalf of the machine. IBM denied this, saying the only human intervention occurred between games. Kasparov demanded a rematch, but IBM had dismantled Deep Blue after its victory and refused the rematch. (Deep Blue (chess computer), Wikipedia)

We can say that the general AI is that of science fiction books and films, that is, a system capable of reasoning, learning concepts, processing them, and performing any task as a human being would. A system of this type would therefore have cognitive abilities comparable (if not superior) to ours, with the ability to face and solve very different problems and in many areas ... The possibility of having an AI of this type still seems very remote and for the most skeptical unreachable.

A restricted AI system basically has only one job to do, in which it can be extremely efficient, but it is incapable of dealing with anything else. (Il Post, 2023 May 10, translated from Italian)

In 2023 AI seems to be the topic of the day, and there is much talk about it.

McKinsey, an international strategic consulting firm, describes in a recent article the performance of ChatGPT, the artificial intelligence model for word processing that is being talked about a lot ... asks Chat GPT to write, in the McKinsey style, the opening paragraph of an article about how artificial will affect the business world. And he finds out AI can do it ... says that, at a time when computers can

Figure 4. AI
Source: Dixit (2023)

re-answer questions by producing original content from the data in their possession, they can now undoubtedly demonstrate creativity.

Voice assistants like Siri, Google Assistant and Alexa are becoming more and more accurate. The first self-driving cars are being developed. In the medical field, artificial intelligence serves as an aid for the diagnosis of rare diseases. And also, to analyze reports, to identify and calibrate effective therapies, to design new drugs. Weather forecasts use AI, and robots driven by AI spread to factories. AI systems are developed to combat fraud and money laundering, to restore images.

The only problem is the reproduction of human hands: the images of hands that the AI picks in the Web are often little detailed or incomplete, and moreover the hands appear in a thousand different perspectives. So, in short, AI is confusing and, as Buzzfeed shows, it puts it at random. (Testa, 2023, translated from Italian)

From March 7, 2023, on the Italian newspaper "Il Foglio", for 30 days small texts are written by ChatGPT:

A challenge: identify all the articles written with this technology. In prize a subscription and a bottle of champagne. A test on artificial intelligence and newspapers. (translated from Italian)

Noam Chomsky, one of the greatest living philosophers and linguists, also writes on AI:

The human mind is not, like ChatGPT and its ilk, a lumbering statistical engine for pattern matching, gorging on hundreds of terabytes of data and extrapolating the most likely conversational response or most probable answer to a scientific question. On the contrary, the human mind is a surprisingly efficient and even elegant system that operates with small amounts of information; it seeks not to infer brute correlations among data points but to create explanations ... Intelligence consists not only of creative conjectures but also of creative criticism. Human-style thought is based on possible explanations and error correction, a process that gradually limits what possibilities can be rationally considered ... But ChatGPT and similar programs are, by design, unlimited in what they can "learn" (which is to say, memorize); they are incapable of distinguishing the possible from the impossible. (Chomsky, 2023)

Many warn of possible risks and stress the importance to prevent people from referring to AI as a person. On May 17, Sam Altman, the CEO of OpenAI, the company behind ChatGPT, is reported to say:

I think if this technology goes wrong, it can go quite wrong ... we want to be vocal about that ... We want to work with the government to prevent that from happening.

He gave several suggestions for how a new agency in the US could regulate the industry – including "a combination of licensing and testing requirements" for AI companies, which he said could be used to regulate the "development and release of AI models above a threshold of capabilities".

He also said firms like OpenAI should be independently audited. (Clayton, 2023)

In a keynote speech at the European Association for Computational Linguistics in Dubrovnik earlier this month, I proposed a novel and tractable first step in responding to LLMs: we should ban them from referring to themselves in the first person. They should not call themselves "I" and they should not refer to themselves and humans as "we."

When people interact with an LLM and are lulled into experiencing it as another person, they are being emotionally defrauded by overestimating the amount of human intentionality encoded in that text. (Munger, 2023)

As a computational system, AI can, for a given set of human-defined goals, make predictions and recommendations or make influencing decisions in real or virtual environments. (Covarrubias-Moreno, 2023)

You've probably read about problems with the current AI models. For example, they aren't necessarily good at understanding the context for a human's request, which leads to some strange results. When you ask an AI to make up something fictional, it can do that well. But when you ask for advice about a trip you want to take, it may suggest hotels that don't exist. (Gates, 2023)

Probably because our most conscious communications take place through words, the most talked about AI applications are those related to text production. But a great expert in the social aspects of technology such as Derrick de Kerckhove - quoted in more detail here in chapter 8.02 (de Kerckhove 2023) - has stresses the ability to produce extremely realistic images, while the author of this book is experimenting for some months the incredible and unprecedented skill of AI to isolate the human voice, as it has been implemented in the video production software *Da Vinci Resolve*, also in the basic version, released for free. So, anyone - with this or other programs featured with this function – can try directly what they have done publishing in October 2023 *Now and Then*, the last song of the Beatles, having completely cleaned up John Lennon's original voice from the instrumental accompaniment (Snapes, 2023). Awesome!

Only a hint here, and more in Chapter 2.

Modern mythologies and narrations of the globalized world often recover the old stories, the gods, the heroes from Greek, Germanic, Indian, Chinese, and Japanese ancient culture, projecting them into future adventures across the galaxies, mixing them with more recent stories of beings created by science, automata, Frankenstein, cyborgs. The development of AI perhaps begins to suggest that these stories might for the first time really take place outside the imagination and the substantial control of humans.

Then, the proposed applications in people's everyday life often manifest themselves at a much more prosaic level. While writing this chapter on AI, I have begun to test some apps on my smartphone. A few hours after the installation, a message comes: "You feel lonely? ChatAI is here for you!"

7. VISITORS AND CREATORS OF CONSISTED, COMFORTING VIRTUAL WORLDS

Riccardo was five years old, in the nineties. He's playing with the original release of *Sim City* on an Amiga computer. Unable to read menus (they are in English, but at that age he can't read them even in his own language, Italian), he helps himself with memory, as children use to do, knowing that clicking on a certain icon or position he can get a certain result. The author of this book, his father, passes by, observes for a while and then tells him, "It seems to me that you are building too much, so you run out of money!" Riccardo promptly answers: "I'll increase taxes!" and with confidence goes to its menu and performs the operation.

In another chapter there will be considerations on how and why, observing scenes like this, someone has fantasized for years about the existence of the "digital natives" as a new emerging race, and other bizarre ideas that, perhaps because as a society we know very little about children, have attracted a great deal of the public opinion.

Here the focus is on the great attraction that to contemplate a world not true but that takes place before the eyes and mind in some way as if it were true, has always exercised on children and even on many adults.

Children playing with dolls and their homes, forts and soldiers, service stations and pirate ships, Meccano and Lego, it's a reconstruction and reworking of situations and social relationships, as a very pleasant exercise in their way towards the knowledge of the world. Railway layouts and other forms of model-building are the evolution of childish games that can become a passion for life, sometimes at great levels of accuracy. The mechanical cribs for centuries amaze for the fact of simulating the movement of water and wind, sun, moon and stars in the sky, people walking and working, and undoubtedly the advent of electrical and electronic devices has contributed, as for the model railways, to the multiplication of increasingly surprising effects.

Digital technology, inside a screen or through VR glasses, is being multiplying this game endlessly: from the first pioneering graphic reconstructions, at the beginning rough and gradually more accurate and likely, in two and three dimensions, to the possibility of building worlds that, based on human indications, grow and develop accordingly (as in *Sim City* and other simulation games), up to virtual environments increasingly controlled by artificial intelligence (as in the metaverse) where the human being is really put in the condition to interact as if it were a real world. Amazing!

Figure 5. Digital world
Source: Godbole (2017)

The strength of the computer is consistency.

If the human programmer has worked well, has been able to devise a well-made plot and put together in an appropriate way the routines elaborated and refined over the years by other programmers, the construction achieves results of great likelihood and can strike in humans the senses of sight and hearing and place them in extremely engaging situations, as and more than in real life. There are video games in which entire cities are rebuilt as if we were really going through them. There are cinematic scenes in which it is almost impossible to distinguish the real environments and actors from those digitally inserted in post-production.

"Sim" software can be a good example, along with historical games like *Civilization*, *Age of Empires*, *Assassin's Creed*, *Battlefield*, *Total War*, and action Adventures (but sometimes the genres intertwine, and it is difficult to distinguish) like *Grand Theft Auto* (GTA), *God of War*, *The Legend of Zelda*, *Star Wars*, *Far Cry*, *Metal Gear* and many, many others.

What is fascinating today for humans, of any age, is something we maybe should think about more than we usually do. It is not only entertainment. It is to have to deal with rules that do not allow us to cheat. That is what video games do, all of them, from the most trivial to the most elaborate, and the best video games go on to do it well, as we continue to play, in all situations.

In an increasingly less knowable real world, humans all need an order within which to move, need to know that there are rules by which they, to their actions, can expect consequential reactions. That is how young children experience the world and, for trials, errors, confirmations, in the reality of life and in their play, process the data through which they begin to move in it, to an ever-greater autonomy. This growing confidence corresponds to pleasure, curiosity, desire to live.

This is the charm of every virtual adventure, but it requires, on the other side, to be careful to the danger, faced with the problems of real life, of seeking refuge in situations that, exaggerating them, can create problems in the psychology of individuals and in social relations.

Here we only begin to mention the narration as a possible substitute for the real world and the problem of digital dependencies, which we will see better in the following chapters. We note however that to offer an easy access to digital environments more and more engaging, also on a sensory level, as in virtual reality and metaverse it happens, to an audience of consumers whose technological competence is most often reduced to taking part in social networks, browsing podcasts and occasionally writing an email, if from a commercial point of view it offers unlimited opportunities, from a social one it could be a serious gamble.

The author of this book, on his Android tablet, sometimes plays *Megapolis*, which is undoubtedly a valid and complete game to build cities, with all the economic infrastructure, connections and a lot of interesting environments and situations. One looks with satisfaction at the streets, houses and skyscrapers, factories and mines, trains and planes traveling the screen. But with this very popular thing today, that the game is for free, but to accelerate it one must pay real money - and if he/she is in a hurry, it can be much money - the question comes up: can't all this in some cases risk becoming a kind of game addiction that hurts the mind and the wallet?

8. OPPORTUNITIES AND STEREOTYPES OF THE CONSUMPTION OF TECHNOLOGY

We've all heard the stereotypes before. The Greatest Generation is "responsible and hard-working"; Baby Boomers are "selfish"; Gen Xers are "cynical and disaffected"; Millennials are "entitled and lazy"; Gen Zers are "civic-minded." Even though these stereotypes are frequently called into question, they linger in the mind, fed by media, politicians, and business experts.

But, while characterizing generations is a common practice, it's often counterproductive. (Suttie, 2021)

When they come to technology, which means machines and software that have rapidly invaded everyone's daily life in just a few years, and whose understanding for many depends on the latest advertisements spread in the market, stereotypes obviously play a major role.

Generational stereotypes are the first that come to mind and much has been studied about them, from several points of view.

Population ageing and technological innovation are two major trends of our time. Virtually every country in the world is experiencing an increase in the proportion of older adults in their population. Worldwide, the number of persons aged 60 years or older is expected to more than double by 2050 and more than triple by 2100 (United Nations [UN] 2017). Simultaneously, the rapid development of new technologies witnessed in recent decades is likely to continue.

Yet, older individuals and technological devices are often seen as worlds apart. (João Mariano et al., 2020)

Baby boom consumers are shown, in contrast to the stereotypes, to have low levels of technology anxiety and high levels of experience of internet and SMS usage ... The results provide evidence of the distortedness of current stereotypes that are used to describe 50-plus consumers. (Niemelä-Nyrhinen 2007)

But also, many are the stereotypes affecting each of us when handling technology, often denying us the real opportunities that a more conscious use could offer.

One of them I like to propose may come as a surprise because it concerns a common behavior, linked to an operation that computers and smartphones perform automatically.

As soon as they are turned on, machines by default try to connect to the Internet, and if for some reason the connection does not work, not being able to be online, we feel lost and limited in our usage. Many switch the device off.

The dependency on the Internet has become a true modern stereotype, as in reality there are thousands of operations that we could perform with a computer offline, of which, due to the constant urge to browse, we risk not even becoming aware.

9. WASTING RESOURCES, FRAMING CATEGORIES, "BUBBLING" ECONOMY

A huge waste of resource is also the result of stereotypes.

First, we are so self-centered in using digital devices, that probably neither consider the unimaginable computing power of a potential collective use, together, if only a minimum part of those who daily argue on social networks agreed on some common goal. A power normally wasted in billions of individual operations that only have the practical effect of enriching the owners of commercial platforms. What, if we learned to do differently?

For now, we have helped to separate the production of wealth from labor even more and too much, which is probably not good for a world where hundreds million people have not enough food and water, and so much money is made with the games of finance and collecting clicks and views online. This is a very complex subject that here can be only mentioned, and something more about will be discussed in Chapter 10.

The software-based program helps you earn passive income by selling products online without owning them. It enables you to generate commissions based on the number of visitors who purchase the affiliate products. (Click Wealth System Reviews, 2023)

During the 90s, the idea that everything online was great and successful made many people extremely rich in a very short time. It was enough that a company had a website to increase its value, and this collective erroneous belief conditioned the real economy for years, up to the so called "dotcom bubble" because of which the tech market lost more than 75 percent of its value by October 2002. Even today, the huge market value of companies based on online user clicks, compared to those that produce real goods, is not at all seen well by many economists.

Operators speak, explain to you, and behave as if they truly know how things are and go. But when it comes to brand new technologies, possibilities that humanity has been experiencing for just a few years, anyone who chooses one direction over another, no matter how skilled and experienced they are, their perspective can be forced at any moment.

There is a constant risk of thinking by stereotypes, by "hearsay", framing people in a generic and irrational way: the old, the young, the "digital natives", the nerds, the "boomers". In the same way it's easy to confuse temporary economic phenomena with long-term trends, basing on preconceived ideas that we find in our mind without having elaborated them, or even without knowing where they come from.

Research does not help us much to understand. Economists' analyses fail to prevent recurrent crises resulting from casual behavior on the markets to which the politics choose not to give effective answers, while so many studies on how people use technology, adults, or young people, are based on abstract data, like the time spent on devices, which means nothing in the end, because we have no information about what people actually do, *how* for example they deal with navigation. That can be some completely different from researchers and readers' way of navigating.

In the meanwhile, each of us on devices, keeping up with the trendiest social media and apps, adhering to stereotypes probably we strongly limit the number of things we could derive from an equipment that we only know to a minimal extent.

And keeping them switched on many hours a day just to surf the Web a little, not only it means to underuse them, but also, it's a huge waste of energy. The mobile phone we keep in our pocket, continuously transmits, and receives data, in connection with antennas, cable networks, satellites, up to finals servers that are located anywhere in the world. Much of these data is advertising emails, or real time notifications from social networks that few really need to go and see whenever the device rings or vibrates. This nonstop and mostly useless connection, multiplied by billions of users, all around the world, at any time of day and night, it is a colossal consumption of electricity that could be saved, if we only connect to the network just when we need to. Probably much more than the standby of television sets, that many recommend turning off, when we don't watch TV, or of other energy wastage.

10. BEYOND THE SCREENS AS MIRRORS AND SHIELDS

A stereotype that quite summarizes a reality today is the image of people of all ages in a public place, a street, a bus, a station, a restaurant, instead of interacting with each other, everyone having their gaze lost in their own mobile phone.

Are smartphone mirrors in which we contemplate ourselves as Narcissus 2.0? Or shields behind which we tend to protect from the dangers and the uncertainties of the exterior world?

These are very empirical thoughts, associations that anyone of us is led to do, confirmed by scientific studies struggling, however, to find their own method and overcome limits. How can we, for example, draw definitive conclusions about *mobile phone usage*, when it can be used in fact in hundreds of different ways?

The selfie phenomenon can be viewed as a symptom and forewarning indication of a deeper globally spreading trend. The somewhat unforeseen development of the Internet toward one of most important phenomenon of the 21st century ... raises some serious questions about its connection to the formation of individual personality.

The issue whether the Internet encourages, supports and enhances the already present self-centered, infantile-regressive and narcissistic tendencies and phenomena will be discussed. Does the available, fast and easy digital interaction without physical presence and validation, as well as the possibility of hiding or taking a false identity, affect the disinhibition from social and ethical constraints and rules, and reduce empathy and the sense of responsibility? (Ercegovac, 2014)

It also depends on whether the focus is on people's habits from a social and statistical point of view, or whether it is, for example, medical research on behavioral disorders.

Little is known about how the interplay between dysfunctional personality characteristics and selfie-related behavior can influence problematic smartphone use ... In the current study, a total of 627 undergraduate students (283 males and 344 females) completed a cross-sectional survey. (Giordano et al., 2019)

We defined PSU (Problematic Smartphone Usage) in accordance with the literature as smart phone use associated with at least some element of dysfunctional use, such as anxiety when the phone was not available, or neglect of other activities. (Yon Sohn et al., 2019)

It is about finding the right methods of investigation and data collection, also considering that the answers derive largely from how the questions are asked.

In 2018, approximately 77 percent of America's inhabitants owned a smartphone (Pew Research Center, 2018), defined here as a mobile phone that performs many of the functions of a computer ... a survey conducted in 2015 showed that 46 percent of Americans reported that they could not live without their smart-phone (Smith, 2015). Similar numbers can be observed in other parts of the (Western) world (OECD, 2017). Therefore, it should come as no surprise that in recent years discussions about the (potential) consequences of (heavy) smartphone use have earned an important place in societal debates.

Our analysis of the literature reveals a predominance of empirical results supporting a negative association. However, this predominance is less outspoken in studies analysing data gathered by paper and pen questionnaires ... In general, when scholars use methods of data gathering which are more susceptible to social desirable behaviour, a non-significant association is found more often. (Amez and Baert, 2020)

As we have pointed out several times, even if people stand with their eyes on a smartphone, we cannot know what exactly they are doing:

88 out of 114 participants started using their smartphone as soon as they were left alone. However, the findings of this study also demonstrate great diversity in smartphone use, in e.g. social media platforms used and motivations for using different apps. These results illustrate that it no longer seems sensible to refer to "screen time" as if it represents a homogeneous phenomenon across youth. (Griffioen et al. 2021)

Professor Daniel Miller said:

Our unique study comprehensively reveals how people of all ages across the world, and in particular older people, are creatively adapting smartphones to work for them, and the social, economic, cultural, educational and health benefits this brings.

We also show how the smartphone is no longer just a device that we use, it's become the place where we live. The flip side of that for human relationships is that any point, whether over a meal, a meeting or other shared activity, a person we're with can just disappear, having 'gone home' to their smartphone. (International study reveals smartphone use around the world, 2021)

The smartphone is also an easy shield at hand, a convenient screen to keep others away:

We've all seen it, and we've probably all done it. Quickly pulling out your phone to look busy so you can avoid eye contact or maybe an awkward conversation.

For some people smartphones have a shield to hide behind to block, avoid, or escape human interaction.

Phubbing is a mashup of phone and snubbing, basically phone snubbing. Body language experts call this "blocking". In 2016 the psychology department at the University of Kent in the UK did a study to find out how common ""phubbing"" really is.

The study found that 26% of people use their phone to block other people 2-3 times a day. Matching that data, 31% of people reported BEING blocked 2-3 times a day. ("Conscious Vibe", 2023)

In my long experience, it often has come to my mind the idea that nowadays average 5-year-old children well perceive that they could do a lot of things with the easy and powerful technological gadgets they have started playing with. But within a few years, they'll learn that they substantially can act only inside a framework of predetermined behaviors and cliches, and that the power of technology is given to them only almost for leisure and consumption, or an inextricable bureaucracy.

The contradiction between what would be possible and what is, it is perhaps one of the deep causes of many specific problems of the present time.

Once upon a time people felt helpless because they didn't have the power in their hands.

Today people feel helpless because they do have the power in their hands - usually we don't even imagine it, but if we think well, in large part it is so! - and they are unable to use it! And this can be much more frustrating and causes more problems in society.

Having the internet in your pocket at all times is basically like being GOD a hundred years ago ... Still, with the infinite world of knowledge at our fingertips, millions of us use this technology mostly to post pictures of our meals and our cats. And to bow out of awkward social situations. ("Conscious Vibe", 2023)

REFERENCES

Amez, S., & Baert, S. (2020). Smartphone use and academic performance: A literature review. *International Journal of Educational Research, 103*, 101618. doi:10.1016/j.ijer.2020.101618

Anderson J. & Rainie, L. (2022, Jun 30). *The metaverse will not fully emerge in the way today's advocates hope.* Pew Research Center.

Bali, M. (2016, Feb. 3). *Knowing the Difference Between Digital Skills and Digital Literacies, and Teaching Both.* International Literary Association. literacyworldwide.org/blog.

Baptiste, A. (2019, Dec 17). Digital Skills vs. Digital Literacy. *Medium.*

Bisogna capirsi su cosa sia "l'intelligenza artificiale." (2023, May 10), *Il Post.*

Bollas, C. (2018). *Meaning and Melancholia: Life in the Age of Bewilderment.* Routledge. doi:10.4324/9781351018500

ChatGPT sul Foglio: per 30 giorni piccoli testi scritti dall'IA sul nostro giornale. (2023, Mar 7). *Il Foglio.* ilfoglio.it/tecnologia/2023/03/07

Chomsky, N. (2023, Mar 8). The False Promise of ChatGPT. *The New York Times.*

Clark, M. (2020). *Dealing with information overload.* accesswdun.com.

Clark, P.A. (2021, Nov. 15). The Metaverse Has Already Arrived. Here's What That Actually Means. *Time.*

Clayton, J. (2023, May 17). *Sam Altman: CEO of OpenAI calls for US to regulate artificial intelligence.* BBC News.

Click Wealth System Reviews - Real Make Money Online Program or Fake Profits Hype? (2023, Jul.). *News Direct Blog.* newsdirect.com/guest-content

Conscious Vibe. (2023, Apr 30). *Using Your Smartphones to Avoid Human Contact (the consequences).* theconsciousvibe.com.

Cottone, N. (2022, Feb 18). Bonus psicologo: l'aiuto fino a 600 euro in dieci domande e risposte. *Il Sole 24ore.*

Covarrubias-Moreno, O. M. (2023). *Artificial Intelligence and Systems Thinking in the Public Sector. In Handbook of Research on Applied Artificial Intelligence and Robotics for Government Processes.* IGI Global.

D'Achille, P. (2021, Sep 24). Un asterisco sul genere. *Accademia della Crusca.* accademiadellacrusca.it/it/consulenza/

de Kerckhove, D. (2023, May 11). Il linguaggio sfidato dagli algoritmi nell'era dell'IA generativa. *Media 2000.*

Deep Blue (chess computer). (n.d.). *Wikipedia.*

Developing Digital Literacy Skills. (n.d). webwise.ie/teachers.

Dixit, P. (2023, Jan. 31). *Why Are AI-Generated Hands So Messed Up?* buzzfeednews.com.

Duffy, B. (2021). *The Generation Myth: Why When You're Born Matters Less Than You Think.* Basic Books.

Fatai, B. (2022, Feb. 9). *What VR looked like in the 90s - The Stone Age of VR.* linkedin.com.

Folena, U. (2023, Mar. 9). Soli, depressi, impasticcati: il malessere di una generazione. *L'Avvenire.*

Gates, B. (2023, Mar. 28). *Here's what the age of AI means for the world, according to Bill Gates.* World Economic Forum. weforum.org/agenda

Ghani, B., Memon, K. R., Han, H., Ariza-Montes, A., & Arjona-Fuentes, J. M. (2022, October 20). Work stress, technological changes, and job insecurity in the retail organization context. *Frontiers in Psychology*, *13*, 918065. doi:10.3389/fpsyg.2022.918065 PMID:36483719

Giordano, C. (2019, Dec). Magic Mirror on the Wall: Selfie-Related Behavior as Mediator of the Relationship Between Narcissism and Problematic Smartphone Use. *ResearchGate.*

Godbole, A. (2017). *Five Steps to Survive Business in Digital Era.* wns.com/perspectives/

Griffioen, N., Scholten, H., Lichtwarck-Aschoff, A., van Rooij, M., & Granic, I. (2021, July 20). Everyone does it—differently: A window into emerging adults' smartphone use. *Humanities & Social Sciences Communications*, *8*(1), 177. doi:10.105741599-021-00863-1

How to cope with information overload as a marketer. (n.d.). etail-week-connect.com.

Illich, I. (1978). *Toward a History of Needs.* Pantheon Books.

International study reveals smartphone use around the world. (2021, May 17). *UCL Global.* ucl.ac.uk/global/news/

Jungst, M. (2022). Effect of Technological Insecurity on Performance Through Emotional Exhaustion: A Moderated Mediation Approach. *International Journal of Technology and Human Interaction*, *18*(1), 1–15. doi:10.4018/IJTHI.300282

L'era del disagio psicologico. (2023, Oct 9). *La Repubblica.*

Leprince-Ringuet, D. (2020, February 26). AI's big problem: Lazy humans just trust the algorithms too much. *ZdNet. Innovation.*

Mariano, J. (2021, Feb 7). Too old for technology? Stereotype threat and technology use by older adults. *Behaviour & Information Technology, 41*(7).

Milivojević, T. & Ercegovac, I. (2014, Jan.). *Selfie or virtual mirror to new Narcissus.* ResearchGate.

Miller, D. (2021). *The Global Smartphone.* UCL Press. doi:10.2307/j.ctv1b0fvh1

Modern Technology as a Status Symbol. (2016, Aug 26). southuniversity.edu/news-and-blog

Munger, K. (2023, May 22). Ban LLMs Using First-Person Pronouns. *Crooked Timber.*

Niemelä-Nyrhinen, N. (2007, August 7). Baby boom consumers and technology: Shooting down stereotypes. *Journal of Consumer Marketing*, *24*(5), 305–312. doi:10.1108/07363760710773120

Roales, F. (2023, Mar 31). The Metaverse Gets the Hollywood Treatment. *Creative Insights.* creativeinsights.gettyimages.com

Rosen, J. (2017, August). Gender quotas for women in national politics: A comparative analysis across development thresholds. *Social Science Research*, *66*, 82–101. doi:10.1016/j.ssresearch.2017.01.008 PMID:28705365

Sandner, D. (2022). The Discomfort in Society or: The Shift of the Socio-structural Boundaries. In *Society and the Unconscious: Cultural Psychological Insights*. Springer. doi:10.1007/978-3-662-66175-8_13

Serafini, M. (2021). *Sostenere la sostenibilità* [Master Thesis]. Università Nicolà Cusano – telematica, Roma.

Snapes, L. (2023, Oct 26). The Beatles: 'final' song Now and Then to be released thanks to AI technology. *The Guardian*.

Sohn, S. Y., Rees, P., Wildridge, B., Kalk, N. J., & Carter, B. (2019). Prevalence of problematic smartphone usage and associated mental health outcomes amongst children and young people: A systematic review, meta-analysis and GRADE of the evidence. *BMC Psychiatry*, *19*(1), 356. doi:10.118612888-019-2350-x PMID:31779637

Stefanoni, F. (2019, Oct 24). Mattarella: «Covid e guerre, il mondo in tre anni cambiato in peggio. Evitare escalation in Medio Oriente». *Il Corriere della Sera*.

Sweeney, P. (2015, February 26). How Globalisation And Technology Drive Insecurity. *Social Europe*.

Testa, A. (2023, Feb 26). Che succede con l'intelligenza artificiale? *Nuovo e utile: teorie e pratiche della creatività*. nuovoeutile.it

ADDITIONAL READING

Ayres, R. U. (2014). *The Bubble Economy: Is Sustainable Growth possible?* The MIT Press. doi:10.7551/mitpress/9957.001.0001

Baker, D. (2010). *Plunder and Blunder: The Rise and Fall of the Bubble Economy*. Berret-Koehler.

Eshet, Y. (2004, January). Digital Literacy: A Conceptual Framework for Survival Skills in the Digital era. *Journal of Educational Multimedia and Hypermedia*, *13*(1).

Goodnight, G. T., & Green, S. (2010, June 16). Rhetoric, Risk, and Markets: The Dot-Com Bubble. *The Quarterly Journal of Speech*, *96*(2).

Gunkel, D. J. (2012). *The Machine Question: Critical Perspectives on AI, Robots, and Ethics*. The MIT Press. doi:10.7551/mitpress/8975.001.0001

Han, B. C. (2021). *The Palliative Society: Pain Today*. Polity Press.

Laursen, B. & Faur, S. (2022, May). What Does it Mean to be Susceptible to Influence? A Brief Primer on Peer Conformity and Developmental Changes that Affect it. *PubMed Central HHS Author Manuscripts*.

Lipson, M. (2021, Sep 1). How Language Classes Are Moving Past the Gender Binary. *The New York Times*.

Mayor, A. (2018). *Gods and Robots: Myths, Machines, and Ancient Dreams of Technology*. Princeton University Press. doi:10.2307/j.ctvc779xn

Mazzucchelli, C. (2023, Mar 16). *ChatGPT: sedotti e abbandonati*. linkedin.com.

Reilly, K. (2011). *Automata and Mimesis on the Stage of Theatre History*. Palgrave Macmillan.

Senejan, W. (2020). *Transcending the Tribe: How to Conquer Conformity, Insecurity, and Reliance on the Approval of Others*. Senejan Enterprises.

Shelly, M. (2018). *Frankenstein; or The Modern Prometheus*. Penguin. (Original work published 1818)

von Weichs, V., Krott, N. R., & Oettingen, G. (2021, June 2). The Self-Regulation of Conformity: Mental Contrasting With Implementation Intentions (MCII). *Frontiers in Psychology*, *12*, 546178. doi:10.3389/fpsyg.2021.546178 PMID:34149487

Chapter 2
Unaware Producers of Information in a World of Narrative:
People and Their Lives, as It Is and as It's Told

ABSTRACT

Stories today are everywhere, and television changed history, telling the same tales to all, worldwide. Mankind is living on narratives, overlapping reality, beyond time, facts, and technologies. Since the 1960s, people have imagined a centralized and oppressive future led by the unapproachable power of a Big Brother, hopefully saved by superheroes, and maybe we cannot take advantage of the possibilities we have to impact the world because we're too busy talking and hearing storytelling about it. Billions of users one by one choose music, movies, news, and publish texts, photos, videos online, not only receivers, but producers and, often unaware, transmitters of information. Surrounded by real and fake information without feeling to control it, we are afraid of what we tell ourselves, for ourselves and for our children, and we cannot take advantage of the latent culture that, if aware, could make us active protagonist in the information society. This chapter explores unaware producers of information in a world of narrative.

1. INTRODUCTION

Today, almost all that we know of the world comes from stories. People like to watch their joys and sorrows told by narrations, and sometimes when reality does not correspond to the pattern of the stories, it's strange to us. The fear of an uncertain and unknown future is confused with entertainment, from old and new media, and online an uncontrollable flow of information and suggestions runs through social networks, mixing the true and the false, and bypassing the "echo chambers" and "filter bubbles" messages of insecurity are magnified, beyond checks and reasoning.

DOI: 10.4018/978-1-6684-8228-5.ch002

Virtual knowledge of reality for mankind begins with television, worldwide. The same stories and cultural models are spread all over the planet, most from a few more developed counties. TV consumption, also in the time of Internet, remains very strong, and its passive nature has hardly marked and still marks the habits of entire generations. People grown up with television find it very difficult to understand the possibilities of means by their nature active, such as PCs and the Web, and probably the Web we know has been severely limited by the television culture of its users.

In the years 2020, with new special effects, the same superheroes are popular of the years 1950 and 60. Their stories come often from ancient traditions, from epic poems and tragedies of the past. And comedy still helps to observe the problems of the world with a healthy smile. Perhaps we have changed much less than we always tell ourselves.

But on the basis of the latent audiovisual culture common to all generations, the citizens of the global world could move much better, as children show us.

2. THE NARRATIVES OF NARRATIVES AND REALITY: DREAMS AND NIGHTMARES LASTING OVER THE YEARS

Stories are everywhere around us, from the ads on TV or music video clips to the more sophisticated stories told by books or movies. Everything comes wrapped in a story, and the means employed to weave the narrative thread are just as important as the story itself. In this context, there is a need to understand the role storytelling plays in contemporary society, which has changed drastically in recent decades. Modern global society is no longer exclusively dominated by the time-tested narrative media such as literature or films because new media such as videogames or social platforms have changed the way we understand, create, and replicate stories. (Mihăeş *et al., 2021)*

When the author was a student at Bologna university, he followed the lectures of Umberto Eco, who used to ask a weird question; do we speak languages or are we spoken by them?

In the neighborhood where I live, in a medium-sized city in northern Italy, among the adjoining houses there are many public gardens, with common spaces where children play. In a point a group frequently meet and, passing by, it is not uncommon to see them engaged in street games of yesteryear, that those who are more than 50 years old remember in their childhood.

I realize that this sounds to me a little strange. I go and write on *Facebook* I have just seen kids playing outdoor at *Un-Due-Tre-Stella* (something like *Statues*, or *Fairy Footsteps* in English countries) and many of my *friends* post comments of wonder.

It's quite natural, but… Why? If we think about it, it is perfectly logical and natural that children who are in the open air, if they somehow know old games, play with them. But this does not correspond to how, in our society, children are usually told, as depending on TV, "digital natives", exposed to online bullying and abuse, and so on. The narrative determines the idea that we have of the youngest - the eventual lesson of our own daughters and sons and grandchildren usually is not enough - and when real kids behave differently, they are the strange.

Once, people used to sing while working. Are we sure, or did we see it in movies?

Sure, if in certain works singing served to make the work lighter and at the same time to give a rhythm, many of today's works, with pressing rhythms determined by algorithms, are less suitable to be sung. But It's the people who don't really sing anymore, if not in karaoke parties, or under the guide of an animator, or it is us who pay less and less attention to what does not correspond to our expectations? Always too much in a hurry to listen, used to frame people in categories from few words or attitudes, we have ideas of reality which not necessarily fit our actual experience. So, it can be that people do not actually sing while working anymore, but it can be also that as we do not expect them to sing, so we do not pay attention to them singing even when they do. We read more and more reality through patterns that automatically, almost unconsciously superimpose on reality itself.

Stories of stories, redundant and obsessive replications of human existences. Not only fictions, but reality shows, economy and politics turned into entertainment with true and false arguing and fighting on live TV. Not only facts or tales from the masters of traditional media, from web producers at any level, but now from everyone, on social networks or instant messaging platforms. Sometimes they are completely harmless and unrealistic, but sometimes surprisingly effective, when they revolve around *influencers* followed by thousands and millions of people, or even when for some reason difficult to assess it happens that they spread with the strength of the group: social battles, more or less valid opinions on culture, customs, politics, environmental issues, and even absolutely bizarre hypotheses on anything that however catch throngs of people.

The success of these narrations does not derive, in the so-called information society, from the validity of information, which few verify, analyze, submit to criticism, but often from prejudices, fears, hopes, ideas of identity of people and groups, sometimes not even based on reality, but on other stories yet.

Big Brother is since many years "the mother" of reality shows on TV, groups of people locked inside houses across the planet and the rest of the world who are passionate about watching what they do, as if it were true. But when George Orwell in 1949 first wrote of it, in the novel *Nineteen Eighty-Four*, it was the perfect representation of a nightmare of the humanity that, just out of World War II, in atomic bombs and in the first immense and inaccessible "electronic brains" saw its future destiny hanging on the will and whims of insurmountable superhuman forces, dictatorships perhaps even more terrible than those that had just been defeated, because governed by technology or even directly by rebellious machines become able to escape from any human control.

A lot of science fiction literature in that period revolves around these topics. And against super threats, in people's imagination come superheroes.

Science fiction encompasses the future of everything and can stimulate cosmic consciousness. Though inspired by the modern scientific vision of reality, science fiction can be traced to ancient myth, with which it shares many features. (Lombardo, 2015)

And it happens that certain stories that passionate and frightened the humanity of the second post-war period, today, with personal computers, the web, and mobile phones, are still incredibly up to date.

By the way, "it is perhaps no coincidence that, contemporary with the work of the precursors of modern computing, such as Babbage and Lovelace, it was the release of Mary Shelley's novel, 'Frankenstein'" (Certi and Toldi, 1986, translated from Italian).

3. THE LANGUAGE AND SOME SENSE OF HISTORY: THE MP3 AND THE PHONOGRAPH

Before we go on talking about the world, technology, and our future, perhaps we need to think a little about the tool we use to talk about it, our own language, that has never, as in recent years, demonstrated all its limits and ambiguities. This is not to draw the umpteenth peremptory conclusions, to affirm an opinion and to counter others, but to keep in mind the slippery terrain on which we move and the ever-looming difficulties of communication, and try to induce in the interlocutor, in the reader, a reasoning that may lead to elaborate new points of view, new keys to understanding reality allowing us to approach it better, possibly together.

Hard work, in times when the measure of an average speech is a 140-character tweet, but still, someone should try to do it, possibly beyond fashions, impressions, and fears, not looking at the world from a porthole, so that the little trends of the present are sometimes absolutized, and the epochal flows cannot be observed.

As we are talking about the changing world, it is important to understand what the stages of change are and to distinguish the important ones. Without any sense of the history, without memory, average people, but even columnists, researchers, politician could be walking into a complete blind spot. That is what often happens today, in times when the huge amount of information would require examining things in depth, but often people stop at the surface, at the single observed phenomenon, at the "headlines."

The discovery of fire, the invention of the wheel, the spread of electricity, have meant for humanity decisive changes in everyday life, work, social relations. Also, the press, the car, the radio, the telephone, the mobile phone; before people lived in a way and then in another.

It does not matter here to list exactly all the discoveries and inventions that have represented a revolution rather than a small change, nor to draw up a ranking for importance along the history. However, given that nowadays there is quite often a cry for epochal changes, especially in reference to the impact of technology, and that usually what people keep in mind are only headlines and slogans from which the public opinion comes up with its own ideas, influencing politics, economics, and relationships, it is important to adopt a certain method. If not, words like "digital natives", or "computational thinking", used lightly by anyone, can do damage.

What is significant for real? Sometimes it is a matter of points of view, and the most important thing is not to always think of observing the world from its center.

Let's take the example of music. From the point of view of a listener the possibility of choosing playlists as we prefer among millions of songs, it's sure something totally new, very typical of the present. But can it be considered the focus of the "revolution"? Maybe a music player looks more at sound cards and electronic effects, allowing musicians today to produce cheap and good works even at home almost as if in professional studios. And who can say if the change due to the appearance of mp3 players was significant more or less than that given by the cassette *walkmans* in the 1980, when music became portable? It was in the 1970 that average people ears began to get accustomed to hi-fidelity, but turntables and phonographs had been invented many years before and probably they were the most innovative of all, making possible for the first time in history to listen to *recorded* music. Previously the only way for people to know songs, operas and ballads was to be just in the place, listening to the musicians and singers playing and singing live. Spotify, Amazon Music and iTunes are nothing compared with that!

Before the development of sound recording and reproduction, only people who had the knowledge to play and create or who were physically located in the same room as the performers, could have access to what we today cherish as canonized musical heritage. (Brusila et al., 2021)

4. FROM ORAL CULTURE TO TELEVISION: THE GLOBAL VIRTUAL ERA BEGINS

To a simple question, possibly a simple answer. When in history average people have become to know the world mainly from a virtual reality, more than from direct experience? There is no doubt: from the widespread presence of television.

Also before there was a reality beyond the physical and lived experience: oral tales, paintings, books, and at some point, also the press, photography, cinema. But they did not fill the time of life and left ample room for imagination, personal reflection, and reworking. From reading the same book, for example, everyone could imagine stories and even very different scenarios, though with illustrations some basic images were shared and common, in the same way as in the traditional iconography that, through painting and sculpture, in churches and chapels had imprinted in the imagination of generations just those figures of Christ, the Madonna, the saints, kings and political and religious leaders.

With cinema, things begin to change substantially. Watching an almost "living" representation of life, people now can locate thinking, desires, dreams somewhere else from daily material existence. It's not only the idea of something beyond life, as it can be Paradise or Hell, Jannah, or Valhalla. Real men and women transform actors and actresses into stars, and some fall in love with them, impossible stories to live only in the imagination, but with an affective involvement similar to that reserved for the real persons. And the virtual and fascinating world that passes on the screen begins to become a touchstone with which people compare their daily life, not only ideas but precise sequences of images, words, events.

Cinema is however still an episodic fact, a one-time thing, amid daily routine, work, school. Television instead enters in all homes, sometimes in all rooms, and literally fills human time. And today

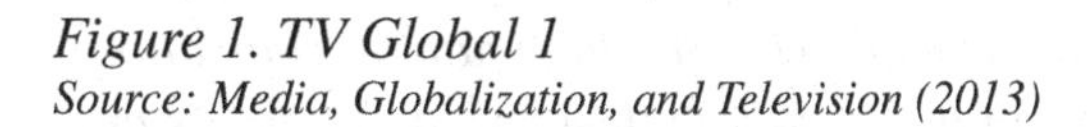

Figure 1. TV Global 1
Source: Media, Globalization, and Television (2013)

Figure 2. TV Global 2
Source: The Globalization of Television (2015)

smartphones are mainly used as an interactive television always and everywhere. As the gramophone has revolutionized the way to listen to music, in the same way television has completely changed for mankind the perception of the world, and it has done so all over the earth, proposing the same messages, stories, settings, values across the entire planet. Netflix and YouTube are nothing compared with this.

In Italy, where until the 1960s inhabitants spoke mostly in dialect (many of which are in fact real languages) often incomprehensible among them, we say that television represented for common people what literature had been in previous centuries for the educated classes; it unified the nation's language. (see, brief but quite exact *The Origins of The Italian Language*, in "Kwintessential").

But all over the world, with the spread everywhere of stories and contents produced especially in the United States of America and in few other more developed countries, with the export of the same successful "formats" in every corner of the planet, a globalization of the imaginary and the thought of billions of people has been produced that perhaps makes it easier today to understand one another among the different cultures of the planet, but also puts at risk the originality and traditions of many marginal cultural and linguistic areas, forcing them to fight to survive. Hence probably also some even violent reactions that have developed against the cultural hegemony, as well as economic of the West.

On the surface, global dissemination of formats may suggest not only the global integration of the economy of the industry but also the standardization of content. A dozen media companies are able to do business worldwide by selling the same idea, and audiences seem to be watching national variations of the same show. At a deeper level, however, formats attest to the fact that television still remains tied to local and national cultures. Bringing up examples of Latin American cases, this article argues that television is simultaneously global and national, shaped by the globalization of media economics and the pull of local and national cultures. (Waisbord, 2004)

The Indian television market has been flooded by adaptations of most of the globally popular brands, such as Big Brother, The X Factor, Dancing with the Stars, The Weakest Link, Fear Factor, and so on.

... Not all formats work well in all markets but as formats are, increasingly, being developed to be accessible in every culture, the power of formats is reflected not only in terms of its presence in cultural markets around the world but in its ability to alter the terms of creative, cultural productions. (Ganguly, 2018)

This is a quite old statement:

For most people in most countries, television remains the central element in their consumption of the cultural industries. A television set (or a better television set) is the main consumer priority for most people in the developing world (and still a high priority elsewhere, as large recent spending on digital high-definition television sets in the richer countries also shows). (Straubhaar, 2007)

But moving forward in the 20s of these century, things don't seem to have changed substantially, despite all discussions and opinions and the current idea that television would be in decline. The sales trend of TV sets, increasingly "smart" and able to connect to multiple channels, is growing steadily and, if what companies spend on advertising on a medium is a trustworthy indicator, in 2023

TV is still popular, with Americans watching more than 2 hours of it a day. But the emergence of YouTube, connected TV (CTVs), and social media have turned the spotlight. Certainly, ad dollars have followed, right? Yes, but less than you'd think.

In 2022, advertisers for more than 12.5K brands spent more than $59b on TV ads, representing a 3% increase from 2021; the number of brands buying TV ads also increased by 3%. ("MediaRadar Blog", 11 Apr 2023)

If a great feature of television is its power of globalizing, another is passivity. Stories, knowledge, emotions, hate and love, all they come from within the box, ready-made, with no need for the spectator to do anything. Outside of work and social duties, the citizen of the information society can observe his or her life literally scrolling ahead. That can be not the best school for active citizenship, nor for introducing to new interactive technologies that we have got in the meantime. And how decades of television habit of the entire world population have affected the development or lack of development of the Internet, is a topic that probably has not been sufficiently thought through.

5. TV AND PEOPLE, SOCIETY, AND THE LACK OF DEVELOPMENT OF THE WEB

Studies and research are mostly about how much and how people watch television, and how TV may affect mental health, relationships with the world, political views. Over time, the changes induced by the multiplication of the channels through which we access television, all in all have not changed things so deeply.

Other than sleeping and working, Americans are more likely to watch television than engage in any other activity. There's new evidence that viewing habits can affect your thinking, political preferences, even cognitive ability ... Some critics have pointed out that the best of the form is equivalent to the most enriching novels. And high-quality programming for children can be educational. But the latest evidence also suggests there can be negative consequences to our abundant watching, particularly when the shows are mostly entertainment. (Rothwell, 2019)

In this article, references are at the effect on children reported during the old experiment of "Sesame Street", from 1969 in the USA, at the average I.Q. decline registered in Norway among the young born in the 1980s, or in Italy among kids more exposed to the signal of Berlusconi's commercial TVs, and at the influence of favorite TV channels on voting trends (although perhaps it can be just political trends that make people to choose one broadcaster rather than another):

They found that children raised in areas with greater access to Mediaset (a standard deviation in signal strength) had lower cognitive scores as adults by the equivalent of 3 to 4 I.Q. points.

People more exposed to Mediaset as children were also less likely to be civically engaged adults and more likely to vote for parties with populist tendencies like Forza Italia and the Five Star Movement ... Exposure to Fox News could increase Republican Party vote shares significantly, and that exposure to MSNBC increased Democratic Party voting share (but with a much weaker effect). (Rothwell, 2019)

Other studies are about the relationships between television viewing behaviors, and attachment, loneliness, depression, and psychological well-being, with particular reference to the so-called "binge-watching".

In a survey conducted by Netflix in February 2014, 73% of people define binge-watching as "watching between 2–6 episodes of the same TV show in one sitting." ("Binge-watching", from Wikipedia)

Past research has found that watching favorite television programs buffers against feelings of loneliness more so than other activities, including eating, surfing the web, listening to music, and watching anything that's on television ... With binge-watching television behavior being the crux of this research, we were interested to find the associations between binge-watching behavior and psychological variables ... We found that participants who scored high in anxious attachment – individuals who are characterized as having a preoccupation with closeness in relationships and fear of abandonment – also reported greater frequencies of engaging in binge-watching television ... Participants high in depression tended to report higher levels of watching television for both ritualistic and instrumental or purposeful motivations ... Interestingly, attachment and depression were positively related to the frequency of binge-watching television, but were not related to the frequency of watching television in general. (Wheeler, 2015)

What is hardly addressed is, in my opinion, the crucial point. In few words: how the habit to television affects the way people approach to new technologies and the web? How maybe in these years we have lost the opportunity to change the world because of the television habits of its inhabitants? That is not only a theoretical problem, neither a matter of what entertainment the most prefer and where next advertising investments will be made. The web is a global system of communication never seen in the history, and how citizens – non only audience or users – use it or don't, are active creators or passive consumers, that can concern any kind of problems and opportunities, social living, relations between peoples and nations, peace and war, life, and death.

Curiously (or not?), looking for studies or simply ideas online on such a subject, we get practically nothing (or maybe I am not able to do the right search on the internet! I have got a little different result using different search engines, but not so much significant).

In essence: it seems that as everyone was expecting the internet to change TV and not vice versa, almost all studies are in that one direction.

In nearly half of 221 primetime episodes analyzed in the study, higher levels of tweeting corresponded with additional viewers tuning in to the programming. The report also showed that the volume of tweets sent about a particular program caused significant changes in ratings among nearly 30 percent of the episodes. (Hirshberg, 2014).

Because the Internet is substantially different from television, the impact of the Internet on a television-dominated culture will be massive. Increased specialization, fragmentation, individualization, and decentralization of societal activity will cause stress to social, economic, and political institutions. Eventually society will adjust to the new communications culture, but it will be a substantially different society from that dominated by television. (Havick, 2000)

Sure? Perhaps you underestimated the strength of a television-dominated culture!

Apparently, it is not considered the possibility that it could instead be television to stifle in the bud the potentialities of the Internet, shaping it for the most as a new interactive space for entertainment, information, and marketing, in which we can take part, but not *make* it, nor to establish a new level of human relationships. Maybe it's also because a TV-like approach to the web cannot easily be verified by submitting a questionnaire to population samples, or with other empirical or experimental methods.

Results showed that students use the digital media majorly to access entertainment information and soft news, while they use the mainstream media to access serious news and to verify information obtained from the digital media. (Salaudeenm & Onyech, 2020)

Different media are compared as sources to *get* information. The small novelty seems to disappear that on the web information, virtually by anyone, can also be *made*!

6. SCIENCE FICTION AND THE HUMANITY SAVED BY SUPERHEROES, NOW AS BEFORE

In these 2020s, in the same way as in the 1960s, superheroes are still well present in the collective imagination. It might seem a small detail but, given the mostly emotional reaction with which, in the absence of a proper widespread culture, public opinion welcomes the frequent real or alleged technological novelties that "change our lives", as well as the great or little problems of the world, maybe starting with superheroes isn't that weird.

According to Wikipedia, the word "Superhero" first appears in 1899. But it is from around 1940 that the world begins to get acquainted with names that are still familiar to all generations: *Superman* (1938), *Batman* (1939) *The Flash*, *Green Lantern*, *Captain America* (1940), *Wonder Woman* (1941).

The *Hulk* (1962, the same year of *Spider-Man*) is a strange kind of superhero, but representative of the times:

Man and War, Man and Technology, finding humanity within, mirror into the dark side of humans, wrestling with the past of the inner self, man's place in world, the role of an individual and individuality in culture... ethical dilemmas... & the individual ... How powerful is the individual? (Frazetti, 2017)

Science fiction is getting more complex, the enemy or monster are no longer just there, the villains to fight, but sometimes develop from within us.

Forbidden Planet, American science-fiction film, released in 1956, that was noted for its groundbreaking and Academy Award-nominated special effects, all-electronic musical score, intelligent script, and robot "Robby" ... The characters, plot, and settings were inspired by William Shakespeare's The Tempest. (Forbidden Planet, Britannica entry)

It was the first science fiction film to depict humans traveling in a faster-than-light starship of their own creation. It was also the first to be set entirely on another planet in interstellar space, far away from Earth. The Robby the Robot character is one of the first film robots that was more than just a mechanical "tin can" on legs; Robby displays a distinct personality and is an integral supporting character in the film ... the Krell machine can create anything by mere thought, but the Krell forgot one thing: "monsters from the id". The machine gave the Krell's subconscious desires free rein with unlimited power, causing their extinction. (Forbidden Planet, Wikipedia entry)

From a very lighter point of view, in the animated stories of the *Jetsons* (1962):

daily life is leisurely, assisted by numerous labor-saving devices, which occasionally break down with humorous results. Despite this, everyone complains of exhausting hard labor and difficulties living with the remaining inconveniences. (The Jetsons, Wikipedia entry)

Many stories were written about the revolt of the machines, and surely one of the most intriguing is that of the computer Hal of *2001: A Space Odyssey* (1968). It is useful also to understand what was in the collective imagination the idea of computers in the 60s.

Science fiction is the most visible and influential form of futurist thinking in contemporary popular culture. (Lombardo, 2015)

Most superheroes of the first seasons are from the United States of America, but from the middle of the 70s a new generation of robotic heroes comes from Japan, such as *Grendizer* and *Mazinger*. They are cartoons aimed especially at the very young, but it is always about saving the earth from monsters and dangers of all kinds.

Some years later, *Dragon Ball* is a saga much more complex, with deep roots in Japanese culture, Shinto and Buddhism, with superheroes to the nth degree fighting against increasingly strong enemies, on earth and in planets. Children from all over the world, but not only children, decree a worldwide success to the story, and the saga multiplies in a continuous succession of dangers so increasingly huge as to be far-fetched, more cathartic than really scary, regularly foiled by heroes. "In 2015, the Japan Anniversary Association officially declared May 9 as 'Goku Day'" (Dragon Ball, official site).

We live in times when, with the prevalence of individualism and the fragmentation of the society, a tendency of people is to gather in virtual communities, around stories, emblematic characters.

Anderson argues that all communities, large or small, are imagined (1983/2006). Every community conceives of itself as a deep, horizontal comradeship, distinguished by languages, performances, and technologies that are real (i.e., they are enacted), yet believed into existence. This belief extends from the "imaginary," narratives that inculcate cultural norms and values into a group of people ... Novels and newspapers (i.e., narrative forms) provide "the technical means for 're-presenting' the kind of imagined community that is the nation" (2006, p. 25) ... The comic provides a field for analyzing imagined communities. Within comics there are ways in which societies re-present themselves, imagining social contexts that reflect sociological, educational, and citizenship realities. (Martin et al., 2023)

In September 2020, we read in BCC Culture:

In the golden age in the US, comics not only were widely read, but they were a medium that allowed much freedom of thought and explored the edges of human psychology through genres such as horror. They also broached questions about ethnicity, gender, and sexuality.

However, all of that ended in the 1950s, when comics became the target of cultural scare-mongering which accused them of undermining the family and Americanness. Many went out of business; those that survived agreed to self-censor and uphold 'American' ideals of decency and masculinity.

The presence of self-censorship in its DNA has made the comic book universe ripe for exploitation across global markets ... Hyper-sexualized but almost entirely sexless, the Marvel movies are emblematic of a blockbuster culture in which a certain degree of celibacy has become the norm. At a time when desperate studios are relying on the success of overly inflated event titles in order to stay afloat, the sheer cost of these juggernauts inevitably dictates their content, requiring the films to appeal not just to the traditional 18-34 demographic, but also younger kids, older adults, and — perhaps most importantly — the fine people of all ages who serve China's censorship bureau. (Laux, 2020)

And in difficult times as those of Pandemic, "Kids Need Superheroes Now More Than Ever". In the subtitle of this article, the suggestion is: "If Captain America can defeat the Red Skull, a child can conquer her anxiety of a Zoom class."

That morning in March, my daughter finally joined the Zoom class, but it was only after her Captain America mask was on securely, her blonde curls sticking out the sides and her blue suit Velcroed in the back. She stood in front of the computer with a new sense of confidence, the smile of a child saved by magical thinking. (Margulies, 2020)

A doubt, a spontaneous question; really can we think our world has changed so much, if we are going to tell and to dream the same heroes of the years 1950?

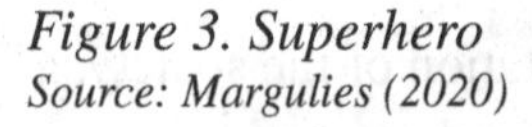

Figure 3. Superhero
Source: Margulies (2020)

7. TRAGEDY, COMEDY, AND EPIC POEMS OF THE MODERN TIMES

The need to rely on increasingly frightening stories, which end up happily ever after, as in most tales that humanity has always told, but often leave behind long trails of suffering, it feeds in present time an endless production for cinema, television, the web channels, that obviously can only be mentioned here, and covers several levels. And these stories are maybe to be considered deeper and more representative of the societies in which we live than many acts and words of politicians and journalists, who often seem to speak and write without having authors of the same standard behind.

When addressing to an adult audience, vampires, zombies, fantasy environments, the Middle Ages, the Romans, the Vikings are told in increasingly realistic productions, often show quite explicit violence and sex. The world, fantastic or inspired by reality, is often represented in a raw and disenchanted way, not hiding the contradictions and indeed sometimes emphasizing that, as in the fantasy of the *Game of Thrones,* or in the stories almost caught up in the news, as *Scandal* or *Gomorra*, there are no good and bad on earth but, in human affairs, beyond the vital impulses, loves and passions, people are all complicated, petty, bad, or full of defects and weaknesses with which in the end all of us must live.

With the holistic approach of postmodernism, there can be evil in good and good in evil. In the popular fantasy texts ... This change easily can be seen in the characters. (Şenel, 2021)

The modern version of an ancient genre, the tragedy, is less addressed to the communities than at the time of the Greeks or Shakespeare, it's more private, even to a certain extent "personalized", and performed not in theaters during special occasions but in houses daily in front of a screen.

Both Oedipus and Jon Snow are tragic heroes in their respective literary materials. (Trivedi, 2020)

A fact is that many like to watch the light-dark side of human nature, as it is also demonstrated by the success of TV programs and podcasts that tell real crimes, with an attention sometimes quite maniacal, an accurate reconstruction of the details even macabre and rough. Watching the reconstruction of violence, it may be a way to exorcise the real violence that, even when it does not directly affect us, we feel surrounding the world we live in.

On the crowded page of Crime TV Shows on Netflix, we read "From real-life documentaries to the comedy side of crime, this roundup features TV shows about corruption, conspiracies and crackdowns. Catch them if you can" (From Netflix web site).

The hunger of the individual for violence is a trigger for the generation of violent content by media, owners of political power, owners of religious power, etc. However, this content is produced considering the individual's sensitivities. Thus, violence is aestheticized. Aesthetics of violence appear in different fields and in different forms. (Erdem & Kocabay-Sener, 2021)

How much the consumption of this production digs into the minds and perception of the world of its viewers is not easy to establish, and the studies cannot analyze well reactions that ultimately remain private, probably a little different for each of the hundreds million people involved. Although they often emerge in reality with more or less unexpected results.

Hayes and Levett (2013) wrote an article about how the crime drama CSI created real biases in jurors during cases that involved forensic science ... The people who watched more crime dramas were more likely to support the death penalty compared to those who didn't watch crime dramas as often . . . those who enjoy crime dramas more expressed more confidence in the justice system. But, it was also found that those who watch more crime dramas are less likely to believe that most people who commit crimes are caught and brought to justice. (Hogan, 2019)

In an article published on "Frontiers in Psychology", the authors wonder:

For example, the death penalty has been abolished in most Western countries a long time ago but is often portrayed or mentioned in US crime shows, which are very popular outside the United States. Previous research suggests that the amount of television viewing can be associated with erroneous perceptions of the use of the death penalty—even when the death penalty is not used in the respective country. (Till et al., 2021)

On another side they are to be located other science fiction sagas such as *Star Trek* and *Star Wars*, probably comparable with another ancient genre, the epic poem. Not by chance they are celebrated more in cinemas, and also in mass gatherings of fans. In them there is a clearer distinction between the good and the bad, and to stay on the side of the good assures people in the end by their inevitable victory.

These stories cater to a more generalist audience, adults, children, nerds, but the overall result is that more and more emotions, fears, hopes, satisfactions have opportunities and reasons to lean on something that however is not the reality of life, as audience in front of movies, but also as virtual protagonists in video games.

Catharsis is the ancient, magic word, corresponding of a need of the human being in front of the difficulties of life. Catharsis is reached by telling stories, and this is probably why, in today's world, which is more problematic than ever, humanity reacts above all by telling stories. From the point of view of the creator of stories, it's presence «is a big reason why some novels just "work," even if the underlying setup doesn't seem that interesting at first. Those novels feel good to read because they create a sense of emotional tension that's then released at the end of the story ». (Jorstad, 2021)

Again, we look at the picture of the very young face of this blogger and read him using ancient Greek terms as *Peripeteia* = Change, *Hamartia* = Failure, Kairos = Timing. We can't help but think about how superficial we are when we think that people today can be so different because they walk having a mobile phone in their hand!

And again, here we emphasize that decades of personal computers, web and smartphones have changed almost for nothing certain basic attitudes of a mankind that, more bewildered then helped in their daily tasks, prefers to imagine to rely on the superheroes of the 40s, rather than really learn to use the latest technologies to take effective control of their lives.

However, having recalled ancient narrative genres that fill our lives today, we cannot fail to mention what in my opinion is perhaps the most current, in which the dynamic, critical, innovative, and positive forces are best expressed: comedy.

The Romans said: "Castigat ridendo mores!" (laughing corrects customs/manners, Wikipedia translation)

We all have the experience that, when for example the debate between politicians from opposing factions becomes entrenched in irreconcilable positions and unbearable to many disillusioned citizens, it is satire that, by highlighting the comic aspects and seemingly addressing issues in a joking manner, appears to illuminate reality with flashes of truth. It can be the sketches of a comedian on TV, or a theatrical performance, or a movie that discusses serious matters or real events highlighting the most paradoxical aspects, observing the facts from a lighthearted and seemingly carefree perspective, avoiding raw and dramatic representation, but still emphasizing the substance of the issues.

In Dario Fo's theater, the audience laughed a lot, but it was socially and politically engaged like few others.

Fo's brilliance in combining urgent political concerns with elements of storytelling, pantomime and grotesque farce, made his plays simultaneously provocative and highly entertaining. It allowed them to embody and communicate what Terry Eagleton describes in another context as "the vulgar cheerfulness of social hope.

This kind of theatre encourages the spectators to an objective and active contemplation of serious issues. According to Fo, his theatre, like traditional, sub-cultural forms, uses grotesque farces because satirical laughter helps avoid the danger of catharsis. (Dario Fo's Politics of Subversive Laughter, "Wire", 2016 Oct. 30)

It can also happen though that, searching for the comedic side, likable aspects are shown also of the "villain" and social criticism risks diluting into a melancholic smile without action, resolving personal discomfort without leading to commitment. For example:

"War Dogs" is a film about horrible people that refuses to own the horribleness. It's too enamored with its glib arms dealer heroes, and although it's packed with scenes that might have inspired moral whiplash in works like "Scarface," "Goodfellas" and "The Wolf of Wall Street". (Zoller Seitz, 2016)

It depends greatly, especially in a fragmented society like today's, on the specific cultural context and how comedy or political satire resonate with the audience:

Because the comprehension of and meaning derived from political humor depend on the cognitive contribution of the audience, future work on political humor's impact ought to link detailed analyses of humorous texts to audience characteristics, psychology, and viewing motivations. (Young, 2014)

The topic is very complex, and here it is important to remember that, whether we laugh in a more or less conscious way about events on which we already have our own opinion, or immerse ourselves in absolutely fantastic and cathartic stories good for an audience of all ages, or even voyeuristically witness extremely realistic and raw representations of reality, in all these ways our understanding of the world develops through what others tell us. It's not about the actual reality, but about its narrative.

Even the obsessive story of the news on TV, which become the pretext for endless speeches by journalists, opinion leaders, experts in various capacities, rather than encouraging the formation of better documented opinions on what is happening in the world, it seems to respond to an increasingly widespread morbid curiosity to observe from every possible angle the spectacular side of the news, whether it is sports, politics, crime.

What makes you think human beings are sentient and aware? There's no evidence for it. Human beings never think for themselves, they find it too uncomfortable. For the most part, members of our species simply repeat what they are told-and become upset if they are exposed to any different view. The characteristic human trait is not awareness but conformity, and the characteristic result is religious warfare. Other animals fight for territory or food; but, uniquely in the animal kingdom, human beings fight for their "beliefs." (Michael Crichton, quotes, The Lost World)

8. TELLING ONLINE THE TRUE AND THE FALSE: ECHO CHAMBERS AND FILTER BUBBLES

In the current day and age, objective facts have less influence on opinions and decisions than personal emotions and beliefs. Many individuals rely on their social networks to gather information thanks to social media's ability to share information rapidly and over a much greater geographic range. However, this creates an overall false balance as people tend to seek out information that is compatible with their existing views and values. They deliberately seek out "facts" and data that specifically support their conclusions and classify any information that contradicts their beliefs as "false news. (Dalkir & Katz, 2020)

With recent headlines around fake news from world leaders and around presidential elections, Twitter and other social media platforms being pressured to detect and label misinformation posted on their platforms, as well as misinformation around COVID-19 and its vaccine, the world has seen an increase in protests, policy changes, and even chaos surrounding this information. (Research Anthology on Fake News, 2021, description)

Educational professionals are now tasked with employing best practices to not only teach basic digital literacy and citizenship skills but also to recognize how technology-immersed learning environments interact with deep fakes and misinformation while equipping students with the tools necessary to recognize authentic and altered content. (Blankenship, 2021)

In a world known above all through narrations, more narrated than lived, the web or better social networks become the perfect space in which all sorts of news are propagated, true, false, proposed by so-called mainstream channels, by the alternative ones, by common people, that interact with billions of other news in ways that are sometimes predictable and sometimes not. And many then carve out small spaces in which to talk about maybe a few things, but that they have the impression of being able to control. Or they choose not to speak at all, as they feel that the environment in which they move is not their own.

The online searches from our browser, the list of friends of which we receive the notifications of the posts, those to which communication arrives of what we write, all are managed by algorithms that, in the immense spaces of networks, first select the references that are based on our previous research, our tastes, as far as possible also our cultural and political preferences. The navigation becomes personalized, and everyone probably has noticed, after searching on Google any consumer product, to receive shortly after an advertising of that product on Facebook.

This happens in networks where the commercial use of data has over time become a science, always on the border and often beyond the rules that the legislators establish to protect our privacy.

To describe the boundaries and limitations of our online movements, scholars have coined terms such as “echo chamber” and “filter bubble”, describing a sort of “comfort zone” in which our network presence is automatically delimited.

Figure 4. Echo Chambers 1
Source: Germain (2021)

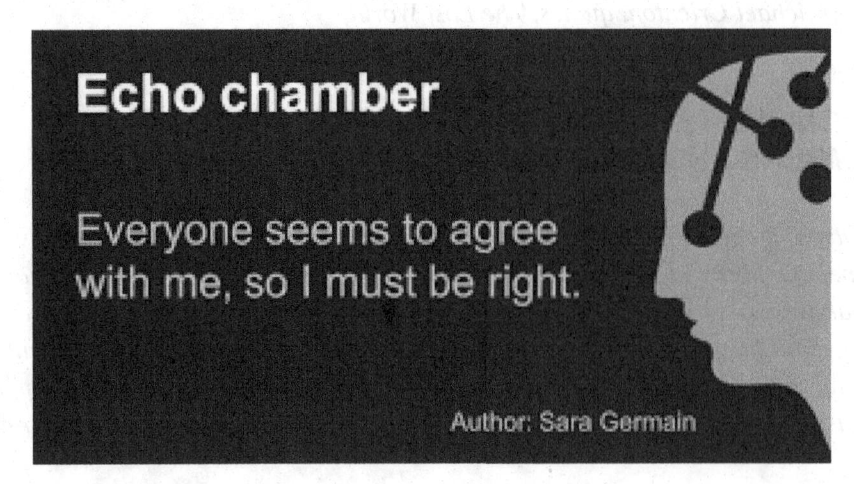

An *echo chamber* is "a bounded, enclosed media space that has the potential to both magnify the messages delivered within it and insulate them from rebuttal" (Jamieson & Capella, 2008, p.76).

The term filter bubble was coined by the activist and entrepreneur Eli Pariser in his book of the same name, to capture his concern that the increasing use of personalisation in the ranking of search engine results and social media feeds would create "a unique universe of information for each of us (2011).

An echo chamber is a form of bubble, but the term does not prejudge why some people might live in such bubbles – it is possible, for example, that some actively chose to, that the situation is a result of demand more than distribution or supply. A filter bubble, on the other hand, is an echo chamber primarily produced by ranking algorithms engaged in passive personalisation without any active choice on our part. (Ross Arguedas et al., 2022).

This does not mean that each of us can only move along predetermined tracks, and yet we must take into account the "web" that, in exchange for services most often for free, providers weave around our surfing and activity in the network. Anyhow, we are not compelled by anyone to stay closed in our bubbles, and also always interacting only with those who agree with us may not be the best solution.

Resonance is not consonance. With my best friends I always argue all the time about everything; it involves hearing a voice that says something different and that makes me answer, a process whereby we both shift and transform into something else. The situation might turn if you say, for example, "You are just a racist idiot" – then closure occurs and I no longer want to be affected. (Hartmut Rosa, in Lijster & Celikates, 2019)

Figure 5. Echo Chambers 2
Source: Definizione Di Echo Chamber (n.d.)

9. UNAWARE PRODUCERS OF INFORMATION IN A SOCIETY OF FEAR: WE ARE AFRAID OF CHILDREN'S SMILES!

Michael Crichton, in his State of Fear, highlights how in industrialized nations, where well-being is widespread and life expectancy is very high, inhabitants live in fear: fear of crime, foreigners, pollution, diseases, food, and technology. And they are nervous, irritable, and depressed. With a series of hardly positive consequences.

We could approach this subject from several points of view, but one example I like to make, particularly significant, and directly connected to the mentioned fact that, regarding our own lives, we increasingly act on the basis not of how we live them, but of how the others tell us.

The privacy laws that many countries have introduced to "protect" minors by preventing the publication of their images without parental consent are producing detrimental and counterproductive effects.

Thought at the beginning with little more than a "courtesy" intention - you use a picture of my baby, please ask my permission - these laws were rapidly distorted in a perverse way by the presence on the network of photos of children in the clandestine and criminal circuits of pedophilia.

It is not the intention of the legislator, nor of the practically unanimous chorus that warns parents to think twice before publishing photos of their children on the web, but the message in the end is clear; the Internet is the place where photos of our children can arouse the morbid appetites of maniacs! To put pictures of kids is dangerous!

Let's think it well! Really? Or don't we risk with this fear of actually hurting our children?

Looking at the picture of the athletic Olympic champion, his wife and their baby with disguised eyes, I wondered; how can I explain to my son or my nephew *why* the face of this child has been so horribly hidden?

Figure 6. Baby
Source: Beneventi (2022)

Because this is a message of violence, of strong fear!

The same is publishing of social network or official school web sites the photos of amusing and instructive activities, with a teacher, a clown, a musician in the middle and all the faces of the kids around hidden by nice yellow points! It is the saddest of the messages, and even sadder is not realizing how unnatural and socially distressing is to internalize and make this type of communication "normal". You haven't got the permission? Don't publish counterproductive images at all!

And what about the smiling images of children who, as a first reaction in many people now, no longer evoke tenderness, love, hope, but the danger of maniacs lurking in the corners of the Internet to perpetrate their horrendous crimes? This way, the morbid thinking is becoming dominant, and probably we are hurting, very badly, our children and ourselves. On the base not of real dangers, but of a shallow narrative.

In practice, to "protect" from a hypothetical danger, which could threaten perhaps one child in a million, the most advanced society are choosing to grow entire generations in a climate of suspicion and fear. And we know that fear is the main cause of discomfort and violence.

We'll deal better in chapter 5 also with the dark sides of the web, where cyber bullying, child pornography and other criminal behaviors are present and can threaten our lives.

But do we really think that to publish pictures of a school activity of feast can be really put someone in danger? More than traveling by car, walking on the street, swimming in the pool, or just existing and living? Statistics tell us that most child abuse occurs in the family or are from relatives and acquaintances. And there are no data that can authorize links between photos published for example on the website of a school and possible activities of pedophiles. Although perhaps just making the publication of these photos in public opinion almost "forbidden" can encourage perverse minds to use them also in this direction.

10. THE LATENT CULTURE AND THE WEB: A HUGE MISSED OPPORTUNITY SO FAR

Television is the common culture of all generations, all around the world. As mostly passive viewers, thanks to that culture we can understand the audiovisual messages we watch, but usually we don't even think that we can use it to produce not trivial content. As we will see better in Chapter 7, children, who are still able, when playing, to pull out what they have inside, show us that, with the easy and powerful means of today, it is quite simple to recover our latent culture of TV viewers and turn it into the ability to make.

But Internet is not only television. As in the case of the personal power of computers, of which as in a film flashback we go to talk in the next chapter, there is no need for deep reasoning, nor for particular scientific investigations, to see how it's difficult, for the inhabitants of a planet all accustomed to the passive modes of television, to move suddenly in an appropriate way within a global environment where vice versa everyone is at the same time, at practically the same level, consumers and producers of information. Under these conditions, in the hand of a substantially illiterate public, consumption and development of the global network can only be uncertain, approximate, determined by the market and advertising more than by technical possibilities. And this is why from the original World Wide Web, open and free, asking initiative and responsibility, the vast majority of the citizens of the information society has been diverted to social networks, structured platforms in which no technological skill is required and whose rules and functioning are decided elsewhere, by a master. They are a very limited version of the web, individualistic, competitive, taking responsibility away, structured so that the elements of

Figure 7. Kids camera

interactivity do not come out of the container, do not open new perspectives for those who go today on the Internet as yesterday watched television.

And it is quite incredible how so many reflections on what will be our "future", even by those who would have the cultural elements to understand and evaluate, do not take into account this decisive original sin.

But latent audiovisual culture is anyhow everywhere, and we could take its scattered elements and remix them to build something new, maybe important, and exciting.

In the following chapters I will try to develop a series of reasoning and observations I hope useful to better define the more general context in which the relationship between humans and technology should be considered, so as not to limit each time to deal empirically and improvise with opportunities and problems. Beyond the sense of discomfort and the difficulty of always leaning, to form our own ideas, to understand and choose, on narratives of narratives.

If traveling in the metaverse can be considered in the end a further step along the way drawn once by television, as for music asking to Alexa to play something is another step of the old story begun when first a person put a record on a phonograph, the idea of continuous novelties to which people should adapt to, which upsets the modern women and men, it can be reasonably resized. Maybe in reality people have more time and ease to feel to themselves, to their personal relationship with others and with the real natural and human world in which they live. And to let the world itself, not only its technical representations, tell directly multiple stories while we live in it: air, water, landscapes, ancient and modern buildings, natural scenery, smells, flavors, touching things and feeling to be touched by the wind, the rain, the sun.

REFERENCES

Beneventi, P. (2022, Feb 23). *Reame del Sospetto e della Paura. sapereambiente.it.*

Binge-watching. (n.d.). Wikipedia. https://en.wikipedia.org/wiki/Binge-watching

Blankenship, R. J. (2021). *Deep Fakes, Fake News, and Misinformation in Online Teaching and Learning Technologies*. IGI Global. doi:10.4018/978-1-7998-6474-5

Brusila, J. (2021). Music, Digitalization, and Democracy. *Popular Music and Society, 45.*

Certi, S & Toldi, F. (1986, Jan). AI: Un passato e un futuro. *Personal Computer*, 1.

Crichton, M. (1997). *The Lost World*. Knopf.

Crichton, M. (2004). *State of Fear*. HarperCollins.

Crime TV Shows. (n.d.). netflix.com.

Dalkir, K., & Katz, R. (2020). *Navigating Fake News, Alternative Facts, and Misinformation in a Post-Truth World*. IGI Global. doi:10.4018/978-1-7998-2543-2

Definizione Di Echo Chamber. (n.d). insidemarketing.it/glossario/

Forbidden Planet. (n.d.a). *Britannica*.

Forbidden Planet. (n.d.b). *Wikipedia*.

Frazetti, D. G. (2017). *Social and Scientific Aspects of The Hulk*. academia.edu.

Ganguly, L. (2018, Feb 27). Global Television Formats and Their Impact on Production Cultures: The Remaking of Music Entertainment Television in India. *Sage Journals*, *20*(1).

Germain, S. (2021). Echo chamber (K. McClintock, Trans.). In C. Gratton, E. Gagnon-St-Pierre, & E. Muszynski (Eds.), Shortcuts: A handy guide to cognitive biases (Vol. 4). Academic Press.

Havick, J. (2000, April). The impact of the Internet on a television-based society. *Technology in Society*, *22*(2), 273–287. doi:10.1016/S0160-791X(00)00008-7

Hirshberg, P. (2014). First the Media, Then Us: How the Internet Changed the Fundamental Nature of the Communication and Its Relationship with the Audience. *Change, 19*.

Hogan, A. (2019). *How crime dramas influence perception of crime* [Undergraduate Honors Thesis]. Butler University. digitalcommons.butler.edu

Jamieson, J. N., & Capella, K. H. (2008). *Echo Chamber: Rush Limbaugh and the Conservative Media Establishment*. Oxford University Press.

Jorstad, L. (2021, Jun 8). Creating Catharsis: How to Write a Story That Works. *The Novel Smithy*.

Laux, C. (2020, Sep 3). Why we no longer need superheroes. *BBC*. bbc.com/culture

Lijster, T., & Celikates, R. (2019). Beyond the Echo-chamber: An Interview with Hartmut Rosa on Resonance and Alienation. Krisis, Journal for Contemporary Philosophy, 39(1).

Lombardo, T. (2015). Dec). Science Fiction: The Evolutionary Mythology of the Future. *Journal of Futures Studies*, *20*(2).

Malick, J. (2016, Oct 30). Dario Fo's Politics of Subversive Laughter. *Wire, The Arts*.

Margulies, M. (2020, Sep 21). Kids Need Superheroes Now More Than Ever: If Captain America can defeat the Red Skull, a child can conquer her anxiety of a Zoom class. *The New York Times*.

Martin, J. (2023). Comics and Community: Exploring the Relationship Between Society, Education, and Citizenship. In *Exploring Comics and Graphic Novels in the Classroom*. IGI Global.

May 9th Is Goku Day! Here's All the Information You Need!! (2021, May 9). Dragon Ball, official site.

Media, Globalization, and Television. (2013, Dec). afghanpopculture.wordpress.com

Mihăeş, L. C. (2021). *Handbook of Research on Contemporary Storytelling Methods Across New Media and Disciplines*. IGI Global. doi:10.4018/978-1-7998-6605-3

Nur Erdem, M. (2020). *Handbook of Research on Aestheticization of Violence, Horror, and Power*. IGI Global.

Research Anthology on Fake News, Political Warfare, and Combatting the Spread of Misinformation. (2021). IGI Global.

Ross Arguedas. (2022). *Echo chambers, filter bubbles, and polarisation: A literature review*. reutersinstitute.politics.ox.ac.uk

Rothwell, J. (2019, Jul 25). You Are What You Watch? The Social Effects of TV. *The New York Times*.

Salaudeenm, M. A., & Onyech, N. (2020). Digital media vs mainstream media: Exploring the influences of media exposure and information preference as correlates of media credibility. *Cogent Arts & Humanities*, *7*(1).

Şenel, S. (2021). Change of Good and Evil Concepts in Fantasy Genre. In *International Perspectives on Rethinking Evil in Film and Television*. IGI Global. doi:10.4018/978-1-7998-4778-6.ch003

Straubhaar, J. D. (2007). *World Television: From Global to Local*. The University of Texas. doi:10.4135/9781452204147

The Globalization of Television. (2015). electricgargle.blogspot.com

The Jetsons. (n.d.). *Wikipedia*. https://en.wikipedia.org/wiki/The_Jetsons

The Origins of The Italian Language. (n.d.). kwintessential.co.uk

The State of TV and Video Advertising. (2022). *MediaRadar Blog*.

Till, B., Arendt, F., & Niederkrotenthaler, T. (2021, July 21). The Relationship Between Crime-Related Television Viewing and Perceptions of the Death Penalty: Results of a Large Cross-Sectional Survey Study. *Frontiers in Psychology*, *12*, 715657. doi:10.3389/fpsyg.2021.715657 PMID:34367036

Trivedi, K. (2020, Aug 27). *Oedipus Rex Tragic Hero Comparison to Jon Snow of Game of Throne*. coursehero.com.

Waisbord, S. (2004, Nov). McTV: Understanding the Global Popularity of Television Formats. *Sage Journals, 5*(4).

Wheeler, S. K. (2015, Apr 20). *The Relationships Between Television Viewing Behaviors, Attachment, Loneliness, Depression, and Psychological WellBeing* [Honors College Theses]. Georgia Southern University. digitalcommons.georgiasouthern.edu

Young, D. G. (2014, Sep 2). Theories and Effects of Political Humor: Discounting Cues, Gateways, and the Impact of Incongruities. In *The Oxford Handbook of Political Communication*. Oxford University Press.

Zoller Seitz, M. (2016, Aug 19). *War Dogs.* rogerebert.com

ADDITIONAL READING

Caitlin Dewey, C. (2022 Nov 7). California's New Child Privacy Law Could Become National Standard. *stateline.org*.

Childhood Exposure to Violence. (n.d.). *healthychildren.org*.

Christmas, C. G. (2020). *Media Ethics: Cases and Moral Reasoning*. Routledge. doi:10.4324/9780429282249

Eco, U. (1976). *A theory of semiotics*. Indiana University Press. doi:10.1007/978-1-349-15849-2

Flaxman, Goel, S., & Rao, J. M. (2016). Filter Bubbles, Echo Chambers, and Online News Consumption. *Public Opinion Quarterly*, *80*(Special Issue), 298–320. doi:10.1093/poq/nfw006

Gligorijević, J. (2019, June). Children's Privacy: The Role of Parental Control and Consent. *Human Rights Law Review*, *19*(2), 201–229. doi:10.1093/hrlr/ngz004

Hartney, E. (2022, Feb 10). The Symptoms and Risks of Television Addiction. *verywellmind.com.*

How Reality Television Influences Teenagers. (2023, April 9). *StudyCorgi.* studycorgi.com.

Influence of Television on the American Society. (2019). *IvyPanda*. ivypanda.com/essays.

Kovach, B., & Rosenstiel, T. (2001). *The Elements of Journalism: What Newspeople Should Know and the Public Should Expect*. Crown Publishers.

Pariser, E. (2011). *The Filter Bubble: What The Internet Is Hiding From You.* Viking/Penguin Press.

Rodowick, D. N. (1995). Audiovisual Culture and Interdisciplinary Knowledge. *New Literary History*, *26*(1), 111–121.

Shaikh, S. J. (2017). Television Versus the Internet for Information Seeking: Lessons From Global Survey Research. *International Journal of Communication*, *11*, 4744–4756.

Sharenting: What parents should consider before posting their children's photos online. (n.d.). usa.kaspersky.com

Shelly, M. (2018). *Frankenstein; or The Modern Prometheus*. Penguin. (Original work published 1818)

Chapter 3
The Intangible Power of New Machines in the Hands of Anyone:
Expertise, Illiteracy, Control

ABSTRACT

PCs and the Internet are systems complex and new, far from the styles of traditional knowledge. During the 1980s and 1990s, crowds of passionate amateurs, often very young, made innovation more than big companies, understanding and inventing, tinkering, and sharing 3D graphics, multimedia, music on devices that challenged them to be smarter: More than machines, infinite sets of possibilities, that people learned more from playing than from attending classes. On video games and home applications it was laid the foundations for a new literacy. With the global mass market, an app for everything, and the migration on the cloud, where managing of data is no longer in the hands of users, the division between producers and consumers seems to be restored, and expertise and control are no more potentially for all, but even at low levels widely returned to the "experts."

1. INTRODUCTION

Personal computers are multi-purpose machines that do not need a network to work. Smartphones are computers in all respects. Under the friendly interfaces, they are very complex devices and the fact that most users use them almost without knowing them, does not help to develop their potential in society. The cloud is a great invention to work better, but the generalized and automatic migration of data into a space managed by providers, is likely to completely remove users control over what they produce.

The story of PCs was written by a collective movement that made them develop far beyond the plans of the industry and the market. There were technicians in this story, but also humanists, visionaries, philosophers, and the contribution of often very young enthusiasts who, playing with machines, discovered possibilities that were not initially imagined by the producers themselves. Because a lot of what we can

DOI: 10.4018/978-1-6684-8228-5.ch003

do with digital devices depends on software. And soon PCs, beyond the calculations of scientists and office applications, they became real tools for artists and performers. Video games have also developed a culture of our time and for many they have been a great stimulus to understanding technology.

The mass use of digital devices, even by an audience that has not received any specific instruction and is getting used to downloading apps that solve every problem instead of humans, it seriously risks bringing us back to that centralized control that was imagined many years ago, much before the invention of the personal computers and the web.

2. PERSONAL COMPUTERS: MULTI-PURPOSE MACHINES EVEN BEFORE AND WITHOUT INTERNET

A personal computer (PC) is a multi-purpose microcomputer whose size, capabilities, and price make it feasible for individual use. Personal computers are intended to be operated directly by an end user, rather than by a computer expert or technician. Unlike large, costly minicomputers and mainframes, time-sharing by many people at the same time is not used with personal computers. . . . During the early 1980s, home computers were further developed for household use, with software for personal productivity, programming and games.

Bulletin board systems and online service providers became more commonly available after 1978. Commercial Internet service providers emerged in the late 1980s, giving public access to the rapidly growing network.

In 1991, the World Wide Web was made available for public use. The combination of powerful personal computers with high-resolution graphics and sound, with the infrastructure provided by the Internet, and the standardization of access methods of the Web browsers, established the foundation for a significant fraction of modern life, from bus time tables through unlimited distribution of free videos through to online user-edited encyclopedias. (Personal computer, Wikipedia entry)

Most users today, if switching on their PC find that for some reason Internet is not available, probably switch off the machine, as if it was temporarily useless.

But what the hell people could do with a personal computer before 1991, if there was not the World Wide Web to connect to?

Two key words in this respect are on the Wikipedia entry.

First: *Time-sharing*.

Throughout the late 1960s and the 1970s, computer terminals were multiplexed onto large institutional mainframe computers (centralized computing systems), which in many implementations sequentially polled the terminals to see whether any additional data was available, or action was requested by the computer user. (Time-sharing, Wikipedia entry)

That's to say that software, process capabilities and data, all were in the mainframes, owned and controlled by few powerful offices and institutions, and remote users, from their screens and keyboard (*terminals*), could access them in some time intervals, shared with other users.

In personal computers, instead, software, process capabilities and data, all were put in a single, local machine.

Second: *Software for personal productivity, programming and games*. It was what users found or could obtain for their personal computer, in order to do what they need. Typically - as described here also in chapter 8 - programs given "in bundle" with machines of the eighties included word processors, painting programs, video games and a music or sound creator in case of machines with dedicated co-processors. Along with the ability to program in BASIC, they were more than enough to encourage the user to try, experiment, do, as well as of course look for other software for various applications.

3. UNDER THE FRIENDLY INTERFACE: PCS (AND SMARTPHONES) ARE VERY COMPLEX SYSTEMS

When computers were as big as rooms or closets and programmed with punch cards, the white-coat technicians who worked with them had nothing in common with ordinary people. Those machines were called also *electronic brains* and were quite frightening (see Hally, 2005).

Between the 1970s and the 80s computers became *personal*, that's to say they entered offices and houses. At the beginning they had few applications, not easy to manage and not in graphic mode. Writing with a word processor software, for example, on the green or amber phosphor screens, the typist had to enter, in addition to the text, a whole series of control characters that would not be printed, to define the features of the font, the lay-out and so on. Many of these control characters (ctrl+B=bold, ctrl+I=Italic), are still used today as keyboard commands, making the work of experienced users faster than using a mouse.

Those early computers, especially when aimed at the home market, were also provided with a so called "hi-level" programming language, the *BASIC* (Beginners' All-purpose Symbolic Instruction Code). Hi-level does not mean that the language is better than others, but that resembles the human languages and for this is generally less powerful, while on the other hand machine codes are much stronger and direct, but not understandable for common users.

BASIC is quite similar to English and, to run on machines, it needs a software interpreter. It made anyone able to "program" a computer, when writing things like "PRINT 2 + 3" and pressing the ENTER key, on the screen appeared the result: "5"! Every line of a classic BASIC "listing" is numbered, and anyone, not only a computer genius, could start practicing:

```
10 INPUT A
20 INPUT B
30 C = A + B
40 PRINT C
```

Magic!

Here we are joking a bit, but with a few tens or hundreds of lines it was quite simple to write a software to perform complex mathematical calculations, or keep the wine list updated in the cellar, and even to program elementary video games.

Someone, taken by enthusiasm, came to call BASIC the "Latin of the future", but by the professionals it was rather defined "spaghetti programming", because it was quite cumbersome. It also depended on the particular BASIC "dialect", because that of Commodore 64 was different from that of Sinclair Spectrum, as well as there were differences between Microsoft BASIC for PC and MSX.

Figure 1. Basic
Source: Turner (2020)

```
10 'This will draw 5 spheres
20 GOTO 160
50 IF VERT GOTO 100
60 CIRCLE (X,Y),R,C,,,.07
70 FOR I = 1 TO 5
80 CIRCLE (X,Y),R,C,,,I*.2:NEXT I
90 IF VERT THEN RETURN
100 CIRCLE (X,Y),R,C,,,1.3
110 CIRCLE (X,Y),R,C,,,1.9
120 CIRCLE (X,Y),R,C,,,3.6
130 CIRCLE (X,Y),R,C,,,9.8
140 IF VERT GOTO 60
150 RETURN
160 CLS:SCREEN 1:COLOR 0,1:KEY OFF:VERT=0
170 X=160:Y=100:C=1:R=50:GOSUB 50
180 X=30:Y=30:C=2:R=30:GOSUB 50
190 X=30:Y=169:GOSUB 50
200 X=289:Y=30:GOSUB 50
210 X=289:Y=169:GOSUB 50
220 LINE (30,30)-(289,169),1
230 LINE (30,169)-(289,30),1
240 LINE (30,169)-(289,30),1,B
250 Z$=INKEY$: IF Z$="" THEN 250
RUN
```

It was an intense but short season, because in 1984 the first MacIntosh was out, and in 1985 Amiga and Atari ST, all with graphic interface and mouse, working and gaming application and no programming language by default.

The author wrote more extensively about this in "When Technology Becomes Popular; A Multimedia, Shared Production for the Information Age", Chapter 2 of the book *Technology and the New Generation of Active Citizens* (Beneventi 2018).

Though more and more familiar, even if commanded with a finger, PCs (and smartphones, that are computers in all respects) are very complex systems.

They appear since decades easy and friendly (at least when everything works fine!), but they have a lot of programs that get installed where and how they want, with their collection of "libraries", of which the most users ignore the existence until for some reason something is missing and then comes the pain! (They came out also computers that allowed people to look inside them, for instance Amiga, but they did not get that success on the market).

In a digital system there are also a lot of *directories* – people know them as "folders", which is a nice metaphor, but not always it helps to understand – in which the users, but also the system itself put a huge amount of data. Knowing where we put our data would be the least, to be able to pick them up when we need them, but to make things "easier", programs have always had their automatic storage folders so that, if we simply accept them and especially if several users access the workstation and don't do everything right, after a while every PC becomes an inextricable tangle.

Anyhow, on PCs an aware user can deal decently with folders, look inside, copy, paste, move documents between directories. But probably many, even not completely clueless, will have wondered, handling an Android device, from what they are occupied all those gigabytes, or why to go and see a single picture that one would know very well where it is, he or she is often forced to pass the whole gallery, with hundreds or thousands of images; connecting an external disk full of pictures to a tablet to view something, it can be a real nightmare!

Anyhow, remaining Apple *iPhone* a world apart, the success of Android over the years has decreed the end of other operating systems for smartphones, as Symbian and Windows phone. And we do not have to worry! The solution, for which market leaders gently assist us to facilitate our "migration", is to put everything into the *cloud*!

4. THE HEAD IN THE CLOUD, THE MISSING NETWORKING, AND THE POWER OF INFORMATION

Please, do you mean that my work, my thoughts, my personal memories, my projects, everything I do using tools with which I now do everything, I have to entrust them completely to a provider that manages them for me? And not because I need for example to be able to access the same data from different devices, or to share them more easily with others, which is why the Cloud was invented and is actually useful. Common users, all users are called to migrate to the Cloud for convenience, for having no thoughts, using complex systems as they were quite simple, managing the power of information without knowing anything of how it works...

Using a computer or a smartphone is now somehow like getting on a plane. Users are not to be educated in any way (who of the passengers is requested to be able to fly an airplane?) and everything is prepared so that they must depend completely on the captain.

The idea of *learning* digital devices has accompanied us in all these decades, and still in schools children are taught about "coding", but the commercial trend has been for several years to increasingly free the users from any kind of responsibility; "There's an App For That" (Apple trademark, from Wired, 2018, Oct 11) And the main narrative is that we can use a science fiction technology at any time in our life, entrusting it practically all of our life, without knowing to read, write, manage it, because someone else is providing all for us!

No dictatorship in history had probably ever dared such a complete domination over people!

We'll consider better in other parts of this book the possible implications regarding individual freedom and democracy. But even from a technical point of view, it is an attitude that makes no sense. Digital gadgets in the real world are not those of the already mentioned *Jetsons* cartoon, that the human pushes a button, and they do everything.

The author of this book, for example, usually lets his current works on the cloud, so that he can deal with them from his desktop PC, or from laptop and phone, but he prefers to save backup copies on external disk drives, not connected to a network.

The danger can be real or hypothetical, but as long as most references in the network address to providers (and as long as the same search for references depends on a provider), it is difficult for example to find testimonies whether it is true or not - as it is been said around - that someone has lost completely all work, or all the music, paid dearly, simultaneously on the iPod, the PC and every other possible devices because of an error of the automatic synchronization. Difficult also because the search directs you first of all to what Apple and Microsoft say.

From the "Guardian", March 18, 2019:

Myspace, the once mighty social network, has lost every single piece of content uploaded to its site before 2016, including millions of songs, photos and videos with no other home on the internet.

The company is blaming a faulty server migration for the mass deletion, which appears to have happened more than a year ago, when the first reports appeared of users unable to access older content. The company has confirmed to online archivists that music has been lost permanently, dashing hopes that a backup could be used to permanently protect the collection for future generations. (Hern, 2019)

Already at the time many were surprised, reading the news, that Myspace still existed, but for a period it had been an absolute reference point for all the people of the Web. And when we talk about more than 50 million songs lost, they were not only placed there as in an online store and so available also elsewhere, because Myspace had been for years the favorite platform by many artists to mark their presence online, many little known, but also several famous singers and groups.

Behind these, in the long queue, are consigned to oblivion records, demos, jam sessions, photos of about 14 million more or less professional musicians, including (as far as I realize that is not decisive) those I had uploaded on the page of my first group back in 2004. (Tomatis, 2019, translated from Italian)

We're going to see better about Myspace as the first important social network in Chapter 4.

Another big risk, more cultural, is to miss, for common users, the difficult concept of *networking*. That is, if we had to choose among all the innovations of our time, probably the most important one, the newest, the one that the citizens of the information society struggle a lot to realize, because in recent decades it has changed its structure and potentialities in a radical way.

In many animal societies, as well as traditionally in most human ones, networks have a center, a head, a tip of a pyramid. The queen of the bees, the head of the herd, the king, the feudal lord, the manager of a company stand at the top and the others descend and are located around. And so also it was the digital information system at the time of mainframe computers.

With personal computers and smartphones, there are indeed huge warehouses and data sorting centers, there are the "giants of the web" that, especially if the others do nothing, can deal with a huge amount of information, but power is potentially available in every single device. A new network, never seen before, extends throughout the planet, more than to the old pyramids similar to the non-hierarchical organization of plants, which can branch, colonize, conquer the territories and the entire planet without the need for leaders (see Mancuso, 2017).

Having the problem of fetching or producing, saving, recovering, sharing large amounts of data between computer disks, external memories, and the network it's not just only a hassle. It's also - like running or bike training - a way to become able, through exercise, to naturally manage new research, knowledge, and work environments in human societies, to which we cannot simply apply the already known models.

More in general, if someone knows how to do something well enough, then it is convenient to find shortcuts to make it better and faster. But if someone who does not know things yet gets used to ready-made shortcuts, he can certainly work quickly and apparently well for a while, but he will never get a real know-how and at the first difficulty he will enter into crisis.

Automating operations on a PC or phone does not help users, and not only in the long term. It can be useful in the immediate to carry out statistically common operations in a seemingly simpler way. But if passing the mouse or the finger I make often happen things that at that moment I do not need, I have

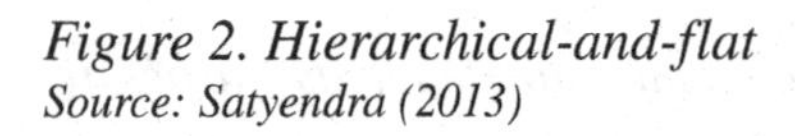

Figure 2. Hierarchical-and-flat
Source: Satyendra (2013)

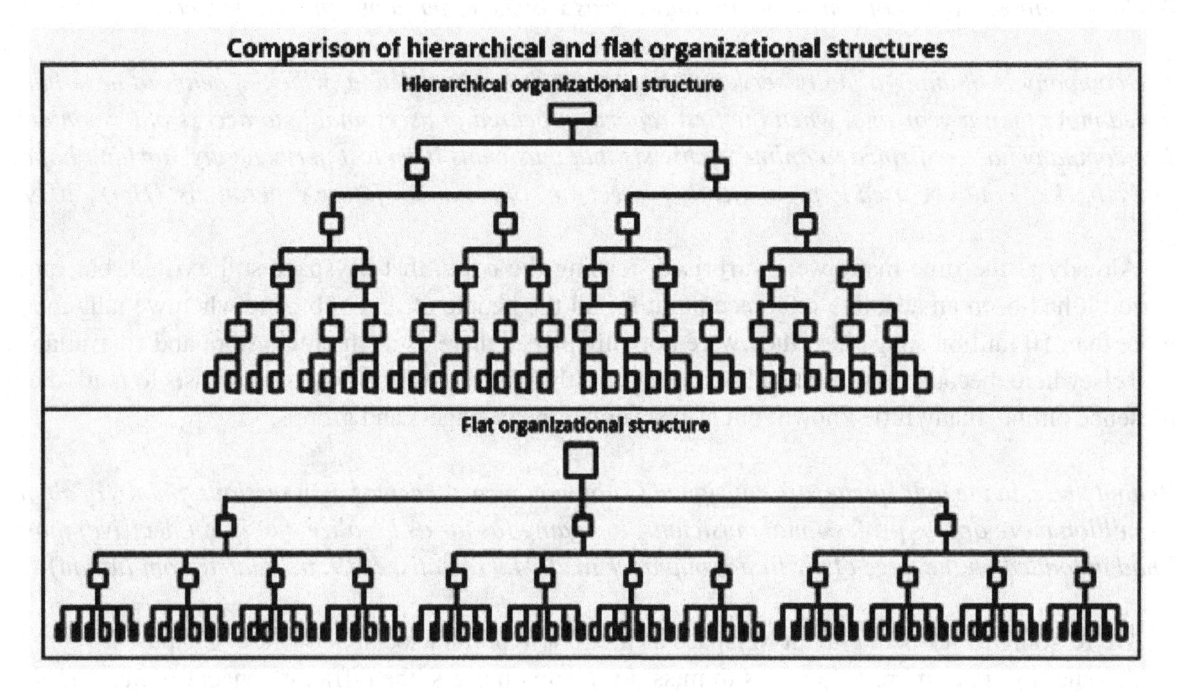

to spend much time finding how to undo automatic operations corresponding to the statistical use of an average user but not to my intentions in that moment. Personally, I find it very annoying.

Still, it's quite irritating in my opinion that, for example, in the properties of a sound file mp3 on Windows, there are by default associated information such as "group" and "album", assuming that it is music downloaded from a network. What if it's a recording instead of a lecture or of a baby's first words? Why do not leave to the user the "responsibility" to decide what kind of sound recording it is, eventually having the possibility of choosing among different preset types?

Advances users have no problems to change default settings on their devices - maybe they don't understand why they have to waste time doing it - but many "basic" users can't or do not dare perform such operations. So, having something associated with the properties of sound files a question like; "It's not a music? Click here!" to have by default information more suitable for the recordings made by us, it would be perhaps a small incentive even in other occasions to go better to specify information on files. And every aware operation with which a user adapts a digital device to his/her needs, it's a small step on the road of recovering technology, against the stress and discomfort of increasingly familiar but fundamentally alien devices that fill our lives.

The contrary, probably, when browsing audio files in the mobile we come across a vocal note that we made on the fly, maybe running down the street, not to forget something that came to mind, and the software attributes it to an "unknown artist" and precedes it with an ad because we don't have a premium account!

Another common and basic example. When typing with the latest versions of *Word 365*, we find the auto-save set by default. It's easier? Maybe. It avoids us, in case of even banally electrical problems to the power supply of the PC, to lose the job that recklessly we have not saved. One thing that has probably happened to everyone and then we should just thank Microsoft for avoiding now this danger.

But Microsoft itself warns us:

Save a Copy before making your changes. That way AutoSave won't overwrite the original file with the changes. If AutoSave did overwrite the file with your changes, see the section below, "I didn't want my changes saved, how do I go back? (from Microsoft support)

Because, saving everything in a cloud space as *OneDrive*, that's to say in every device connected, the problem can be, in case of errors, to lose a good version of our document and not to be able to recover it. But how many users in fact go and see the advice "save a copy?"

In this example, not to have a problem that could easily be avoided if everyone learned to periodically save their work, as well as they learn to look left and right when crossing a street (it is called road education, or education to the use of a PC), another problem is created at a superior level, perhaps more difficult to understand for users who, pampered with a series of automatic operations that "statistically" make things seemingly easier, in this way can hardly improve their awareness of the systems they use. In other words, how to deal with all saving problems, it's something that every user should learn well starting from the beginning, as a part of the basic digital literacy, and auto saving would be a possibility to be chosen, not to be refused if we don't like it.

These are all small things that make a person at a computer not feel free, but somehow under guardianship, even just hovering between icons, menus, prompts of a machine that continually winks at the use it presumes most likely, so that every personal choice becomes a nuisance, having to waste time eliminating the unsolicited automatic alien choices that should "help".

We can guess that in a society in which "for convenience" everyone is given a wheelchair, there will be probably a great part of the population unable to walk!

Nonstop networking also requires a number of precautions against network vulnerabilities (see e.g. Morrow 2018), with possible problems in case of a hacker attack on a server in some remote countries, or other technical problems of communications.

So, why depending totally on a network, when local stores drives are available, very cheap, and we can keep them sure in a drawer in our house or office?

It's true that even a PC hard drive may not work well, or the user may no longer remember where he or she hid the external memories in a "safe place". But knowing that the errors are ours and that we can correct them, it is different from having to trust for everything in a Big Brother who sees and provides for us.

This continuous "facilitating" the use of digital gadgets, so that humans go on using them without ever understanding how they work, in addition to fueling in many users the underlying sense of discomfort with technology, it certainly encourages the tendency to frequently renew one's equipment, perhaps in the secret hope of finally understanding something. This can be good for economy, but it also has an impact on culture, politics, and the life in general, as everything now goes through electronic gadgets.

Digital systems are complex and necessary in the society, and it is not only a matter of market, but of literacy, that's what make citizens free. Delaying, evading, not recognizing this central problem of our time can be very dangerous.

5. ONCE UPON A TIME ROOKIES INVENTED THE DIGITAL ERA: BEYOND THE INDUSTRY AND MARKET

It is not said here that the pioneers of the digital age were all and totally naive, but certainly many of them were very young and did not have all the certifications. Though at the beginning, of course, there were engineers.

Federico Faggin had joined Olivetti at the age of 19 and had been working at one of the world's first programmable desktop electronic calculators, the *Olivetti Programma 101*, ten of which were bought by NASA and used to plan the Apollo 11 first landing on the Moon. From Italy to Silicon Valley, he joined Intel Corporation, that was then working at a joint venture with the Japanese Busicom for a computer processor with data processing logic and control all included on a single integrated circuit. He entered in a team with Ted Hoff, Masatoshi Shima and Stanley Mazor, and they made the world's first commercially produced *microprocessor*, the Intel 4004, released in 1971 and sold for US$60.

In the User Manual of the Intel 8080, 1975, we find not only technical indications, but also an accurate explanation on what a microprocessor is:

Today, Intel offers the systems designer a new alternative ... the microcomputer. Utilizing the technologies and experience gained in becoming the world's largest supplier of LSI memory components, Intel has made the power of the digital computer available at the integrated circuit level. . . . A microcomputer chip set replaces dozens of random logic elements, thus reducing the cost as well as the size of your system. (From Intel 8080 User Manual)

Here is the full list of the indicated applications: Intelligent Terminals, Gaming Machines, Cash Registers, Accounting and Billing Machines, Telephone Switching Control, Numerically Controlled Machines, Process Control.

We realize that a missing item could be just "personal computer". Because at that time nobody had thought yet of putting a microprocessor inside a box to build a machine network-independent and not dedicated to a specific function.

It was Ed Roberts, in New Mexico, who assembled the Altair 8800, designed in 1974 and featured on the cover of the magazine "Popular Electronics" of January 1975. The personal *computer* was officially born when the young Bill Gates and Paul Allen arrived at Albuquerque carrying the BASIC language with which the machine can be programmed. A souvenir of that meeting is the famous mug shot of Bill Gates, when he was stopped by the police for speeding, in 1977.

Even back in high school I knew I could design computers with half as many chips as the companies were selling them with. I taught myself, but I had taught myself in a way that forced me to learn all sorts of trickiness. Because you try to make valuable what you're good at. I was good at making things with very few parts by using all sorts of tricks — almost the equivalent of mathematics — so I valued products that were made with very few parts.

That helped in two ways. When you are a startup or an individual on your own, you don't have very much money, so the fewer parts you have to buy, the better. When you design with very few parts, everything is so clean and orderly you can understand it more deeply in your head, and that causes you to have fewer bugs. You live and sleep with every little detail of the product. (Steve Wozniak, in Tindle, 2019)

Figure 3. Bill Gates
Source: Wikimedia

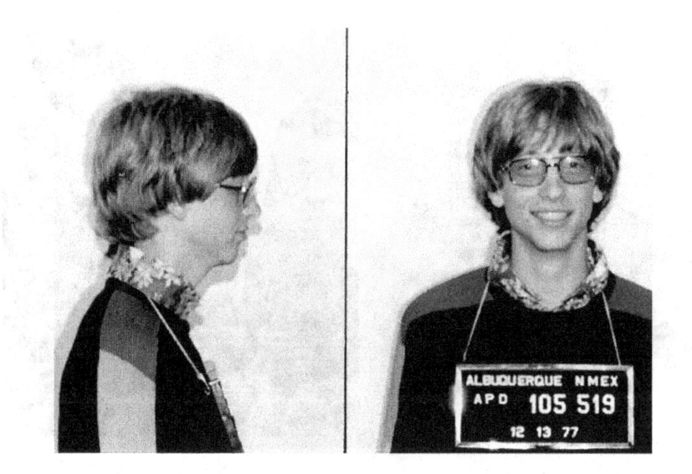

6. THE PHILOSOPHER, THE PROGRAMMER, THE MERE USERS

The audience loves dualism, rivalries, oppositions in characters. In every good story with two protagonists, to make the contrast evident and immediately visible, there are a short and a tall, a fat and a thin, a white and a black, a blond and a brown: Laurel & Hardy, Starsky & Hutch, Micky Mouse & Goofy.

In the society of spectacle, if individual figures appear strongly charismatic (as Jeff Bezos, Mark Zuckerberg, Elon Musk) dualism and opposition probably add something more. So, the most famous companies of the digital revolution start as two and opposing, Microsoft and Apple, both having a double head: Bill Gates & Paul Allen, Steve Jobs & Steve Wozniak.

Multiple rounds of conversations through people in the tech circuit who knew Allen followed and the Allen-Gates duo created Q-DOS (an acronym for Quick and Dirty Operating System) to meet IBM's requirements. This was later re-named MS DOS.

In a brilliant business decision that would make itself obvious only in hindsight, Allen "licensed" it to IBM. What it meant was that if any IBM clones emerge in the future, Microsoft could license MS DOS to those entities as well. Entities that mimicked IBM emerged. And Microsoft sold MS DOS to them. Allen put the organisation on a path to grow into the juggernaut that it is now. (Assisi, 2018)

By the way, Q-DOS was not "created" by Microsoft, but bought, fixed and developed, as it would later happen with *Internet Explorer*, *Power Point* and several other successful software. Its original programmer was Tim Paterson:

86-DOS (known internally as QDOS) . . . is a discontinued operating system developed and marketed by Seattle Computer Products (SCP) for its Intel 8086-based computer kit. . . . The system was licensed and then purchased by Microsoft and developed further as MS-DOS and PC DOS. (86-DOS, Wikipedia entry)

Figure 4. Apple One
Source: Original Apple computer built by Steve Jobs and Steve Wozniak sells for $400k (2021)

Apple co-founder Steve Jobs and his childhood friend Steve Wozniak started the company in Jobs' garage in 1976. They were both passionate about technology and had a shared vision of creating a company that would change the world. They raised money from family and friends to start Apple, and Jobs took on the role of CEO while Wozniak served as the company's chief technology officer. (Cache, "List Foundation", 2022, Oct 17)

Where the Apple I had been Steve Wozniak's hobbyist project, the Apple II was his hobbyist project with Steve Jobs pushing him on. Apple II was their company's first consumer product, as in a computer that was designed to be used right out of the box, instead of having to be assembled by technology fans. (Gallagher, 2023)

Without relying on one's own personal history and limitations as if they were valid for everyone - a vice common especially to certain popularizers of mass philosophy when they talk about technology - I too can bring my experience of non-technical that at certain times to realize projects worked with technicians.

Knowing how to use some author programs and software to make websites, though without writing code but graphically, it is not like using a word processor or a video editor, because the result of the work will not be a final product, a text, a movie, but another software that others will see on a screen, which they will click on, and which will work more or less well depending on what we have done. One must take into account several possibilities and variables and the field is that of *programming*.

It can be a very simple thing, accessible even to a child - I did it in kindergarten schools - when we decide for example that a figure, a shape, enter a certain way into the screen, with a movement, a speed, a shadow and a color, possibly a sound and goes to put itself right there, beside or behind other figures, or a text... It is to tell the machine what it must do.

The fact instead that almost all the people managing computers only think themselves as mere *users*, has created many problems when dealing with software that require, even in a very small part, an approach as programmers. And this has also created strong bottlenecks on the market, with the practically monopolistic development and the stereotypical use of only a few applications, which in practice allow users, so to speak, to program without taking the responsibility of programmers. I apologize for this simplification, but perhaps it helps us a little to understand the strange case of software as *PowerPoint* and *WordPress,* that we will see better in chapter 8, speaking of the value of "soft diversity".

And anyhow it is beautiful and extremely instructive to play the part of the advanced user who, testing up to a certain level hardware and software, discovers, imagines, guesses possibilities, and then can confront with the programming technician to see how far his insights can be realized... This happened on a mass level in the heroic years of the first PCs and the birth of the Web, when technology for many was accompanied with hope. And this has happened much less for several years, and it is not by chance that now technology is accompanied more often for many with resignation.

In the "Stanford Encyclopedia of Philosophy" computer science is considered as a mathematical, engineering, and scientific discipline, from a point of view not only technical but also philosophical:

Between the 1960s and the 1970s, computer science emerged as an academic discipline independent from its older siblings, mathematics and physics, and with it the problem of defining its epistemological status as influenced by mathematical, empirical, and engineering methods.

The complex nature of computer programs ensures that many of the conceptual questions raised by the philosophy of computer science have related ones in the philosophy of mathematics, the philosophy of empirical sciences, and the philosophy of technology. (The Philosophy of Computer, 2013-2021)

7. MORE THAN MACHINES, INFINITE SETS OF POSSIBILITIES, DEPENDING ON SOFTWARE

This is a concept that, from different points of view, is repeated several times in these chapters. Because it is the cultural turning point, the focus of the revolution that, not understood, can cause many problems. That is exactly what is happening in our societies.

That is, in a nutshell; those who design and build PCs, tablets and smartphones basically they cannot teach others how to use these machines. Because, unlike all other machines built throughout the history of mankind, it does not count with what ideas, intentions, purposes the machine was designed and built, but it all depends on something added after, even from someone who has absolutely nothing to do with the original manufacturer. What these machines do, it depends essentially on *software*.

This true and fundamental fact seems to be the hardest for people to understand, and it's natural, being an epochal change in the relationship between man and technology. But we risk going on experiencing a lot of problems that we will never be able to solve, if we do not at least try to figure out what the core of the issue is.

Certain specific uses of digital machines, linked to certain software for example at work, they can and must obviously be learned, also by attending specific courses, but machines as such, they cannot be learned from courses, because they are infinite sets of possibilities. And how - differently from the past - each of us can approach this infinite but often indistinct power that envelops us, it's something that should got well, as these machines and software are at the center of the global social organization and all of us, willing or unwilling, use them.

Many big problems of the present are probably given just by applying old methods of education, training, certification to completely new objects, with the result that the so-called "digital skills" of much of the population, after decades they are still mostly very limited.

This arguments are also developed in other parts of this book, and in particular in Chapter 5.

Regardless of the field in which you work, developing general technological abilities and the digital skills important to your industry can help you perform your work responsibilities more efficiently. Understanding the basic use of technological systems allows you to adapt faster to emerging technologies and digital workflows. Digital tools ranging from smart devices to software clients are important in businesses across a broad range of industries, making them important for modern individuals. (Preston, 2023)

But this is only the surface of an iceberg whose shape and features broadly depend on its uncertain navigation across a still unknown ocean, of which we have explored only the waters closer to the coasts, with the eye more to the ports and the lighthouses that we already know, rather than to the immensity of the horizon that we have in front.

This argument will also be developed in chapter 6 of this book.

8. GRAPHICS 2D AND 3D, MUSIC, MULTIMEDIA: WHEN COMPUTING DEVICES TURNED INTO ART

By heart, I remember an ancient example of computer art, when I was still a boy and personal computers were still to come. It was on a TV program, showing a quite old graphic artist able to mix fantastic shapes and colors moving and transforming on a screen. The voice over said; «He does not know anything of computer science! »

How personal computers turned from office machines into powerful multimedia stations is something that deserves a deeper reflection. Indeed, for years it has gone on playing on the misunderstanding of more or less serious uses and worthy of consideration, and the overall result is that few people today really know what a personal computer is.

In the early 90's it happened that using Amiga, a multimedia, multitasking computer, capable of extraordinary graphic and sound processing, I used to meet serious PC owners who knew nothing about it, but they told me with a smirk that mine was only a video game machine. Then, just to print a few pages in color, they had to took the opportunity to go to lunch, because their "professional" computers were not able to perform more than one operation at a time, while with my "toy" I could write a text, having a complex graphic elaboration in background, playing a music and format a floppy disk at the same time, as well as naturally printing, slowly, my documents. But no matter what I see, it matters what I believe, especially when I can make judgments about something I do not know!

Today, after many years, we've all learned that "gaming" PCs are often much more powerful and performing than normal ones, but the idea, as a basic training, of exploring the endless sets of possibilities that are digital machines, is still quite far from common sense. It's obviously not about learning to do everything, but maybe it could be useful at least to know that they exist. Beyond that misunderstood culture of competence and specialization that would take us all very good in our field and practically illiterate in all the others, because of which the natural curiosity that as children we all have to look around, observe, possibly choose, with adulthood it's sacrificed to the need to cultivate each only the knowledge and skills related to our own work. And in times when according to the software the ways change to use machines, this can be an important cultural limitation.

We have already mention that machines intended primarily for the home market, as the basic versions of Amiga in fact were (but also previous 8-bit computers as Commodore 64, the best-selling model in history, the MSX family, BBC Master and similar), having sound and graphic co-processors, they were often sold with different applications "in bundle", showing several processing possibilities. Sound was not at that time for listening to music (mp3 they were still yet to come), but for making it, or processing voices and noises.

In that season, crowd of young people, who by age have not yet forgotten how human children play, explore search and discover, but who also do not yet have time and intelligence all absorbed by work, they take those machines in their hand and not only talk about the latest application launched on the market, but in many cases they *create* the market, with ideas and proposals that large companies are not even able to imagine.

2D painting and animation programs, 3D modeling software, musical processors and sequencers, they are proposed and launched by the first emerging software houses, but also by individual enthusiasts, people whose way of thinking meets that of machines and, having to fight with memory limits measured in *kbytes* on floppy disks or even music cassettes, they write and run incredible programs that revolutionize the idea itself of computer.

In 1984, even if the real further revolution which would have made the digital machines really accessible to everyone, that is the graphical interfaces, still were only taking the first steps, an advertisement of Olivetti on newspapers declared; "Orwell was wrong!" And the most used word for PCs was "friendly".

We are going to see more in detail in chapter 8 a list of software examples to get a broader picture of the horizons opening in front of the users of the second 80s and 90s, when the former "electronic brains" of scientists in white coats and the sad office devices as they were the first successful PCs on the market, as if by magic they turned into machines for artists, who seemed to place no limit to creativity.

Not only we don't have just to press a button, waiting for the machine to do everything, but in defining all the details of a three-dimensional figure that appears and then moves in a space (shape and size, texture, "reverse kinematic"), in describing the properties of textual, graphic, sound objects that are seen or heard in a multimedia, we are recovering, even if in a virtual environment, ancient gestures of craftsmen of whom the industrial society seemed to be about to erase even the memory.

3-dimensional modeling, beyond a certain level, was not for all, but with many software, often given for free in old or limited versions, anyone could try elementary works that already gave an idea of the possibilities, observe from any point of view, turning, approaching, moving away a person, a building, an airplane, and apply the skin, the body, and decide if the surfaces had to be bright, opaque, hairy.

Multimedia software was a very simple way of becoming the authors of something people were beginning to experience every day, words, figures, sounds, that together go to compose a work different from those we knew before, because we have links, hyperlinks, and can navigate it in ways every time potentially different. Some authoring programs are simple, do not need any particular skill, and thinking of different elements and their features, even the most inexperienced after a while begins without realizing it to reason a bit like a programmer, to manage "objects", with their properties.

With the first graders:

The animator takes a notebook and places a pencil, an eraser, a glue stick, a coin, a mobile phone... He asks the children, "What have I put on the notebook page?" They answer: "A pencil, an eraser, a coin..." Yes, but how could you say with a single word? I put many..." "Objects!"

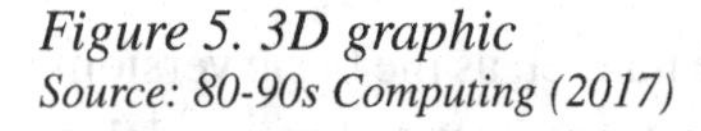

Figure 5. 3D graphic
Source: 80-90s Computing (2017)

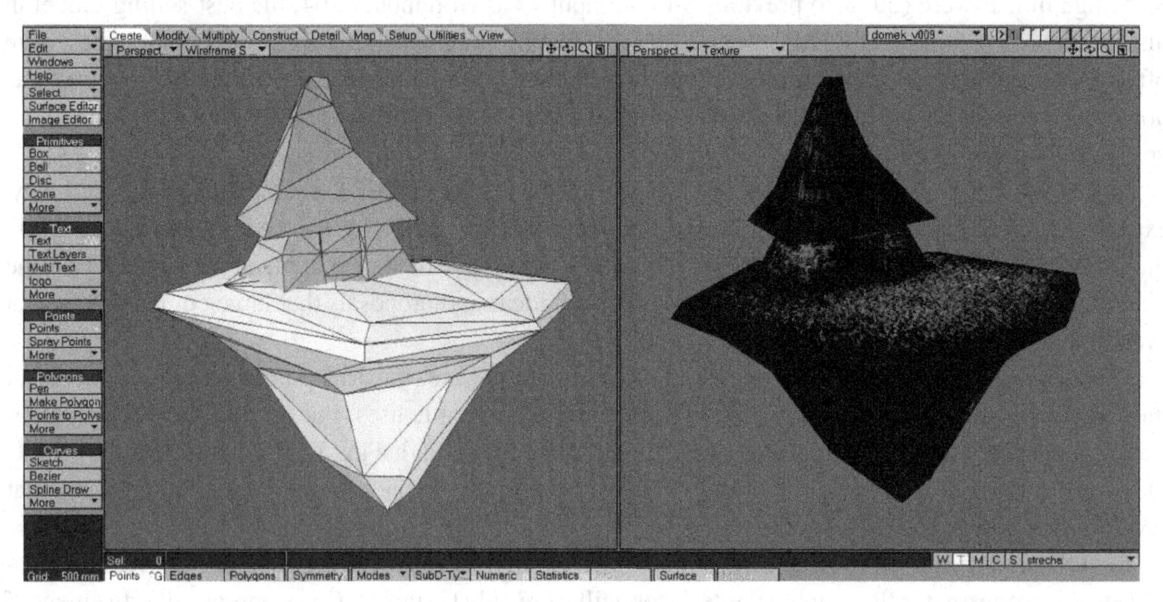

The animator then takes the objects and moves them on the page, removes some, others he adds, puts one in front of another.... Passing to the "page" of the computer, the objects are taken with the mouse and things work the same." (Beneventi-Conati 2010, p. 206, translated from Italian)

Yet, exploring photographic images with curiosity, and applying corrections, filters, deformations, transformations; trying, even without having the hand of a Giotto or a Michelangelo, to insert in photos and drawings perfect geometries, symmetries, transparencies. With the personal computer we can all be artists, at levels previously unimaginable.

So, that's the way they do it!

It's the phrase I heard spoken, identical, by two children of two different groups, fourth and fifth grade, who went out and entered the room, observing from afar some simple effects a teacher was trying on a computer using a drawing program of those I call *true*. That's like saying; I understand what I see in video games, something that with a software like this I can start now to do by myself too! They said this by looking at a screen from a distance for a few seconds, after years of using a program like *Paint*, without understanding the link – very typical of a school exercise! - between the images they produced at school and those they were used to consuming in their normal life.

And listening to their own voices processed, whose intriguing design they could also see on the screen, so they described them the children of a kindergarten school:

The girl's voice was strange, as in space, that of robots. . . . It was in a cave, that another noise was heard. . . . When there's nothing in a room, then it echoes. . . . Manuela's voice was like a lion. . . ! There are many children! Perhaps the heads, many. . . ! We learned to change voices! (Beneventi 1999, p. 94, translated from Italian)

Good editing video programs also for amateurs came a little later, needing a much stronger processing power, but they also give the possibility to cut, paste, overlap, mix, not only in a much more precise and "physical" way than with old magnetic tapes, but even better than with film, as if we could touch it more!

From the idea of computer doing everything for us, automatically, like in the *Jetsons* cartoons of the '60s, to the idea of computer as a tool allowing us to touch and modify things deeply, with our fingers and mind. Entirely new perspectives were opening for human genius and creativity. Or not?

9. VIDEO GAMES AND MEDIA LITERACY

Although gaming was once primarily used for personal entertainment, video games and other similar technologies are now being utilized across various disciplines such as education and engineering. As digital technologies become more integral to everyday life, it is imperative to explore the underlying effects they have on society and within these fields. (Dubbels, 2018)

As they are *games*, luckily in this case there are no to many didactics through which someone believes that they should be taught. Children as well as adults are free to approach them in the most natural way, however they wish. And they learn them, discover the internal rules around which they are organized, the strategies to complete them.

Video games are probably the way humans can most easily learn to use digital machines, and this is not so difficult to understand for mobile phones, that all manage without attending courses, just playing with what they have under their fingers and going sometimes to read some instructions. But also, those who know PCs well often approach a word processor, a video editing, or a concept map software as they were video games.

While on the one hand we all form a solid though often unaware audiovisual culture watching movies, TV series and commercials (if not, we would not understand them) on the other hand, entire generations have grown up learning interactivity with digital machines through video games. It's not good for the citizens of the information society, the fact that in schools, in information courses, in the "certifications" that are required at work, little account is taken of this, as well as of the so called "media convergence", because of which in many cases the medium or the machine we use becomes a secondary factor, since we can access the same content or even perform the same operations using devices traditionally considered different; PCs and tablets, phones, video game consoles, audiovisual equipment, TVs and more, and naturally, in a more traditionally unidirectional way, newspapers, books, radio.

Good computer and video games like System Shock 2, Deus Ex, Pikmin, Rise of Nations, Neverwinter Nights, and Xenosaga: Episode 1 are learning machines. They get themselves learned and learned well, so that they get played long and hard by a great many people. This is how they and their designers survive and perpetuate themselves. If a game cannot be learned and even mastered at a certain level, it won't get played by enough people, and the company that makes it will go broke. Good learning in games is a capitalist-driven Darwinian process of selection of the fittest. (Gee, 2003)

It is not the graphics or the special effects that make the success of a game, but its playability. This is why certain educational games fail in a place where the usual boring content is reproduced under a shining digital guise, while seemingly unappealing games have been very successful, such as those in

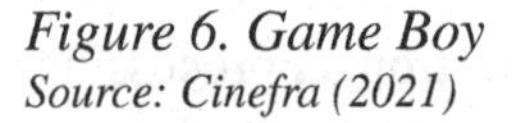
Figure 6. Game Boy
Source: Cinefra (2021)

black and white of the old *Game Boy* that, behind the appearance of a children's toy, was a concentrate of extremely innovative ideas.

Video games, in their extreme variety and diversity, draw on all human culture, extracting every element that can enter an interactive story, of which the player is the protagonist.

The public opinion is often captured especially by those in which there is a component of violence, asking themselves questions about their possible negative influence on kids, but there are memory games, mathematical games, games that stimulate knowledge of history and nature, games of pure skill and, as often happens in the manifestations of human culture, even those in which negative aspects are concentrated, they probably are the effect and not cause of real problems present in society. And if the life of some children takes place according to the schedule of the school and other commitments of all kinds, they do not have the way to play with other kids and spend the little free time in the house almost only between TV and video games, obviously *that* is the problem. And of course, having a predominantly virtual, though "interactive" experience of the world - as we also saw in Chapter 2, talking about global narratives - may not be the best way, for any human being of any age, to build a harmonious and balanced personality.

But in the end, if there is no addiction, if there is no exaggeration, many agree, even scientist, that video games can be a great thing:

Believe it not, scientific research confirms video games are good for you (video games are sports, after all). (Barone, 2023)

Students in the 21st century are learning by doing and playing. Teachers need to incorporate technology into everyday tasks. Games assist students in the learning process. Once students have learned a task through the playing process, they will remember this much easier and longer than simply doing a worksheet. Research shows students enjoy interactive and engaging activities and will choose these types of activities over pencil and paper types of activities. Teachers must prepare students for the future which involves more critical thinking and technological types of skills. Traditional teaching methods and styles have underused technology tools and pedagogical methods. The 2020 Covid pandemic and remote learning delivery style assisted teachers in developing new tools and methods to reach and teach all students with various and diverse needs. (Lane, 2022)

Being familiar with many situations of video games, as well as with the special effects of the movies they see on television, especially children are able to easily understand what they have the opportunity to do by themselves, using appropriately the apps they have available for PCs and smartphones.

If the effects are within programs in which we can manage, vary, process, export to other programs to do other things, without needing special explanations, the child, but also the attentive adult, understand the procedures applied, at higher levels, by the information professionals, and they easily start to play, to build a bridge between the technology they consume and the one they can handle directly. This is called *literacy*.

But if the effects are in a context of pure immediate fun, simple clicks from a ready catalog, to make for example strange selfies with the phone, or the approach to the software is purely scholastic, so that things are learned in the precise order proposed by the teacher and there is little space to play and experiment, then it can happen that, after years spent with the mobile phone in hand or diligently performing the procedures in the computer room, between the technology we consume and the technology with which we do things, that connection can be never established. And to kids never it happens to say; «So, that's the way they do it! »

10. AN APP FOR EVERYTHING: THE NEW SHAPES OF DIGITAL DIVIDE

Download the app!

I don't know if it's the same all over the world, but in my experience, this is a relentless chorus from TV commercials. To order food, book a trip, manage a bank account, processing videos, solve all the problems in the world!

The children and grandchildren of television, the de-responsible citizens of the information society, are strongly called to giving back definitively to those who manage search engines and networks that centralized control that was behind the perfect world of the Jetsons cartoons.

Probably we must also review the concept of "digital divide", which for a long time has been associated, in a somewhat superficial way, to the material availability of means and internet access. Of course, there is a fundamental difference between having the means available and not having them at all. But when the means are there, there is just as much between knowing how to use them, or not. And taking it for granted, as an indisputable postulate, that the diffusion of digital devices and broadband connection automatically favor an effective and productive use of the means of communication, is at least a great naivety.

As important as the concept of digital transformations is for businesses, the truth is that the phrase has made it to the top of the list of buzzwords that most leaders have come to ignore, hate, or misunderstand. . . . In fact, the term "digital," in and of itself, can be a word that leads to miscommunication. Jim Swanson, CIO of Johnson & Johnson, warns that "Digital is a loaded word that means many things to many people." The best way to unload what this means is to clearly define exactly what the process entails for your team. Swanson advises, "when you discuss digital transformation, unpack what it means." (Koelsch, n.d.)

In general, from the point of view of the market, there is no need to educate the public on the use of new machines, to overcome the old television stereotypes about a future of automated consumption, because billions of humans all with a mobile phone in their hands just to that "future", in some respects, are now approaching…

I write this obviously with a certain amount of irony, but that's what evidently happened at some point.

As we have seen in Chapter 2, in the years 2020 a part of the collective imagination has returned to coincide in a surprising way with that of the 1960s, and so the consumption patterns, confirming a clear division between producers and consumers that, at least at the level of information production, in the 1980s and 1990s it had begun to falter dangerously.

In fact, in the absence of a widespread education adequate to the use of digital devices whose diffusion has been left almost exclusively to the market, despite the texts and videos of dissemination, courses, instruction manuals, tutorials that theoretically would allow anyone to manage them in a conscious and appropriate way, things then often happen based on stereotypes that escape rational categories, and are often difficult to study:

When presented with websites for two online hotels, individuals planning for a hypothetical city visit were more likely to select the more functional (utilitarian) option when viewing on a desktop, and the more pleasure-based (hedonic) option when viewing on a tablet. . . . Despite similarities in input mechanisms of desktops and laptops, there was no significant relationship between the number of desktops frequently used and confidence in using a laptop or vice versa. Similarly, despite both smartphones and tablets being operated via touchscreen, there was no significant relationship between using a smartphone frequently and confidence in using a tablet or vice versa. . . . Laptops, desktops and smartphones were considered to be similarly utilitarian, while tablets were seen as significantly less utilitarian than other devices. . . . Smartphones and tablets have markedly different profiles to each other, whilst laptops and desktops are more similar to each other.

Existing literature is therefore unable to quantify when and why the device used to respond to a questionnaire will shape the captured responses. (Steeds et al., 2021)

For some important tasks it is useful indeed to have dedicated apps. Here the author, after many not so exciting experiences, he finally came across a software on mobile phone managing a bank account in an excellent way. Worth it, to be able to easily perform remotely all the possible controls and operations, it is his/her own checking account, a basic and very personal thing. Useful as well it can be to connect directly to car insurance, or to our "digital identity" on public administration and so on. But to have an app for every point of shopping, every service one can use once a year and other similar "facilities", when all those functions would be easily accessible from their websites, it looks a bit insane. But why to use a single application (the web browser) to perform any operation we need, when we can fill our smartphone with an infinite number of programs that we practically never use?

Companies spend a fortune squeezing their logos into magazine and TV ads, and yet with an app they can have their brand in our pockets 24/7 at virtually zero cost. . . . Furthermore, you'll almost always need an account with these apps, and that's a great way to track your browsing and purchasing habits. It's cheap data collection for these companies, with tailored recommendations to lure you back into their app. . . . These apps are all about capturing your long term business and building up that advertising profile, rather than offering us a superior service. (Triggs, 2017)

If people want to needlessly fill their phones with nothing, they are of course free to do it. The problem is that in this way, from the idea of a global and universal network that connects everything, which still a large part of the citizens of the information society has not yet learned to use, we return directly to the phone number! The apps connecting directly, always, destroy the very concept of network, that is one of the bases, perhaps the main one, of the literacy of the present time.

But also apps that *do something* are not always an element of progress and are likely to cause damage.

Dealing for example with a complete piece of software with which, as we learn it, we can apply effects to our photographs, it is not the same as going and using many different apps, each good, maybe great, for each effect or group of effects. And kids who grow up now getting used to choose ready made processing tools in catalogs, to be applied to pictures or sounds with a click, just in the way set by the authors of the apps themselves, they are certainly less stimulated to look for new and original solutions, as it happens when the same effects are taken from within a software that allows and also suggests other possibilities and combinations of processing according to the intention of the human, his desire to seek, to experience.

Even the exchange of ideas and solutions within the peer group, which is the key of youth creativity, as well as the development in sometimes unpredictable directions of the software, when individual apps do everything and satisfy, it becomes useless, superfluous, nonsense.

So, with complex systems as computers and smartphones for everyone, no literacy about using them, and automatic solutions upstream by the supplier, market rules seem to be restored with a clear division between producers and consumers and knowledge returned to the "experts".

But this process is not irreversible. On the contrary, by their nature, as we have seen and underlined and as at other times it has been more evident, digital means favor underground and unpredictable currents of thought and action. Even in a highly industrialized field such as that of video games, which moves huge economic interests, reality does not always correspond to the current narrative and artisan, artist activities are vital, and not only underground:

The videogame industry, we're invariably told, is a multibillion-dollar, high-tech business conducted by large corporations in North America, Europe, and East Asia. But, in reality, most videogames today are made by small clusters of people working on shoestring budgets, relying on existing, freely available software platforms, and hoping, often in vain, to rise to stardom—in short, people working like artists.

Cultural industries don't come from nowhere. They come from cultural fields. The videogame industry, as the exclusive site of legitimate videogame production, does not exist—at least not in the manner that we are used to imagining it. It is instead entangled with and dependent on the skills, communities, and innovations of a broader field of cultural production.

Before there were videogame companies, people made videogames. Beyond the limits of videogame companies, people make videogames. Beneath and holding up the foundations of global videogame production, a vast range of people in a vast range of contexts make videogames. (Keogh, 2023)

REFERENCES

80-90s Computing: One guy and his life with old computers of all kinds. (2017, Jan 8). swarmik.tumblr.com

DOS. (n.d.). Wikipedia. https://en.wikipedia.org/wiki/86-DOS

Assisi, C. (2018, Oct 20). Paul Allen the artist versus Bill Gates the entrepreneur. *Founding Fuel.*

Barone, R. (2023, Jan 8). *Yes, Video Games are Good...for Your Mind and Body.* idtech.com/blog

Beneventi, P. (1999). *Come usare il computer con bambini e ragazzi*. Sonda.

Beneventi, P. (2018). *Technology and the New Generation of Active Citizens*. IGI Global. doi:10.4018/978-1-5225-3770-0

Beneventi, P. & Conati, D. (n.d.). *Nuova Guida di Animazione Teatrale: A Scuola e nel Tempo Libero.* Sonda.

Bill Gates Mugshot. (n.d.) Wikimedia. https://commons.wikimedia.org/wiki/File:Bill_Gates_mugshot.png

Cathie. (2022, Oct 17). The Visionary And The Genius: The Story Of Steve Jobs And Steve Wozniak. *List Foundation.*

Chen, B. X. (2010, Oct 11). Apple Registers Trademark for 'There's an App for That'. *Wired.*

Cinefra, V. (2021). *Game Boy, artista trasforma la console in una vera opera d'arte.* spaziogames.it/notizie

Dubbels, B. R. (2018). *Exploring the Cognitive, Social, Cultural, and Psychological Aspects of Gaming and Simulations.* IGI Global.

Gallagher, W. (2023, Apr 17). *How Apple owes everything to its 1977 Apple II computer.* appleinsider.com/.

Gee, J. M. (2003, October). What video games have to teach us about learning and literacy. *Computers in Entertainment, 1*(1), 20. doi:10.1145/950566.950595

Hally, M. (2005). *Electronic Brains: Stories from the Dawn of the Computer Age*. Joseph Henry Press.

Hern, A. (2019, Mar 18). Myspace loses all content uploaded before 2016. *The Guardian.*

Intel 8080 Microcomputer Systems Users Manual. (1975, Sep.). Intel.

Jamie Mahoney, J., & Buttrey, K. M. (2022). Using Gamification to Improve Literacy Skills. In *Handbook of Research on Acquiring 21st Century Literacy Skills Through Game-Based Learning*. IGI Global. doi:10.4018/978-1-7998-7271-9.ch015

Keogh, B. (2023). *The Videogame Industry Does Not Exist: Why We Should Think Beyond Commercial Game Production*. The MIT Press. doi:10.7551/mitpress/14513.001.0001

Koelsch, E. (n.d.). Challenging the Overuse and Misuse of 'Digital Transformation'. *The National CIO Review*.

Mancuso, S. (2017). *Plant Revolution*. Giunti.

Morrow, T. (2018, Mar 5). *12 Risks, Threats, & Vulnerabilities in Moving to the Cloud*. Software Engineering Institute, Carnegie Mellon University.

Original Apple computer built by Steve Jobs and Steve Wozniak sells for $400k. (2021, Nov 10). moneycontrol.com/news/trends

Personal Computer. (n.d.). Wikipedia. https://en.wikipedia.org/wiki/Personal_computer

Preston, R. (2023, Jun 8). *What Are Digital Skills? (And Why They're Important)*. indeed.com/career-advice/career-development

Satyendra. (2013 Dec 8). *Comparison between Hierarchical and Flat Organization Structures*. ispatguru.com

Steeds, M., Clinch, S., & Jay, C. (2021, August-December). Device uses and device stereotypes. *Computers in Human Behavior Reports*, *4*, 100100. doi:10.1016/j.chbr.2021.100100

The Philosophy of Computer Science. (2013-2021). *Stanford Encyclopedia of Philosophy*.

Time-sharing. (n.d.). Wikipedia. https://en.wikipedia.org/wiki/Time-sharing

Tindle, A. (2019, Aug 12). *The Steve Wozniak Guide to Building Better Software: Software development insights from the man who started the personal computing revolution*. medium.com.

Tomatis, J. (2019, Mar 19). Perché la cancellazione di MySpace è terrificante. *Giornale della musica*.

Triggs, R. (2017, March 18). *Do we really want an app for everything?* androidauthority.com.

Turner, R. (2020). *Microsoft Open-Sources GW-BASIC*. devblogs.microsoft.com/commandline

ADDITIONAL READING

Are Video Games Good for You and Your Brain? (2022, Nov 15). *Health Essentials*. health.clevelandclinic.org

Cooper, R., & Zimmerman, M. (n.d.). Do Video Games Influence Violent Behavior? *Michigan Youth Violence Prevention Center*. yvpc.sph.umich.edu

Griffiths, M. (2005, July 16). Video games and health. *BMJ (Clinical Research Ed.)*, *331*(7509), 122–123. doi:10.1136/bmj.331.7509.122 PMID:16020833

Hern, A. (2020, Jul 22). Playing video games doesn't lead to violent behaviour, study shows. *The Guardian*.

Horban, O. & Martych, R. (2020). Phenomenon of Videogame Culture in Modern Society. *Studia Warmińskie, 56*.

Kickmeier-Rust, M. D., & .... (2011). A Psycho-Pedagogical Framework for Multi-Adaptive Educational Games. *International Journal of Game-Based Learning*, 1.

Layton R. (2023, Feb 28). Mobile vs. desktop usage: What percentage of internet traffic is mobile in 2023?. allconnect.com/

Lai, J., & Widmar, N. O. (2020, October 3). Revisiting the Digital Divide in the COVID-19 Era. *Applied Economic Perspectives and Policy*, *43*(1).

Why tomorrow's professions will be increasingly scientific yet also more humanistic. (2021, Apr 12). morningfuture.com

Michael Latzer. (2013). Media Convergence. In *Handbook on the Digital Creative Economy*. Edward Elgar Publishing.

Shaw, A. (2010). What Is Video Game Culture? Cultural Studies and Game Studies. *Games and Culture*, *5*(4), 403–424. doi:10.1177/1555412009360414

Szymon Zbigniew Olejarnik, S. Z., & Romano, D. (2023, July 5). Is playing violent video games a risk factor for aggressive behaviour? Adding narcissism, self-esteem and PEGI ratings to the debate. *Frontiers in Psychology*, *14*. PMID:37476087

Rachini, M. (2021 Mar 19) *Nintendo's Game Boy systems were stepping stones to smartphones, says video game historian*. cbc.ca/radio/day6.

Vilasís-Pamos, J., & Pérez-Latorre, Ó. (2022). Gamer Identity and Social Class: An Analysis of Barcelona Teenagers' Discourses on Videogame Culture and Gaming Practices. [ijoc.org]. *International Journal of Communication*, *16*.

Violent video games found not to be associated with adolescent aggression. (2019, Feb 13). University of Oxford. ox.ac.uk/news/ Myspace, the once mighty social network

Chapter 4
Senses, Thought, Connections, and Disconnections of a Divided Experience:
Broken Communities in Social Networks

ABSTRACT

For many citizens of the information society, there is no more coincidence between how they know the world and their sensitive experience. Images not respecting shapes and proportions, words making no sentences; more than powerful extension of human senses and skills, digital gadgets are often prosthesis to compensate for increasing inabilities. Educated by the old school and television (on any platform, TV it is!) and by the market, the most in new interactive systems interact basically with themselves. The medium is the message and on widespread Narcissism and consumerism many try to make from their online addiction a lucrative job. "Hyperconnectivity" enables sorts of electronic hive minds across the network of social media. But spending time and personal resources in virtual worlds that we do not control, we don't have an ESC key for our real lives.

1. INTRODUCTION

In the "always connected" daily experience of present days, many times there are, on the contrary, disconnections between different areas of our experience, the physical senses and even similar messages passing through not so different means. We tend to accept messages also when they are in contradiction with our perception, or our knowledge, even when we could intervene to correct them.

Internet is perhaps the greatest opportunity for democracy in history, but for generations grown and educated by television it is generally a lost opportunity and in some people the presence in social networks can even cause addiction. Screen protected communication and virtual identities intersect, and merge, and things are observed on the web never seen, that someone has described as Electronic Hive Minds.

DOI: 10.4018/978-1-6684-8228-5.ch004

Lately, widespread narcissism and confrontational attitude are making the main social networks less and less social, with fewer connections, more opposing sides, and the accentuation of the link to influencers and brands of reference. Certain behaviors we get used to on the web create problems, when applied in real life, and the difficulty that many have in dealing with familiar and even relatively simple media as photography and video, matching them to knowledge and lived experience, it poses questions about the possibility to manage in a serene and productive way technically much more complex and directly less accessible experiences like virtual reality and the metaverse.

2. TECHNOLOGY, SENSES, AND FEELING

On October 8, 2013, a gunman entered a crowded San Francisco commuter train and drew a .45-caliber pistol. He raised his weapon, put it down to wipe his nose, and then took aim at the passengers.

None of the passengers noticed because they were attending to something far more interesting than present reality. They were subsumed by their smartphones and by the network beyond. These were among the most connected commuters in all of history. On the other side of their little screens, passengers had access to much of the world's media and many of the planet's people. They were not especially connected to the moment or to one another. They were somewhere else.

Only when the gunman opened fire did anyone look up. By then, 20-year-old Justin Valdez was mortally wounded. (Hirshberg, 2014)

The video made with a phone by an average user is not intended to be watched also on a television set and so it is normally taken vertical, though this often means to leave a lot of "sky" upon the subject, half display occupied for example by the ceiling and more important information (a hand, an arm, other persons) missing on the left and on the right, or frenziedly searched with nervous and frequent movements that disturb the view. When everything could have been easily framed perfectly simply turning the device horizontal and still.

This is a typical situation of the time of "all connected"; not to connect, in our minds, the videos we take by ourselves using phones with the videos we watch from professional productions on huge TV screens, as if they were on totally different planets; not to connect the quality of the device (so emphasized in the advertisement, that in some case made us choose just that device) with the quality we go actually to get in our own shots.

On the small displays of phones most pictures seem to be good, but often it is enough to watch them on a tablet or laptop screen to realize that the pictures are much more moved or blurred than we thought. This is generally not so important, as they are things to be consumed in a short exchange with relatives and friends, or on social networks with virtual but not less domestic friends, and the fact of having a device capable of 4K videos does not make many of us think at all that our product could be of quality.

If then it happens that by chance we filmed something interesting for the news of a true TV, a car accident, a flood, a fire, and in the absence of other images the national broadcast corporation is to use just our footage, instead of leaving a black or at least opaque frame on the sides of the vertical shot on the TV screen, in order to make the scene well visible, often they fill all the horizontal big display of

TVs with something on the sides like a magnified and blurred mirror of the original picture, so that it is hard to distinguish the images of the original flood taken in vertical format from the digital flood mirrored all around. Information is confused, communication is quite nothing, but probably they know that TV audience doesn't like empty spaces in screens and wants the TV display to be always filled with a colored, moving image.

Even when old videos are shown in a wrong format, it is more important to fill the screen, and the majority doesn't even notice that basketball players appear short and sluggish! The consumption of the technological medium, the potential quality of the 4K led display is so strong, that we do not even notice when it provides us with distorted or unrecognizable images.

The medium is the message, Marshall McLuhan said in the 1960s, and human senses can do they nothing but bow to it? His words seem to fit exactly the present time, but perhaps in a not-so-distant future other humans will smile at this bizarre human confusion in communication around the years 2020!

In the electric age, when our central nervous system is technologically extended to involve us in the whole of mankind and to incorporate the whole of mankind in us, we necessarily participate, in depth, in the consequences of our every action. It is no longer possible to adopt the aloof and dissociated role of the literate Westerner. (McLuhan, 1964)

All media work us over completely. They are so pervasive in their personal, political, economic, aesthetic, psychological, moral, ethical, and social consequences that they leave no part of us untouched, unaffected, unaltered. The medium is the massage. (McLuhan, 1967)

When I once asked why a whole movie in a cinema hall had been projected in a wrong format, with all women and men and cars ridiculously thin and tall, many around, that had no noticed that, said to me; "But you are an *expert*!"

An "expert"? If the ball is round or oval, it is not the same game, the same sport, every child knows it!

It happens apparently - I try to put it briefly - that for most citizens of the consumer society 2.0 (or 4.0. or 5.0, the number is random and the "dot zero" in mathematics not by chance means nothing!) the relationship with reality is no longer based on what we know about the world and what our senses communicate to us, but it is as given by the context, the medium through which reality itself is filtered at that moment. The medium prevails over the message and we, addicted to the essentially passive attitude of the TV viewer, do not find it natural to intervene to correct any mistakes. Maybe in our mind we know that Audrey Hepburn was not so short and fat and even that the fault is of the 3:4 format of the old film now reproduced in 16:9, but in fact we accept to see the distorted image, and to this distorted perception we get used as perhaps normal when watching TV.

Similarly, in other contexts it may then be normal not to listen to our hearing, our taste, or to the feeling of malaise that grows inside us in a situation in which we perceive there is something wrong.

Today, machine translations from a language to another generally work pretty well, but sometimes sensational linguistic errors occur, when words are ambiguous or slang, or artificial intelligence does not understand the context. At least in the cases in which there's a human who knows the destination language and automatic translation is for speed and convenience, it would be enough to read, and manually correct, but in many cases this do not happen.

Figure 1. Aspect ratio
Source: Working with aspect ratio (2023)

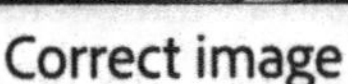

So, we get used to images with wrong proportions and meaningless sentences. And our experience is driven to normally break into non-communicating departments, which do not require that the idea of the world we have in a context corresponds to that we have in another... Especially using technology, the way how we approach reality is more and more often according to the device, the platform, the procedures we get used to. We are passive consumers, we take what others give us, we do not even imagine that we can have new opportunities and responsibilities than watching and following the rules of games that in any case are not depending on us.

But is this the right way to be real, alive, confident persons in the choices we make, in relationships with other people, at work, in social, political and private life? What would a psychologist say?

3. HOMELESS AT HOME, EXTENSIONS, AND PROSTHESIS

It is the essence of alienation that people find themselves homeless in the very territories they call home. Aliens are "others," strangers who roam the edges of their own well-being. (Henricks, 2016)

Traditionally, the typical alienation of the information society is associated with "consumption of escape-type content from the mass media". (Pietilä, 1970)

Studies on visual perception describe the mechanisms in general, and its ambiguous character, so that, in addition to the "photographic recording" by the eyes, the brain always performs a reconstruction work.

Basing on how the brain achieves vision processing in living organisms, in "deep learning", a *convolutional neural network* (CNN) is a class of artificial neural network most commonly applied to analyze visual imagery:

We construct an aspect ratio estimator whose input is a (possibly distorted) image and output is a scalar value of aspect ratio. Since estimation of aspect ratio from image can be regarded as regression problem, we modeled the estimator by CNN. Once we have a reliable estimate of aspect ratio of an image, the correction can be done straightforwardly by inverse stretching. (Sakurai, 2017)

Something similar is evidently done by the human brain to which CNNs are inspired, that somehow corrects wrong images also in case of a mistaken format in TV, so that for people it's possible to watch movies in another aspect ratio than the original as if they were right. But not to realize the error at all, it seems to be quite unnatural, as well as ignoring the recurring problem in literature.

We can find online several articles and texts on aspect ratio that tell everything on different format, how to choose a format for our own purposes, what kind of pictures are allowed or convenient on the different platforms, and how to fix incorrect aspect ratio in different environments of course. But generally there are no mentions of people who do not realize the aspect ratio error. Maybe this is not a problem, or maybe it is something so absurd that we do not know how to study it. But having so many people who don't get upset when to their eyes images are transmitted not matching what they know about reality, it is not a normal thing!

Here we are to another related argument, what people can do with media, as if everyone were aware of the tools and able to choose and use them.

Out of working contexts, where the correct use of just those machines and software is important for production processes, so that people are properly trained and learn to use just them, in everyday life, as well as often in school, for decades someone has been telling us and describing what wonderful things we could do with technology, hardware, and software, with an endless list of articles, courses, tutorials, ads, discussions in forums and chats online. Time passes, with all those things almost no one has done anything, but instead of wondering why so many people go on not using technology as they could, not paying real attention at all those suggestions, someone continues to write and tell us what we could do with other new technologies, new hardware, and software...

This is fully in line with the discourse of the world and life told rather than lived, but to me personally it seems a bit insane. Or not?

That some too handy technologies can be an element of disturbance and waste of resources in working time, it's a known fact.

I've concluded that more than 90% of people waste between 15%-40% of their workday as a result of technologies created in the digital revolution. This means that most employees miss 2-5 months of work a year. It begs the question; Despite the great advances brought on by the technological revolution, can we also navigate the enormous dysfunctions to our productivity that come with it? (Gonzalez Rodriguez, 2020)

But how a lot of opportunities offered by technology, for instance in education, are lost because users are left alone with them after a shallow, scholastic information, or because they, with that type of instructions, cannot in fact overcome their condition of semi-literate, this seems one of those problems that, under the eyes of all, we deliberately choose to ignore.

Here we often come to considerations about the inadequacy of the training of citizens on digital technologies, practically left in the hands of the market. Still, it is difficult to understand the general attitude whereby, if the experts have provided instructions for use, all it's fine, even if then nothing happens in the real world with those instructions and technologies.

From a social point of view, other problems come when technology is not used, as it could, as a powerful extension of human senses and skills, but in fact as a prosthesis to compensate for increasing inabilities. An example before everyone's eyes is the difficulty, especially of the youngest, to orient themselves in a car travel without satellite navigation.

But humans are sensitive animals. When we talk of social discomfort, we should take into account also the general loss of the ability to listen to our living environment using our senses, feeling with our body the real world, reading the stories it tells, if not inserted into the patterns of the artificial stories that the generations of consumers continually tell one another. The direct relationship with the reality is more and more often been replaced by its narration, photographs, vidéos, words quickly written, and read in a tweet.

4. THE WEB AND DEMOCRACY

The Internet (or internet) is the global system of interconnected computer networks that uses the Internet protocol suite (TCP/IP) to communicate between networks and devices. It is a network of networks that consists of private, public, academic, business, and government networks of local to global scope, linked by a broad array of electronic, wireless, and optical networking technologies. (Internet, Wikipedia entry)

The World Wide Web (WWW), commonly known as the Web, is an information system enabling information to be shared over the Internet through simplified ways meant to appeal to users beyond IT (Information Technology) "specialists" and hobbyists, as well as documents and other web resources. (World Wide Web, Wikipedia entry)

After this summary, there will still be those who between the two things will make confusion, as it is quite natural. But it does not matter here to explain what exactly the global network is, whose technical characteristics one can go to study in detail, but rather to stimulate some reflections that can be useful to ordinary citizens to understand it and use it possibly better, and to scholars to eventually do research on some aspects of it.

We have already mentioned the metaverse and virtual worlds, the cloud, and the social networks, and how we are probably wasting many of the possibilities that the Web offers us, and also the fact that a personal computer can work very well even if it is not connected to a network.

It is not a systematic, chronological, consequential treatment, but the arguments are approached, if we can say so, according to "blocks of experience", trying to make so that the author's point of view, anything but neutral, not hinder an examination of the issues by the reader the most possible wide and serene, with the constant suggestion to remember that today we are not only external spectators of all this but also easily, more or less, the protagonists.

Then, we must remember that, starting a speech, we cannot be sure that the others automatically follow us, and that to the words they assign the same meaning or connotations that we attribute to them.

According to the *Cambridge Dictionary* online, *connotation* is "a feeling or idea that is suggested by a particular word although it need not be a part of the word's meaning, or something suggested by an object or situation". The definition of *Oxford Learner's Dictionaries* is much more concise: "An idea suggested by a word in addition to its main meaning."

There is in any case a fundamental ambiguity, a strong component of subjectivity in human language and communication processes, which can never be eliminated, neither using the human intelligence, nor even the artificial one.

I wrote, many years ago:

Figure 2. Web democracy stock, alternative
Source: Our Democracy Is Only As Good As The Information That Voters Have (2022)

The Internet, for better or for worse, is probably the biggest opportunity for democracy that the world has ever known because practically anyone, not just those who hold political and economic power, as it has been until now, can inform anyone else about anything. There can be no filter, veto, or censorship like in the press and television. The silence of potential channels of information cannot be bought because they are practically infinite. If we consider that censorship on media is one of the first things that dictatorships impose, we can realize how potentially "revolutionary" the Internet is, if we don't use it solely as a kind of interactive TV. (Beneventi 1999, p. 172, translated from Italian).

Speaking of "democracy", I had in mind above all a situation in which all the citizens are in the condition to take an active part in the life of their community, with ideas and actions. I did not think in particular of a centralized or federal state, of a parliamentary or presidential republic, or even of a monarchy, as in Europe one may not think much about it, but there are still many.

Published in the same year, *Digital Democracy* starts like this:

The focus of this book is a critical exploration of the potential for new information and communication technologies (ICTs), such as the internet, to contribute to "strong democracy" based around citizen-to-citizen deliberation and strengthened links between governments and the governed. (Hague & Loader, 1999)

Not directly from this sentence, but going on reading the text, we see that the authors look above all at how the network can change the relationship between citizens and *those* institutions, the ones they know and are present in their territories, favoring interactive ways before impossible.

It is always about democracy, but not exactly from the same point of view.

We read in the web pages of CERN, the European Organization for Nuclear Research where the WWW first began to run:

Tim Berners-Lee wrote the first proposal for the World Wide Web in March 1989 and his second proposal in May 1990. Together with Belgian systems engineer Robert Cailliau, this was formalised as a management proposal in November 1990. (From CERN web site)

The web is more a social creation than a technical one. I designed it for a social effect - to help people work together - and not as a technical toy. (Berners-Lee & Fischetti, 2000)

The early web community produced some revolutionary ideas that are now spreading far beyond the technology sector:

Decentralisation: No permission is needed from a central authority to post anything on the web.

Non-discrimination: If I pay to connect to the internet with a certain quality of service, and you pay to connect with that or a greater quality of service, then we can both communicate at the same level. This principle of equity is also known as Net Neutrality.

Bottom-up design: Instead of code being written and controlled by a small group of experts, it was developed in full view of everyone, encouraging maximum participation and experimentation.

Universality: For anyone to be able to publish anything on the web, all the computers involved have to speak the same languages to each other, no matter what different hardware people are using; where they live; or what cultural and political beliefs they have. (Berners-Lee, 2012)

In 2019, Berners-Lee writes:

Today, 30 years on from my original proposal for an information management system, half the world is online. It's a moment to celebrate how far we've come, but also an opportunity to reflect on how far we have yet to go.

The web has become a public square, a library, a doctor's office, a shop, a school, a design studio, an office, a cinema, a bank, and so much more. Of course with every new feature, every new website, the divide between those who are online and those who are not increases, making it all the more imperative to make the web available for everyone.

And while the web has created opportunity, given marginalised groups a voice, and made our daily lives easier, it has also created opportunity for scammers, given a voice to those who spread hatred, and made all kinds of crime easier to commit. (Berners-Lee, 2019)

5. ONLINE BRAINS

Talking about the web in the end is like talking about the world and so we could say anything. But sure, it has not only changed the way in which information is made, but also daily human behaviors, and not of a small part of people of this or that community, but of most of the inhabitants of the planet, that now have other habits, use other gestures and activate other areas of the brain;

The Internet is the most widespread and rapidly adopted technology in the history of humanity. In only decades, Internet use has completely re-invented the ways in which we search for information, consume media and entertainment, and manage our social networks and relationships. With the even more recent advent of smartphones, Internet access has become portable and ubiquitous to the point at which the population of the developed world can be considered "online" ... even simple interactions with the Internet through the smartphone's touchscreen interface have been demonstrated to bring about sustained neurocognitive alterations due to neural changes in cortical regions associated with sensory and motor processing of the hand and thumb. (Firth at al., 2019)

Not to overestimate the role of "technologies" as a factor of change, it is not necessary to be a neuroscientist to assume that the same can be said of any human activity involving sensory and motor processing of body and mind never practiced before, as for example to start playing piano or guitar, or driving a bicycle. On the other hand, we are talking about billions of people that do all the same gestures and activate just those specific areas of their brains...

Another question that sometimes arises is whether there may be significant differences in the functioning of the brain between those who have learned to use digital media only at some point in their lives and those who, like the so-called "digital natives", are born into it. At a first sight intriguing, it is an issue which, in addition to not being in any way experimentally testable, is generally posed by people that wonder when seeing how several few-year-old babies handles seemingly naturally gadgets that for (some of) their parents and grandparents present a lot of difficulties.

Apart from the fact that (other) parents and grandparents are those who those gadgets have invented, children play naturally with so many things and evidently digital devices in some of their functions lend themselves to being played with relative ease. Children who, we should remember, in the first three years of life normally learn from scratch to speak a language, sometimes more than one - that maybe it's a little more complicated than clicking on a screen - and nobody is surprised!

Anyhow, during an experiment conducted in 2009 at UCLA in Los Angeles (Small & Vorgan, 2015) two groups of people had their brain scanned, of experienced web surfers and newbies.

The brain activity of the first group was much more extensive than that of the others, particularly in one region of the left frontal lobe ... six days later ... the neophytes had spent an hour a day doing web searches. It was enough this short period of "training" to have also in the second group an activation very similar to the first. (Bormetti, 2019, p. 38-39, translated from Italian)

In people of all ages

Smartphones have introduced widespread and habitual "checking" behaviours, characterized by quick but frequent inspections of the device for incoming information from news, social media, or personal contacts ... education providers are beginning to perceive detrimental effects of the Internet on children's attention ... hyperlinks, notifications, and prompts providing a limitless stream of different forms of digital media, thus encouraging us to interact with multiple inputs simultaneously, but only on a shallow level, in a behavioural pattern termed "media multi-tasking". (Firth et al., 2019)

This may be one of the reasons why for teachers to get a sustained attention from a group of children today, it appears more complicated than in past.

6. SOCIAL NETWORK ADDICTION

More than 1 billion people worldwide regularly use social networking services (SNSs), such as Facebook, Twitter, and Instagram, which are virtual communities where users interact and build online and real-life relationships. (Wang, 2021)

It's a totally new experience in the history of humanity, so even experts can say little definitive, if not formulate hypotheses, observing, studying.

In many cases users organize themselves in communities, pages, interest groups, which often do not really work. We will see in other chapters how commercial platforms would not be the best environment where to develop effective collaboration among humans and how in other contexts virtual enterprises can be set up better, but one fact is that in this early decades of human adventure in the cyber-world it is in commercial social networks that the majority have chosen to stay.

Faced with a multitude of individual and group behaviors that are not easy to understand in their nuances, researchers try to organize observations as scientifically as possible, but the bases and criteria of this science itself must be found, defined, and cannot completely rely, for example from a psychological point of view, on the knowledge and skills of those who have hitherto dealt almost exclusively with the problems of individuals, with rare incursions in the past on the suggestive but slippery terrain of mass psychopathologies, in times when media communication was one-way.

Internationally, over 1.7 billion people visit Facebook every month ... differential effects of active and passive Facebook use: Facebook contentment (a wellbeing enhancing effect) and Facebook depression (a wellbeing diminishing effect). (Joseph et al., 2021)

Results showed that while posting food photos were associated with social activity, posting selfies were associated with shyness. Narcissists were more likely to involve in posting both food photos and selfies. (Leung & Wan, 2022)

Perfectionistic self-presentation is a major constituent of young people's identity development and may intensify during the transition to college ... The study was conducted on 578 Indian students who belonged to the age range of 18-24 years ... Instagram is a major online platform where perfectionistic self-presentation is portrayed to salvage the deflated self-esteem. (Ubaradka et al., 2023)

Internet addiction (IA) is typically defined as a condition where an individual has lost control of their Internet use and proceeds to use the Internet excessively to the point where he/she experiences problematic consequences which ultimately have a negative effect on his/her life. (Bozoglan 2019)

Although not formally recognized as a diagnosis, SNS (social network site) addiction shares many similarities with those of other addictions, including tolerance, withdrawal, conflict, salience, relapse, and mood modification ... A key distinction between normal over-engagement in social networking

Figure 3. Click copyright indications
Source: Wegmann et al. (2015)

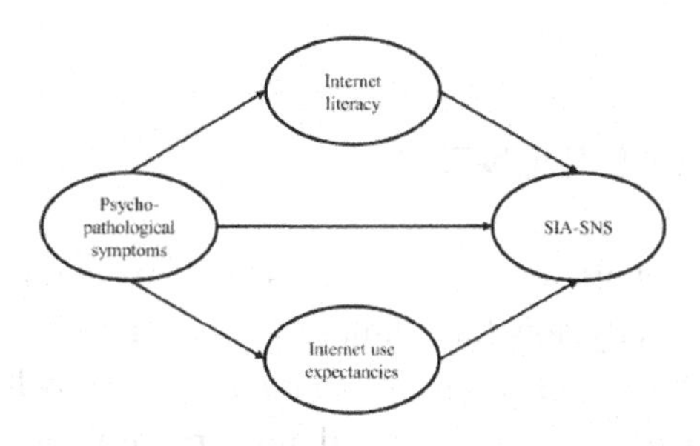

(occasionally experienced by many) and SNS addiction is that the latter ... becomes uncontrolled and compulsive ... SNS users seek feedback, and they get it from hundreds of people—instantly. It could be argued that the platforms are designed to get users "hooked." (Andreassen, 2015)

Communication on social media might be a replacement of spending valuable time on face-to-face communication ... SNS users can compare themselves with other users or celebrities on dimensions that are relevant to self-worth such as attractiveness or social connectedness ... Intense SNS use increases the likelihood of being exposed to and engaging in highly self-worth endangering online communication, such as cyberbullying, grooming by strangers, and sexting. (Appel et al., 2019)

SNS use may be reinforced by experienced gratification and relief from negative feelings. Individual competences in handling the Internet may be preventive for the development of SIA-SNS. (Wegmann et al., 2015)

Studies have begun to be conducted about cultural and gender differences that can influence internet addiction. And by now, we can find many online articles on the "digital detox":

In February, news broke that Salesforce CEO Marc Benioff had taken a 'digital detox': 10 tech-free days at a French Polynesian resort ... Digital mindfulness may be more practical for some people, in

Figure 4. Click copyright indications
Source: Wegmann et al. (2015)

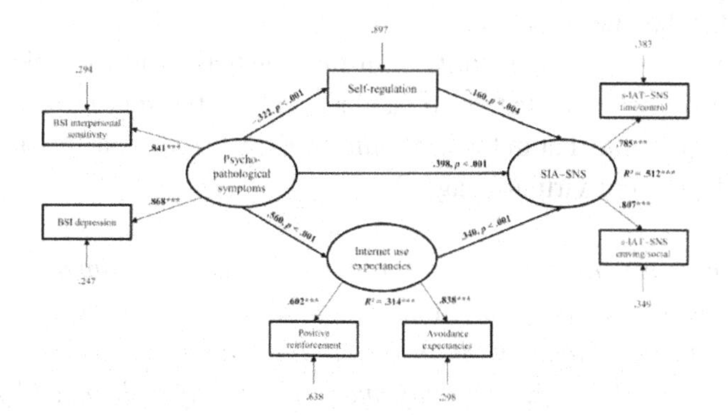

lieu of a full detox: less worry about cutting tech out entirely, and more focus on being intentional with its use. (Epstein, 2023)

7. PERSONAL AND VIRTUAL IDENTITIES

People migrate from one social network to another, often stay in many posting the same content in different spaces, and we do not know exactly how for example to attend a platform ordered for professionalism like *LinkedIn* or to pay money for a greater visibility on *Facebook* really leads to improvements from the work point of view. There is a general sense of no need, no commitment, in being on social networks, so that, even when many people are involved in a discussion, either because the topic is interesting, or the profile in which it takes place is of someone famous, normally it happens that, with the fact of having said his own with one or more comments, the participation can be considered closed.

Even when with an explicit message one requires a contribution of ideas and actions for some project for which he/she is seeking support, perhaps because such a request appears on the wall of a chat, the impression is that often people, friends, colleagues, do not understand the message completely. That's to say; one is looking for people to participate in something and others do not say yes or no, do not give their opinion, but they put a "like" to the message, maybe a little heart, and then disappear. Have they really read what was written and understood the message?

Still, it happens with articles published in online magazines, or blogs. There is a space for comments, where they would remain visible always and directly related to the article. But if the link to the article has been put for example on Facebook, others prefer to write their comments there, where they pile up in a much more confusing way on the profile, in the group or on the page where the text in quoted, and after a few days will be difficult to be traced. That is, the convenience of commenting immediately, in the first space I meet, without considering that, going instead to publish in the space where the article is actually published, my comment could enrich the article itself and improve the overall discussion on the topic.

We're as constantly distracted, in a hurry, with too much to do. And lightly we do not use simple tricks that would allow our ideas on the global network not to go regularly dispersed, to maybe make memory, to grow together. Probably, the possibility that those ideas can eventually grow together is something we do not even consider. But maybe, if it entered our horizon, it could make us many things less stressful, simpler, and fun.

It is the basic difference between the culture of sharing, so every intervention added to the others often leads naturally to a superior synthesis, and the culture of competition, so instead the unique purpose is to mark each one's intervention, possibly better than the others, after which all return to their starting point, as if in practice they had never spoken.

Something seems to happen to our identities, in the nowhere land of social networks, where the avatar of our "stories" overlaps with what we are and not only in the sense that for others in the end we are what we publish. Is it possible that in the long run, by expressing a substantial part of us online, we tend in some ways to adapt to our virtual images?

The identity construction is a personal and psychological process that involves body indwelling and, profoundly, the connection with primary emotional and relational experiences ... The experience of who I am is deeply related to the way I look and to the group I belong to, as they suggest what the other see and reflect about me. As a result, one's own body image is strongly influenced by self-esteem and self-

evaluation, and strictly linked to the evaluation provided by the others. Moreover, it can be powerfully affected by cultural messages and societal/media standards of appearance and attractiveness ... Research investigating the process of identity construction in adolescence is increasingly exploring the Internet environment. (Boursier and Manna, 2019)

Digital technologies, such as social media platforms like Facebook, Twitter, Snapchat, and Instagram are designed to bring people together, yet they may have the opposite effect ... isolate them from the social life. It also does not allow them to spend enough time with their family members ... Actively encourages social comparisons, as its miles plagued by records which could effortlessly be used as metrics of obvious social success (e.g., friends, likes, shares, fans and so forth). These metrics are problematic in themselves, because if adolescents don't get enough likes to a comment or picture they have posted, or if someone has more likes or friends than them, it can make them feel inferior ... To only see an extremely edited 'highlight reel' of other people's lives ... this kind of negative social comparisons may experience higher levels of depression and anxiety in adolescents. (Saptasagar, 2022)

In adolescence, one of the key moments is the discovery of sex. It is difficult to assess the global impact on the internet on the most recent generations, where not only one can easily find pornographic content once much more difficult to obtain, but also where anyone, using web cameras, can expose themselves and perform, alone, in couple, in groups, and in sex chats interact with others who do the same. There are people of all ages who actively participate in this, and some become very popular, as real influencers. And from several years words and ideas are spreading by many people as "phone-sex" and "cyber-sex".

So, the "virtual" touches, contaminates, perhaps transforms, even the most personal, private, intimate aspects of people's lives.

Increased usage of the Internet has given rise to a new challenge to marriages: That of online infidelity, which is perceived to be as traumatic as actual infidelity. (Mao and Raguram, 2009)

The last decade has witnessed a revolution in the ways that singles meet other singles. In the "era of isolation", the Internet offers displays of a wide array of eligible single men and women, allowing the user to form romantic encounters and helping to break through gender norms and to form new rules for dating. (Seifert and Miara, 2019)

Cybersex is often used as a collective term for all sorts of sexually related entertainment, information, and personal contact offers available in computer networks respective "in cyberspace." It is also understood to be a computer-mediated interpersonal interaction in which the participants are sexually motivated, meaning they are seeking sexual arousal and satisfaction. Types are virtual-reality-based cybersex, video-based cybersex, and text-based cybersex. From a technical perspective, two sub-forms of text-based cybersex are differentiated: tinysex and erotic chat. (Choudhary, 2019)

The purpose of this study was to compare male and female college students in four countries (Canada, Germany, Sweden, and the U.S.) ... recent experiences with six types of online sexual activities (OSA): sexual information, sexual entertainment, sexual contacts, sexual minority communities, sexual products, and sex work. (Döring et al., 2017)

One thing that academic studies don't often remember is that web pages with pornographic and sexual content are about 30% of the total.

2015, worldwide, there were more than 2 billion web searches for porn. • 20 percent of mobile-device searches are for porn. • 90 percent of boys and 60 percent of girls are exposed to Internet porn by age 18. (Castleman, 2016)

A vast array of platforms are used in the sex industry. This presents opportunities for sex workers such as access to large customer markets, opportunities for homeworking, building brand recognition and a dedicated fan base and access to peer support. (Swords et al., n.d., p. 287)

8. GLOBAL "ELECTRONIC HIVE MINDS"

Besides addictions affecting the individuals, which in digital domains pose problems that also occur in other contexts, there are other, totally new phenomena made possible only today by the daily interactions of billions of people, in environments and in ways that, until a few decades ago, humanity had never known, that probably we should think of, and understand, and maybe worry about. A very suggestive image is that of *Electronic Hive Minds* on social media.

People communicate not only what they imagine they are purposely sharing but also unintentionally leak information, which allows others to glimpse a sense of the subconscious and unconscious at a macro level.

An electronic hive mind is enabled by humanity's hyperconnectivity through ICT technologies that enable them to share information and digital contents (and moneys and physical contents) in near real-time. This history-making enablement enables people from a wide geographical area (global) to interconnect. The human tendencies to filter information to see generally what they prefer and their confirmation bias (a form of built-in cognitive bias) may mean that people may "mind-meld" with other homophilous thinkers (those who prefer others with similar likes) regarding particular in-world phenomena, for short bursty periods or for longer term ones. The "hive" aspects of this suggest some sort of organization, with people and small groups and larger groups playing unique roles within the hive—to enable information collection, decision making, and leadership, among other needs. (Hai-Jew, 2019)

We have mentioned in Chapter 2 the so called "echo chambers" in which users are attracted as in a comfort zone on the internet, filtered and shaped according to their interests, research, attendance. But while perhaps our collective, social, and political thinking is moving towards ways that recall a hive, it is also strong the pressure to compete and emerge individually among the indistinct mass, as the master chefs on television or the *influencers*. When networked activity, whatever it is, brings thousands of followers and millions of views, automatic advertising mechanisms allow a very small number of users to convert their dependence into a lucrative job and earn even important money from their presence on social media. And for the others, likes are anyhow a reward for narcissism, which helps, compensates, and motivates.

Figure 5. Hive mind

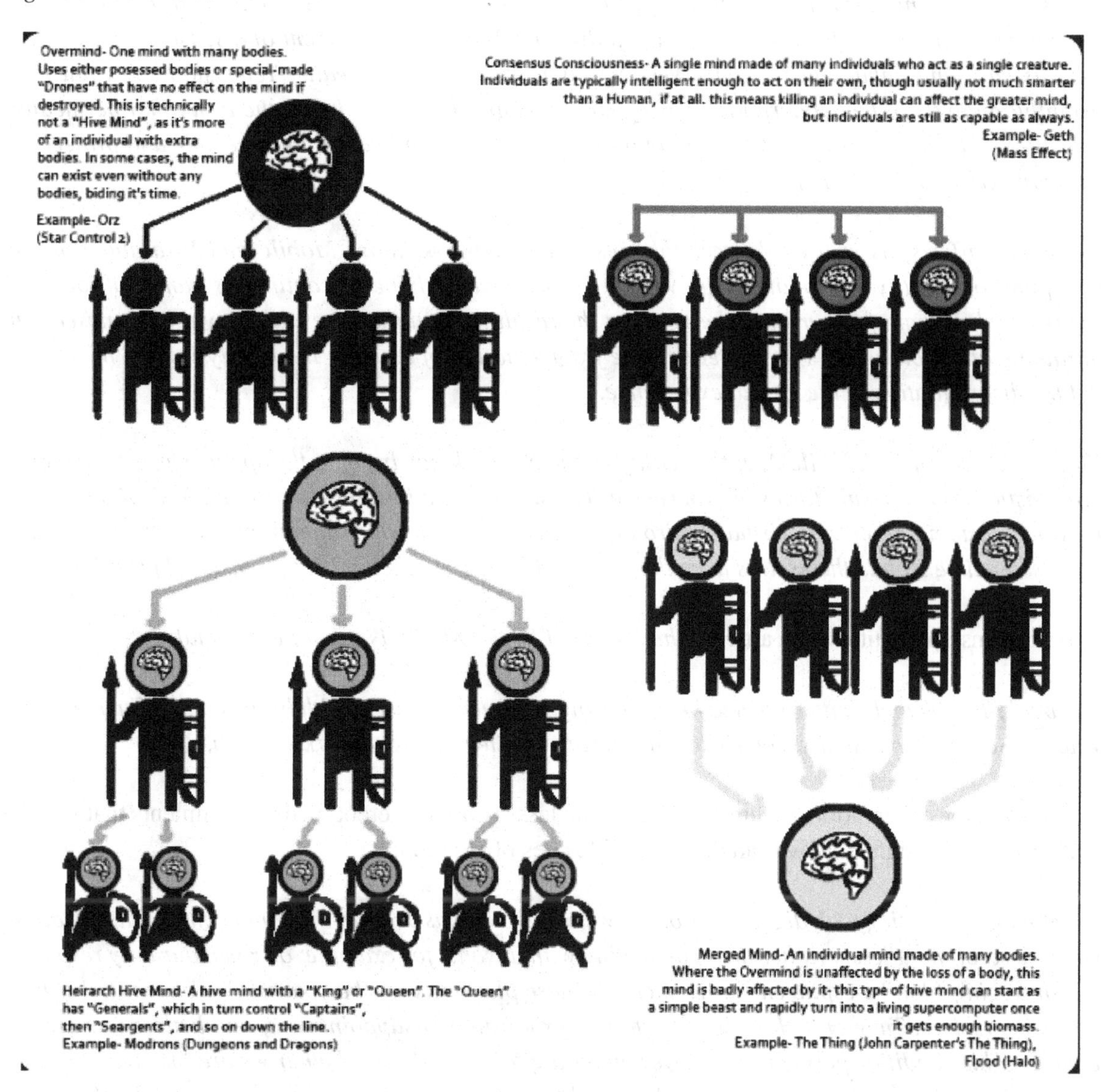

Social media, once called 'Web 2.0', has allowed ordinary people to step into the realm of celebrity by giving them the power of influence and voices that cannot be ignored ... a vast literature on the culture of influence and celebrity on social media has emerged to redefine the contours of the traditional definition of celebrity. (Chikhi, 2021)

On the most successful platforms of recent years, users reinforce the narcissism built around their own images, in a context in which the network, the web, the connections are placed in the background, behind blurred and indefinite trails of followers. In *Tik Tok*, the first thing that strikes the occasional visitor is a gallery of ostentatious physicality, an exhibition of people according to recurrent and repetitive patterns in which it seems incredible that someone can find his/her own original and personal way of proposing, but that's what many try to do.

Narcissism and consumerism ... people are pushed to focus on their own biographies and self-promotion to the point of creating a false self within the individual and the development of a sense of dissatisfaction, dis-ease and unhappiness ... The New Narcissus in the Age of Reality Television constitutes an insightful analysis of the modern ideology of greatness, perfection or 'being the best', that permeates society - an ideology that overwhelms and ultimately drives the individual to dissemble and project an artificial self. (Collins, 2017)

The screen affects, as well as the technologies of the Network, those Mobile and Wearable, on the perception of identity and relationality with the other giving shape to continuous games of identity. The research is that of the unity of the ego, but the result is often the pure withdrawal into oneself, an inordinate attention to one's own interests, the fragmentation of identity, the paralysis from mirroring and the disorientation of the virtual experience.

With the advent of the Mobile Age, the reality of the Network has become the space where to exercise narcissistic and rewarding forms of experience. The screen, with its icons, defines a physical perimeter on which custom and private virtual environments take shape in which the individual can mirror and at the same time isolate themselves from the real world. (Mazzucchelli, 2015, translated from Italian)

As it sums up the title of an article, *The Future of Social Media Is a Lot Less Social.*

Facebook, TikTok and Twitter seem to be increasingly connecting users with brands and influencers. To restore a sense of community, some users are trying smaller social networks. (Chen, 2023)

But from the observation of our moving less and less at ease in stereotyped environments that induce conformity and resignation, we can draw possible cues of reaction:

Sometimes, interacting with digital platforms, we want to be passive—in those moments of dissociation when we scroll mindlessly rather than connecting with anyone, for example, or when our only response is a shrugging "lol." Despite encouragement by these platforms to "be yourself," we want to be anyone but ourselves. Tung-Hui Hu calls this state of exhaustion, disappointment, and listlessness digital lethargy. This condition permeates our lives under digital capitalism, whether we are "users," who are what they click, or racialized workers in Asia and the Global South. Far from being a state of apathy, however, lethargy may hold the potential for social change.

Hu explores digital lethargy through a series of works by contemporary artists, writers, and performers. (Hu, 2022)

9. A STRANGE DIGITAL UNIVERSE WHERE PEOPLE NEVER DIE

I think not to be the only one to have noticed that, even years after a person died, Facebook go on suggesting wishing him or her a happy birthday! Overall, it's a little troubling.

If Facebook is made aware that a person has passed away, it's our policy to memorialize the account. Memorialized accounts are a place for friends and family to gather and share memories after a person has passed away. Memorializing an account also helps keep it secure by preventing anyone from logging into it.

If you're a legacy contact, learn how to manage a memorialized account. If you'd like to report a deceased person's account to be memorialized, please contact us. (From Facebook Help Center)

Facebook announced Thursday a policy that allows you to designate a "legacy contact", who'll be allowed to "pin a post on your Timeline" after your death, such as a funeral announcement. The contact won't be able to log in as you or read your private messages, but will be allowed to respond to new friend requests, update your cover and profile photos, archive your Facebook posts and photos. (Linshi, 2022)

So now we wonder what happens if one, having other things to do in his life, forgets to designate a legacy contact who manages his Facebook account after his death! Who can make him rest in peace even in the social network? Ex-wife, current girlfriend, children, siblings, parents, favorite friends?

And - how it is true, obviously I don't know- we can also come across messages like this:

Someone memorialized my murdered son's account and went in and deleted everything that included evidence of crimes. I suspect who the guilty parties are but I want facebook to restore everything and I should be the manager of that account and I want to sue the person (s) involved in this deliberate fraud. However, I cannot find any way to contact facebook or get them to respond to me! (from Facebook, "STOP FACEBOOK UNVERIFIED MEMORIALIZED ACCOUNTS" Group, 2022)

Normality is to go now, June 2023, and look up for example at Seymour Papert, the creator of programming language LOGO, who died in 2016. As evidently no one has "memorialized" his profile, I find it just like all my other friends' accounts. I can guess he's no longer with us from some wishes I read like "Happy birthday, Seymour, wherever you are!". The same happens in other profiles of friends I know they are dead, where, beside some commemorative messages, appropriate and heartwarming, there are also the wishes of obviously distant friends who after years do not know yet about the death, but even other messages clearly of advertising. On the profile of a woman, I read of the podcast of psychiatrists who sponsor their channel, and on Papert's even that of a lady who suggests the miraculous diet thanks to which in 30 days she lost... judging by the photos something like 100 kilograms! This is not good at all!

After a long search, I finally found a profile with the inscription "memorialized", of a man. Apart from the name, I don't understand it, as it's in Arabic, but it puzzles me a little the blue button on the right of the page; if I want, I can still ask his friendship!

What in this case is probably an unintended effect of the system, it could even become in the future a much more intentional and precise project;

The ancient human dream of eternal life can be achieved through technology: i.e. human digital immortality. A day will come when the entire technical capabilities will allow personalities to be copied into a computer. Thus immortality could be provided in a virtualized form, heaving being replaced with a super computer. (Scarlat, 2017)

At the present, from the participation and interaction of billions of humans in social media and in the web more in general, we would probably find a lot of paradoxical and surreal situations, as well as a huge amount of good ideas, solutions for the problems of the world, and totally ranting dreams. But it is very difficult to know what really important happens and which are the influences on daily life of people and on society. The elements that we can record statistically are the number of visualizations, the likes, and for the rest we can only make assumptions.

The participatory web phenomenon has emerged so quickly and widely that research has generally focused on various features, user responses, and design characteristics much more than on theoretical explanations for the underlying causes and contingent effects associated with their use. (Walther & Jang, 2012)

Results from the studies showed that interactivity comprises three correlated but distinct dimensions: active control, two-way communication, and synchronicity. (Liu, 2003)

10. EXPLORING MULTIPLE REALITIES, BUT THERE IS NO ESC KEY IN TRUE LIFE

June 3, 2023. A case has affected Italian public opinion, of a young man, who murdered his girlfriend, seven months pregnant.

The body is there in front of the eyes. Alessandro what does he do? He runs on the Internet ... asks the oracle how to erase the evidence, how to make the blood disappear, how to eliminate from cell phones the memories of Whatsapp ... the tragic story of this murder betrays all the existential disability of those who have become accustomed to facing life as a challenge on social networks ... dramatic confusion between reality and metaverse, or whatever we want to call this alternative dimension in which you just press "esc" to stop everything and enter reset mode. (Massini, 2023, translation from Italian)

The hypothesis is strong, but not so unlikely. Can the habit of living a large part of time, emotions, dreams, thoughts in an alternative universe alter in some individuals the way they deal with reality, to the point of not making them aware of the real consequences of certain actions? Or rather, is it possible that whatever we do, even a murder, almost as for a conditioned reflex, we instinctively search for a solution online?

Virtual and augmented reality is a further extension of the "universes" that technology can create all around us, so that our perception of the world can be enhanced, or shifted, or displaced… It depends on situations and attitudes, and probably we cannot apply the same patterns to different people.

Today's learners are accustomed to multimedia learning environments and have come to expect a certain level of technology integrated into their curricula. Virtual Reality (VR) technology enables students to become immersed within a 360-degree view experience of scenes that have been completely digitally created, whilst no longer viewing the real world around them. (Yilmaz et al. 2019)

The problem, very usual, is that, alongside the descriptions and narratives that intertwine online of what it *could be* - the user, the child, the elderly, the disabled person can take advantage of... in theory

- often based on postulates that correspond in the end to clichés, we have at disposal limited scientific studies, and on actual experience there is little information and reflection. In fact, having technology doesn't mean at all that people use it in everyday activities, even when it would take very little.

A trivial example, from my own experience, better covered in chapter 7.

There are photographers and video makers who take and publish wonderful photos and videos of insects, which we can all admire online.

There are children who observe insects in the garden near the school and, since about 20 years - that is when compact digital cameras even economic were available, capable of discrete macro photography - they can take pictures, directly or with an adult help, some of which look (almost) as good as those of photographers. I have led hundreds of children to do something like this, always with excellent results. They see better the insects on the spot, then review them magnified on a screen, discover and know with surprise and pleasure the living nature around, are keen to study, draw, tell stories, just from the action of enhancing their exploration with cameras. Putting together living experience and technology, we can also share online our photographs and videos with other kids, schools, or even scientists, and sometimes our picture are better of some we find on serious web pages. Children are satisfied of what they can get from their experience and from technology, for school and for fun, easily, naturally, as true actors of knowledge, builders of a small part of the information society.

Probably, I may have not been good at telling all this, or have found myself too alone, publishing photos and videos - not even problems of privacy, when just insects and spiders are shown and of the children, we hear only the voices around! – trying to address teachers, parents, and the public to watch them, in which it's clear that those pictures were taken in a very normal school activity, even sometimes by people not expert at all.

Still, in front of the pictures of photographers in books, magazines and online, the most look at them as if we normal people could not even try to get something like this, and instructions for beginning to observe insects still are given to children or adults only suggesting, like forty years ago, to go and see them with a magnifying glass!

Nothing against magnifying glasses, but how can we talk about harmoniously and effectively incorporating augmented reality and metaverse into our lives, if we still have so many problems to do it with video, photo cameras and mobile phones?

We often here mention the word "disconnection" referring to our virtual and real experience. A problem of technical tools is that often we use them not in addition, but in partial or complete replacement of senses. Anyone of us should have notices that, when taking pictures for example of a show, of a touristic site, we tend to pay less attention to the real thing, and we remember it less than when not using a camera. And watch photos and videos later is not enough to compensate for the lack of attention in the presence. The more we use technological extensions of the senses, the more we should try somehow to compensate for this attitude.

A group of students were taken to an art museum, and in between they took photographs of the exhibits and others just looked at them. The next day the memory was drawn that the participants had objects seen/photographed ... The group he had photographed remembered fewer objects and fewer details. (Bormetti, 2019, p. 46-47, translated from Italian)

And not only we should try to do it more in first person, as we now have the tools to do it, not always waiting for an explanation of all to come from teachers, scientists, and psychologists, but

Figure 6. Boy with camera
Source: Beneventi

Figure 7. Camera with insect
Source: Beneventi

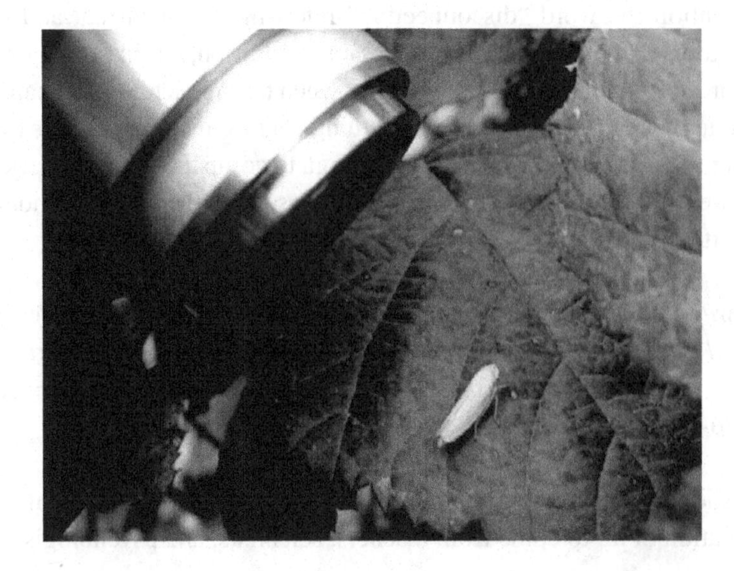

Figure 8. Children photographing insects
Source: Beneventi

The ever-increasing influence of the virtual world or Internet cultures demands to read its complex relationship with human existence in a digital world. Theory of psychoanalysis, specifically object-relation theory can be called forth to analyze this multifaceted relationship. Within the light of this theory, Internet cultures are acting as "objects" like games, memes, chat rooms, social net etc. and the virtual world can be interpreted as the "object world". (Akmam & Huq, 2019)

I do not know if it is because the objects in which we habitually divide our experience are less and less touching one another, but there is also the question, repeatedly mentioned, that we often behave as if everything were born today, and in times when we celebrate the infinite possibilities of electronic memories, we live more and more in a continuous present, and just human memory seems to be out of the game.

As we have already seen for artificial intelligence, also the discourse on different digital realities is not so new as according to some mass disclosure we would be led to believe.

The immersive multimedia history began with the concept of virtual reality. In the late 1960s, some of the developer's needs (programmers and artists) were to create experiences digitally made through interactive multimedia. This became known as virtual reality since they produce 'near-to-reality' outputs. Currently, virtual reality can be seen as computer-created environment that users can experience through the senses of sight, hearing and touch. Immersive multimedia is a combination of multimedia elements and Interactivity in virtual reality. On other hand, the Immersion concept and practice is redefining several areas like education, live production industries, arts, and providing new experiences in publics through a combination of creative development and technical innovation. (Soares & Simão, 2019)

And of course, powerful applications of these technologies are possible, available, and even practised. Although the average level of the increasingly disconnected discussions on social networks suggests that most citizen user consumers on the planet have no idea of that.

Augmented reality (AR) is an extension of extended reality that superimposes virtual images onto real world view. It has been implemented across a versatile range of fields including education, entertainment, military, and much more. Unlike virtual reality (VR), AR focuses on enhancing the real-world view and enriching people with a better way to display the learning content in an attractive way. AR provides content simulation and interaction which can display textual data in a more immersive way which can retain learner's concentration for longer periods of time ... Mentally differently abled children require special attention right from their childhood ... AR-based learning would make their learning much more easier through the personalized and immersive platform. (Geetha et al., 2019)

The marking feature of the present is ubiquity, as in the loss of spatial and temporal coordinates and the gain of a presence-absence that new technologies allow us to live – both positively and negatively. The body is the core of this electronic, virtual, and increased involvement. In this phase we're living in, the author suggests we introduce the neologism "metrobody" to identify this new hybrid condition undertaken by the body. (Cipolletta, 2019)

Advances in immersive virtual reality (VR) and wearable augmented reality (AR) technology have provided new opportunities to design interventions targeting the core deficits associated with ASD (Autism Spectrum Disorder) and supporting optimal functional outcomes. (Turnacioglu et al., 2019)

Deftly applied automation can buy back time and cognitive resources for operators, decreasing the chances of human error, but technology also has the potential to become less of a tool and more of a crutch if operational fundamentals and basic seafaring skills are forsaken to automation. Operators must be able to rely on their own "sea sense," developed through experience and mentoring, and use technology to accomplish specific objectives rather than defer to automation as the default decision-maker. (Culley, 2021)

REFERENCES

A short history of the web. (n.d.). home.cern/science/computing/birth-web/short-history-web.

Akmam, J., & Huq, N. (2019). Living Parallel-ly in Real and Virtual: Internet as an Extension of Self. In *Multigenerational Online Behavior and Media Use: Concepts, Methodologies, Tools, and Applications*. IGI Global. doi:10.4018/978-1-5225-7909-0.ch031

Appel, M. (2019, Oct 16). Are Social Media Ruining Our Lives? A Review of Meta-Analytic Evidence. *Sage Journals, Review of General Psychology.*

Beneventi, P. (1999). *Come usare il computer con bambini e ragazzi.* Sonda.

Berners-Lee, T. (2012). History of the Web. *World Wide Web Foundation.* webfoundation.org.

Berners-Lee, T. (2019, March 12). 30 years on, what's next #ForTheWeb*? Web Foundation.*

Berners-Lee, T., & Fischetti, M. (2000). *Weaving the Web: The Original Design and Ultimate Destiny of the World Wide Web.* Harper.

Bormetti, M. (2019). *Egophonia: Gli smartphone fra noi e la vita.* Hoepli.

Boursier, V., & Manna, V. (2019). Relational Body Identities: Body Image Control Through Self-Portraits – A Revision of the Body Image Control in Photos Questionnaire. In *Intimacy and Developing Personal Relationships in the Virtual World.* IGI Global. doi:10.4018/978-1-5225-4047-2.ch003

Bozoglan, B. (2019). *Multifaceted Approach to Digital Addiction and Its Treatment.* IGI Global. doi:10.4018/978-1-5225-8449-0

Castleman, M. (2016, Nov 3). *Dueling Statistics: How Much of the Internet Is Porn?* psychologytoday.com/us/blog/all-about-sex.

Chen, B. X. (2023, Apr 19). The Future of Social Media Is a Lot Less Social, *New York Times.*

Chikhi, I. (2021, May 27). *Financial Influencers and Social Media: The Role of Valuable and Trusted Content in Creating a New Form of Authenticity* [Student Theses]. Baruch College, City University of New York. academicworks.cuny.edu

Choudhary, A. (2019). Cybersex. In *Intimacy and Developing Personal Relationships in the Virtual World.* IGI Global. doi:10.4018/978-1-5225-4047-2.ch011

Cipolletta, G. (2019). Ubiquitous Bodies: A "Metrobodily" Transition From Real to Virtual. In *Virtual and Augmented Reality in Mental Health Treatment.* IGI Global. doi:10.4018/978-1-5225-7168-1.ch001

Collins, M. E. (2017). *The New Narcissus in the Age of Reality Television.* Routledge. doi:10.4324/9781315463490

Culley, K. E. (2021). *Mariners or Machines: Who's at the Helm? Shifting Roles and Responsibilities on Navy Warships. In Human Factors Issues and the Impact of Technology on Society.* IGI Global. doi:10.4018/978-1-7998-6453-0.ch009

Döring, N. (2017, Aug). *Online Sexual Activity Experiences Among College Students: A Four-Country Comparison.* pubmed.ncbi.nlm.nih.gov

Early Mapping. (2019). "Electronic Hive Minds" on the Web and Internet. In *Electronic Hive Minds on Social Media: Emerging Research and Opportunities.* IGI Global.

Epstein, S. (2023, March 15). It's harder than ever to step away from our devices, which are so entwined in our lives. Is it fruitless to even try? *BBC.* bbc.com/worklife/article

Facebook. (n.d.). *Help Center*. Facebook.

Firth, J., Torous, J., Stubbs, B., Firth, J. A., Steiner, G. Z., Smith, L., Alvarez-Jimenez, M., Gleeson, J., Vancampfort, D., Armitage, C. J., & Sarris, J. (2019, June). The "online brain": How the Internet may be changing our cognition. *World Psychiatry; Official Journal of the World Psychiatric Association (WPA)*, *18*(2), 119–129. doi:10.1002/wps.20617 PMID:31059635

Geetha, S. (2021). Augmented Reality Application: AR Learning Platform for Primary Education. In *Multimedia and Sensory Input for Augmented, Mixed, and Virtual Reality*. IGI Global. doi:10.4018/978-1-7998-4703-8.ch006

Gonzalez Rodriguez, J. L. (2020, August 24). When Technology Turns Into Wasted Time: How To Get Your Productivity Back At Work. *Forbes*.

Guazzaroni, G. (2019). *Virtual and Augmented Reality in Mental Health Treatment*. IGI Global. doi:10.4018/978-1-5225-7168-1

Hague, B. N., & Loader, B. D. (1999). *Digital Democracy: Discourse and Decision Making in the Information Age*. Routledge.

Henricks, T. (2016, Apr 4). The Broken Self: Rethinking the Idea of Alienation. *Psychology Today, Spirituality*.

Hirshberg, P. (2014). First the Media, Then Us: How the Internet Changed the Fundamental Nature of the Communication and Its Relationship with the Audience. *Change*, *19*.

Hu, T.-H. (2022). *Digital Lethargy: Dispatches from an Age of Disconnection*. The MIT Press. doi:10.7551/mitpress/14336.001.0001

Joseph, J. J. (2021). Facebook Depression or Facebook Contentment: The Relation Between Facebook Use and Well-Being. In *Research Anthology on Mental Health Stigma, Education, and Treatment*. IGI Global. doi:10.4018/978-1-7998-8544-3.ch061

Leung, W. C., & Wan, A. (2022). My Little Joy in Life: Posting Food on Instagram. In *Research Anthology on Usage, Identity, and Impact of Social Media on Society and Culture*. IGI Global. doi:10.4018/978-1-6684-6307-9.ch057

Linshi, J. (2015, February 12). Here's What Happens to Your Facebook Account After You Die. *Time*.

Liu, Y. (2003, June). Developing a Scale to Measure the Interactivity of Websites. *Journal of Advertising Research*, *43*(2), 207–216. doi:10.2501/JAR-43-2-207-216

Mao, A., & Raguram, A. (2009, October-December). Online infidelity: The new challenge to marriages. *Indian Journal of Psychiatry*, *51*(4), 302–304. doi:10.4103/0019-5545.58299 PMID:20048458

Massini, S. (2023, Jun 2). La Radice del male. *La Repubblica*.

Mazzucchelli, C. (2015). *E guardo il mondo da un display*. Delos Digital.

McLuhan, M. (1964). *Understanding Media: The Extensions of Man*. McGraw Hill.

McLuhan, M., & Fiore, Q. (1967). *The Medium Is the Massage: An Inventory of Effects*. Random House.

Our democracy is only as good as the information that voters have. (2022). ippi.org.il

Pietilä, V. (1970). Alienation and Use of the Mass Media. *Acta Sociologica, 13*(4), 237-252.

Popescu, F., & Scarlat, C. (2017). *Human Digital Immortality: Where Human Old Dreams and New Technologies Meet. In Research Paradigms and Contemporary Perspectives on Human-Technology Interaction*. IGI Global. doi:10.4018/978-1-5225-1868-6.ch012

Sakurai, R. (2017). *Correcting aspect ratio distortion of natural images by convolutional neural network*. ieeexplore.ieee.org/document/7992894. 14th International Conference on Ubiquitous Robots and Ambient Intelligence (URAI)

Saptasagar, K. A. (2022). Effects of Digital Technology on Adolescents: Pros and Cons. In *Impact and Role of Digital Technologies in Adolescent Lives*. IGI Global. doi:10.4018/978-1-7998-8318-0.ch002

Schou Andreassen, C. (2015). Online Social Network Site Addiction: A Comprehensive Review. *Current Addiction Reports*, *2*(2), pages175–184. doi:10.100740429-015-0056-9

Seifert, T., & Miara, I. (2019). The Effect of Social Networks on Relationships Outside the Network. In *Intimacy and Developing Personal Relationships in the Virtual World*. IGI Global. doi:10.4018/978-1-5225-4047-2.ch012

Small, G., & Vorgan, G. (2015). iBrain: Surviving the Technological Alteration of the Modern Mind. *Education Review*.

Soares, C., & Simão, E. (2019). Immersive Multimedia in Information Revolution. In *Trends, Experiences, and Perspectives in Immersive Multimedia and Augmented Reality*. IGI Global. doi:10.4018/978-1-5225-5696-1.ch009

Stop Facebook Unverified Memorialized Accounts. (2022). Facebook.

Swords, J., Laing, M., & Cook, I. R. (2021). Platforms, sex work and their interconnectedness. *Sage Journals. Sexualities*, *26*(3), 277–297. doi:10.1177/13634607211023013

Turnacioglu, S. (2019). The State of Virtual and Augmented Reality Therapy for Autism Spectrum Disorder (ASD). In *Virtual and Augmented Reality in Mental Health Treatment*. IGI Global. doi:10.4018/978-1-5225-7168-1.ch008

Ubaradka, A., Fathima, A., & Batra, S. (2023). Psychological Correlates of Perfectionistic Self-Presentation Among Social Media Users. *International Journal of Cyber Behavior, Psychology and Learning*, *13*(1), 1–13. doi:10.4018/IJCBPL.324089

Uzelli Yilmaz, D. (2020). Nursing Education in the Era of Virtual Reality. In *Virtual and Augmented Reality in Education, Art, and Museums*. IGI Global. doi:10.4018/978-1-7998-1796-3.ch003

Walther, J. B., & Jang, J.-W. (2012). Communication Processes in Participatory Websites. *Journal of Computer-Mediated Communication*, *18*(1), 2–15. doi:10.1111/j.1083-6101.2012.01592.x

Wegmann, E., Stodt, B., & Brand, M. (2015). Addictive use of social networking sites can be explained by the interaction of Internet use expectancies, Internet literacy, and psychopathological symptoms. *Journal of Behavioral Addictions*, *4*(3), 155–162. doi:10.1556/2006.4.2015.021 PMID:26551905

What is your favorite type of Hive Mind? (n.d.). reddit.com/r/sciencefiction/

Working with aspect ratio. (2023, Aug 23). helpx.adobe.com/il_he/premiere-pro

ADDITIONAL READING

Frison, E., & Eggermont, S. (2017). Browsing, posting, and liking on Instagram: The reciprocal relationships between different types of Instagram use and adolescents' depressed mood. *Cyberpsychology, Behavior, and Social Networking*, *20*(10), 603–609. doi:10.1089/cyber.2017.0156 PMID:29039700

Laconi, S., Kaliszewska-Czeremska, K., Gnisci, A., Sergi, I., Barke, A., Jeromin, F., Groth, J., Gamez-Guadix, M., Ozcan, N. K., Demetrovics, Z., Király, O., Siomos, K., Floros, G., & Kuss, D. J. (2018, July). Cross-cultural study of Problematic Internet Use in nine European countries. *Computers in Human Behavior*, *84*, 430–440. doi:10.1016/j.chb.2018.03.020

Mauri, M., Cipresso, P., Balgera, A., Villamira, M., & Riva, G. (2011). Why is Facebook so successful? Psychophysiological measures describe a core flow state while using Facebook. *Cyberpsychology, Behavior, and Social Networking*, *14*(12), 723–731. doi:10.1089/cyber.2010.0377 PMID:21879884

Orr, E. S. (2009). The influence of shyness on the use of Facebook in an undergraduate sample. *Cyberpsychology, Behavior, and Social Networking*, *12*(3). PMID:19250019

Sariyska, R., Reuter, M., Bey, K., Sha, P., Li, M., Chen, Y.-F., Liu, W.-Y., Zhu, Y.-K., Li, C.-B., Suárez-Rivillas, A., Feldmann, M., Hellmann, M., Keiper, J., Markett, S., Young, K. S., & Montag, C. (2014, April-May). Self-esteem, personality and Internet Addiction: A cross-cultural comparison study. *Personality and Individual Differences*, *61–62*, 28–33. doi:10.1016/j.paid.2014.01.001

Turel, O., He, Q., Xue, G., Xiao, L., & Bechara, A. (2014). Examination of neural systems sub-serving Facebook "addiction". *Psychological Reports*, *115*(3), 675–695. doi:10.2466/18.PR0.115c31z8 PMID:25489985

Turel, O., Serenko, & Giles. (2011, December). Integrating technology addiction and use: An empirical investigation of online auction users. *Management Information Systems Quarterly*, *35*(4), 1043–1061. doi:10.2307/41409972

Verduyn, P., Lee, D. S., Park, J., Shablack, H., Orvell, A., Bayer, J., Ybarra, O., Jonides, J., & Kross, E. (2015). Passive Facebook usage undermines affective well-being: Experimental and longitudinal evidence. *Journal of Experimental Psychology. General*, *144*(2), 480–488. doi:10.1037/xge0000057 PMID:25706656

Wang, T., Wong, J. Y. H., Wang, M. P., Li, A. C. Y., Kim, S. S., & Lee, J. J. (2021, December). Effects of Social Networking Service (SNS) Addiction on Mental Health Status in Chinese University Students: Structural Equation Modeling Approach Using a Cross-sectional Online Survey. *Journal of Medical Internet Research*, *23*(12), e26733. doi:10.2196/26733 PMID:34889760

Chapter 5
The Spirit of the Information Society, Technologies, and Citizens:
Consumers, Hackers, the Shipwreck of the Web

ABSTRACT

Since years the hackers' movement warns about it. For a huge cultural misunderstanding, we are going on trying to learn new technologies according to the rules of the old school or using them as if we could learn directly from the market. The most cannot properly use the present devices too powerful and easy, and many ideas on the future come from science fiction. It's difficult to understand that the Web is made by each of us and depends on what we put in it, more than on our visits online. Once the Internet was attended by a small vanguard capable of managing websites and blogs, gathering in communities, innovating audiovisual and media, sharing experiences and knowledge. Since several years we are billions crowded in networks much more commercial than social, where no technical skills or references to reality are required: Really "ready" for the incoming metaverse, AI and the Web3?

1. INTRODUCTION

In latest decades, the huge amount of information and novelties has led to some bizarre observations and predictions about a "future" that often, instead, has taken different directions, sometimes beyond imagination.

There is a big underlying cultural problem in our society. We are still accustomed to the idea of a coded knowledge that is transmitted by teachers to students and attested through certifications, while recent technological evolution is inducing the widespread production of a new and much more dynamic culture. It's what hackers have described as the contradiction between the academy and the monastic

DOI: 10.4018/978-1-6684-8228-5.ch005

school. This leads to confusion, power struggles, cultural barriers, which often hinder the resolution of important and vital problems on the global planet.

The web, for example, one of the greatest invention in history, after the first pioneering phase inevitably led by a narrow vanguard, has reached the mass of consumer citizens in the form of a global supermarket, an often inextricable bureaucracy, and for the daily use of general public but private and rigid commercial spaces such as social networks, to which everyone is admitted, but from which the possibility of really affecting society is minimal, if not for a small group of *influencers*, selected according to competitive methods that have little correspondence to the nature and potential of the medium. Though, some forms of popular culture appear and spread.

Metaverse and artificial intelligence are also proposed in mainly commercial ways that risk limiting their potential. In fact, to the fascinating descriptions that the avant-garde makes of what we could do using new technologies, often it corresponds in the real world a tired repeating always the same things, simply using different means. And some descriptions for example of a highly decentralized web 3 appear out of reach of increasingly passive citizens, accustomed to downloading apps that free them from any choice and responsibility. This is a significant threat to democracy.

2. WHEN BOOKS WERE TO BE SOON REPLACED BY VIDEO CASSETTES...

When the author was still very young, many commentators already ruled the next death of the book. The designated killer, at that time, was indicated in video cassettes.

What, please? Do you mean that, instead of writing a book, in the "future" people will be always making films, with screenplays, cameras, actors, editors? But do you ever think about what you write?

In the so-called information society, since decades, the more and more increasing amount of information we all have at our disposal does not prevent us from directing entire seasons of the cultural debate literally on nothing, with a diminished ability to understand reality, an increasing loneliness of individuals, who feel small and powerless in the face of a world whose working mechanisms are beyond our comprehension.

Today it's chatting with artificial intelligence, that feeds on the words that humans think and write, on how they repeat, chase, and enter in relationship with one another. Overwhelmed by this flood of words, living and sentient people with their bodies, emotions, thoughts, and the natural and artificial environment in which they live, they seem to lose meaning, and it may be strong the temptation to give up once and for all and rely on the impersonal ability of machines to use at this point our logic and grammar better than us. While apparently, judging by the enormous blunders that appear in an increasing number of published texts, at all levels, almost no one now reads and corrects the errors of artificial intelligence for example in translations. It seems to be an unconditional surrender that certainly does not promote effective communication and does not make people happier.

Many things appear to happen without a purpose, we do not set ourselves goals, as if everything was already decided by someone or something greater than ourselves. And if that something is an artificial intelligence, the situation is perfect to remove from us any residual responsibility once more.

We could make our human intelligence work a bit more. To think not superficially, wonder whether it is really possible for books to be replaced by video cassettes or something like this, or whether it is really possible for machines to think for themselves, and not on the basis of human material, for example books and newspaper articles, with which they have been informed by humans:

Whereas humans are limited in the kinds of explanations we can rationally conjecture, machine learning systems can learn both that the earth is flat and that the earth is round – They trade merely in probabilities that change over time. (Chomsky, 2023)

3. PLATO'S ACADEMY AND THE MONASTIC SCHOOL: A HUGE DIGITAL MISUNDERSTANDING?

From Wikipedia:

A hacker is a person skilled in information technology who uses their technical knowledge to achieve a goal or overcome an obstacle, within a computerized system by non-standard means. Though the term hacker has become associated in popular culture with a security hacker – someone who utilizes their technical know-how of bugs or exploits to break into computer systems and access data which would otherwise be inaccessible to them – hacking can also be utilized by legitimate figures in legal situations. (Hacker: Wikipedia entry)

The hacker ethic is a philosophy and set of moral values within hacker culture. Practitioners believe that sharing information and data with others is an ethical imperative. The hacker ethic is related to the concept of freedom of information, as well as the political theories of anti-authoritarianism, socialism, liberalism, anarchism, and libertarianism. (Hacker ethic: Wikipedia entry)

In 2001, inspired by the famous title by Max Weber *The Protestant Ethic and the Spirit of Capitalism,* Finnish philosopher Pekka Himanen wrote *The Hacker Ethic and the Spirit of the Information Age*. It is a small book very useful to understand a big contradiction of present times.

We have already mentioned here in chapters 1 and 2 how, rather than following the dreams of the 1990s, our societies awkwardly evoke the nightmares of the 1950s, born from the world war and nuclear build-up, long before the appearance of the personal computers and the web.

Himanem identified the problem in education: the way in which the possible digital revolution started between the 1970s and the 1990s and promoted by a minority vanguard, was then transmitted to the mass of consumers, with the widespread dissemination first of personal computers and then of mobile devices among all the inhabitants of the planet.

A chapter is titled "The Academy and the Monastery":

Figure 1. Hacker ethic
Source: Supremecreature (2012)

In the original hacker money ethic, the new economy's governing attitude, "which seeks profit rationally and systematically" (Weber's description of the spirit of old capitalism, which still applies well to our lime),' is challenged by the open model in which the hacker gives his or her creation freely for others to use, test, and develop further. (Himanem, 2001)

Himanem makes the example of Linux, the operating system born from the non-profit shared work of hundreds of independent programmers, that is in direct competition, often preferred to Windows in network management, without having a direction or a group to make decisions, but basing all on a new and different organization of the work.

It is the bazaar against the cathedral, according to the definition by Eric Steven Raymond (Raymond, 1999).

Although a technologist himself, Raymond emphasizes that Linux's real innovation was not technical but social: it was the new, completely open social manner in which it was developed. (Himanem, 2001)

Another possible allegory for the open-source model is again the academy ... Scientists, too, release their work openly to others for their use, testing, and further development. Their research is based on the idea of an open and self-correcting process ... It is a continuation of the synusia of Plato's Academy, which also included the idea of approaching the truth through critical dialogue." The scientific ethic entails a model in which theories are developed collectively and their flaws are perceived and gradually removed by means of criticism provided by the entire scientific community". Of course, scientists, too, have chosen this model not only for ethical reasons but also because it has proved to be the most successful way of creating scientific knowledge. All of our understanding of nature is based on this academic or scientific model. (Himanem, 2001)

The ethos of the original academic and the hacker model—well summed up by Plato's idea that no free person should learn anything like a slave" is totally different from that of the monastery school, the spirit of which was summed up by Benedict's monastic rule: "It belongeth to the master to speak and to teach; it becometh the disciple to be silent and to listen." The irony is that currently the academy tends to model its learning structure on the monastic sender-receiver model ... the result is a computerized monastery school. (Himanem, 2001)

That is probably the point! Yet visible since that time (2001), the trend has never stopped and, if it's easy to understand why companies born from nothing and become extremely powerful within a few years, have an interest in feeding a neoliberal ideology that favors huge profits for them, much less understandable it is the underestimation of this enormous contradiction on the part of culture, of the intellectuals. The few dissonant voices in academia and alternative movements have not had the way to make themselves heard so far, or perhaps have not been able to give themselves, for their diffusion, the same efficiency in communication that the groups working on Linux have managed to give themselves.

But in the meanwhile, curious things are happening in society:

In the early days of the computer underground, regulated and lifelong employment was the norm in society. Those who opted out from this legally secure arrangement were true outliers. But over the last thirty years or so, an ever larger segment of the workforce has had to make a living under the same precarious conditions as the hacker. In the so-called "gig economy," everyone is an outsider. "Open" is the sibling word to "outside." (Söderberg, 2022, p. 189-190)

4. THE FUTURE AND IMAGINATION, VARIABLES, AND POSSIBLE FIXED POINTS

No one has a crystal ball in which to see the future, so humans have always been trying to imagine it, and they like to do that. From the nineteenth century writers began to create science fiction novels, to which in the twentieth century the stories were added of cinema and television, that have passionate multitudes.

If the authors can play on feelings, passions, aspirations, ideas that in some ways are constant in the history of humanity, as demonstrated by literature over centuries and millennia, it is much more difficult to imagine the technology of the future, and the risk of anachronism is always present. So, in science fiction stories, in a context of space travel between galaxies that maybe humanity will never really live, technological elements are put typical of the time when the book or the film was released and that already after a few decades appear irremediably old and dated.

For example, on a distant planet, having taken shots of the mysterious and possibly hostile aliens, space travellers must wait, to see them, that the film is developed! Or on the starship accelerating at the speed of light, the monitors are cathode ray tubes, and the computer memories are reel recorders. In the cartoon set in the years 3000, the memory of the android robot is contained in a floppy disk!

The legendary "computer" with which for decades only the characters of *Star Trek* have spoken, now is experienced every day talking with *Siri*, *Alexa*, *ChatGPT*. But that in the future all of us will all be able to interact with computers by touching with speed dexterity and precision their transparent screens, as we see in *Avatar* and other films, without combining disasters, it's something I do personally doubt.

On some things we can reason, find a methodology, and perhaps some firm points can be established. For example, *handwriting* has basic movements that do not change, regardless of the instrument we use - goose feather pen, brush, nib, fountain, ball or touch screen pen, finger - and of the *hardware* - paper, parchment, wax, blackboard, touch screen. It depends on how our arm, hand, fingers are made. It's a fixed point, and we can reasonably imagine, describe, show in a fiction, humans in the future handwriting more or less in the same way.

Solid-state storage memories maybe are something like this, ultimate, as data published in the past on different media - paper for text and images, magnetic tapes and vinyl discs for audio, film and magnetic tapes for movies and videos - are put together in a single container which does not contain mechanical parts.

Apart from the fact that digital coding can occur in an infinite number of different ways, or *formats* – like the files which we are used to recognize from the extension of names - and this can be a big problem, as described in subchapter 5.07, it is mechanics that determines the object shape, and the way the human user must handle it. In a film camera, the shape is given by the film format: 35, 60 x 60, 60 x 90 mm; a VHS o U-matic video camera must be large, while a mini-DV one can be quite small, but all must have a compartment and a drag mechanism for the cassette.

Solid-state memories do not need mechanics. Reflex and mirrorless photo cameras look like old film cameras, a bit by tradition, and also to share\ the lenses, as well as video cameras resemble to their cassette ancestors for ergonomics. But photos and movies today are taken mainly with smartphones, whose shape is determined by other factors: the need to be kept at the ear as phones, to be touched as graphics interfaces, to be taken possibly in a pocket.

So, we can imagine a future in which humans will capture images using gadgets of any shape, with inside solid-state memories, and that there's no going back from this. Probably, cards to be put inside devices, pen drives that connect directly, hard drives with or without a cable, changing the interfaces and the modes of wi-fi transmission and maybe a little bit the shape, they all are models that we can project into the future, without the risk of excessive technical anachronisms.

5. ARCHAIC MODELS OF EDUCATION FOR NEW MEANS, COURSES, CERTIFICATIONS, CLICHÉS

Many stories of the "future" tell of empires, geniuses of evil, brave captains, and heroes, today as it has always been in the history of humanity, since when epic poems were not written, but heard by the voice of singers and bards.

When the ECDL (European Computer Driving Licence) was established, I immediately wrote a small article: "My computer is a bicycle and I drive it without a license" (Beneventi, 2001).

That licence was an "official" recognition of the skills provided by the previous "private" Microsoft license. "Basic" skills on computer are about office, including the very specialized competences on spreadsheets and data bases. But why? And then "optional" skills were added for example for audiovisual, with a surreal list of "basic" competences about video and music, that not even a whole team of technicians at the end of their career…

Among the ICT instruments, in the forms that Italian school requires - I am basing on that one I had to fill last year, when working in a primary school - there are not photo and video cameras and - very curious - not event printers! Of course, they are quoted screens, all possible imaginable!

It seems that technology is considered only on the side of consumption, of the "education" that is to be given to students by someone else. Devices are not considered for what anyone can do, create, being active.

And PCs, in those forms, are even indicated as "individual" devices. Individual? Have they ever seen kids really *working* on personal computers, on their own? Kids are natural, collective *hackers*! And any adult can learn a lot from their original solutions.

Apparently, it has nothing to do with what we are talking about, but I like to quote here the drawing of a nine-year-old girl, after an exit to observe small animals (using photographic and video *technology* to see better). There is a ladybug, red with its black dots, with its mouth biting a triangular shape, red with black dots: "What is this?"

The girl looks at me in amazement, "How can't you understand? It's a ladybug eating a watermelon!"

Thus, children establish relationships, play and can "change the world", as we will see in more detail in chapter 7 of this book.

If a citizen of the mid-20th century had seen someone searching and finding information about anything in real time, simply typing or pronouncing one or more words on a mobile, he or she would have thought it was a miracle, or a devilry. But we know that not everyone is equally good at research on the internet, and many teachers complain that their students do not really know how a good search should be done.

Stanford researchers find students have trouble judging the credibility of information online.

Education scholars say youth are duped by sponsored content and don't always recognize political bias of social messages. (Donald, 2016)

We know also that not always we can take for granted being online. In the video I coordinated from afar in the time of the pandemic, the children of a 5th grade in Milan remember that when they had school online there was always something wrong with connections for someone. But in UK too

Over a quarter (27%) of university students were unable to access online learning during the Covid-19 lockdown, according to new research which suggests that disabled students and those from poorer backgrounds were worst affected.

The survey, which was carried out in July by the National Union of Students (NUS), found that disruptions to studies arose from a lack of IT equipment and software, insufficient course materials, and poor internet connections. (Packham, 2020)

Back to the main interest here, it is not so much to what we take from the web, but to what we put into it, because it is what we all upload online that make the web what it is and marks its difference from other works of human genius.

6. AND TECHNOLOGY MOVED ONLINE: GRAPHIC SITE BUILDERS

From a personal computer or a smartphone any end user, without need to be a technician, can access the web, watch, and download content made by others, and also put online his/her content.

This fact that we all are the authors of the web, that the web is largely composed of documents uploaded by ordinary people, I do not know how clear it is to the multitude of its users, perhaps because of the "TV deformation" mentioned in these pages on several occasions, or also because we mostly interact with the internet through social networks.

When we "post" our photos and videos, when we start a discussion or partake in those of others, we are actually just "filling shelves", or walls, that have been arranged and set up by someone else, and many behave as if they were with a small group of friends, rather than potentially in contact with the whole world. There can be attention and care for messages, hoping of attracting and gaining followers, but also many aspiring *influencers* behave much more as competitors than as publishers.

Social networks, which are commercial enterprises that earn sometimes very well, profiling and redistributing our data for marketing, they are mostly organized to get the widest possible audience, even those who are completely ignorant of hardware and software. But nowhere is it established that the web must be only a quick library for information or a fun park for bored consumers.

The first websites were set up by people who knew the programming language used on the internet, namely HTML. It's a high-level language, that's to say commands and instructions are practically in English and the syntax is not particularly difficult. But dealing well with it it's not for everyone and the only fact of learning and writing it, knowing that if you miss a comma or a space the software does not work, drastically narrowed the field of possible authors of websites. However, as it had been for writing, drawing, pagination, for which everything had been simplified with the introduction of the graphical

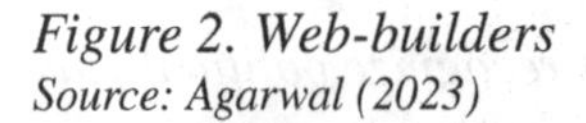
Figure 2. Web-builders
Source: Agarwal (2023)

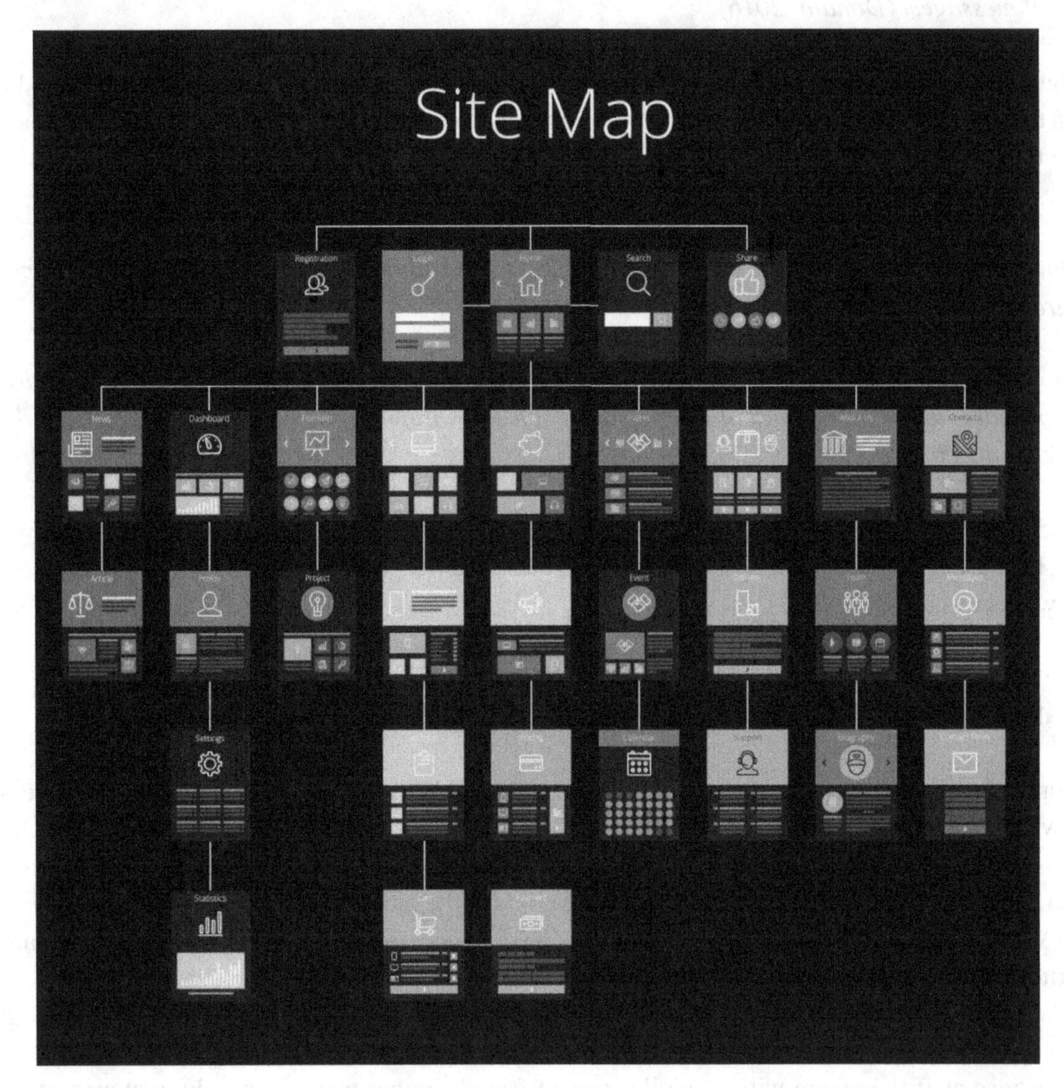

interface and the so-called WYSIWYG (WhatYouSeeIsWhatYouGet) programs, the same happened for websites; the code is hidden below, and the author simply manages objects on the screen.

So, websites began to be an ideal environment for the work of artists rather than programmers, even if they include many technical elements, such as the management of links and navigation, data bases, embedded videos, eventual electronic commerce systems, and so on.

Between 1995 and 2000 *FrontPage* was a popular software by Microsoft (originally by Vermeer Technologies) to set up web sites, and professionals preferred things like *DreamWeaver* and *Fireworks*, (by Macromedia and then Adobe). The author of this book, after having used other tools taken by magazines, whose name now he does not remember, found himself using *WebPlus* by Serif (of Nottingham, of course!). All these programs allow you to work in a graphic way and, if necessary, to intervene more in-depth using HTML.

There would not be a "basic way" of making a website, but potentially endless, as infinite are the human activities that through web pages can be made present and accessible on the internet. Nevertheless, maybe because of the increasing online business and the consequent look for the most effective "formulas" to attract visitors and make money, websites building is quite subjected to fashions.

For several years *Flash* (by Macromedia, then Adobe, officially dead at the end of 2020) was a software used to make animated graphics online and, in the times when it became popular, almost every website, including the most professional, those showing latest trends and the "state of art", had a well visible button; "stop the animation!", so that a user could go beyond the beautiful and often completely useless displays of the webmaster's graphic expertise which inevitably opened home pages, and finally access the content. Java applets were a possible good alternative for *Flash*, that was not well read on some browsers, and never supported by the iPhone, and it could be interesting to know something more of all that story.

Before 1996, the web was a static, dull place. But the accidental creation of Flash turned it into a cacophony of noise, colour, and controversy, presaging the modern web. (Bedingfield, 2019)

Since several years, the language HTML5 allow web masters to add anything, included animated graphic to websites with no need of add-ons, and more and more platforms on the market offer different solutions for self-made professional looking websites:

As website builders continue to evolve, we expect an increase in the number of advanced site-building "wizards." By automating the development process, site owners can dedicate themselves to a purely administrative and overseeing role.

Since this technology is so effective, web agencies may start lowering the cost of their design services ... When it's so easy for regular users to create their own sites. This is reflected in the decline of the US web design industry, which has decreased by 3.1% between 2017 and 2022.

Furthermore, although the popularity of website builders is growing, CMSs (Content Management Systems) shouldn't be overlooked. WordPress currently powers 35% of all websites, steadily increasing from 33.6% in 2021.

Considering other platforms, CMS have now created 45% of all mobile web page. (Hernandez, 2022)

From the point of view of the users who think to build their own website, in the 2020s, it's quite easy to go looking for an online software and, having the content, to set up their pages in a few minutes, I would say, and in few hours for sure. In completely graphic environments, without knowing anything of coding, they can harness all the power of HTML5, galleries, animations, hyperlinks, chose among a wide choice of templates of every sort, replace existing sample texts and pictures with their own, move something here and there, delete or adding pages, adjust buttons and links, and all is done, looking almost professional.

The sites made with *WordPress* probably will look much like one another than those made with *Wix*, that is less constraining the occasional web master into pre-defined patterns. For these two and for other platforms as *Webador*, *Weebly*, *Site123*, *Jimdo*, *Web.com*, *Square Space*, *GoDaddy*, *Shopify* (specific for e-commerce), Webflow and others, the basic services are all for free for a while, or even forever with limitation of memory, speed, and functions, and without the possibility of registering your own domain, but with the possibility of doing excellent things. If you want more, there are several subscription formulas.

Online site builders are used more and more, they have a lot of ready-made functionalities and can help to save time, but we need to see if their schemes match what we need.

The author of this book, who is not a great webmaster, but has his own ideas, has returned to use a traditional offline graphics software and makes his web sites that, even though below they have the power of HTML5, some people tell him that they look like those of the 90s!

7. COMMUNITIES FOR A WEB TOGETHER: MYSPACE

At the start of this history, when all these possibilities weren't there yet, to help people who were not skilled programmers to stay on the internet, communities began to develop where users can meet and collaborate. Among those of success:

GeoCities was more than just a hosting service, however: with community-oriented features and tools to make the creation of websites easier, it could be seen as the forefather of social media. In 1999, the site was the third-most popular on the web. (Shoam, 2022)

Then it came *Myspace*, that we have already mentioned in Chapter 3, for the unfortunate loss of millions of music, one of the worst shipwrecks in the history of the web. But it had been the most popular and successful social network from 2005 to 2008.

Myspace is a free, advertising-supported service that allows users to create Web "profile" pages that feature photographs, express their interests, and, most importantly, link to other people's profiles. The site can be used to keep in touch with friends, "meet" and become friends with new people, or find potential romantic partners. Members must be at least 13 years old, and the profiles of members younger than 16 cannot be viewed by members older than 18, in order to reduce access by potential sexual predators. (Myspace, Britannica entry)

The idea was just to give to everyone, not only to expert and advanced users, the possibility of managing a real web site, set up just in the way everyone prefers, not having to manage each his/her own domain and all the web mastering, but within a ready platform, in which it is possible to meet many other people who do the same things and connect with those who share activities and interests. Very beautiful, but also a bit difficult, because the culture of reconciling and comparing their own ideas and creativity with the others, taking responsibility for what is published, for generations grown up with television, we have already said and repeated that it is not easy to be improvised overnight. It is no coincidence that in recent years the most popular social networks, such as Instagram and Tik Tok, without any problem of presentation and paging, basically managed by the system, they focus on the immediate publication of individual content, simply compared to those of the others, and the networking is limited to the users we follow and those whom we are followed by. That's all, folks!

In *MySpace*

Figure 3. MySpace
Source: Codecademy Team (2020)

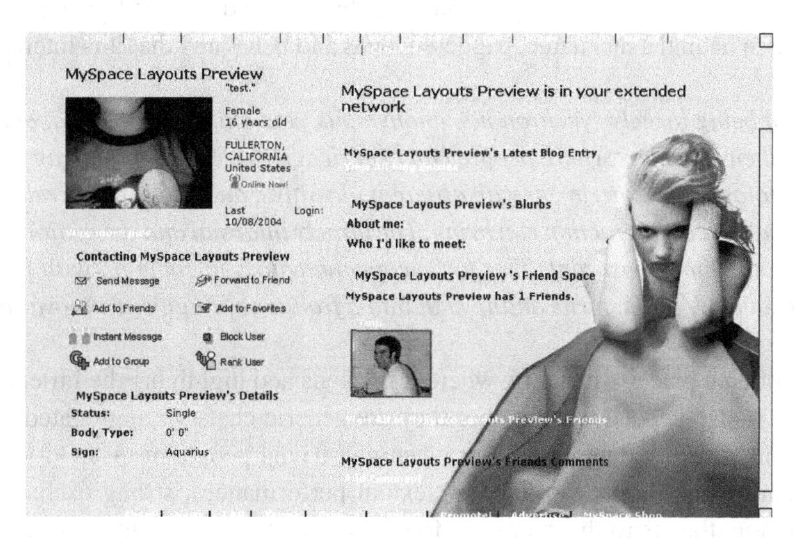

Findings showed a clear pattern of use of the site for creating and developing personal identities and relationships online. Findings show a high degree of control by users over private information ... MySpace as a social networking site, a communication tool, and a means of self–disclosure and identity formation. (Jones et al., 2008)

Various commentators have tried to analyse the rapid and shining rise and steady downfall and decline of the once most popular social media site of all. Some reasons for its fall and consistent user decline were seen in a lack of technical innovations, an area where the competitor social media site Facebook made points and invested heavily. MySpace users were also flooded with pop-up banners and other forms of online advertisement that damaged its reputation and annoyed many of its users. Vandalism, phishing, malware and spam were further problems that also emerged on MySpace and gave it a reputation of being an unsafe site. (Allgaier, 2018)

For a time, it was the musicians who kept the platform alive. Artists such as Nicki Minaj, the Arctic Monkeys, Dev, Lily Allen, or even Adele, were discovered through this portal and remained a bit attached to it. Another reason for initial survival was that the Myspace was the only one that allowed a player of songs to listen and download in real time. But in the end the performers were forced to give up too. Navigation through Myspace became increasingly difficult. Paradoxically because of one of its previous merits: great customization. (Digital Education Lab, 2018, translated from Italian)

8. FROM CHAT LINES TO SOCIAL NETWORKS, COMMON AND PUBLIC PEOPLE ON THE INTERNET

Chat lines were a very innovative experience in human communities. It began probably for the possibility of working together from far that some people the first times met online, as we all have experience it is possible and even necessary to do, after the global pandemic of Covid 19. There were not cameras at the beginning, it was only possible to communicate by text, and the limit, or possibility, to act also anonymously, hidden behind a nickname, triggered ideas and behaviors that it is interesting to consider.

Due to its nature of being largely synchronous, anonymous, and mainly text-based, online chat offers a social interactional environment where people can experience the feeling of making new friends or acquaintances, psychologically experiment with different identities, and explore new relationships without the shyness that face-to-face interaction can bring. The largely informal and recreational nature of online chat, together with the time constraints that force communicators to come up with interesting ways to sustain efficient communication, turns online chat into a frontier of linguistic innovation. (Gong, 2008)

Chat lines are often a place of banality, where it thickens and highlights the littleness of certain human relationships. It also depends on whether they are generic chats, or aggregated for interests, age, geographical locations, topics, intentions. But when non-trivial people meet, in "rooms" or in private conversations, then unique things can happen, textual performances, strong exchanges of emotions, flights of imagination, thanks to the evocative force and power of the written word, used in a totally new context. Timing makes the difference with other more traditional media such as letters, because instant communication forces people to be more truthful, or more liar. But above all it is intriguing that you don't know who's really on the other side. Curiosity then, danger too, which is very limited indeed as long as the relationship remains virtual.

Figure 4. Chat lines
Source: Chatting with Friends Online

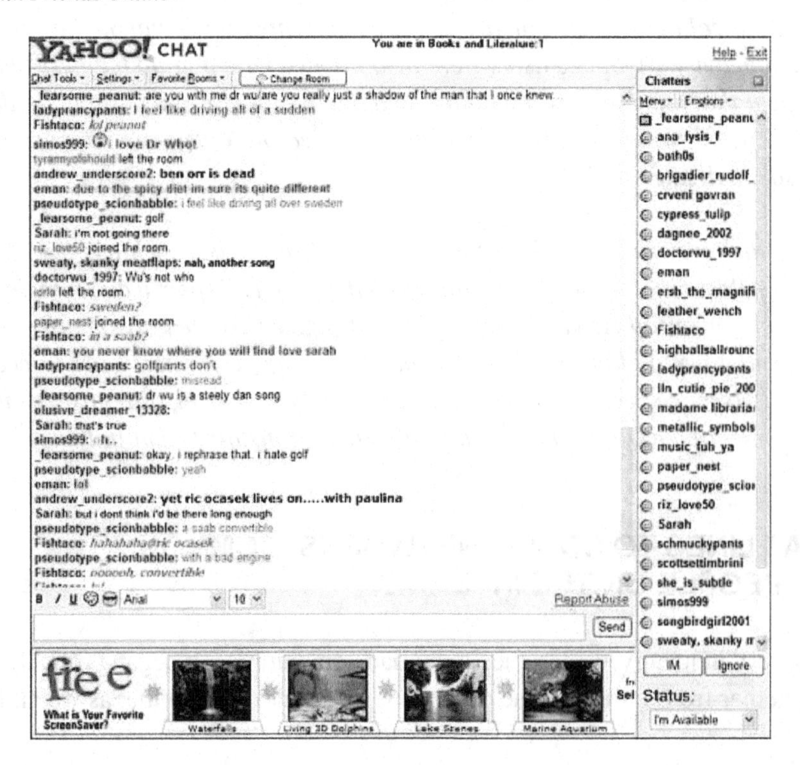

But then people in some cases really meet, make friends, have sex, fall in love. And then everything changes, or nothing changes, it still depends on how we are, how we propose ourselves, how each of us, not only online but in real life, deal with relationships with other humans. That have found, relationships, with the internet, a whole new ground on which they can be developed.

Due to their audiovisual anonymity and asynchronicity, social media have the potential to enhance self-disclosure, and thereby facilitate closeness among existing friends. (Desjarlais, 2020)

In classic chat lines people are anonymous, by definition. On social networks, which can be considered extensions of chat lines with many other functions, people mostly present themselves with name and surname, with their real identity. Or not?

On social networks, ordinary people, even without any technological preparation and even, if they don't want, without worrying of their virtual space at all, can enter and simply write or, very easily, take and upload photos and videos from their computer or mobile phone, inserting them in the schemes set up by the platform administrators. It is certainly not an "evolution" of the Web; indeed, it is probably its reduction to a minimum - we only have to give our name and some basic data, a picture, an email, as to obtain an identity card to the registry office - but it's within the reach of anyone, of any age, from anywhere on the planet. However, it sounds a bit grotesque when, hardly knowing how to write a tweet, some people feel themselves up to date with "technology".

Then, so many and various are the ways of managing our presence in those spaces, our activities, and "friends", that any general speech can only be false or otherwise partial. It depends on how we are, not on "technology". But one thing is certain; the fact that we are always theoretically connected with the whole world does not mean at all that communication between people in our societies is improving, On the contrary, many signs indicate that we are going in the opposite direction altogether, with increasing difficulties in the relationships between people and groups.

On how people stand in social networks, we have seen in chapter 4 that there are several studies related to well-being and mental health, but one fact that can leave quite baffled is how many politicians, or bankers, or managers of multinationals, that is people who count a lot, for some years also mark their presence on social networks in a similar way of ordinary people, posting improvised statements also on topics that once were managed by issuing official press releases, after having well measured the words. But their words, unlike those of ordinary people, can immediately affect the society, the economy, peace, and war. This is what some authors call the "selfie democracy".

Politicians who use digital media appeal to the same fantasies of digital connection, access, and participation peddled by Silicon Valley ... describes the conflation of gender and technology that contributed to Hillary Clinton's defeat in 2016, chronicles the Biden campaign's early digital stumbles in 2020, and recounts the TikTok campaign that may have spoiled a Trump rally ... Although Obama and Trump may seem diametrically opposed in both style and substance, they both used mobile digital media in ways that reshaped the presidency and promised a new kind of digital democracy. Obama used data and digital media to connect to citizens without intermediaries; Trump followed this strategy to its most extreme conclusion. What were the January 6 insurrectionists doing, as they livestreamed themselves and their cohorts attacking the Capitol, but practicing their own brand of selfie democracy? (Losh, 2022)

Social movements have been transformed in the last decade by social networks, where the dynamics of the social protests have evolved and have been structured and viralized through social media. They are no longer just conversations between activists that stay on social platforms. The cyberactivism that takes place on Twitter or Instagram can also play a significant role in general society by influencing government decision making or shaping the relationships between citizens. (Holgado-Ruiz et al., 2023)

Social media brings to the forefront two very important factors to today's politics: the prominent role of the internet and the importance of personalisation which is closely tied to a tendency of political candidates to overexpose their private lives ... The interest tends to fall on the candidate's lifestyle; on their personal characteristics and their most intimate surroundings, which blurs the line between the public and private spheres. (Hernández-Santaolalla, 2023)

But,

Does social media help facilitate activism that leads to social change? What are the strengths and limitations of social media in creating and maintaining a social movement? (Brown et al., 2023)

In general, the attention of observers and research seems addressed more to the potentiality and immediate results of some mass actions on social network, that on the long-term effects of the shift in these virtual contexts of much of political, social and cultural debate. It's more difficult to do a search on it, but we can notice empirically that if for battles on individual themes strongly identifying online mobilization can be fast and effective, when projects require more complex aggregations and a theoretical elaboration to be developed over time, on both political and cultural issues, things almost never go on for as long as necessary.

In fact, to an increasing use of the Web or a part of it, it corresponds in society and in citizens a growing political impotence, a flattening of the debate on extremely simplified slogans or symbols (everything must be in a headline, or in a tweet), and a general tendency not to compare different ideas to come at common syntheses, but to stand in defense each of their pre-constituted positions; Theoretically immense possibilities and general barbarization in reality.

9. BLOGS: A BIG LOST OPPORTUNITY?

In the so-called information society, there are two examples that demonstrate, by their simple existence, how personal technology development can potentially erase the traditional division between producers and consumers of information. Not surprisingly, both are today somehow out of the trendy mass consumption practices, and considered by many "obsolete". My idea is that this confirms that we are in a time of substantial regression, but obviously others can think differently.

The first example are CDs, DVDs, Blu-rays, of audio, video and multimedia.

Let's avoid for now any other discourse (so I refer to chapter 6) and look only at the final objects.

We find them still on sale in shops and online with the works of music and cinema published and distributed by the large entertainment industry. We can take them in hand, look at the case with a cover of images and writings, open the case and take the disc with its label and put it in the appropriate reader device or in our PC, if we still have a PC equipped with a disk reader. Music discs sound very good and video discs, in addition to the movie, they have menus with extra content, scenes from backstage and so on.

Then we go instead to see a disc made by ordinary people. If well done, it has a label, an illustrated case and, inside, two or more audio channels and spectacular menus with the main and extra content.

That's to say: having on one hand industrial products, made by companies that bill billions, and on the other amateur products, made by common people, or a school, with any computer, cheap software, a printer and a CD burner costing few tens dollars or euros, practically they are the same!

Can maybe be this the reason why the burners are often removed from PCs, to avoid that, simply looking at the final products, we come up with strange ideas?

The second example are blogs.

Working on a WordPress based platform, on Blogger or other free providers, anyone can produce a magazine online that, if graphics and details are properly considered, is very similar in appearance to a professional product. And this fact, alone, can induce anyone to reflect on how certain boundaries, once uncrossable and still by the most considered very well defined, today can be much weaker, thanks to easy, economic, powerful technologies.

Our small home-made personal blog hardly can reach the views of the online page of a national newspaper and, at least if we work alone, cannot compete in terms of content. But, also in front of the mantra so often repeated about how the system of information deceives us, doesn't tell us the truth, etc., the question can be;_why "common people" haven't looked for a way yet to organize another kind of information, putting together ideas, skills, and experiences in visible and well-done publications, instead of dispersing in millions of individualistic and losing streams in social networks? Are we sure that, learning to use in another way the incredibly powerful devices we have in hand, it could be anyhow impossible? Or couldn't it be all a matter of attitude?

Figure 5. Blog
Source: Cosa significa blog?

The author of this book has experience of online publications both personal and professional, meaning for "professional" that for the things you write someone pays you. The work of the author is practically the same, and even the fact in a professional context to manage the publication in first person, or to entrust it to an editorial staff, depends not on technical reasons, but on the choices of the publisher.

In practice, blogs are the proof that today - apart from the not small problem that without a financial base no one can expect people to work for free, but how much "free work" we do publishing our content on social networks! - if we are not able to organize on the Web an alternative information to that of which we complain, the fault in the end is ours. And yet to say for example that blogs are "outdated", in practice it means creating an alibi for not even looking for it, to keep away from us the responsibility for a situation that depends essentially on our inability to work together.

But we are living now in the age of Narcissus, who for his nature, is "disconnected" (Recalcati, 2014), and this can explain in a single, simple image, the substantial failure of all our connections through technological means, and why they do not produce, in the whole of our society, a perception of greater control over reality, but vice versa an overall sense of loneliness and resignation not to be able to act on things. Let's think of it!

Online articles comparing proper websites, blogs, and social media are usually oriented to the analysis of the pros and cons of the different platforms from the point of view of promoting an activity. It is difficult to find studies on motivations, attitudes, intentions, cultural background, on who and why. And we keep always doing the same things. But maybe the games aren't already all done

The worldwide popularity and trend for the search term "blogging" has been constant for the past 5 years. It's declining in some countries (increasing in many more countries). (Agarwal, 2023)

Many business owners are foregoing traditional websites to allow social pages to act as their sole online presence ... Customers expect businesses to have websites, not just social media accounts ... 63 percent of customers primarily turn to a company's website to initially engage with it. (from WordPress web site, 2019)

By the way, a third example of the possible big ongoing changes in the information society would be the PDF books with which anyone today can do "self-publishing", with or without a final printing. But the author is working now at this book, with an important publishing house...

Obviously, I'm joking. Let's never take ourselves too seriously!

10. VIDEO GAMES AND THE METAVERSE: ONLINE AS AUDIENCE

It's an old story. The idea of being for example in a city of ancient Greek, Roman, Chinese, Indian, per-Columbian civilizations, and moving by observing the houses, streets, things and people as if we were there, has always rightly fascinated the builders of 3D and virtual reality, that from the time of the first analogous interactive laser discs (before CD ROMs, in 1978) try to propose adventures of this type. Some reconstructions can be very useful, especially when for example in archaeological sites are accompanied by the observation of what remains of ancient real cities.

Very impressive; the visitors, the students, it is as if they were there!

But in fact, they are not there, that's just a story, and as far as we know, it could all be false, depending on the seriousness, honesty, sincerity of the story tellers, and their ability to rebuild an environment where no one really was. From this point of view video games are much better. As immersive and realistic as they are, we know at the start that nothing is true and that everything is just a game to make us have fun, and to test our ability.

Imagine a virtual world where billions of people live, work, shop, learn and interact with each other – all from the comfort of their couches in the physical world.

In this world, the computer screens we use today to connect to a worldwide web of information have become portals to a 3D virtual realm that's palpable ... Digital facsimiles of ourselves, or avatars, move freely from one experience to another, taking our identities and our money with us ... It must be underscored that the metaverse is still a set of possibilities, not a reality ... who will control it, what it will encompass and how much of an impact it will have on our lives – is still up for debate ... Metaverse skeptics view it as merely an extension of the digital experiences we have today but not transformative – and potentially something worse: a magnifier of the current social media ills, including disinformation campaigns, addictive behavior and tendencies toward violence. (Tucci & Needle, 2023)

Neal Stephenson famously coined the term "metaverse" in his 1992 novel Snow Crash, where it referred to a 3D virtual world inhabited by avatars of real people ... The metaverse is tough to explain for one reason: it doesn't necessarily exist. It's partly a dream for the future of the internet and partly a neat way to encapsulate some current trends in online infrastructure, including the growth of real-time 3D worlds. (Robertson and Peters, 2021)

I foresee old wine in new bottles. The positives and negatives are the same as with games and the Internet: There are some small harms in regard to aggression but more harms in regard to being social and experiencing communities in real space, being less present and less connected with each other. (Dmitri Williams, quoted in Anderson & Rainie, 2022)

In past centuries, literature was shared among a little group of people on earth, those few who could read and write. For the majority of illiterates, the written word represented a power they had no access to, the law, the revealed truths of religion.

In some future, for digital consumers who today for everything need a special app, the metaverse would easily be a virtual space that almost all can enter, but on which the most probably will not have any power, immersed in realities created by others, whose rules of participation are dictated by the landlords. Even if hundred million people take part in those virtual environments, they would live experiences that a small elite has arranged for them, inside an immersive and interactive substitute of reality out of their control.

It's like describing a world saying that everyone will be poets, where most people can't in fact even write a shopping list! Like today; a few make Hollywood movies and series, and all the rest make reels!

11. THE OLD ROOTS OF ARTIFICIAL INTELLIGENCE

Curiously, at least for those who believe that the world moves each new day in newness, looking around on the web for "AI" and "CAI" as keywords, one can come across an article just entitled *AI in CAI: An Artificial-Intelligence Approach to Computer-Assisted Instruction*. The journal was called "IEEE Transactions on Man-Machine Systems and ceased, with that name at least, in 1970. (Carbonell 1970)

Since people often talk about artificial intelligence in relation to school and education, it is not bad to mention here the old idea of teaching machines, on several occasions resumed along decades, that in collective imagination is easily connected to a world of machines and "cold" scientists that oversees, coordinates, disposes of humans, in a somehow "objective" way; aptitude tests, IQ measurements, final irrevocable judgments.

Teaching machines were originally mechanical devices that presented educational materials and taught students. They were first invented by Sidney L. Pressey in the mid-1920s. His machine originally administered multiple-choice questions. The machine could be set so it moved on only when the student got the right answer. (Teaching machine entry, Wikipedia)

In the years 1950, Burrhus Frederic Skinner, the father of Behaviorism psychological theory, «described his machine as a frame of incomplete textual or numeric problems that appear in a square window with sliders that are used to move the opening over each problem. When the student completed one problem, he or she checked the response by turning a crank to reveal the correct answer. The machine was able to sense the setting of the slider, and, if the student's answer was correct, moved a new problem into the window.

Decades later, modern technology has revived an old concept and responded to Skinner's appeal for a keyboard, not to mention microprocessors that convey information at the speed of light ... Technology has transformed the old teaching machines into CAI (computer-assisted instruction) that allows students to gain basic and advanced skills in a more engaging manner. Programs for school children, college students, military personnel, and employees in business and industry are only a mouse-click away. (Davis Lazarus 2005)

CAI was also described as "system which is capable of writing computer programs" (Koffman & Blount, 1975).

CAI is also the acronym of "Conversational Artificial Intelligence", that brings us back to our days:

Refers to the use of messaging apps, speech-based assistants (Amazon Alexa, Google Assistant etc.) and chatbots to automate communication using Natural Language Processing and enhanced machine learning through a spoken or typed interface which creates personalized experiences at scale. (Conversational Artificial Intelligence (CAI), definition)

Another acronym for CAI is "Content Authenticity Initiative"

A community of media and tech companies, NGOs, academics, and others working to promote adoption of an open industry standard for content authenticity and provenance ... Our open-source tools allow you to integrate secure provenance signals into your products. Empower your users to share and consume tamper-evident context about changes to content over time, including identity info, types of edits used, and more. (Content Authenticity Initiative, home page)

By the way, when is Alexa Listening?

Echo devices are designed by default to detect only the sound waves of your chosen wake word, and everything else is ignored. (How Alexa works, from Amazon web site)

But sometimes things happen that leave us a bit puzzled, as when pictures were published on the internet of a young woman sitting on the toilet

Not taken by a person, but by development versions of iRobot's Roomba J7 series robot vacuum. They were then sent to Scale AI, a startup that contracts workers around the world to label audio, photo, and video data used to train artificial intelligence. (Guo, 2022)

12. FROM POPULAR CULTURE NEW COMMUNICATIONS WAYS? (AND SPIES AMONG US!)

In today_Web the success of a website, a blog, a page is generally measured according to the rules of SEO (Search Engine Optimization) and the number or "unique visitors". The goal is to attract visitors who pass by and induce them to stay a few minutes more on the page, increasing the value of any advertising hosted. But there are scientific, personal, community, specialized, artistic, religious, only for joke sites, with no ads, where people can be invited directly, or go as they know what happens there, or a particular work can be done.

In general, it seems reasonable to say that, as humanity uses the web just since about 30 years, it is a little early (and a bit integralist) for someone to establish that into the internet people "must" follow certain rules to set up his/her own pages.

However, for different purposes, it occurs that some models are successful.

There are *Youtubers* really good who, whatever the topic they work about, offer productions with beautiful shots, rhythm, ideas and effects. They take advantage of the new opportunity given by having today all easily at disposal the technical means of production and dissemination (a fact we little talk about) and substantially follow the good rules of the audiovisual communication. Of this also we little talk about, while the attention of the public is more oriented to the supposed differences among the different platforms (*YouTube* rather than *Instagram* or *TikTok*, or what else) and to the "rules" that should be followed to be there effectively, including the format of the videos to "adapt" to the platforms. Another time, the truth is out there, and everyone seems to talk about what really nobody knows.

There are then *Podcasters* that maybe sometimes are not so good in audiovisual communication, but have the ability of investigating subjects and speaking well about them. Some productions of theirs can appear long and monotonic, but they are popular as their audience listen to them from the mobile while cooking, or on bed during a siesta. If they fall asleep, they start over the next day.

There are *TikTokers we* don't know whether they are successful because they dance well, or because they dance in underwear. But if at a certain point they understand what the others like of their perfor-

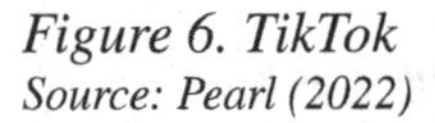

Figure 6. TikTok
Source: Pearl (2022)

mances and work well, maybe some original form of communication can arise, and their success can last over time.

Actually, we are faced with a myriad of productions, some completely amateur, others that after being successful find sponsors, others behind which there is a design work of a much more professional type but, apart from knowing them directly, any general discourse, however, risks talking about something else, about stereotypes, and every research can only be extremely partial and misleading. We can tell, but we cannot draw conclusions, and above all we cannot do it now, at a time when in fact very few have the cultural and technical skills to talk about it with full knowledge of the facts.

In the first quarter of 2023 "TikTok has surpassed Instagram as the most downloaded app and has taken the top spot on the consumer spend chart" (from "OhMyDigital", 2023).

But TikTok comes from China, and in times of complicated international relations mobile devices and apps can become dangerous bridgeheads in the pockets of the unsuspecting citizens on planet earth:

U.S. Commerce Secretary Gina Raimondo said on April 26, 2023, that Chinese cloud computing companies such as Huawei Cloud and Alibaba Cloud could pose a threat to U.S. security. (Panettieri, 2023)

The UK ban on installing and using social media app TikTok on government devices brings our country's policy in line with that of other jurisdictions including the US and member states of the European Union ... Jamie Moles, senior technical manager at ExtraHop*, said: "I'm a security expert who downloaded and used TikTok when it came out like so many others ... I removed it as soon as it became clear that the app could harvest anything from my phone including contacts – GPS data, authentication info from other apps, and so on.*

Having this app on your phone is tantamount to giving the Chinese government the keys to our economy. (Jowitt, 2023)

13. THE CONTRADICTORY ROAD TO THE WEB3

Here is a list of the features of the incoming Web3:

Decentralized, Blockchain-based (data management on a broadly distributed, peer-to-peer network); Cryptocurrency-enabled; Semantically organized (the system can learn words in the same way a human would); Autonomous and artificially intelligent (Essex et al., 2023).

As the Web3 is supposed to grow from the present Web2, it is an interesting question, again; how decentralization can be originated from inside a social context of consumers more and more used to do things downloading an app from everything?

"Don't trust, verify" is the catchphrase of bitcoiners who would rather rely on mathematics to safeguard their wealth than the whims of central bankers and governments. And yet, paradoxically, convincing web users that they can trust such trustless technology is proving to be a greater undertaking than web3 developers might have imagined. (Wintermeyer, 2022)

How the economy works is something that ordinary people have never understood well, and even less understand at a time when much of the wealth is not originated by work, agriculture, industry, services, but by financial games. Even less do they understand, when they see the difference widening dramatically on earth between who earns more and more and who less and less. And, although not clearly, they realize that empires are made on the time that just ordinary people spend online to do they don't know well what.

But what could happen if ordinary people were to agree globally on an all-out click strike? Would the world entire economy collapse? Or perhaps we would still have to eat, to dress, to move with the means of transport, in the real world?

Central bankers may not be the most trustworthy people on this earth, but somehow, we all know what it means to earn and spend dollars or euros. How can billion people, all over the world, who barely can handle their emails rely on cryptocurrencies?

It is common, in tech circles, to hear a business pitch that is simultaneously simple and baffling. "It is going to be like "x" [insert the name of any successful business], but on a blockchain ... A blockchain

Figure 7. Blockchain-cryptocurrency
Source: Föderale Blockchain Infrastruktur Asyl

is a database that contains the history of whatever information it was designed to store. It is made up of a string of "blocks" of information that build on top of one another in an immutable chain. Bitcoin, one of the first blockchains, was built in 2009. It stores data on transactions in bitcoin, providing proof of who owns what at any time. What distinguishes a blockchain from other databases is that its ledger is distributed, publicly available and replicated on thousands of computers—or "nodes"—around the world. Rather than a centralised entity, like a bank or a tech platform, ensuring that the ledger is accurate, it is verified by a decentralised network of individuals. (Jaso, 2021)

Presenting the top 10 Cryptocurrencies Of 2023, Forbes Advisor writes:

Cryptocurrency is decentralized digital money that's based on blockchain technology. You may be familiar with the most popular versions, Bitcoin and Ethereum, but there are more than 9,000 different cryptocurrencies in circulation.

A cryptocurrency is a digital, encrypted, and decentralized medium of exchange. Unlike the U.S. Dollar or the Euro, there is no central authority that manages and maintains the value of a cryptocurrency. Instead, these tasks are broadly distributed among a cryptocurrency's users via the internet.

You can use crypto to buy regular goods and services, although most people invest in cryptocurrencies as they would in other assets, like stocks or precious metals. While cryptocurrency is a novel and exciting asset class, purchasing it can be risky as you must take on a fair amount of research to understand how each system works fully. (Ashford, 2023)

Sure, a naive earner, saver, consumer, can ask some questions like these: What in the end makes the value of a cryptocurrency? Who in real world accepts cryptocurrency payments? How can I change my cryptocurrency into dollars or euros? Who guarantees me that cryptocurrency will exist and will have value over time? Isn't that another bubble of digital times likely to burst at some point?

These are questions that, together with many other reasons for uncertainty, loom over our future. And luckily, according to the current narration, technology is to simplify our lives!

The major downside to cryptocurrency is the risk of loss, which is even more difficult to manage when a crypto company is holding your coins. In November 2022, crypto exchange FTX suffered a major liquidity crisis, and filed for Chapter 11. In July 2022, two major crypto trading platforms, Voyager and Celsius, declared bankruptcy. (Rosenberg, 2023)

REFERENCES

Agarwal, A. (2023, Jun 29). *The Future of Blogging: Are Blogs Still Relevant in 2023 And Beyond?* bloggerspassion.com.

Allgaier. (2018, Jul). MySpace. researchgate.net.

Anderson, J. & Rainie, L. (2022, Jun 30). pewresearch.org.

Ashford, K. (2023, Feb 16). What Is Cryptocurrency? *Forbes Advisor.*

Bedingfield, W. (2019, Sep 19). *The rise and fall of Flash, the annoying plugin that shaped the modern web.* wired.co.uk

Beneventi, P. (2001). *La Patente - Il mio Computer è una Bicicletta e si Guida senza Patente!* paolo-beneventi.it/Biblioteca

Brown, S. J. (2023). Social Media and Social Movements: Strengths, Challenges, and Implications for the Future. In *Research Anthology on Social Media's Influence on Government, Politics, and Social Movements*. IGI Global.

Carbonell, J. B. (1970, Dec). AI in CAI: An Artificial-Intelligence Approach to Computer-Assisted Instruction. *IEEE Transactions on Man-Machine Systems, MMS-11*(4).

Chatting with Friends Online. (n.d.). flylib.com/books/en/2.932.1.169/1/

Chomsky, N. (2023, Mar 8). The False Promise of ChatGPT. *The New York Times.*

Codecademy Team. (2020, Feb 14). *MySpace and the Coding Legacy it Left Behind.* codecademy.com/resources/blog/

Content Authenticity Initiative. (n.d.). *Authentic storytelling through digital content provenance.* contentauthenticity.org.

Conversational Artificial Intelligence (CAI). (n.d.). voiceflow.com.

Cosa significa blog? (n.d.). wikibit.it/b/cosa-significa-blog-1997/

Davis Lazarus, B. (2005). Programmed Instruction Overview. In *Encyclopedia of Distance Learning*. IGI Global. doi:10.4018/978-1-59140-555-9.ch230

Desjarlais, M. (2020). Online Self-Disclosure: Opportunities for Enriching Existing Friendships. In *The Psychology and Dynamics Behind Social Media Interactions*. IGI Global.

Digital Education Lab. (2018, Dec. 18). *Che fine ha fatto Myspace, il primo Social di successo nel web?* digitaleducationlab.it/blog.

Donald, B. (2016, Nov 22). Stanford researchers find students have trouble judging the credibility of information online. *Research Stories.*

Essex, D. (n.d.). *What is Web 3.0 (Web3)? Definition, guide and history.* techtarget.com.

Gong, W., & Ooi, V. B. Y. (2008). Innovations and Motivations in Online Chat. In *Handbook of Research on Computer Mediated Communication*. IGI Global. doi:10.4018/978-1-59904-863-5.ch065

Guo, E. (2022, Dec 19). *A Roomba recorded a woman on the toilet. How did screenshots end up on Facebook?* technologyreview.com.

Hernandez, I. (2022, Oct 21). *The Current State of Website Builders (Overview & Comparisons).* dreamhost.com.

Hernández-Santaolalla, V. (2023). The Social Media Politicians: Personalisation, Authenticity, and Memes. In *Research Anthology on Social Media's Influence on Government, Politics, and Social Movements*. IGI Global.

Himanen, P. (2001). *The Hacker Ethic and the Spirit of the Information Age*. Random House.

Holgado-Ruiz, L. (2023). Activism in the Digital Age: Social Movements Analysis Using User-Generated Content in Social Media. In *Research Anthology on Social Media's Influence on Government, Politics, and Social Movements*. IGI Global.

Jones, S. (2008). *Whose Space is MySpace? A Content Analysis of MySpace Profiles.* researchgate.net.

Jowitt, T. (2023, Mar 15). *TikTok Mulls Split From Beijing-Based ByteDance – Report.* silicon.co.uk

Koffman, E. B., & Blount, S. (1975). Artificial intelligence and automatic programming in CAI. *Artificial Intelligence*, *6*(3), 215–234. doi:10.1016/0004-3702(75)90001-6

Losh, E. (2022). *Selfie Democracy: The New Digital Politics of Disruption and Insurrection*. The MIT Press. doi:10.7551/mitpress/14334.001.0001

Packham, A. (2020, Sep 8). One in four students unable to access online learning during lockdown – survey. *The Guardian*.

Panettieri, J. (2023, Apr 27). *Huawei: Banned and Permitted In Which Countries? List and FAQ.* channele2e.com.

Pearl, M. (2022, Dec 23). *TikTok admits to spying on U.S. users as effort to ban the app heats up.* mashable.com/article.

Rabideau, C. (2019, March 24). *Website vs. Social Media: Which Is Better for Your Brand?* wordpress.com/go/digital-marketing.

Raymond, E. S. (1999). *The Cathedral and the Bazaar*. O'Reilly. doi:10.100712130-999-1026-0

Recalcati, M. (2014). *L'ora di lezione. Per un'erotica dell'insegnamento*. Einaudi.

Robertson, A. & Peters, J. (2021, Oct 4). *What is the metaverse, and do I have to care?* theverge.com.

Rosemberg, E. (2023, Feb 28). *What Happens When A Crypto Exchange Goes Bankrupt?* investopedia.com.

Shoam, A. (2022, Feb 22). *What Ever Happened to GeoCities?* Techspot.com.

Sitemap generator. (n.d.). lucidchart.com/pages/examples

Söderberg, J. (2022). *Resistance to the Current: The Dialectics of Hacking*. The MIT Press. doi:10.7551/mitpress/13466.001.0001

Supremecreature. (2012, Oct 9). *The Hacker Ethic.* supremecreature.wordpress.com

The Instagram vs. TikTok Showdown Continues Plus 9 Other Updates. (2023, Apr 3). ohmydigitalagency.com.au

Tucci, L., & Needle, D. (2023, Sep 18). *What is the metaverse? An explanation and in-depth guide.* techtarget.com.

What to make of cryptocurrencies and blockchains. (2018, Aug 30). *The Economist.*

Wintermeyer, L. (2022, Aug 25). Web3 Will Make Or Break Social Media. *Forbes Digital Assets.*

ADDITIONAL READING

AIContentfy team. (2023, Nov 6). The impact of social media on blogging. *aicontentfy.com.*

Allen, H. J. (2022, Sep). The Superficial Allure of Crypto. *International Monetary Fund.* imf.org/en/Publications

Bassett, A. (2021, Mar 22). The Good, the Bad, and the Ugly of Online Communities. *shondaland.com.*

BeerC. (2020, Jan 7). The Rise of Online Communities. blog.gwi.com

Brandtzæg, P. B. (2012, July). Social Networking Sites: Their Users and Social Implications - A Longitudinal Study. *Journal of Computer-Mediated Communication, 17*(4), 1. doi:10.1111/j.1083-6101.2012.01580.x

Coffey, L. (2023, Nov 8), Art Schools Get Creative Tackling AI. *Inside Higher Education.*

Crompton, H., & Burke, D. (2023, April 24). Artificial intelligence in higher education: The state of the field. *International Journal of Educational Technology in Higher Education, 20*(1), 22. doi:10.118641239-023-00392-8

D'anastasio, C. (2022, Jan). Video Games Already Do What the Metaverse Just Promises. *Wired.*

Dafermos, G., & Söderberg, J. (2009). The hacker movement as a continuation of labour struggle. *Capital and Class, 33*(1), 53–73. doi:10.1177/030981680909700104

Delir, S., & Albanese, M. (2015). Data Management in Pervasive Systems. In *Data Management in Pervasive Systems* (pp. 195–209). Springer.

Dhingraa, M., & Mudgal, R. K. (2019). Historical Evolution of Social Media: An Overview. In *International Conference on Advances in Engineering Science Management & Technology (ICAESMT).* Uttaranchal University. 10.2139srn.3395665

Ferreira, J. J. (2023, Sep 28). Ethics and the dark side of online communities: mapping the field and a research agenda. *Inf Syst E-Bus Manage.*

Gilbert, C. (2013). Blogging in the global society: cultural, political and geographical aspects, *The Australian Library Journal, 62*(2).

Goswami, A., & Kumar, A. (2017). Challenges in the Analysis of Online Social Networks: A Data Collection Tool Perspective. *Wireless Personal Communications, 9*(3), 4015–4061. doi:10.100711277-017-4712-3

Jimenez, L. & Boser U. (2021, Sep) Future of Testing in Education: Artificial Intelligence. *american-progress.org*

Lunceford, B. L. (2006). *Democracy and the Hacker Movement: Information Technologies and Political Action* [Doctor of Philosophy Thesis]. The Pennsylvania State University, The Graduate School Department of Communication Arts and Sciences.

Makarov, I. (2022, March 23). *Cryptocurrencies and decentralized finance (DeFi).* brookings.edu

Martineau, K. (2019, Apr). Teaching machines to reason about what they see. *MIT News.*

Morris, M., & Ogan, C. (1996). The Internet as Mass Medium. *Journal of Computer-Mediated Communication, 1*(4), 0. doi:10.1111/j.1083-6101.1996.tb00174.x

Siripurapu, A. & Berman, N. (2023, Feb 28). *Cryptocurrencies, Digital Dollars, and the Future of Money.* Council on Foreign Relations.

Thevenot, G. (2007). Blogging as a social media. *Tourism and Hospitality Research*, *7*(3/4), 287–289. doi:10.1057/palgrave.thr.6050062

Zhang, E. (2021). *Decentralize The Hacker Movement.* hidorahacks.medium.com

Chapter 6
Technique and Behaviors, Trendy, Useful, Correct:
From Unified Procedures to Unified Thinking?

ABSTRACT

We often use technology not according to what it allows us to do, but to the idea that we have of it. More than the competence of users, it counts the faith in reference brands and commercial policies. So, useless products selling well on the market, mandatory updates of services without a reason, and the general resignation to the fact that humans may not understand or choose the future but adapt to it, and always run, even when we have machines that can run for us! We worry about cybersecurity, but we can no longer live without the control of many little big brothers, who also monitor our thinking, establish what is politically correct and address the groupthink of many. Without a new philosophical vision of the relationship between humans and media, we will never achieve what is technically possible, or we'll have anyhow virtual and physical realities out of control.

1. INTRODUCTION

Technological industry is driven above all by marketing. Useless products are sold attracting the attention of the public and useful ones are unsuccessful because nobody knows them. The rapid change of media and formats also affects the cultural production and dissemination. When optical discs are removed from many computers, the first decades of digital culture risk never being known by the ordinary users, as mostly production was released on CD and DVD. And the new knowledge is not collected in libraries, but allowed to vanish, at the whim of the market.

Instead of a single Big Brother who controls everything, as the one imagined at the dawn of the technological revolution, probably there are many small brothers, who live now within all of us. Fundamental human skills not corresponding to mass fashion, such as cursive writing, are considered by

DOI: 10.4018/978-1-6684-8228-5.ch006

many obsolete and useless their teaching in schools, and the "convenience" of online communications is also imposed in situations where human activities take place in person. Algorithms often drive work relationships as an objective technical fact, and in the "dark web" cyberbullying and new crimes grow, as almost inevitable threats, in a society that to compulsive and semi-illiterate consumption is sacrificing awareness and active citizenship. And the current technological determinism probably extends to the whole set of human relationships, also with the automatic shortcuts of the "politically correct".

T The technically given possibility of a potentially democratic control from below, can generate by the established power exaggerated responses, as in the case of WikiLeaks, while the attention of the public is continuously driven somewhere else, to the "next" launch of multiple novelties that, every time, are expected to change our lives.

2. TECHNOLOGY AND FAITH

In 1999 I was at the book fair in Turin, presenting *Come usare il computer con bambini e ragazzi* (How to use the computer with children and teenagers). Beyond the very handbook title, the work was based much on my concrete work in schools, even in kindergarten, on the responses of real children and young people, on their ability to play with certain software, to discover its potential, well beyond the idea of learning to do all the same things in the same way.

A teacher is talking to me, she is interested, we are comparing the mutual experience. At one point, I let slip a sentence about some Windows problems, and the frost drops. The teacher makes a strange, dark, scandalized face, and silently walks away…

I did not want to denigrate the operating system at that time as successful as ever but, as it is used among those who deal with computer science and practice, I made those observations about the defects of a software that are an essential part of the life and development of the software itself, whose periodic updates not by chance list every few months the defects of previous versions and the corrections made to fix them. Clear that not all users' comments are welcomed by developers, that anyone has his own ideas and preferences, but in any case, it should not make a matter of faith.

That is what often happens instead, with too many people who, today as and more than before, seem not to need to understand, but to *believe* in "technology".

In 2012 Apple removed their SuperDrives from iMacs, to make them "thinner". Then, optical discs were removed from Mac Pro and finally MacBook pro in 2016. The external Super Drive has been the best-selling accessory for Macs in many markets for years, until it has been no longer supported with M1 Macs, from 2020.

Aside from the fact that it's not so clear why a desktop computer should be *thinner*, since we don't have to put it in a bag or carry it on a plane, and it may be that with our furniture It looks better a sturdy one, I personally had the problem that a part of my activity was just to make DVD videos with children.

We are going to see in detail in chapter 7 why from an educational point of view I do think that to work for a DVD is better for kids than to post instant reels on TikTok. But more in general, having many different tools at disposal, I'd like to be free of choosing among them, according to my taste and needs. I understand that in front a substantial technological change, it's up to me to equip myself looking for external devices allowing me to convert for example old analog video formats to digital. If several years ago I had a PC with a card inside dedicated to this, I know that obviously producers can't go on manufacturing PCs with devices inbuilt completely out to date.

Figure 1. Blu-ray sales
Source: Blu-Ray Media and Devices

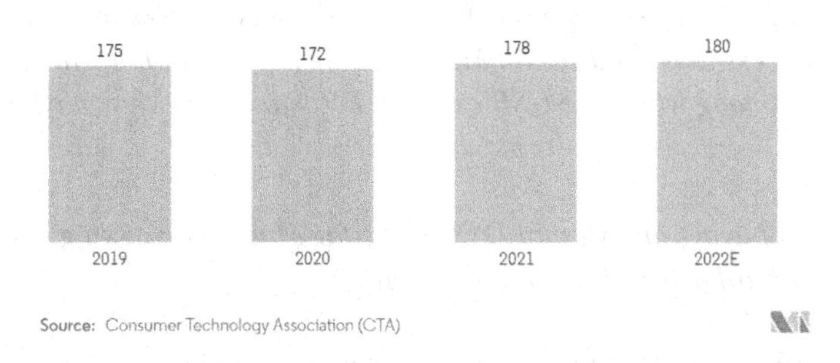

But here we are talking about the same digital technology and about media that not in 2012, but still today, 2023, are produced and sold on the market. Moreover, after a period when sales worldwide were declining, after 2020 they seem to have started to rise again and, also thanks to the new 4K mastered disks, the forecasts from 2023 to 2028 are of a growing market. (BLU-RAY MEDIA AND DEVICES, from MordorIntelligence web site)

How can we define the fact of thinking separate the PC market from that of the still alive readers of optical disks, if not *ideology*? We have spoken here on several occasions of a disconnected world divided into watertight compartments…

Going back to that 2012, I am complaining about Apple choices with a teacher who, like me, uses to works on video with his students. I expect he can understand my point of view: to take our videos from cameras and smartphones and put them into a computer, edit them in a movie, make a DVD with a burning software with its label and box with a graphic program and a printer, just like those of the major companies, and finally watch it, in the screen of the computer itself, without the need of plugging an uncomfortable external device, which also spoils me the aesthetics of the new PC so beautiful and thin!

But the teacher is a longtime Apple fan, loyal as only Apple fans can be.

Question: “Why Apple does remove discs from table PCs? I’d like to use Apple PCs and I still use discs!”

Answer: “I do not use optical discs as memory anymore!”

Surrealistic!

First, am not asking what *you* do with optical disks, and what *you* do with them can’t be anyhow a criterion by which all the users of the world are deprived of a feature that maybe someone could use.

Second, here we are not talking about mass memories, but about the *standard* of digital publications of the last 30 years, that’s to say audio CDs, CDs and DVDs video. It happens that at some point a manufacturer decides that, as in the future of its marketing there are other choices, everything that has been done before is not accessible by their PCs anymore! So average users simply forget that optical discs can be read or written with computers, and these few stubborn ones who know and still want to deal with discs, they must find a solution by themselves, adding external devices, so that they can keep the link with the past and a present declared obsolete by a commercial company.

It's a bit like if, since the publishing houses decided to publish the books digitally, the public libraries closed and only scholars and researchers could read paper books in dedicated, special locations!

As Apple kills off the optical drive in its MacBook Pro and MacBook Air to maintain super-thin profiles, users are left with no ways to play or copy DVDs on Mac directly. However, the removal of DVD drive doesn't mean blocked access to DVD discs on Mac. Despite the lack of built-in optical drive, there are workarounds available, among which the USB external DVD drive for Mac maybe the easiest. (Brown, 2023, May 19)

To watch movies without buying an external DVD drive for Mac and carrying a stack of discs, simply copy DVDs to computer hard drive. (Brown, 2023, Sep 7)

Excellent! But to copy the DVD to the disc without buying the player, I guess I'll have to borrow it!

3. VANISHING LIBRARIES: BIG BROTHERS ARE INSIDE US

I need to repeat: It is not like floppy disks, micro drives, cassette readers or other media, transitory, interchangeable, tried, used, replaced by others who perform the same function better. CD ROM and DVDs have been for decades the main physical support of digital culture, official publications for home music and cinema, more occasional ones attached to the distribution of newspapers and magazines, timid and uncertain attempts of an original multimedia publishing, and not least many and mostly unknown local craft productions of amateurs, artists, schools, communities, made possible by the availability of low-priced disc writers, of which allegedly only a small part have been distributed and that, because of the problems first of size (too big for the original web) and then of format (often not readable online) is little present on the network.

The problem had also arisen with music and video cassettes, not so much the industrial ones, available also as records, films, or in the archives of televisions, but the self-produced, whose only chance to survive, as well as keeping old recorders and readers hoping they won't break, is to be digitized. The slogan with which the USB video digitizers are proposed on the market is since years something like this: "from VHS to DVD"! And now that even the writers on PCs are becoming rare, I would say that the absurdity of the situation is well synthesized.

If for analogic production, there are actual problems of compatibility, there is no technical reason to keep away the public from works published in the years on digital discs, and the only reason to gather everything into the cloud seems to be that in this way everything remains stored in virtual places of which providers and not users have keys.

The question if this digital cultural production, professional or not, also with direct participation of subjects that in history never had been recognized as producers of culture, is to be somehow available as books in libraries, or marketed as goods, or quietly forgotten at all, it should be one of the central themes of the cultural debate today but, in fact, little is said about it. Something more we'll write about in chapter 8.0: The Library and the Store.

But in such a context, to have or not to have, even by chance, something in your device that as invites you to go and see what other people have produced over the time, it can make the difference. Today, those who already know things, the expert, the artist, the creative, the *elite*, may go to look for certain works, and even, to remain at our example, add disc players to their computers, But who arrives now, the youngest, the general public who do not find the readers embedded, may not even know that certain production exists, or that he/she can not only listen to music and watch videos on other devices, as a CD and Blu-ray player, but also see them *inside*, as only a PC may allow to do. It was *playing* and discovering unforeseen possibilities, choosing among tools, and not following only the suggestions of the market, that the generation between the years 70 and 90s made the first digital revolution. It was because they were able to go far beyond what the industry was programming for them. And beyond the conformist choices of most bewildered users, that preferred to use illegal copies of *Word*, even when with computer it was given free *Lotus Word Pro*.

Getting used only to standard ways of using machines and software that fill so an important part of the lives of billions of citizens, it is not without repercussions on the quality of social life. People become less and less capable to choose and to face problems independently, seek security only in ready solutions, do not compare with the others and take side:

In the last decades there have been two major changes in the social and economic life that has affected masses: the internet revolution and the rise in inequality ... Evidence from social psychology, neuroscience, econometrics, and experimental economics indicates that people observe those around themselves and select a reference group with whom they compare themselves. The reference group is basically used as a standard to evaluate oneself and the outcome of that engagement reflects on one's sense of well-being. Consequently, people's decisions are influenced by the decisions and actions of this reference group. This indicates the presence of what is called peer effects which can also referred to as social interactions effects. (Ünay Tamgaç, 2019)

The number of big brothers depends on how many of them you invite to surveil you. Yes, it is you yourself that invite them. It is you who let them put yourself under their looking glass in exchange for comfort and pleasure. Indeed, these big brothers are not the Orwellian villain who is devoid of any goodness. They constantly monitor you to know you personally as a unique individual, so that they can maximize serving you. (Maulana, 2019)

Here we are to give a series of examples, not systematic as it's impossible, but rather evocative, of how certain clichés, habits, automatisms of behavior and thinking related to the widespread use of technology, without us realizing it, they come to influence more and more many moments of our individual and social life, towards a growing and worrying conformism, alignment on fundamentalist positions and an increasingly uniformity of thought.

4. HIDDEN OR MISUNDERSTOOD PRODUCTS ON THE MARKET

In recent decades, several products that were to be "revolutionary" have been launched on the market and have had no success. Others had it for a short time, until people realized they were of no use. Others failed, because almost no one noticed that they existed.

Some "ghost" products on the market could have, if known, led average customers to do something more than simply buying devices and using them for only a small part of their potential. It's still the original sin of the old industrial society market organization: to sell new machines to be consumed ac-

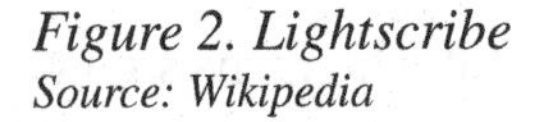
Figure 2. Lightscribe
Source: Wikipedia

cording to poor and standard uses, without exploring their "infinite sets of possibilities". This causes a huge waste of resources and is an obstacle to innovation or progress from the permanent condition of waiting for the next novelty, hoping to finally figure something out.

Who knows, for example, what is "Lightscribe"?

Again, something related to optical disk, I beg your pardon. But for about 10 years, at the beginning of the new millennium, on many if not all disc writers inbuilt in desktop and laptop PCs there was that little mark printed on:

LightScribe is an optical disc recording technology that was created by the Hewlett-Packard Company. It uses specially coated recordable CD and DVD media to produce laser-etched labels with text or graphics, as opposed to stick-on labels and printable discs. (Lightscribe: Wikipedia entry)

We are obviously speaking about those strange people who had fun with homemade CDs and DVDs, a minority, a protected species, but those discs were beautiful, elegant, a possibly choice for quality, good-looking products.

I personally liked the idea and, after I saw that my HP computers had it, I immediately searched on the shelves of many stores for lightscribe disks. I never found them.

A simple question, as I am not an expert of marketing: How can we say at some point that something on the market doesn't work, if the customers have not been informed at all about it? In this case, when people still used to look at the store shelves to know about novelties, was it so complicated have normal disks, printable disks, and Lightscribe disks one next to the other, so that customers, just at a first look, could have ideas?

I found then, and I still can find Lightscribe disks in online shops, and I use sometimes the lightscribe writers I have on my old HP PC.

Another example, on how it can also happen that substantially meaningless products are marketed with success as technological innovation. And it's still about DVDs, pardon again!

As I have been making videos during all my life, I'm still trying to find a technical reason for the production, for many years, in millions of pieces, of cameras that used, as a storage medium, the mini-DVD. Uncomfortable to hold in hand, inferior in quality to the cameras with cassettes, encoded in a format that made it very difficult the edition, they had the "convenience" that you could take the little disc and put it into a DVD player to watch what you had shot on your home television: from having to connect camera and television with an audio-video cable, something that changed your life completely!

In my humble opinion, the operation was aimed at an amateur video audience that is supposed to be constantly illiterate over time, managing once Super 8 film cameras and then analogue video Betamax, VHS and 8mm, and then digital SD, HD, 4k devices and finally smartphones, in the exact same way, that's to say, but exceptions, completely unaware of what they do. Being the DVD read by a laser beam, it was probably an invitation to customers to feel themselves up to date with the latest technology, a step towards the future…

Still in the audio video industry, the houses constantly offer in competition new products on the market, spend a lot of money on research, kill devices that came out just a few months before, and prevent users in the end from being really updated and practically force them to buy randomly. Technically – I am speaking naively as a quite advanced user who makes semi-professional videos - it's hard to understand why they are already offering me, in Summer 2023, a wide choice of 8K TVs, that cost absurd figures and with which I can actually watch nothing, as 8K videos in the world still almost do not exist.

From the point of view of video communications, the planet has not yet completed the transition for broadcasting content to a standard HD video and still, few are the possibilities to really take advantage of the more recent 4K technology. Moreover, most users have only a theoretical idea of what it means to watch a video in one resolution rather than another, and evidently also in this case the narration prevails over human senses, if the reference device for many is above all the mobile phone.

On the on the 6-inch displays of a smartphone, whatever are the resolution of the original audiovisual and the screen, the human eye can hardly distinguish between an SD and a 4K video. But this is something that usually remains implied, and it seems that all the explanations we find online about what TV or monitor to choose, they take for granted that everyone knows that the more resolution increases, the more we need a large screen to appreciate it. It is a bit like those detailed lists on all the software that teachers can use in schools, that never seem to take into account how many teachers are still in fact uncomfortable simply using a computer.

The medium is the message. And more than technology the statements count, the advertising, what sellers tell us and what we tell us by ourselves, not having the courage to admit that we are just following the stream, in the era of Narcissus.

After a long search online (but I'm probably the one who can't look for well), I finally found a little hint like this: "While 4K displays may one day be cheap enough and smartphones fast enough to use them, human beings will still be unable to tell, assuming that we don't get upgrades for our eyes at the same time" (Butler, 2022).

5. USELESS AND OUTDATED HUMAN ABILITIES?

For some years now, there have been recurrent interventions in the direction of no longer teaching cursive writing in school (almost nobody uses it!), or even to make handwriting superfluous or optional, in times when everyone writes on screens.

Apart from bizarre future scenarios in which humans will be fantastic app users but will no longer know how to make their signature or hang on the door handle an iPad with the words "I'll be right back!", it is absolutely incredible how one can superficially think that a human ability fruit of evolution in thousands of years (but given to every single human on the earth only since a few decades, with the mass school) can now be questioned on the basis of the supposed preferences of the majority.

Cursive writing involves areas of the brain other than writing in block letters, which today's humanity has active and would no longer be activated, we do not know with what consequences. Cursive writing, brush writing, handwriting in general, is probably one of the foundations of our current civilization.

Data analysis showed that cursive handwriting primed the brain for learning by synchronizing brain waves in the theta rhythm range (4-7 Hz) and stimulating more electrical activity in the brain's parietal lobe and central regions. "Existing literature suggests that such oscillatory neuronal activity in these particular brain areas is important for memory and for the encoding of new information and, therefore, provides the brain with optimal conditions for learning ... A lot of senses are activated by pressing the pen on paper, seeing the letters you write, and hearing the sound you make while writing. These sense experiences create contact between different parts of the brain and open the brain up for learning." (Bergland, 2020)

Cursive writing in primary school shows that the group of children who had teaching sessions focused on cursive writing showed a more stable performance through time in a two-letter-search task ... Historical documents like the Constitution are written in cursive. In schools, kids are asked to read pictures of different historical documents and the children are unable to. When children are not taught to write in cursive and are not exposed to it, they can't read it, either. This is harmful to education as well as jobs dealing with historical documents and memorabilia when graduate students cannot interpret the documents. (Harp, 2021)

Cursive writing is also one of the activities more tied to the personality of each individual, it is studied and analyzed by psychologists, probably for some it is an intimate and deep way of expressing oneself. And to consider handwriting from a purely functional point of view reveals an extremely dangerous and integralist conception, as well as a fundamental ignorance of the world of communication today, in which during last century the only medium not extinguished seems to be still the paper book, and no one can know if in a few years our texts will be written with a real or virtual keyboard, with fingers, dictated or what else, and especially in which codes and on what media exactly.

Accustomed to unbridled consumerism and competition, we look for continuous shortcuts, the new way of doing things that makes the old one useless and obsolete.

But is it true that people use so much digital keyboards, or it is another story that, by force of telling us, ends up believing?

Figure 3. Handwriting
Source: Marani (2016)

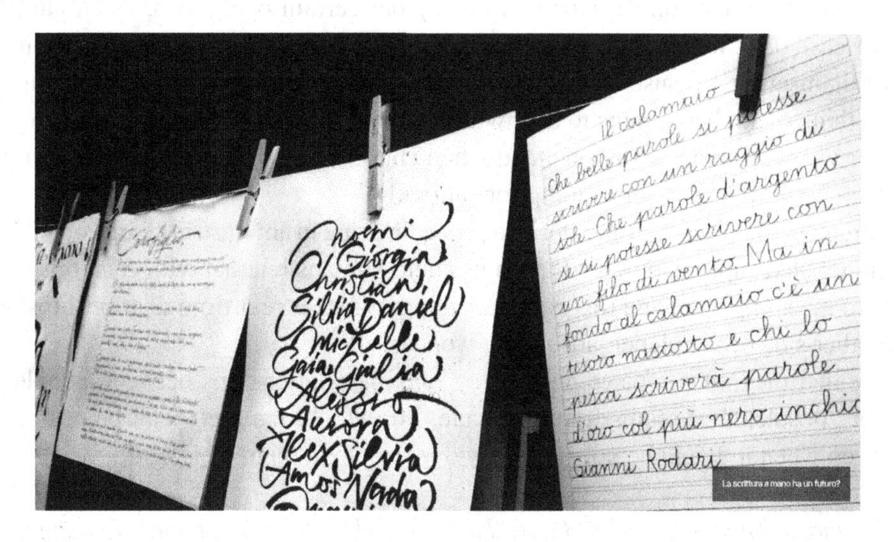

The delegates noted with interest that everyone at the table had chosen to use pens, not laptops, to make notes. One reason for this could be that writing plays a social role in our lives, said Dominic Wyse, professor of early childhood and primary education at UCL ... He believes handwriting gives children similar skills to those gained through music – resilience, creativity and the ability to interact socially. "We are not just talking about mechanical skills here," he said. "We are talking about how children learn. We are making them ready for life ... For Idress, this is key: making sure we help children choose the right tool for the task in hand – whether that's a pen, a laptop, or something else ... The school has created something called the pen licence. It allows younger children to move from using a pencil to pen once they've reached a certain standard. "There's a lot of excitement about reaching that pen licence stage." (Larsson, 2018)

6. FORCED REMOTE CONNECTIONS EVEN TO NEXT DOOR: ESCAPE FROM RESPONSIBILITY?

I don't know how it is in the rest of the world. In Italy, since some years the enrollment at the first grade of the primary school must take place online and the school secretariats do not perform that function. It is part of the general digitization of the relationship between the citizen and the public administration but, since it is compulsory - parents cannot avoid enrolling their children in school, even if they choose to educate them at home - the state should ensure registration even if they cannot or will not use the electronic tool. This is convenient, fast, precise but, as happens for example with train tickets, it could also be possible to address directly to the school next door, having the digital procedures performed by an employee. Why not? When direct human relation is easy, and it can help to solve together problems of any kind, difficult to preview at all, when the standard digital procedure does not work well, or is not well understood, or not well thought out. It is quite absurd that the automatic procedure is the only possible one.

The same, I find bizarre, at the supermarket as well as at the bank, to see employees who assist customers in using machines "on their own" to carry out certain operations, as an alternative to the bank counter or cash desk with human operators. A paradoxical aspect is that these "helpers" work in the end against themselves, because the function of the vending machines is to take the place of human workers. Many think that, if one wants to deal with the bank digitally, he or she does it at home from a PC, or wherever wants from a smartphone, and when chooses to go personally to the office, is to deal in person with an employee. The same going for shopping.

Machines, archives, data bases, computerized procedures are in any case in charge of all the operations at school, station, bank, supermarket, and machines help humans interact with each other even when it is not possible to meet in person and this is a great thing, it makes real-time relationships possible with people on the other side of the planet: absolutely wonderful!

But thinking that they *must* replace humans by making relationships between people in the same room useless or "obsolete", it seems frankly insane. So, why? Men are social beings and "robotize" relationships even when it would be not necessary does not help them feel good.

Humans need humans. Anyone who has changed a plane ticket with an automated phone teller, or plodded through a digital pharmacy order is sympathetic to this fact. If only a human were on the other side of that receiver—how much easier would it be to get that ticket or that prescription? In an increasingly digital world, this seemingly mundane point about the role of humans in our lives becomes profound ... Digital platforms are a part of our everyday but they must serve humans rather than compromise our natural social instinct. (Hirsh-Pasek, K. et al., 2018)

It would be interesting to find out why, having a technology that we can drive in any direction and adapt to different situations, we tend to look for rigid solutions that force everyone to behave in the same way, even when this for some means discomfort?

I do not know if someone has conducted a serious investigation among the employees of the bank or supermarket asking why, instead of doing them a job, they now help us to get it done by the machines; or if someone asked the school secretary why my son's data is not entered by her, who knows better than me how to do it. I tell them her and, in a few minutes, we solve everything, without stress for anyone.

I remember when a hotel clerk in Valencia told me that she could not correct the wrong data of my booking by adding a day, because the software did not allow it. She told me with a resigned air that it was because of technology. I replied that probably it was because of a human error in writing the software. It wasn't her fault, and I made a new reservation.

Hiding behind a technical, objective procedure, which is not up to us, it avoids people from taking responsibility. And today we live in a society where, for a variety of reasons, most flee from responsibilities. So, instead of using technology to really improve our lives, adjusting and programming it in a way that is flexible and adaptable, we often take advantage of the rigidity of its use in a superficial and approximate way, to build around us fences of alibi. To the user, citizen, person, in the end it only remains to accept. And this habit of adjusting in so many cases to something outside, beyond our reach, without a real need, it ends up applying not only to the practical things of life driven by technology, but probably also - let's see a little further - to words, speeches, thoughts, in many automatic manifestations of the "groupthink" and the "politically correct".

By the way:

Recently a photo posted by the Instagram page- Good News Movement- introduced social media users to the Dutch practice of "Kletskassa." This practice enables a special checkout lane that allows people to engage in a conversation with the cashier and help combat loneliness. Many senior citizens prefer these slower checkout lanes as a relief from their mundane routines, and it has helped thousands with five minutes of kindness. Here's why this trend became popularised among the Dutch and why it needs to reflect in other systems as well. (Mohan Kumar, 2022)

7. OLD STORIES IN NEW LOOKING SHAPES: DOCTOR DIGITAL AND MR. ALGORITHM

How many times, to describe for example the hard-working conditions of the so-called "riders" who deliver meals and goods at home, we hear that the fault is of the algorithm! There are also, in several countries, court judgments on the matter.

According to Article 22 GDPR, an individual has the right "not to be subject to a decision based solely on automated processing, including profiling", which produces legal effects concerning him or her or similarly significantly affects him or her. However, fully automated decision-making is allowed when necessary for entering into, or performance of, a contract ... The right to obtain information on the logic used for automated decision-making cannot be identified with the right to know the algorithm itself. Firstly, the algorithm may constitute a trade secret, which may determine the greater or lesser profitability of the business. And secondly, accessing the algorithm – or algorithms, as it is common to use multiple algorithms – would be absolutely counterproductive and confusing, insofar as it may consist of pages and pages of indecipherable codes. (Ginès i Fabrellas, 2021)

In mathematics and computer science, an algorithm is a finite sequence of rigorous instructions, typically used to solve a class of specific problems or to perform a computation. (Algorithm, Wikipedia entry)

Figure 4. Algorithm
Source: Lum and Chowdhury (2021)

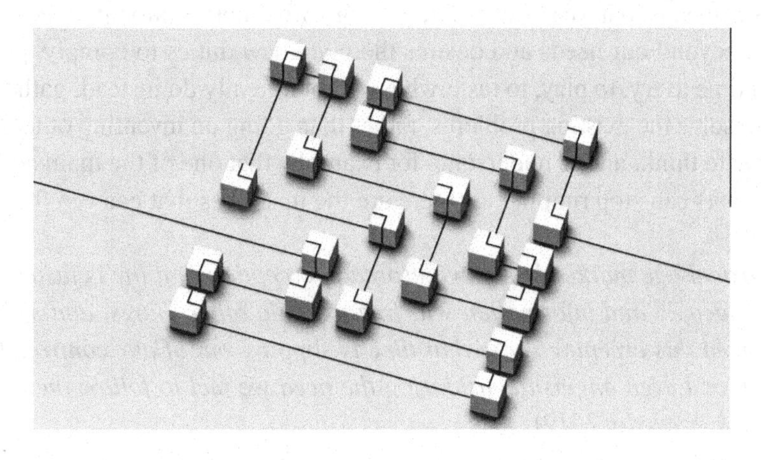

In the current narrative, for example journalism, we often hear about an algorithm almost as a higher entity not subjected to the rules and laws of humans.

But who gives the instructions, and with which intentions and goals? Is should be evident that, without entering in technical detail of how to write the software or how to address artificial intelligence, algorithms are going to be more and more a matter of trade union negotiations: how can workers take part in the definition of the algorithms, so as to safeguard rights and working conditions?

Workers and managers are not passive recipients of algorithmic results; they could find ways to develop a functioning understanding of algorithmic systems, work around issues such as trust, and align the system to their needs and interests ... Since a common culture obsessed with efficiency and extraction of maximum value from workers has long existed, there is a risk of siloing algorithmic competencies into a small number of organizational members ... Algorithmic management is a sociotechnical phenomenon. This means that while algorithms have a central bearing on how work is managed, their outcomes in transforming management and relationships between workers and managers are socially constructed and enacted. (Hossein Jarrahi et al., 2021)

Employers have established broad rights to use technology to gather data on workers and their performance, to exclude others from accessing that data, and to use that data to refine their managerial strategies. Through these means, companies have suppressed workers' ability to organize and unionize, thereby driving down wages and eroding working conditions. (Rogers, 2023)

Laws focused on data protection, data privacy, data security and data ownership have unintentionally failed to protect core human values, including privacy. And, as our collective obsession with data has grown, we have, to our peril, lost sight of what's truly at stake in relation to technological development—our dignity and autonomy as people. (Renieris, 2023)

Algorithms, as a narrative, are probably one the latest, updated representations of the one-way behaviors we tend to adopt in our social life, that make us less responsible of our actions, starting from the incredible interpretation of the old futurist myth of speed, that most understand as the need to always run, all of us, more and more.

Always running it means to have no relaxing, staying with others, dialoguing, pursuing our interests, because constantly, beyond our needs and desires there are new duties to comply, procedures to learn. So that we have no time to try, to play, to taste what we could really do instead, gathering the resources and collaborating to solve the existing problems, rather than going on inventing others. Always running, we have not the time to think, and to understand for example, that one of the main advantages of digital time is just that humans can stop running, as there are the machines that can run for us!

We live in a paradoxical age marked by the widespread perception that life is faster than it used to be, that quick access to people and information will free us to do other things, and simultaneously, most of us have experienced this creeping sense that time is slipping out of our control. That perception is a source of concern and even anguish considering the need we feel to follow the pace "imposed" by technology. (Santos & Azevedo, 2019)

A major theme of this book is that the rhythm of our lives, the very meaning of work and leisure, is being reconfigured by digitalization. But at this juncture, it is helpful to consider other, often overlooked, dimensions to and causes of harriedness ... How people spend their time matters for quality of life, irrespective of the income generated, as economists and even governments have begun to grasp ... The inexorable increase in the pace of life is viewed as a perverse symptom of late modernity, leading to increasing pressure and stress. Understanding why time pressures have increased is a critical social question not least because of the consequences for physical and mental health outcomes. (Wajcman, 2014)

Today's societies are the ones that have the most facilitators of everyday dynamics, cars, washing machines and dishwashers, piped water systems, ovens, stoves, etc. - which apparently saves time, which means people should have more time available, but the general complaint is lack of time.

The initial thesis is that the time spent on the screens (television, tablet, smartphone and computers) intensifies the use of time, making people never having "in-between times", that is, free time between tasks or displacements because the person has the smartphone and with it saturates your time, it fills. In such a way the screen-time is full, that leads individuals and societies to a state of sedation - society sedated by screens. (Oliveira, 2019)

Towards algorithms, knowing what we are talking about, we can also have a more interesting attitude. Here just a hint, starting from the fact that a certain point humans have produced machines that can learn.

Learning algorithms learn to participate in communication, and they can do so because they do not need to understand what people have in mind.

For the same reason, people can themselves learn from their interactions with learning algorithms, even if they don't understand them ... Archaeological research shows that at the beginnings of writing, especially nonalphabetic writing, lists were very common. Ancient written documents practically never

Figure 5. Ancient lists
Source: King Lists (n.d.)

had a narrative form and did not reproduce discourse ... they wrote for administrative and economic purposes. (Esposito, 2022)

Again, about the very post-modern problem that afflicts the whole of our society: It's not that we tell too much, tell everything, tell just to tell?

8. THE CLEAR AND DARK WEB: TRUTH AND FEAR ARE OUT THERE

The Dark Web is a known hub that hosts myriad illegal activities behind the veil of anonymity for its users. For years now, law enforcement has been struggling to track these illicit activities and put them to an end. However, the depth and anonymity of the Dark Web has made these efforts difficult, and as cyber criminals have more advanced technologies available to them, the struggle appears to only have the potential to worsen. Law enforcement and government organizations also have emerging technologies on their side, however. It is essential for these organizations to stay up to date on these emerging technologies, such as computational intelligence, in order to put a stop to the illicit activities and behaviors presented in the Dark Web. (Rawat et al., 2022)

The words "dark web" are scary, they evoke images internalized from science fiction narratives, amplified by the exponential growth of the power of technology around us that we do not know how to control. In reality, the so called "surface web", despite being an enormous dataset, it only comprises a small portion of the content of the global network. As in an iceberg, the invisible part below the surface is far more extensive.

The Clear Web, also called Surface Web, Indexed Web, Visible Web, Indexable Web or Lightnet, is the region of the Internet that most of us are familiar with. This can be easily accessed from any browser and is regularly crawled and indexed by search engines including Bing, Google, and Yahoo. It can seem like a huge amount of information, but the Clear Web is just 4% of the total size of the World Wide Web ... Many people don't realize that the Deep Web comprises mostly benign sites, like those of your password-protected email account, Twitter, Snapchat, or Facebook messenger, certain parts of paid subscription services like Netflix, and sites that can be accessed only through an online form as it can only be encrypted via application program interfaces. A significant part of Deep Web also involves instant messaging and secure data and file sharing services, like Google drive, Syncplicity and Dropbox. (Kumar, 2021)

To access the dark sites you need a special browser such as Tor Browser, which can establish the secure and encrypted connection on the Tor network ... can mask our IP but can nothing against cyber attacks, sites .onion spy and against malware that often circulate on hidden sites ... Surfing the dark web is very dangerous: even just a wrong click to commit a crime or find yourself in a sea of trouble ... use a security suite equipped with dark web analysis. (Vanni, 2022, translated from Italian)

During latest decades, International organizations have often been involved in campaigns against the dangers that children may face from the careless use of technology.

Figure 6. Dark web
Source: Vanni (2022)

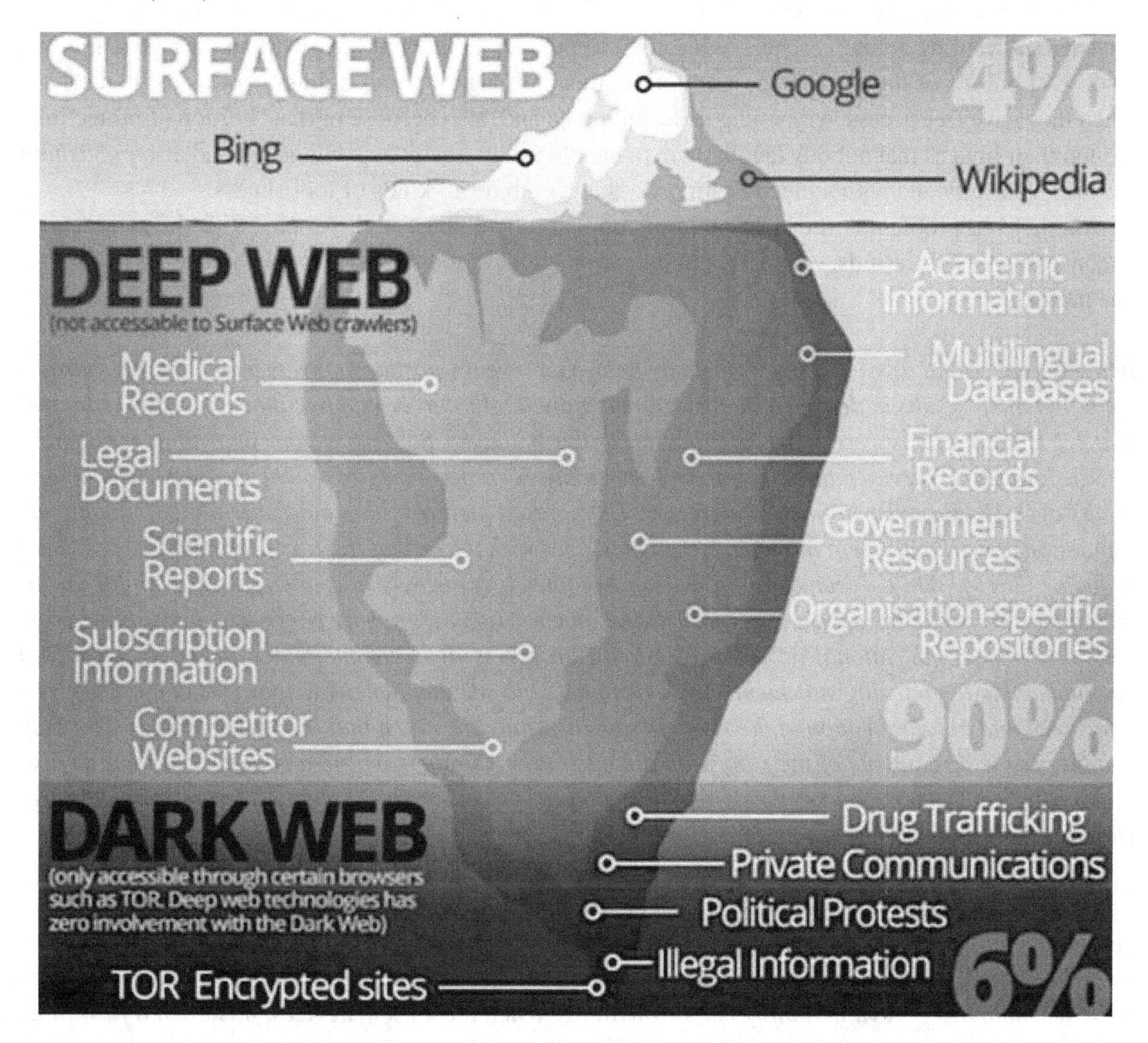

*New types of risk in cyberspace are growing with the emergence of new devices, such as mobile internet access, peer-to-peer (P2P) file sharing, instant messaging, chat rooms, multi-player interactive games and web cameras. The impact on children was highlighted at a meeting arranged by the organization End Child Prostitution, Child Pornography, and Trafficking of Children for Sexual Purposes (ECPAT), based in Thailand, and the United Nations Children's Fund (UNICEF) during WSIS in Tunis. (Yasser El-Bably, 2021)*_

However, often confusion is made, putting in a unique speech the images of abused and exploited children circulating in the dark web (testimonies of truly horrible crimes), the possibility for kids to make bad meetings on the network, with maniacs who, behind the screen, pretend to be peers ((absolutely real danger, to which every girl or boy must be aware), and the publication of photos of children taken in normal life situations and posted on the Web. This is – let's think of it! – probably much less dangerous than walking down the street, eating at the school canteen, going to the park with grandparents. And feeding certain irrational fears this is hurtful to children, as we also pointed out in chapter 2.08.

Then, preventing adults, teachers, educators, to publish pictures of kids without permission, it can be correct but it's of little, when most of compromising images are put online by the kids themselves, when they have free access very young to social media and, also because of that "cordon of protection" around their images that nobody taught them to handle safely – selecting, choosing, and also *publishing* pictures, carefully and with a precise purpose - they combine all kinds of foolishness.

Another big problem is the circulation of intimate photos that adult people, with the same guilty unconsciousness of the kids, carelessly put into circulation, or that are widespread by friends and previous partners:

Image-based sexual abuse (IBSA), commonly known as revenge pornography, is a type of cyberharassment that often results in detrimental effects to an individual's career and livelihood. . . . It is estimated that 1.2 trillion photos were taken in 2017; out of those images, 85% were from smartphones (Richter, 2017). In a 2015 survey that looked into "commonly regretted types of social media posts" among adults ages 18 and older in the United States, 14% shared pictures that could potentially impact their reputation at work; 10% sent intimate, sexual messages with a fear that their privacy could be breached (YouGov, 2015). While documentation culture becomes increasingly normalized with popular social media platforms like Instagram, Tik Tok, Twitter, and YouTube, a growing concern is how online presence can impact educational and/or professional prospects. It is commonplace to see social media accounts include prefacing statements in the account's bio section, declaring thoughts and opinions as one's own and not a reflection of the views of any institution in which that user is associated. Not only should people be cautious of their individual contributions to their online identities, but there is also the fear of what others can say or do without consent. Cyberbullying only exasperates this concern. (Rood & Schriner, 2022)

Cyber-security, just like physical-security, depends on layers or controls that prevent unauthorized access, especially policies, procedures, and technologies. Humans are involved at every layer. Humans write these policies. Humans carry out these procedures. Humans design, create, install, and maintain these technologies ... A vulnerability can be anything. When it comes to devices, it is often a flaw in its programming of some kind. These vulnerabilities are sometimes discovered and exploited by hackers before the equipment manufacturer even becomes aware of the problem. When manufacturers do become aware, however, they usually release new software to patch the vulnerability, but these are not always installed by the organizations who use the manufacturer's equipment in their network. (Crumbaugh, 2019)

9. CYBERBULLYING, BUSINESS AND POLITICS, COPS AND ROBBERS ONLINE

It depends on the behavior of the single users, who threaten other users, of the companies to which we confidently rely, who illegally use our data, of the same governments, which in certain cases through the network exercise control over citizens. And when it happens that they are the citizens to use the power of the global network against governments, then the reactions may be very strong, as it has happened in the case of WikiLeaks.

Cyberbullying remains an elusive social problem for all because cyberbullying has been associated with school shootings, suicides, and other violence among adolescents. (Michael Pittaro, 2020)

Cyberbullying is currently a global problem aggravated by the constraints generated by the pandemic COVID-19 pandemic. In this sense, leaders of international organizations (e.g., ONU, WHO, UNICEF - Board Chair, end Violence Against Children African Child Policy Forum), committed to the protection of children, they signed a document in which they share the concern about this type of violence, appealing for action and promising support to protect children from violence and reduce the impact of COVID-19 on children in all countries and communities. (Carvalho Relva, 2023)

In a society where it's normal that unknown people attack you heavily in chat if you dare to call "caterpillar" a larva of Hymenoptera - by the way, butterfly and moth caterpillars have from two to five prolegs, and if we meet one with more, it's a sawfly! - talking about cyberbullying as a problem of the internet is quite outlandish. Of course, there it takes place, but it certainly does not derive from there. Watertight compartments, difficulty in establishing connections, identity of people often in the balance, competition at any level as a permanent way of managing human relationships: we live in a global bullying factory. And the spaces on the web, especially for people whose "education" to manage them has been left to the market, they are obviously where, individually or as participants in a *groupthink*, the various forms of social aggression more immediately manifest themselves.

Cyberbullying is bullying with the use of digital technologies. It can take place on social media, messaging platforms, gaming platforms and mobile phones. It is repeated behaviour, aimed at scaring, angering or shaming those who are targeted. Examples include:

- *spreading lies about or posting embarrassing photos or videos of someone on social media*

- *sending hurtful, abusive or threatening messages, images or videos via messaging platforms*

- *impersonating someone and sending mean messages to others on their behalf or through fake accounts.*

Face-to-face bullying and cyberbullying can often happen alongside each other. But cyberbullying leaves a digital footprint – a record that can prove useful and provide evidence to help stop the abuse. (Cyberbullying, From official Unicef web site)

The first objective of the present study was to describe the nature of cyber aggression and victimization among emerging adults by focusing on what digital technologies are used and the relationship between the perpetrator and the victim. The second objective of the present study was to investigate the longitudinal, reciprocal relationships between cyber victimization, cyber aggression, suicidal ideation, non-suicidal self-harm, depression, loneliness, anxiety, and grade point average among emerging adults over four years, using cross-lagged modeling. (Wright, 2020)

Digital footprint is a key point of any online experience. For some years websites warn us about cookies, the data that record our navigation, allowing us to leave only the most technical ones, or others that will be used for commercial purposes. We all have experience of advertising of products or

Figure 7. Digital footprint
Source: Digital Nation (2019)

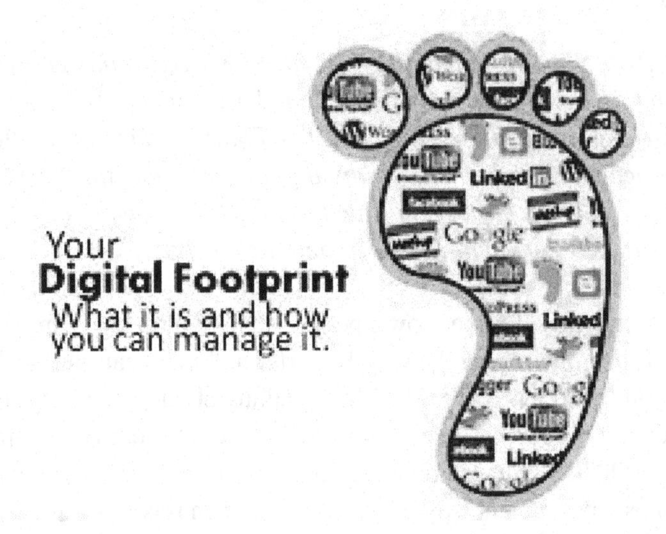

services that arrive to us immediately after we have searched them on the internet, through channels that apparently have nothing to do with the one where we have carried out the search. Today browsers allow also anonymous navigation, leaving less traces, and even not particularly experienced users can easily activate a VPN (Virtual Private Network), provided by the browser itself, by antivirus programs or coming as dedicated software, so that, browsing online, we do not show our actual *IP address*, but another one, dummy, from our country or even from any other part of the world. Against wild advertising this seems to work, but often, as profiling software sees the VPN in our machine, there are searches we can't do, links we can't establish, or we get warned that if we want to watch the champions league match, we must turn the VPN off.

Some websites try to look right inside our computer, steal, or illegally use data and images, and of these attempts the diligent antivirus programs inform us, often warning that the new specific form of intrusion requires additional protection that is not yet part of our subscription.

The current idea is that the risk is above all linked to bad sites such as the pornographic ones, but in some cases, we may find that spying on us are directly governments:

Although the paper does not name and shame, the risks mentioned by the Commission are reminiscent of recent news from the US, where last month a lawsuit was filed against New York-based start-up Clearview AI, after it was found that the company sold information scraped from social-media networks to law-enforcement agencies across the country.

Clearview AI gathered photos without citizens' consent – three billion pictures, in fact, which were taken from sites like Facebook, Twitter, YouTube, and others.

Turning to the EU's other major competitor in technology, China, it is equally easy to point the finger. The Chinese government has been using facial recognition for a long time, often to the detriment of its citizens.

Recently, for instance, it was found that the authorities had set up gate-like scanning systems to record biometric, three-dimensional images, as well as the smartphone fingerprints of Muslims living in the country's Xinjiang province, to track the population's movements.

The EU is keen not to allow this type of application. Ursula von der Leyen, the president of the Commission, said: "I want that digital Europe reflects the best of Europe – open, fair, diverse, democratic, and confident." (Leprince-Ringuet, 2020)

Looking through our PC can also be understood in a literal sense:

If you are paranoid about people seeing things they should not while you're working, you may be wondering if you need a physical camera cover over your computer lens.

Several high-profile public figures have been known to use webcam covers, which are typically plastic sliders or a piece of tape that go over a lens. Former FBI Director James Comey told NPR he has done it. In a 2016 photo posted to his Facebook account, Meta CEO Mark Zuckerberg appeared to be using a sticker on his laptop camera. Should you do the same? (Torres, 2022)

Accustomed to passive citizenship and the idea of a Big Brother above us, however, we do not generally consider that, given the interactivity of digital systems and the growing "democratization" of the means, increasingly powerful and economic, this fact of someone who watches over us can be potentially overturn.

Anonymous is decentralized international activist and hacktivist collective and movement primarily known for its various cyberattacks against several governments, government institutions and government agencies, corporations and the Church of Scientology. (Anonymous, Wikipedia entry)

Hacktivists can be defined as politically motivated hackers. Hacktivists are different from other types of hackers because their motivations are driven by the pursuit of social change, as opposed to seeking profit or intellectual pursuit. Hacktivism is a new controversial form of civic participation, which will most likely continue to have an impact on the Internet and the world. (Mikhaylova, 2014)

Anonymous seeks mass awareness and revolution against what the organization perceives as corrupt entities, while attempting to maintain anonymity. (Timeline of events associated with Anonymous, from Wikipedia)

Although "outlaws", those of Anonymous are not necessarily perceived as the "bad guys", and indeed in certain circumstances their intervention is viewed with sympathy by a part of public opinion, when, for example, in times of frequent cyber battles between the West Countries and Russia, certain of their actions gave the idea of being more effective of those led by government and military.

And how frightening for the "power" and governments can be an effective use of the global network "from below", it is demonstrated by the case of WikiLeaks.

Some federal prosecutors disagreed with decision to charge Assange under Espionage Act ... Part of the concern among Justice Department veterans was that prosecutors had looked at the same evidence for years during the Obama administration and determined such charges were a bad idea, in large part because Assange's conduct was too similar to that of reporters at established news organizations. (The Washington Post, May 24, 2019)

On this case everyone can document himself and obviously make his own opinion, but the doubt is that much has counted the value for say "symbolic" of the story: what can it happen if, instead of living fearing any sort of control by the Big Brother, citizens learn that they can be the controllers themselves?

10. "LIKES" AND FLAGS, THE GROUPTHINK, AND THE SHORTCUTS OF POLITICALLY CORRECT

This contribution studies the debated terms "politically correct" and "cancel culture" on Twitter and in particular investigates the meaning that people give when they label something or someone as politically correct or indicate a case of cancel culture in the Italian context ... A textual analysis of a corpus of tweets selected through a set of hashtags was carried out to identify thematic clusters to understand features and meanings given to these expressions, along with their ways of using in the various situations and contexts. The main results show different meanings of the term, in the negative sense as a limitation of freedom of speech, and in a positive sense as the exclusion of some terms that may offend some people or groups. (Felaco et al., 2023)

Coming directly to the point, I start from the discomfort, strong, my personal and of many, faced with the attempts to correct in "inclusive" sense in my case the Italian language, replacing while writing the male and female final desinences (in Italian neutral gender is no longer present) with improbable Schwa characters or asterisks.

Since the gender of terms is often given not only by the final ending (*attore* = actor, *attrice* = actress, and so "attor*", what the hell is it?), and that the correction cannot be applied coherently even to all articles, pronouns, adjectives connected, without going crazy, the final result in my opinion is only an empty and rather clumsy exhibition of "fairness" by inserting here and there "flags" that only serve to satisfy the ego of the writer and her/his *groupthink*: look how good and inclusive we are!

The reader then can approve, laugh, get angry, but in no case pronounce words written like this, and I found all this personally quite offensive to me.

According to the highest authority in Italian language, the *Accademia della Crusca*, solutions such as asterisks and Schwa are however forcing, due to the impossibility of rendering them on the phonetic plane. (D'Achille, 2021). That is: you can write, but you can't read it.

Again, we find moving in a castle of ideology often coming from a far past. Free market is a myth of the 18th Century, velocity is from Futurism, 100 years ago, and the idea that all is based on competition makes us to think that "inclusion" means removing things that could divide people, as well as "technical progress" means forcing people to use new tools and procedures instead of the old ones. But removing is not inclusion and replacing is not necessarily progress.

Inclusion can be, instead of stopping to celebrate Christmas not to "offend" the faithful of other religions, to celebrate together - who wants, of course - all the feasts of any religion and community. And to add new tools and procedures so that people have more possibilities to choose, that is progress.

We live in a planet where, while in certain countries "pink quotas" are imposed in elective assemblies and companies' boards, from the media, TV, advertising, in a context of general commodification of everything and everyone, female models proposed worldwide are often and willingly still based, as and more than before, on the exhibition and commodification of the women's body (or its total negation, which is the other side of the same coin). And discrimination against women, violence against women, murders of women, are on the increase not only among the Taliban, but in all the democracies of the civilized western countries.

Accustomed to participating in social life with "likes" online, we often *list* the software we could use, the rules we should follow, the goals we would reach, and then we don't care in fact of the results, moving only as commentators, dispersed in a quantity of Facebook and Whatsapp groups, losing the capacity of really acting on reality.

11. WHAT IS TECHNICALLY POSSIBLE, AND WE WILL NEVER ACHIEVE

Digital traces are left online for years of an infinite number of interventions, words, images, with which we contribute to an overall nothing that is continually renewed and forgets itself. Every now and then Facebook reminds us of things that we published five, twelve years ago, and sometimes by re-publishing them in new posts they get more attention than the original ones.

The form of technological determinism of that I suffered led me to think that there was only one way to exploit the potential of digital, which in my head was the best: that to allow all users to become producers, triggering a virtuous circle so that every product could become the starting material for other products and any environment could have become part of more rich and complex ones.

After nearly thirty years of trying to create digital transformation environments (i.e. educational software) I think I have reached a banal awareness: it is not sufficient that something is technically possible to be realized. Everything I thought and understood about the characteristics of digital probably remains true, helps to understand the potential, but it is not enough to ensure a sensible use and aimed at the development of all. (Guastavigna & Penge, 2020, translated from Italian)

However, while even those who had imagined and dreamed now think substantially that they have failed and get by posting pictures of kittens, the world does not go on only with the obsolete narratives of market, advertising, SEO, metaverse as the amusement park of the future, accessible to the races of merchants, combined with stronger pre-technological categories as nationalism, fear of the different and the stranger, defense of "traditional" values, search for keywords through which define the "enemy" and gather around the figures of charismatic leaders, and other features that make the "digital" society extremely similar to all other preceding in human history. And instead of reacting to an ever-increasing complexity by looking for improbable easy, elementary shortcuts, we probably would need a new global thought capable of attacking complexity, a new philosophy adapted to the times, so that if we speak for example of virtual reality, we can't just always tell around stories of students who will learn the Middle Ages or ancient Rome as if they were living there…

At the start of the 21st century, humanity faces data that it alone cannot process without the aid of even more technology ... "Immersive," "spatialized," and "embodied" media—where the participant feels to be inside of the experience rather than an external viewer observing action within a frame ... Virtual Reality (VR) and Augmented Reality (AR), and sometimes Extended Reality (XR), creates a head-scratching and exhilarating nexus of participation and observation, action and reaction, dread and awe. For many, its myriad "launches" into the public sphere have often proven underwhelming, frustrating, or lacking longevity or long-range utility. Extended inquiry into the media from a philosophical layer, and a very quick list of small victories and failures, may foster new discussion around what is missing and what is possible. (Malicki-Sanchez, 2020)

REFERENCES

Algorithm. (n.d.). In *Wikipedia*.

Anonymous. (n.d.). In *Wikipedia*.

Bergland, C. (2020, October 2). Why Cursive Handwriting Is Good for Your Brain. *Psychology Today*.

Blu-Ray media and devices market size & share analysis - growth trends & forecasts (2023 - 2028). (n.d.). mordorintelligence.com.

Brown, B. (2023, Sep 7). *How to Copy a DVD (Protected/Homemade) on a Mac with Best Quality.* macxdvd.com.

Butler, S. (2022, Feb 25). *Why Don't Smartphones Have 4K Screens Yet?* Howtogeek.com.

Carvalho Relva, I. (2023). Cyberbullying: A Form of Peer Violence in the Digital Era. In *Handbook of Research on Bullying in Media and Beyond*. IGI Global.

Crumbaugh, J. (2019). Common Mistakes in Delivering Cybersecurity Awareness. In *Cybersecurity Education for Awareness and Compliance*. IGI Global. doi:10.4018/978-1-5225-7847-5.ch002

Cyberbullying: What is it and how to stop it. (n.d.). *Unicef.* unicef.org/end-violence/how-to-stop-cyberbullying

D'Achille, P. (2021, Sep 24). Un asterisco sul genere. *Accademia della Crusca.* accademiadellacrusca.it/it/consulenza/

Devlin Barrett, D. (2019, May 24). Some federal prosecutors disagreed with decision to charge Assange under Espionage Act. *The Washington Post*.

Digital Nation. (2019 Oct 18). Your Digital Footprint Matters. *Facebook*.

El-Bably, A. Y. (2021). Combating the Exploitation of Children in Cyberspace: Technical Mechanisms to Protect Children from Sexual Content. In *Combating the Exploitation of Children in Cyberspace: Emerging Research and Opportunities*. IGI Global. doi:10.4018/978-1-7998-2360-5.ch003

Esposito, E. (2022). *Artificial Communication: How Algorithms Produce Social Intelligence*. The MIT Press. doi:10.7551/mitpress/14189.001.0001

Felaco, C. (2023). I Correct or Canceling You: Political Correctness and Cancel Culture on Social Media – The Case of Twitter Communication in Italy. In *Research Anthology on Social Media's Influence on Government, Politics, and Social Movements*. IGI Global.

Ginès i Fabrellas, A. (2021, Feb 9). Do riders have the right to know the algorithm? *Do Better*.

Guastavigna, M. & Penge, S. (2020). *Tecnologie per lo sviluppo umano: Dialogo tra Marco Guastavigna e Stefano Penge*. Creative Commons Licence BY – SA 4.0.

Harp, K. (2021, Mar 31). *Teaching cursive writing helps improve brain development, should be required in schools*. Columbiamissourian.com.

Hirsh-Pasek, K. (2018). *The New Humanism: Technology should enhance, not replace, human interactions*. brookings.edu/articles.

Jarrahi, M. H. (2021, Jul 1). Algorithmic management in a work context. *Sage Journals*.

King List: Egyptian Chronology and Material Relating to Surviving Ancient King Lists. (n.d.). ancientegyptfoundation.org

Kumar, S. (2021). The Deep Web and Children Cyber Exploitation: Criminal Activities and Methods – Challenges of Investigation: Solutions. In *Combating the Exploitation of Children in Cyberspace: Emerging Research and Opportunities*. IGI Global. doi:10.4018/978-1-7998-2360-5.ch002

Larsson, N. (2018, Apr 5). Putting pen to paper: the schools nurturing a love of the written word. *The Guardian*.

Lee Rood, M., & Schriner, J. (2022). The Internet Never Forgets: Image-Based Sexual Abuse and the Workplace. In *Research Anthology on Child and Domestic Abuse and Its Prevention*. IGI Global. doi:10.4018/978-1-6684-5598-2.ch032

Leprince-Ringuet, D. (2020, Feb. 24). AI: It's time to tame the algorithms and this is how we'll do it, says Europe. *ZDNet*.

Lightscribe. (n.d.). In *Wikipedia*.

Lum, K. & Chowdhury, R. (2021, Feb 26). What is an "algorithm"? It depends whom you ask. *MIT Technology Review*.

Malicki-Sanchez, K. (2020). Out of Our Minds: Ontology and Embodied Media in a Post-Human Paradigm. In *Handbook of Research on the Global Impacts and Roles of Immersive Media*. IGI Global. doi:10.4018/978-1-7998-2433-6.ch002

Marani, G. (2016). *La calligrafia al tempo del digitale. Un convegno internazionale a Milano*. Artribune. artribune.com/editoria

Maulana, I. (2019). Big Brothers Are Seducing You: Consumerism, Surveillance, and the Agency of Consumers. In *Handbook of Research on Consumption, Media, and Popular Culture in the Global Age*. IGI Global. doi:10.4018/978-1-5225-8491-9.ch004

Mikhaylova, G. M. S. (2014, Dec). *The "Anonymous" Movement: Hacktivism as an Emerging Form of Political Participation* [Master's thesis]. Texas State University.

Mohan Kumar, L. (2022, Dec 24). Kletskassa': Know How This Dutch Supermarket's Slow-Moving Cash Counters Are Helping Combat Loneliness Among Elderly. *The Logical Indian Crew*.

Oliveira, L. (2019). Sedated by the Screen: Social Use of Time in the Age of Mediated Acceleration. In *Managing screen time in an online society*. IGI Global. doi:10.4018/978-1-5225-8163-5.ch001

Pittaro, M. (2020). Cyberbullying in Adolescence: Victimization and Adolescence. In *Developing Safer Online Environments for Children: Tools and Policies for Combatting Cyber Aggression*. IGI Global. doi:10.4018/978-1-7998-1684-3.ch006

Rawat, R. (2022). *Using Computational Intelligence for the Dark Web and Illicit Behavior Detection*. IGI Global. doi:10.4018/978-1-6684-6444-1

Renieris, E. M. (2023). *Beyond Data: Reclaiming Human Rights at the Dawn of the Metaverse*. The MIT Press. doi:10.7551/mitpress/14119.001.0001

Rogers, B. (2023). *Data and Democracy at Work: Advanced Information Technologies, Labor Law, and the New Working Class*. The MIT Press. doi:10.7551/mitpress/11253.001.0001

Santos, I. N., & Azevedo, J. (2019). Running after time: temporality, technology, and power. In *Managing screen time in an online society*. IGI Global. doi:10.4018/978-1-5225-8163-5.ch002

Tezcan, U. T. (2019). Popular Culture and Peer Effects in Consumption: Survey of Economic Consequences. In *Handbook of Research on Consumption, Media, and Popular Culture in the Global Age*. IGI Global. doi:10.4018/978-1-5225-8491-9.ch002

Timeline of events associated with Anonymous. (n.d.). In *Wikipedia*.

Torres, M. (2022, Oct 20). Do We Really Need To Cover Up Our Laptop Camera Lens For Privacy? *Huffpost*.

Vanni, G. (2022, Aug 1). Dark web: cos'è, che contenuti si trovano, perché è pericoloso. *HTML.it Magazine*. html.it/approfondimenti/.

Wajcman, J. (2014). The Time–Pressure Paradox. In *Pressed for Time: The Acceleration of Life in Digital Capitalism*. The University of Chicago Press.

Wright, M. F. (2020). Negative Psychological Outcomes Associated With Emerging Adults' Cyber Aggression Involvement. In *Recent Advances in Digital Media Impacts on Identity, Sexuality, and Relationships*. IGI Global. doi:10.4018/978-1-7998-1063-6.ch001

ADDITIONAL READING

Butler, S., Moore, L. J., & Moore, M. C. (1984, July). Optical-Disc Technology: Future Implications for Teaching Sociology. *Teaching Sociology, 11*(4), 439–454. doi:10.2307/1317800

Chotiner, I. (2021, Jun 3). The Purpose of Political Correctness: A conversation with the columnist Nesrine Malik about who makes the changing rules of public speech. *The New Yorker.*

Digital culture – Access issues. (2020, Jun). *European Parliamentary Research Service.*

Duggan, M. (2017, Jul 11). Online Harassment 2017. *Pew Research Center*. pewresearch.org/internet

Eco, U. (2023). *L'era della comunicazione: Dai giornali a Wikileaks*. La Nave di Teseo.

Hinduja, S., & Patchin, W. (2008). Cyberbullying: An Exploratory Analysis of Factors Related to Offending and Victimization. *Deviant Behavior, 29*(2), 129–156. doi:10.1080/01639620701457816

Lee, M. K. (2018, Mar 8). Understanding perception of algorithmic decisions: Fairness, trust, and emotion in response to algorithmic management. *Big Data & Society*. journals.sagepub.com/doi/full

Lipson, M. (2021, Sep 1). How Language Classes Are Moving Past the Gender Binary. *The New York Times.*

Louv, R. (2008). *Last Child in the Woods, Saving our Children from Nature-Deficit Disorder*. Algonquin Books.

Murray. (2022). The Reliability of Optical Disks. *Murray's Blog: About the things I make and do*. blog.ligos.net/

Notar, C. E. (2013). Cyberbullying: A Review of the Literature. *Universal Journal of Educational Research, 1*(1), 1–9. doi:10.13189/ujer.2013.010101

Parent-Rocheleau, X., & Parker, S. K. (2022, September). Algorithms as work designers: How algorithmic management influences the design of jobs. *Human Resource Management Review, 32*(3), 100838. doi:10.1016/j.hrmr.2021.100838

Paul, P. (2023, Jun 1). Political Correctness Used to Be Funny. Now It's No Joke. *The New York Times.*

Petrov, V. V., Kryuchin, A. A., Shanoylo, S. M., & Sidorenko, V. I. (2003). Optical Disks as a Basis of Modern Paperless Data Processing, Processing. *Cybernetics and Systems Analysis, 39*(5), 777–782. doi:10.1023/B:CASA.0000012098.70754.13

Phillips, C. (2022, Sep 13). *The Psychology of Groupthink and the Desperate, Dangerous Desire for Social Acceptance.* pbs.org/independentlens/blog

Silva, H. (2023, Jul 20). *My child, the algorithm.* thebookseller.com.

Chapter 7
Children and the Clothes of the Digital Emperor:
The Ball, the Doll, the Smartphone, the Animals...

ABSTRACT

If not forced by the adults into unnatural life situations and left free to play together with their peers, If not forced by the adults into unnatural life situations and let free to play together with their peers, children can more easily move beyond the cliches. They don't see oppositions among digital devices, outdoor games, body exercises, nature adventures, puppet shows. Children as they are, and not as described by adults who often don't know them, don't pay a real attention to them and think to "protect" them erasing their smiles from social communication. Children that today can not only be observed but, thanks to powerful, easy and intuitive tools, can tell in person that the king is naked, producing and publishing content almost on their own, showing how to overcome some dead spots of the present, and a possible human pathway to the future, that an active use of technology makes possible. Unless we change and become like little children, we will never enter the kingdom of heaven!

1. INTRODUCTION

Children are multimedia beings, naturally, inside. Beyond the clumsy descriptions of adults in crisis with technology, looking for an alibi and telling tales like that of "digital natives", with computers and smartphones children simply play, as well as with toys and so many objects and moments and topics of life. And playing probably they have a more suitable attitude to understand machines that "tell stories".

Growing up, conforming to adult models, children generally lose their ability to play creatively with the world, and with digital tools too. But perhaps it is precisely by knowing and valuing the natural approach of children and their point of view that today we can find solutions to many problems of present time.

We know, we write, we sometimes complain about children as consumers. But little is known about children as *producers* of culture.

DOI: 10.4018/978-1-6684-8228-5.ch007

It can be useful to consider some examples of how children can reconcile nature, body, technology, in a harmonious and productive way, collaborating, doing together. To observe insects and other animals in the gardens, make original videos, discover by playing the endless possibilities of computers. Children can teach us much and today more than ever they can be a hope for the future. Rather than projecting on them all our insecurities and thinking to have to save them from any sort of dangers, making them grow in a context of anxiety, suspicion and fear, we should dispose ourselves to observe and learn from them not supposed innate digital skills, but their creativity, sociality, joy of living, and especially the ability, when put in the appropriate conditions, to do and live together, in peace.

2. THE AMAZING CULTURAL PERFORMANCES OF BABIES: OUT OF HIERARCHIES

In the middle of the domestic and non-school spaces in which it acts, the child (every child, today, in our village), experiences and knows itself and the other, the world, with an approach that is not improper to define "multimedia" ... The child is a multimedia being because the logic it uses ... is based on the collaboration-integration of a wide variety of means (telephone, radio, recorder, television, newspaper, book, picture albums, toy, etc.), within which the traditional hierarchies of cognition and use are lacking ... Its way of being multimedia is absolutely natural. (Maragliano, 1996)

I like much this "old" definition, these words, and many times I have said it to Roberto Maragliano himself: "At that time, you did see exactly!"

Rather than other definitions that dwell on external phenomena, even on objects, as if they were the protagonists, like the nefarious "digital natives", this goes exactly to the point, which is how naturally the mind and knowledge of children work: *the lack of hierarchies.*

Hierarchies are the first thing that comes into crisis in times of transformation, like those we have been experiencing since the last decades of the last century, with the digital revolution.

And just the return in the society - for market, or political or whatever reasons - of an anachronistic and rigid system of rules, hierarchies and certifications, probably it's causing that short circuit that makes our present time so contradictory, between humans and technology, that's the central subject of these pages. We have seen in chapter 5 how we are insisting on treating and teaching means that would lead us straight into the future according to the ancient rules of the transmissive knowledge...

I knew a child who at the age of four did not speak yet but knew how to find on YouTube the videos of sirens of police, firemen, ambulances from all the world, America, Europe, Russia, China.

How did he do it? We'll never know! He did it naturally, quickly, and I probably would have film him and then watch in slow motion the gestures of his fingers on the touch screen. I probably missed an opportunity to try to understand.

By the way, they are a lot of occasions we all miss not to take, watch, and share videos of young babies exploring and discovering the world applying their methods, strategies, ideas. By looking at them collectively and documenting things almost as they happen, with a mean of reproduction of reality as complete as video, we could have much more material and understand them deeper, together, than illustrious but few scientists of the past, who had to limit themselves to some samples and, describing in written words what they saw, probably lost important details, such as facial expressions, gestures, postures.

Figure 1. Children computer
Source: Beneventi

What we will never discover about children - who are destined to remain essentially unknown, but whose privacy is respected - we will probably know about cats, whose online catalog of situations of any kind, for an attentive observer, is now an endless mine for an extremely thorough knowledge of their cognitive behaviors and styles!

Going back to that child of the sirens on the web, he probably didn't know either how he did and growing up he learned to talk and begun to ask adults to type in for his research, for example "scary streets"! Then he learned to write and of course now he uses the keyboard himself, having lost completely his first baby style of browsing.

Observing, presumably from afar, children playing with digital keyboards, or moving fingers with agility on touch screens – some humans apparently consider playing with a keyboard or a touch screen a sign of great intelligence! - authors began to tell the story of the "digital natives", a new generation that, just by growing up in technology, can teach the world everything on tablets and mobile phones.

Today's students ... have spent their entire lives surrounded by and using computers, videogames, digital music players, video cams, cell phones, and all the other toys and tools of the digital age ... It is very likely that our students' brains have physically changed – and are different from ours – as a result of how they grew up. But whether or not this is literally true, we can say with certainty that their thinking patterns have changed. I will get to how they have changed in a minute. (Prensky, 2001)

3. NOT NECESSARILY REALITY: MATCH THE PATTERNS

It was curious Prensky's contextual definition of "digital immigrants" for previous generations, in which it seems he does not consider that, if many who were grown reading books have actually had to learn the new means in their adult age, just some "immigrants" are the ones who those means have invented. That's to say: they were "immigrants" as Bill Gates and Steve Jobs those who created the digital world!

Anyway, ideas like that of digital natives have the power to catch many people in a public opinion always looking for easy and quick resumes for many aspects of reality, and probably it's an alibi in this case to justify the common trouble in communicating with the youngest. Years later, in Italy, we read:

The natives experience directly the pedagogy of trial and error, more than a historical or systematic and sequential approach to knowledge like ours. Moreover, the sharing with peers, the cooperation, the use of different approaches to the problem, and of multiple codes and interpretation plans to solve it, differentiate them radically compared to us. It is an "open source" and cooperative approach to objects culture which is well represented by the way young people share music, knowledge, and online experiences through the most diverse technological communication tools (MSN Messenger, Wikipedia, Skype, iPod and podcasting, blogs). (Ferri, 2011 translated from Italian)

My first instinctive answer would be that also my cats play with touch screens and "write" on keyboards, but not for this if the Wi-Fi doesn't work, I ask them for help! Talking of trials and errors and sharing, and even of "open source", about children's *play*, it can be suggestive, except that children are not aware of this attitude and, otherwise educated in the school, are normally destined to lose it. And above all, it is a general attitude, not related to the "digital". Babies, today as always, in the first two or three years of life learn to walk, understand and speak one language from scratch or even more, in cases of bilingual family or community, or migrations, which is probably a little more complicated than fiddling on a tablet, and nobody is surprised. They also become able from personal direct experience to connect in their mind environments, sounds, flavors, recognize the natural and man-made objects of their world, with also technological devices that are a simply a part of the whole, as family and friends, toys, food, plants and flowers, the sky, the animals.

When a child on his own seems to surf the Web with ease, not only it does not do it better than an adult, but probably it does it completely differently and, if not somehow helped, it will lose at some point that ability to play the Web as a child, without learning the way to use it an adult. It is not by chance that many teachers complain that their students in high schools do not know how to do well an internet search.

The idea of "digital natives" as an effect of exposure to the media from birth, suggests the acquisition of permanent skills, independent of education and naturally superior those of previous generations, but it is based on assumptions that no one has ever demonstrated.

What is suggested here in following pages, instead, is that by helping children grow up without losing the ability to play the world, indeed by maintaining and developing it, so that it is not erased by the taking over of adult thought - something that already happens to a minority, in brilliant people, in the artists - the whole of society could benefit from it, because it is the most positive attitude towards new technologies as well. And the first step is the recognition, by adults and even by children themselves, of the validity of their natural approach to reality, of which the digital media are an aspect and not the center around which everything must rotate. It can be misleading to speak of digital school, digital identity, digital citizenship, etc., as if the "digital" was more important than humans.

Nei Segni di una Foglia (In the Signs of a Leaf) is a collaborative notebook about nature and environment workshops with children, published in Milan, with no specific date provided, but sure it was out in 1989 or 1990. It features contributions from esteemed authors, with a deep understanding of the true children's culture, among which the most renowned is Bruno Munari (I worked with his group and with him a little too), and the one I am more familiar with is Marco Geronimi: people who when they think, act and write not agitate ideas, but touches reality, and attending and reading them is intense, important, and helps to understand the youngest from the unusual and inspiring point of view of genius.

But at some point, I read a notation that leaves me puzzled, on certain changes that scientists are observing in the mental mechanisms of today's (of 1990) children.

An 18-month-old child handling an instrument such as the remote control ... performs algebraic operations without knowing it: he works on about ten variables (on or off, different channels, color, brightness, sound volume...) ... is able to obtain an image that is very close, if not equal to that obtained through an automatic system of tuning. It means that that child, who still cannot read and write, who probably speaks at 18 months still rudimentary, has acquired from exposure to this new environment a new and different competence, very early, absolutely different from the one that founded the way of thinking of us, being born and raised in a different environment. (Munari et al., 1989, p.17, translated from Italian)

They catch the eye striking analogies with the speeches that will be made about "digital natives", but starting in this case from a TV remote control! The reference is to a study by Swiss researchers, and emphasis is placed on the word "different". But different from what?

If scientist can certify some results of their tests, can they really call them "competences"? Do they have similar tests on babies who grow up in contact with animals, live in large families, travel by car, follow the row of ants or observe the development of the branches of a tree? (see Munari 1978). What behaviors and cognitive styles, for example in language development, as well as in interactions with the others, may be seriously linked in the future for those babies to having handled so young a remote control? We cannot know. But among a lot of operations, algebraic and not, that any baby performs every moment in its life, we put the attention on those that appear weird to us as they don't match our patterns and expectations, and often they are related to "technology".

I am instinctively amazed, just a couple of years later, looking at my 18-month-old child, Riccardo, his first time in front of a computer screen, using the mouse, properly taking and moving virtual objects as if he knows what he's doing! But how much of this does an 18-month-old kid do, with toys, dolls, other humans, animals, that nobody notices because it's not about technology?

Frankly, I don't think that handling a mouse at 18 months gave Riccardo so strong an advantage to me, about digital devices. More important for him it was probably to grow up from an early age in contact not with only one system "to learn", but with many. That mouse was of an Amiga computer, but later, 3 years old, he had discovered that, through key combinations, on the LCD display of the old laptop Olivetti *M10* he could get simple graphic symbols: a car, an airplane, a cottage. And he also liked much

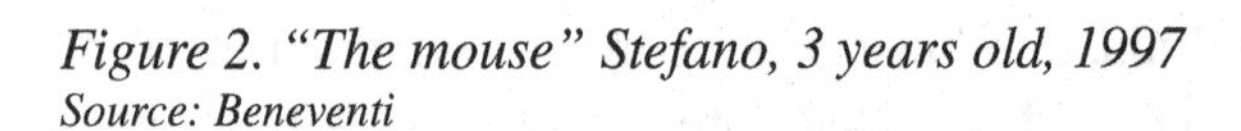

Figure 2. "The mouse" Stefano, 3 years old, 1997
Source: Beneventi

to type random on the keyboard and ask me: "What have I written?" "Asofjosvjdsfiodgyewb!" Fun! I have also a video of the same period, with him explaining how to take colors from the palette and draw on the screen with a painting program on MSX2. In the following years, he could play with his father's PC, his brother's iMac, and his own Amiga, on which at eight years he customized windows and icons ("Look how beautiful it is: there is more space!") and installed programs, copying them from CD ROMs. And when he had grown and could choose, he obviously bought himself a video game console!

4. BEYOND CHILDREN AS CONSUMERS IN DIGITAL MARKET: THE BASIS OF RESEARCH

Media consumption is a term in "sociology" that describes the individuals that organize information on the basis of the use of produced goods, rather than on the axis of services and production. Mediums that fall under the scope of media consumption include radio, television, computer, mobile phones, newspaper, and magazine formats. The usage patterns and applications of these tools are internet, music, movies, games, etc. Among children between the ages of 5 and 8, those who do not use computers represent a small percentage of 10%. Even within this age group, a large majority know how to use computers. More than half of children under the age of 8 have played games and watched videos at least once via a smartphone, iPod, iPad or similar device. According to a US study, children spend about 9 hours a day on the screen. Besides this, despite all the options, listening to music and watching television for children and young people continue to be a favorite activity. (Köksalan et al., 2019)

9 hours a day? Let's say everything else is accurate and that this number is an oversight!

However, for several decades, children have been an important group of consumers, including of technology, and a large part of the market is targeted at them. They are often unique children, above

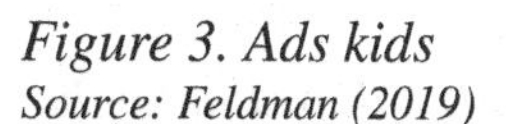

Figure 3. Ads kids
Source: Feldman (2019)

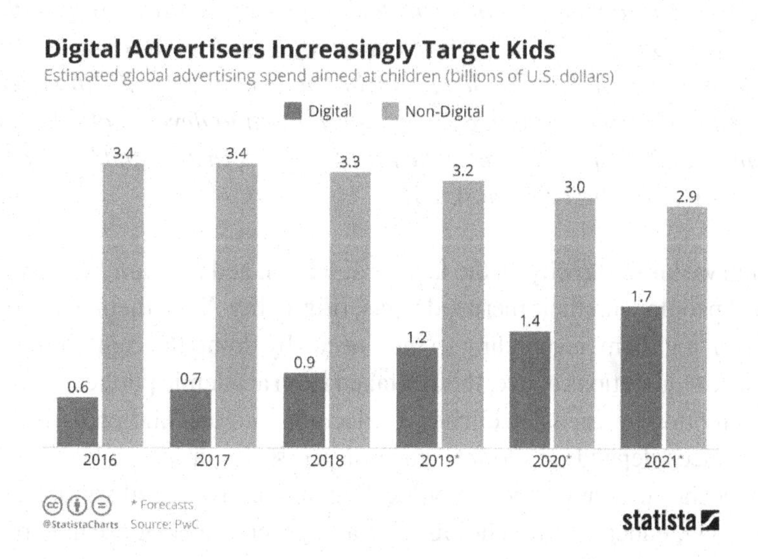

all in the families of economically stronger countries, have a social life planned outside the school and little time to spend playing freely with friends. In the seventies and eighties of the last century they grew with television, then they were among the main recipients of the market of home computers and dedicated consoles, video games, and in the new century more and more also of entertainment software for mobile phones.

The influence of children is also extended in the more general consumption of families, in forms which, although not generalized, are quite widespread:

Observe a child and parent in a store. That high-pitched whining you'll hear coming from the cereal aisle is more than just the pleadings of single kid bent on getting a box of Fruit Loops into the shopping cart. It is the sound of thousands of hours of market research, of an immense coordination of people, ideas and resources, of decades of social and economic change all rolled into a single, Mommy, pleeease!

If it's within [kids'] reach, they will touch it, and if they touch it, there's at least a chance that Mom or Dad will relent and buy it, writes retail anthropologist, Paco Underhill. The ideal placement of popular books and videos, he continues, should be on the lower shelves so the little ones can grab Barney or Teletubbies unimpeded by Mom or Dad, who possibly take a dim view of hypercommercialized critters. (Cook, in Shah, 2010)

Children's experiences are increasingly characterised by the use of digital technologies, disrupting the divide between the physical and virtual world. The digital environment provides children with many opportunities, but it also exposes them to risks. Participation in the digital environment must therefore be balanced with protection, ensuring that children have the knowledge, skills and resilience to identify and manage digital risks ... School closures and digital teaching and learning due to the COVID-19 pandemic repositioned these issues high on the policy agenda. To ensure learning was not disrupted for their children, many families around the OECD, specifically the most disadvantaged, faced several challenges such as access to suitable devices and broadband connectivity. (Children and digital technologies, n.d.)

Positive aspects of social media include allowing children to be brought up as multicultural individuals, enabling education and training environments to design for purposes, using as the main or supplementary source of education, a great power in creating and sharing information. Its negative aspects include leading to a reduction of their academic, social, and cognitive skills in the early periods when children were exposed to the social media, causing the children to develop obesity, mostly bringing up as consumption-centered individuals, perceive the world as a screenshot, and have low critical, creative, and reflective thinking skills. (Dilci & Eranıl, 2019)

There are children we know directly, in the family, at school, and to whom we hardly refer by hearsay, because they are real people with their merits, defects, originality. With them we know the difficulty of interacting, accompanying them, responding to their needs by doing the right things.

But also from the few quotations above, though taken from academic publications, we realize that the speech about children often proceeds by clichés. Collecting data on children as consumers, we should also consider that choices depend on the influence of peers, the fashion and mass media, the family dynamics, the socioeconomic status, and many local, national, or cultural variables. The topic is very interesting for marketing, education, psychology, but any general discourse can hardly fit the real chil-

Figure 4. Global kids tablets market

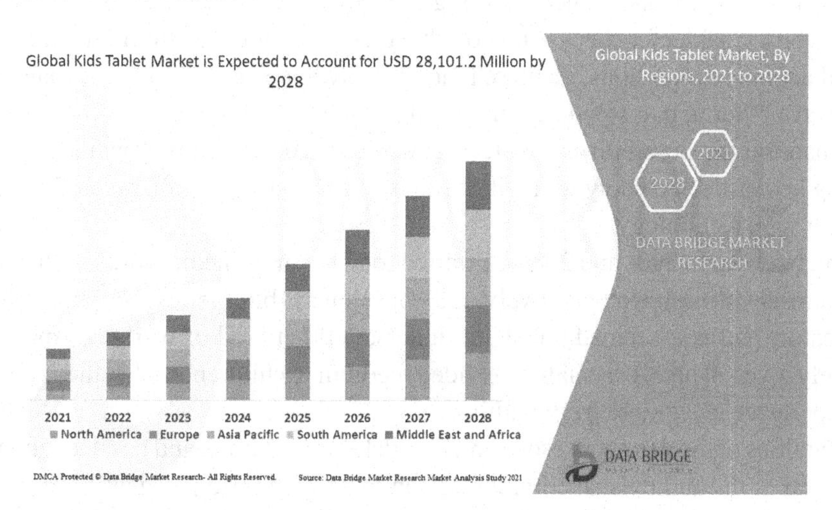

dren we meet, and often stereotypical images attached to children in general, they affect real educational models, social expectations. And it is not nice for children to deal with adults who, instead of listening to them, consider them according to generic consumerist schemes.

Here I refer above all to the children I have been personally meeting in more than 40 years of educational experience, in particular by setting up multi-disciplinary workshops in schools, as an external expert, and other situations. That is to say thousands of kids, from the age of three, in different parts of the world, from the early 80s until the present.

After having observed almost always the same reactions of excitement, desire to do, sincere satisfaction for the mere fact of participating, cooperation inside the group, regardless of the subject of the workshop (theater, storytelling, nature, video, computer, or other), it is probably worth to understand why of this general success and, given the huge number of cases, the consistency of the results, and the availability of a wide documentation, we can identify constants and variables in the approach of the educator, as well as in the responses of children, and draw a theory good for the science of education.

The problem can be how to extract, evaluate, communicate data that, being human activities in many cases unpredictable and original, are placed more on the level of artistic manifestations than, to say, of sessions of psychology.

However, if we want to understand humans, we can't just look at behaviors that are easier for scientists to record, and we have to work out serious methods of investigation for even the most complex ones. A thousand studies of certain conditioned behaviors, for example, which are documented similar in humans and mice, can tell us a lot about our insecurities, fears, ancestral instincts, but they will never help to understand how Leonardo da Vinci and Shakespeare can exist and not even that thing that, manifesting itself in various forms, we call *love*.

I don't rely only on memory - when we tell each other things in words, every time we change them a little - and not even on written notes that, at the moment you take them, overlap an interpretation to what happens, but especially on audio and video documents that I have collected in a systematic and constant way. They are obviously not the whole reality, but of reality they return some moments in a quite "objective" way. From the point of view of scientific research, I have to keep in mind that other things happened before or after, or outside the frame or far from the microphone, and that in the work of editing I had to apply forcing and choices (editing is necessary if we want to communicate, but original documents must be available, for checks and possible reconsiderations). But so, we are dealing now with real words, real actions, expressions, glances, that probably match to reality more than crossed boxes or programmed answers for a, b, c solutions on a form.

Having at disposal the possibility of collecting audiovisual data on our own since several decades, and considering how little and badly we do it, it is in my opinion a sign of a rather perverse relationship we go on having with technology.

At one point, between the 90s and 2000s, I started to make multimedia works with children, in which the children themselves participated actively and consciously, but then we stopped, because the adult audience, educators and not, seemed unable to understand that kind of works. In more recent times, I have increasingly given in hand especially the video medium to children, so that they can use it firsthand, telling their experience even more from within.

But the difficulties of the daughters, sons and grandchildren of book and passive television in actively using the potential of the audiovisual communication in daily life and in scientific research, it must not be an alibi for not deepening this research method. Also because we can not only talk about kids in a new and much more direct way, sharing with anyone the sources of our reflections, but even call kids themselves to take part in the talk, managing directly the same means and language of communication.

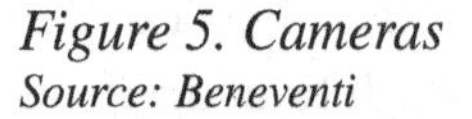

Figure 5. Cameras
Source: Beneventi

5. PICTURES OF INSECTS AND SPIDERS: FROM THE SCHOOLYARD TO THE INTERNET

The Children's Virtual Museum of Small Animals is a website where multimedia documents are collected, based on the real experience of groups of children from many parts of the world. There, people can find photos and videos of insects and spiders, with scientific names and classification, place and date of discovery, and age of the class, group, or single kid who found it. (Beneventi, 2013)

It is almost 20 years since we began to go looking for insects in schoolyards. Recently (summer 2023) I was out with a group of kids in the natural area around an archaeological museum on the shore of Garda Lake, where testimonies of ancient human settlements are collected, from the time before the Romans to the Middle Ages. Nature, history, the experience of looking among the grass and in the mud, on the leaves and barks of the trees, next to ancient ruins of a village of stilts and a castle, with in hand cameras and smartphones that help us to see better, to enlarge, remember the details. It's a global multimedia experience, taking place in the physical and natural world, involving the senses, emotion, collaboration with the others, technology, used both locally (devices to capture images and store them) and globally, because we can share our observations, make it available on the Web.

We are aware authors of information, that we verify, select, in case process (cutting frames, correcting lights) and then we put online, where we can find similar photos and videos of others with whom we are, or we can easily be in contact. We can write to the authors of the other images, children or teenagers like us, photographers, or professional video makers, send emails, contact them on their profiles in social networks: "We liked your images, go to this address to see ours!" And we can look also for scientists and professional entomologists as advisors.

The adults who are amazed about "digital natives", only watching children who tinker on tablets, and see it as a break, a division between generations, probably they should observe a little how here a whole process of knowledge and communication takes place in an absolutely natural way, with nature and technology getting along, as well as adults and children.

Even those who do not know a correct use of cameras - many teachers don't - just go close, hold their hand still, and in many cases they can get images of absolute quality. And it does not matter so much to use this or that technology, to adopt an educational method, the skill and charisma of the teacher. The "secret" is working together, in groups, as certain teams of good professionals and artists, and scientists do, but naturally children as well, if put in the right conditions.

Sometimes we have to overcome obstacles due to bad habits, to the fact that many kids grown up as puppies of consumers begin soon to lose their ability to know the world by playing, how it's typical of babies. But starting with insects it can be great, perhaps also because there are no stereotypes of consumption related to children and insects. Usually, it is enough to show 5 minutes of videos of other children who had a similar experience, look at the images, listen to the voices, and there is no need to add anything.

Did you like what you saw? Let's go to do it!

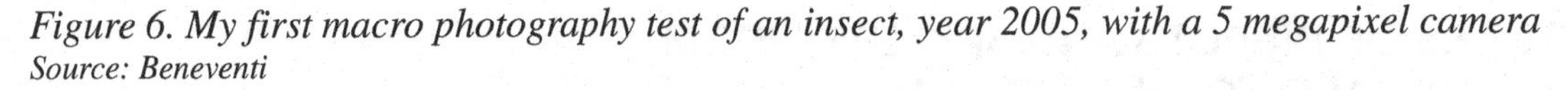

Figure 6. My first macro photography test of an insect, year 2005, with a 5 megapixel camera
Source: Beneventi

6. CHILDREN AS FILM MAKERS, AND THE LATENT AUDIOVISUAL CULTURE, COMMON TO ALL GENERATIONS

In 2017, I am asked for a video documentation of the last step of an educational project in a primary and a middle school in my town, Brescia, Italy. The goal is to make a nearly professional product. Instead of just going and filming the kids and their lab supervisors, as they draw conclusions about the experience, I give the camera directly in the hands of the kids, all, in turn. Holding it mainly on a tripod and a with few basic instructions, they make a decent and, in some parts, original video.

In 2018, during a workshop with an afternoon group in a school of Siena with students from 11 to 14, I have the occasion of having filmed by the kids themselves all a path lasting 12 meetings, from the first, when we were introduced, through the making of a fiction film, until the final conversation of the group with a professional TV producer of RAI, the powerful Italian state television, as he and the kids were colleagues.

I don't "teach" kids how to make videos. With all the television they've seen, they know very well, somewhere in their mind, how to make a video. Indeed, with all the television we have seen, we all know it: it is a latent culture, transversal to all generations. The problem is that both us and the children, when we take a camera or a mobile phone in hand and make videos, we generally think that not being professionals our videos will come out anyway bad. We have grow up with the idea that quality depends on means and skills that we do not have, that we must attend schools and courses, receive diplomas and certifications. Of course, directing a feature film requires study, experience, and skills. But to make good photos and shots, with the extraordinary machines that are there today, absolutely not! We don't need someone to *explain* all the tricks. Maybe it is enough to understand why our shots of the party, or the trip are so often unwatchable and learn those three rules, no more, so that they next time will be much better. That's all? Of course! Today an amateur can get very beautiful photos or videos, even without knowing anything about technique. And this is one of greatest changes in our times. Just the change that, so attached to the old idea of a sharp division between producers and consumers, we often cannot see!

The kids taught me how to teach video making to kids!

I had begun in the early 80s, but probably I fine-tuned my "typical and ultimate" introductory workshop when in 2007 I had a three-day experience in a poor and problematic neighborhood of Havana,

Cuba. I was there with two cameras and a tripod, a video projector, a laptop with editing software, and a bunch of kids that were anything but digital natives, as they had in fact never held a mobile phone in hand. But maybe because they didn't have their mind and imagination full of publicity, as the brats of the rich Western countries, they were very curious, careful, and eager to play. They were used to watch television, of course, that's the mother of all our virtual knowledge of the world.

To put the camera on the tripod, to play to shoot one another exploring the faces, smiles, gestures; to have first very simple interviews and then, for say, some dialogue between hands or feet, eyes and fingers; enjoy the amazing digital effects inbuilt in cameras in that period, symmetries, balls, accelerations and slowdowns, which children see live in the "mirror" screen and, while laughing like crazy, they start moving accordingly, in an increasingly precise and appropriate way. And if they are Cuban children and then you put on a music, it immediately looks like a video clip!

Those effects – that sometimes we find now in some web camera or mobile software, as additional jokes - to take kids into the game of making videos right away at high levels, they were good more than a whole series of lessons. But after a while they were cut off in cameras by the "market". And neither the market nor the school has ever indicated a model of camera suitable for educational use, by the way!

Anyhow, even without effects, the "magic" is simply to put a group of kids behind a real camera, on a tripod. It has not to be a professional machine, but if it's just a bit like that, it's better at first. More important is that the tripod is good, that's to say heavy enough so kids can pan.

Using the tripod makes the children enter another game, an activity completely different from the usual horrible takes, too fast, blurred and without cuts with which, from the time of Super 8 until 4K smartphones any kid, or adult, confirms to himself that his footage can only be a disaster.

Not the single child, in the beginning, but the group of children, because children play well together. They pay more attention, observe, and advise each other, and try to do better, or in a slightly different way.

The perfect number for the first experience of kids behind a camera is three: one to watch the screen and set up the frame, the second to wear headphones, so that if people around is chatting or making unnecessary noises, he/she can say: "silent, please!", and the third, when everything is ready, to clap hands in front of the lens and shout "Action!"

After the game has started, initially a little stiff and then more and more loose, the children gradually begin to behave in an increasingly appropriate way to what, beyond their play, they are doing. Gestures as a director to move and position people, raise the voices; camera movements with attention and precision, pans above all (at the beginning it is better never zooming!). You look them in face, you film them in backstage scenes where all can see the commitment and awareness they put. If they do not know something, before eventually asking the adult, they consult each other. And after being used to the tripod, taking camera in hand, they hold it in a completely different way, and the same they do with mobile phones.

I have backstage videos of middle school students at work, making that fiction film in Siena, or a documentary on their school in Brescia, shooting together with two or three video and photo cameras and several mobiles at the same time, covering all the space and the points of view, adjusting body and arms to a wall or a bench to have shot the most stable as possible. I have pans by kids of primary schools slow and extremely accurate, even two-handed (by two girls, it was great!), with an ability to also dominate the use of the devices physically, as it is thought that only professionals or artists can do. This in Italy, in Cuba, anywhere, when children are called to have a true play (in the sense of how children *play*) with video making.

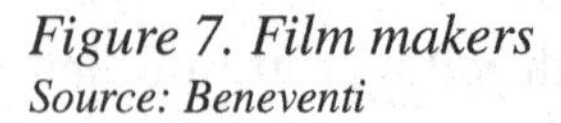

Figure 7. Film makers
Source: Beneventi

What about the stereotypes of the kids taking selfies for Tik Tok? That also is a fact, but not the only, and probably not what they prefer, if they can choose.

7. THE PERSONAL COMPUTER, A GROUP PLAY MACHINE THAT CHILDREN CAN TEACH HOW TO USE

To all my students I have always talked about "computer science of the mind" also because I am convinced that an approach centered on the human mind is the only one that can reassure those who are afraid of computer science and of the same mathematics ... poor computer science, without computers ... children realize that playing with themselves ... become masters of their own body and its extraordinary possibilities, mathematics and computer science become an extension of very positive experiences. (Lariccia, 2010, translated from Italian)

Children like computers not because children are digital beings but, on the contrary, because children probably see computers as many adults cannot see them: "machines that tell stories". (Penge, 2017, translated from Italian)

By telling and making computers (and phones, of course) tell stories, with children we can discover functions and possibilities of digital machines that most of the shy and reverent adult users do not even imagine.

Audio processing software – few know it – all fascinate children with the chance to see on the screen the shape, the drawing of their voices, that can be selected with the mouse to apply the most varied and fantastic effects. Actually, there's not a lot of literature on this, but since I've been testing it for over 30 years with all the groups of children that I work with, I think I can say that so it is.

Something I have already reported about in chapter 3.07. In this kind of programs kids are particularly able to work and discover things by themselves, without a teacher, just trying and playing together.

Among the available programs, all addressed to adult or even professional users – the market and the school haven't probably realized yet that this can interest children and very few things have been proposed for them over the years, and very limited - I like one, *Goldwave*, shareware, in English, having two good features. First, the oscilloscope, even full screen, so that children can see their voices drawing "live" on the screen. And sometimes the shape of vowels and consonants resemble the graphic of the alphabet: amazing! It's not easy to keep a clear and steady voice, we notice from the signs on the screen changing. But it is voice training, and listening to our body, while we learn that to get a regular graphic from "eeee", "sssssss" "aaaaa" or "mmmmm" is easier than from "ffffff". To be tested, using stamp function on PC to collect screenshots, and labeled with the notes of the group of children.

The second great feature of that software is that, from a wide series of preset effects, we have the possibility of changing parameters, with sliders, numbers or other, and save the new effect with another name. In fact, I do not know that program deeply and often, after leaving a group of kids 9 or 11 years old playing with it, they discover new functions that I didn't know.

Figure 8. Goldwave
Source: Workshop with kids

No image file Uploaded to
e-Editorial Discovery Submission System!

!WARNING!

Please provide suitable image during proofing.
Otherwise this figure (and any reference to it)
will be cut from the final published document.

One day, many years ago, the already mentioned Riccardo came from school, 8 or 9 years old, and said, smiling: «Today the teacher taught us to turn on a computer! » And in 2022, filling out a bureaucratic form for a school job, I discovered that computers for the Italian Ministry of Education are still classified as "individual" machines! Please? Digital machines/sets of possibilities can be learnt much better in group, just as good programmers, hackers and also children do, with teachers who can help them to organize the work as a whole in a way they alone hardly are able to do. And so, each one doing what is the best for him, the collaboration between generations can be easy and natural.

To watch kids between 9 and 14 working on their own with a multimedia authoring software, it was a real "masterclass" during the 90s, tested on several occasions in schools, fairs, events. And one could understand the deep meaning of the word "workshop". With younger children, playing with computer to write books or multimedia works, even when the final product was put together by an adult, the kids could realize directly on the field how digital means can allow anyone of them to take part in a real production, easily and with fun.

Next quotes are not from academic articles, but from the voices of five years old and first grade children, in multimedia videos (sequential stories made at the computer) and hyper-textual works.

Ospitaletto (Brescia), Italy, kindergarten, 1997:

Teacher: - What did we do with your drawings?

Kid 1: - We put them into the computer!

Kid 2: - To make a book!

Stefano: - We made a cartoon with the computer!

Giada: - We also told a story!

Child 3: - We took one drawing and then another came out and the first disappeared, and then other one ... always different!

Sara: - We were doing as a cartoon theme song!

Mattia: - We learned to use computers to make cartoons, to do important things!

Child 5: - The books, to make books!

Child 2: - It's like an album!

Teacher: - And now, what we see?

Child 1: All the figures we made! (Beneventi, 1999, p. 92, translated from Italian)

Children:

"You press the buttons, and then they show you what you want to do". "Computers are not only for playing, but also for doing things for work!". "As my daddy's got one, so I know it a little bit". (From Le Fiabe, la TV e il Computer, book and multimedia video, Kindergarten, Ospitaletto, BS, Italy 1997, translated from Italian).

"Today we saw pictures on the computer, then we gave the voices and you showed us some strange effects". "We were talking in the microphone and there were drawings on the computer screen". "There were lines that showed our voice when it was low and when it was high". "You even let us see the sound waves!". "And then it (the voice) was reversed and we didn't understand anything it said!" "You were showing us on the computer things going around, and then images coming out!" "We took the photos from the computer and transformed them!" "We changed faces, we could choose anything we wanted, nose, mouth, half man and half woman..." "With voices you cut the pieces, put them back together..." (From MM "La Natura e noi", Collebeato, BS, Italy 2003, first grade).

Children used also simple and intuitive but strong morphing programs, in few minutes learning to change their own faces or even some famous pictures like the Gioconda, that time when - the kids said - she had eaten a lemon! We applied morphing also telling the story of Odysseus and Circe at kindergarten, turning sailors into pigs...

Stop! It seems we are talking about a parallel world, where people and kids naturally use the means in an active and productive way, learning every day something new, without the need of forgetting and "replacing" what they did before, collaborating in friendship and serenity with peers and with the educators. And "digital" does not mean compulsive behaviors with mobile phones on social networks and the need of defending someone against every sort of dangers, while all around bullying is growing inevitable and brigades of psychologists are sent to in school to save the children from attention deficit

Figure 9. Gioconda lemon
Source: Workshop with kids

and discomfort. Our experience and narration of media seem often to tell different stories that hardly meet each other.

We constantly repeat ourselves that the world is changing very rapidly, but probably we are failing to keep up with the continuous and "external" (not depending on our choices) replacement of means and technologies in so many aspects of our lives, so that often we take refuge in rigid and substantially immobile mental and behavior patterns. That we are at the same time consumers and producers of information, so that we must take on new responsibilities, but also, we can face changings more quietly, and that children may be examples for the whole of society about how to deal with this new situation, it is hard to realize.

8. UNLESS WE BECOME LIKE LITTLE CHILDREN, WE WILL NEVER MAKE PEACE WITH TECHNOLOGY!

Here we recall the example, mentioned in chapter 6.04, of the little girl who drew a ladybird eating a watermelon.

Children are the masters of connections!

In a compartmentalized world, where clumsy inhabitants could suddenly move between everything, setting a potentially infinite number of links, but they are bewildered of this, the naturalness with which children can do it is maybe a key towards a future not so irremediably conditioned by how we imagined it in the past.

During the 1970s, an important cultural movement, with children at the center as "masters", it was in Italy the so-called "animazione teatrale". The words have correspondences in languages as French and Spanish, less in English. As well as to moving objects or drawings in the shack of a puppeteer or on a screen, *animazione* refers directly to the Latin etymology of the term: *anima = soul*. So, *Animare* may stand for "give a soul", in a group of people give life, lead to some action.

Animazione teatrale was based on free bodily expression, the play of children that becomes a cultural proposal against the difficulties of communication and relationships in the society. Working with children, from the years 1960, in France and later in Italy the term begun to be used in education, to mean that children do not learn things only from adults but, appropriately solicited, they "pull them out" from themselves, individually but especially collectively, freeing their resources of knowing the world through their body, play, interaction with thew others. As it is natural in early childhood, when babies take on their own from the environment, without someone *teaching* them, what they need to learn to walk, talk, play, but not in traditional school, where children are led to change their approach to the world and to adapt increasingly to codified models of knowledge and culture, given by the adults.

Children have a strong need for "deconstructing and restructuring" the reality, to pretend, playing, that things are not exactly as they are, especially in a world, like the present, in which every toy comes to them "with the instructions" ... It's important that children learn to organize their time and their own game through moments of true autonomy. Because, without it, they simply will not ever grow. (Beneventi & Conati, 2010, translated from Italian, p. 28).

Project DEFY is an international network of schools without teachers. Its founder, Abhijit Sinha, asks: "Do you think that children are stupid?"

At Project DEFY, a holistic education organisation based in Bengaluru, India, we don't think that any human beings, young or old, are "empty vessels". We believe that everyone has their own skills, talents and dreams that are waiting to be unleashed. Based on the principles of experiential learning and a self-designed education, our "Nook" learning spaces enable everyone to find their calling and chase their dreams.

We believe that traditional education models are actively blocking learning, by ignoring the learners' personal needs and interests because the education system was designed for the sole purpose of creating like-unleashedminded, like-behaving, unquestioning factory workers. The result? A world where all we care about is getting a job, building a house, owning a car while we continuously contribute to or ignore problems that surround us. Classrooms did not exist 400 years ago. They will not exist 100 years from now. (Sinha, 2019)

The idea that the kids can be of inspiration for all is not so new: "Unless we change and become like little children, we will never enter the kingdom of heaven!" (Matthew 18:3)

So, young children take a crayon, a ball, a doll, a smartphone, a camera, a robot, and simply begin to play with them, according to what that "device" and its features suggest. Especially if they can play together, they easily learn to use things well, know and imagine the world. They can be "digital natives" as they are natural natives, theatrical natives, sports natives, draw natives, puppeteers native, and in general human natives. But they can't practice solutions on their own, they don't even know that they have the solutions. Generally, growing, they conform their behaviors to those of the adults around.

To maintain the natural ability to play and imagine that in their early years amazes adults with strong messages of hope, they need first to be safe, not to suffer dramatically, as it often happens, the consequences of wars, famine, climate change, forced migration. And then they need to be recognized. When an adult shows attention to a child, and gives it confidence to do something, that child is happy.

If the adults pay attention to what children are capable of doing together, the children themselves grow aware that in their natural attitude towards the world there is something good, and that they don't have to deny what they are in order to grow up. And an adult confirmation of what children are and feel can maybe keep a few psychological problems afar from many of them.

As we'll see also in chapter 9, section 6, beyond the ambiguous technology of "screens" (often lazily used in schools as books, only to receive other people's content), other digital toys are much better suited to letting children enter directly into the "future", building it, commanding it, like 3D printing, robots, drones.

Arduino. 3D printing. Wearable tech. What is all this stuff? ... The technologies we talk about in this book for the most part arose out of a do-it-yourself, "hacker" or "maker" culture. ... How young is too young to make things? Obviously, little kids have always made things, and probably everyone's parents have some strange dried-out thing in a drawer as a memento of past artistic endeavors. Where is the line between "playing" and "making"? Or is there a line, and does it matter? (Horvath & Cameron, 2015)

Sixth grade students participating in a four-hour hands-on technology enriched space science camp acquired more positive dispositions toward space science. Topics related to the Parker Solar Probe mission, the Apollo 11 moon mission and Mars spacecraft were taught through innovative technology experiences such as augmented reality, virtual reality, 3D printing, robotics and drones. Analysis of pre-post data revealed that space science camp participants exhibited significant gains in their dispositions toward space science. ... Implications of these findings for expectations regarding potential contributions of informal learning to formal science concepts are discussed. (Christensen et al., 2019)

Educational Robotics (ER) has revealed several benefits in the educational context, not only helping the teaching of disciplines ... Teamwork and problem solving have been used as approaches to stimulate some students' skills, such as analyze, manipulate, execute, debug, re-execute, and practice. These skills can assist the learning of theoretical content thought practices activities. ... We identified Papert ideas, where students are encouraged to take more responsibility for their learning). (Souza et al., 2018)

Interacting with machines in this technology of doing, as well as with pictures and software on computers, children easily find original and creative solutions, so that the results often go far beyond learning and repeating what a teacher can tell. And at once a school activity becomes search and discovery together.

Children free to live their childhood, today as never they can suggest answers to adults able to listen to them and to become like them, to enter the kingdom of heaven.

9. THE DESIRE FOR PROTECTION OF THE YOUNGEST MUST NOT GENERATE A SOCIETY OF FEAR

We have been living for a long time - and now we are so addicted and resigned that we do not even realize it - in an ugly and sad fairy tale in which a wicked wizard king systematically erases, disfigures, deforms, and hides from the sight of the villagers the eyes, the faces, the smiles of children. What were once images of hope, joy, confidence in the future, in the now twisted minds of the subjects of that wizard king mostly evoke suspicion and fear ... "Mother, father, grandfather, teacher! Why are the eyes of that child erased?" "You must know, my child, that we have privacy laws that protect minors". "So, children like me in our society are 'minors', meaning that they count less? And the smile of a child is something that in adults like you causes fear, alarm, insecurity?" (Beneventi, 2022, translated from Italian)

I have already written of this, in chapter 2.08, of the laws and regulations on privacy that can be counterproductive and harm a whole generation of kids. In the society of "tag behaviors", automatic signals beyond context and intention, also to answer to the natural pampering of a child who is not our son or grandson, it may be considered unseemly. But in this way, are we protecting children for real dangers, or rather are we making them grow up in a sad and cuddle-less world, where it will be more difficult for them, growing up, manage emotional relationships, love, and sex? When we sometimes observe disconcerted certain incomprehensible, violent, or very tough behavior by adolescents, perhaps we should consider that they are growing in a context where completely natural and innocent manifestations how to embrace a person to express joy and empathy, are more and more strictly "privatized", reserved for "authorized persons", and otherwise automatically associated with danger and perversion. And when in the refusal of an adult to respond to his/her spontaneous embrace the child feels - as it can happen, given the times - embarrassment and fear, he/she will feel offended, rejected, not understanding why. We are saving appearances, but we are not protecting that boy or girl, we are in fact hurting them!

Figure 10. Paint
Source: Beneventi

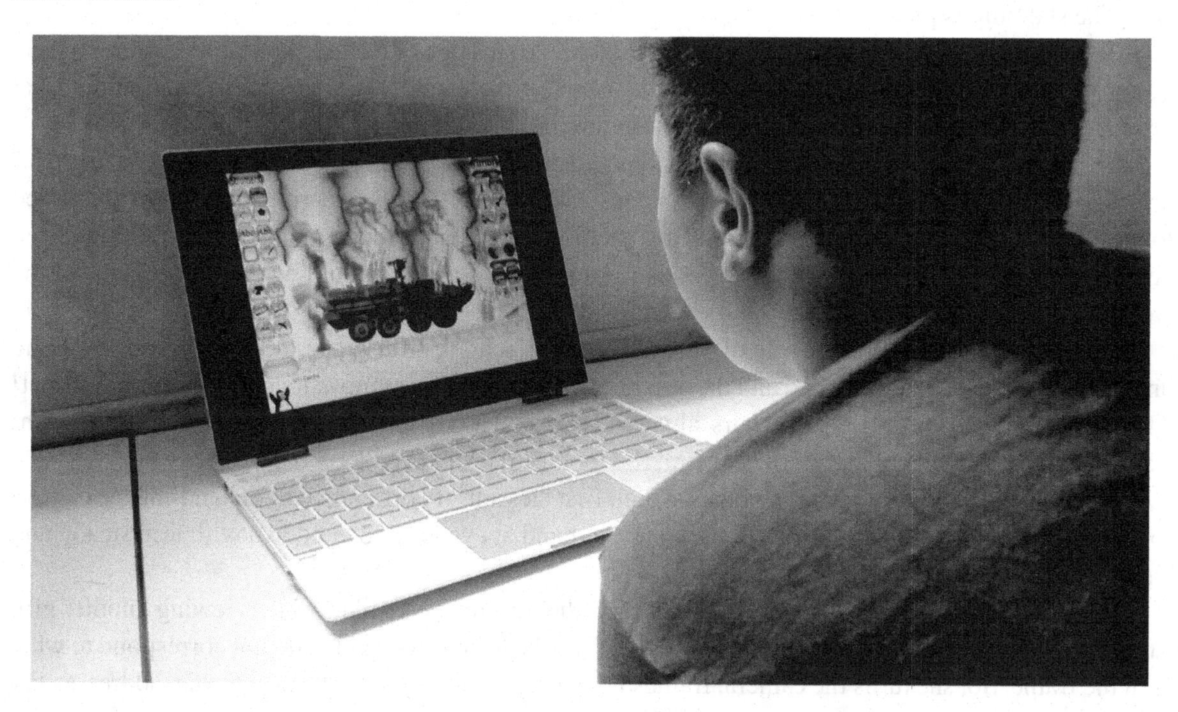

Also for this it is important to come out from the narrations and listen, watch to the messages that the true kids can send us almost directly, today as before it was impossible. Asking for all permissions according to the law, but let's go back to look at the smiles of children!

In this respect, to educate kids from an early age to be aware producers of information, selecting and choosing the images to be shared also online, starting with those of the insects in the school yard, and even more those of their activities at school, it is probably a great way to make them grow more attentive in the management of their own images and worthiness, when as teenagers they begin to share things independently on social networks. It is not by keeping them away from the world until the very last moment that we can protect them, but by accustoming them to move inside it, in a careful, self-respecting and serene way.

10. REAL CHILDREN COMMUNITIES FROM THEIR VIDEOS: HOPE AND A NEW STYLE IN COMMUNICATION

2006, Provaglio (Brescia) Italy. The group of the first grade is mirroring in the TV set, connected to a camera. At the beginning they crowd in front of the screen, but when they understand where the eye of video really is, they go in front of the lens. There's the "ball" effects and the kids, all alone, fine tune their faces into the frame, and some of them even "rebound" in it.

2007, Barrio La Timba, La Habana, Cuba. After three days of video workshops, kids who did not have experience of technology are making the final interviews, to the mates and to the teacher. Having the camera in hand, the girl sitting on the ground is leveraging her elbows against her belly to keep it still. The shooting is perfect!

2010, Cagliari, Italy. During a book fair for children, groups of 5 or 6 children completely improvised go for 40 minutes with two cameras to make the *News* of the event. There is a bit to cut, but the final product gives the idea, from an original point of view!

2017, Brescia, Italy. The girl is looking serious and engaged, watching the display with care and panning very slowly with the tripod's handle, with her schoolmate at the side wearing the headset connected to the camera. The faces slide of children from a multi-ethnic neighborhood in northern Italy: European, African, Middle and Far East, in a few seconds from a fourth class that could be an encyclopedia of the world's ethnic groups!

2018, Brescia, Italy. Other couple of kids of the same school, fifth grade, now in the yard walking and, having one the camera in hand and the other the headphones, must move together carefully. Perfect! Then they even manage to climb the stairs, always in two, and it is not something that a teacher can teach! Thanks to the optical stabilizer of the camera, the footage doesn't even look bad!

2018, Pyrgos, Greece. 6th grade students at their first "lesson" try different way of handling the camera to get each a slightly different shot of their mates: in hand at eye level, hand down with arm steady and rigid, on the tripod, on the floor...

2019, Calenzano (Florence), Italy. In the library, the girl, ten years old, is interviewing another girl. Framing the partner, she realizes that the words that will be heard in the video do not correspond to what is in the frame. So, she turns the camera, frames now herself and, holding the new frame, addresses her partner again and repeats the question, in profile!

Another group of girls, of twelve, being in a library, think of a story in which a girl who can't read is taught about the letters of the alphabet and another who can't use the mobile is taught about surfing the web with a smartphone. They do everything alone, and only when going for the final editing of the video, the adult educators can listen to the dialog.

Are you sure this is right for me? I think I can get better from myself, than from a phone...

In this coffer, but with bars, you can see everything the world offers, gives you, but you can't use it, so, you feel alone, closed.

I had always the will of learning, and now that I have a chance, I feel wasted! You should apply a little less with technology. Why don't you read a book, sometimes? It shouldn't be bad for you! I've changed my mind; I think that technology is not the only way to learn. In fact, it is not a way to learn!

We have just finished our video, better than the Insta Stories!

I greet my mother, father, my cousins and my kitten! (from the author's video workshops with kids, translated from Italian, 2019)

In literature since decades one can find descriptions about children and media, television, digital gadgets, how these media determine the imagination, culture, cognitive styles of the youngest.

A curious fact is that most of the observations and examples refer to the individual child in front of the screen. It is true that this describes a situation that often occurs, the only child, or two or three broth-

Figure 11. TV ball
Source: Beneventi

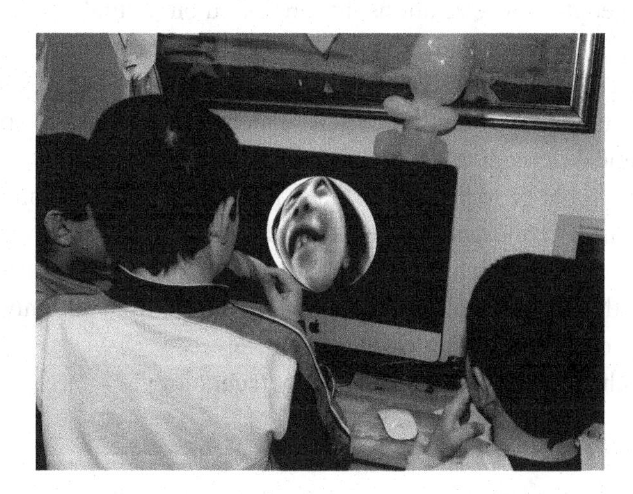

ers who in their home seat hours in front of the television (as it was in the recent past, and often today) or isolate themselves from the rest of the world glued to tablets and mobile phones, all intent on video games or bizarre network explorations. But can we say from this picture that we have a comprehensive idea of the relationships of children with media? What about, for example, children in school watching TV ads together? Or making TV, as in the examples above?

It's hard to talk about children looking at them superficially from the outside, or consider their way of participating in society only through tests and questionnaires, especially when administered individually. Besides the family and social contexts, as well as the school, in which they are considered on the basis of learning and behavior within a structure to which they must adapt, it is above all the "social" aspects of the life of children that should be considered, also because, in the end, it is above all in the group of peers that the thought and culture of kids is formed (although, curiously, this concept well present in the common sense appears little studied or highlighted in the literature). School, street, sport, music, internet groups.

That's to say that children can be understood better not from laboratory observations, but from the living knowledge of what happens when kids interact, inside and outside the school, in situations in which they are alone with themselves or in which, on the contrary, they are supervised by adults. It depends also on how the adults pose, as traditional teachers, sports coaches, technical facilitators, or "animators", able to help the kids to express themselves serenely, recovering their playing abilities.

The variables are many, it is a world to be explored, in order to identify its characteristic features, on the basis of which *then* we will be able to draw maps. Some great educators, for not many decades, have begun to describe it, with the humility of starting not from what adults would like to teach the children, but from what children are, and observing how they grow, play, learn, with an attitude like that of anthropologists, who watching other human groups try to understand their culture.

Since some years in the present, as not before, anthropologists have the chance of giving to the "tribal peoples", and the children, the possibility of talking almost directly about themselves, using not only verbal and graphic codes, but also audiovisuals, as a universal, shared, multi-directional language.

To begin to consider the youngest not only according to easy patterns, but listening to the true messages they send us, as so far the adult society has never done, it opens to a non-authoritarian approach, to a dialogue if not between equals - for better or for worse, children depend on adults and have them as models - at least among people whose relationships are based on mutual respect.

In this context, we can easily watch their actual behavior, learning, cognitive styles - that, given similar circumstances, repeat in a similar way, with variations to be considered - but also we can probably face better problems such as bullying or attention deficit, which it seems hard to solve only with sermons, repression and psychological or medical interventions on the individuals.

A first important step should be to have soon ready a "collection of the collections" of adequate audiovisual documents on and by children, from which finally derive a common method of collecting and sorting data and observations, on which to compare ideas, opinions, educational strategies, in a debate that, given the nature of the documentation on which it is based, may not only be among experts, but involve the whole of the society, including children themselves.

This would be a real change today made possible by technology!

REFERENCES

Almomani, S. (2022). *Unesco Reports 244M Children will not start school this year.* worldforgottenchildren.org.

Beneventi, P. (1999). *Come usare il computer con bambini e ragazzi*. Sonda.

Beneventi, P. (2013). The Children's Virtual Museum of Small Animals: From the Schoolyard to the Internet. In *Handbook of Research on Didactic Strategies and Technologies for Education: Incorporating Advancements*. IGI Global. doi:10.4018/978-1-4666-2122-0.ch001

Beneventi, P. (2022). Feb 23. In *Reame del Sospetto e della Paura*. Sapereambiente.

Beneventi, P. & Conati, D. (n.d.). *Nuova Guida di Animazione Teatrale: A Scuola e nel Tempo Libero*. Sonda.

Bowens, J. A. (2022). Developing Digital Presence for the Online Learning Environment: A Focus on Digital AVC. In *Pedagogy, Presence, and Motivation in Online Education*. IGI Global. doi:10.4018/978-1-7998-8077-6.ch003

Children and digital technologies: Trends and outcomes. (n.d.). *Education in the Digital Age: Healthy and Happy Children*. oecd-ilibrary.org/sites.

Christensen, R. et al. (2019). Creating Technology Enriched Activities to Enhance Middle School Students' Interest in STEM. *EdMedia + Innovate Learning*, Jun 24

Cook, D., in Shah, A. (2010, November 21). Children as Consumers. *Global Issues (Washington, D.C.)*. globalissues.org/article/237

Dilci, T., & Eranıl, A. K. (2019). *Handbook of Research on Children's Consumption of Digital Media*. IGI Global.

Feldman, S. (2019, Jul 24). *Digital Advertisers Increasingly Target Kids*. statista.com.

Ferri, P. (2011). *I nativi digitali, una razza in via di evoluzione*. Cronache Editoriali.

Global Kids Tablet Market - Industry Trends and Forecast to 2028. (n.d.). databridgemarketresearch.com/reports

Horvath J. & Cameron, R. (2015). *The New Shop Class: Getting Started with 3D Printing, Arduino, and Wearable Tech*. New York: APress.

Köksalan, B., & … . (2019). Media Consuming in Children: Child Development, Babyhood (0-2), Early Childhood, Interests. In *Handbook of Research on Children's Consumption of Digital Media*. IGI Global.

Lariccia, G. (2010). *Informatica della Mente. Carignano (TO)*. Book-Jay.

Maragliano, R. (1996). *Esseri Multimediali: Immagini del Bambino di Fine Millennio*. La Nuova Italia.

Matthew 18:3. *Gospel*.

Munari, B. (1978). *Disegnare un Albero*. Zanichelli.

Munari, B. (1989). *Nei Disegni di una Foglia: Ambiente, lezione numero uno*. Comune di Milano – Cariplo.

Penge, S. (2017). *Lingua, programmi e creatività: Coding con le materie umanistiche*. Anicia.

Prensky, M. (2001, Oct). Digital Natives, Digital Immigrants. *On the Horizon*, *9*(5).

Shah, A. (2010, November 21). Children as Consumers. *Global Issues (Washington, D.C.)*. globalissues.org/article/237

Sinha, A. (2019). *Project Defy*. Academic Press.

Souza, I. et al. (2018). A Systematic Review on the use of LEGO® Robotics in Education. *researchgate.net*/publication

ADDITIONAL READING

Ahmad Dar, W. (2021). Constructivism, Pluralism, and Pedagogy From Below in India: An Integrative Role of Educational Anthropology. In *Ethical Research Approaches to Indigenous Knowledge Education*. IGI Global.

Beneventi, P., & Conati, D. (2010). *Nuova Guida di Animazione Teatrale*. Sonda.

Canadian Paediatric Society. (2017, Oct 9). Screen time and young children: Promoting health and development in a digital world. *Paediatrics & Child Health*, Volume 22, Issue 8, December 2017, Pages 461–468.

Di Bari, C. (2023). *I nativi digitali non esistono: Educare a un uso consapevole, creativo e responsabile dei media digitali*. Uppa.

Ferri, P. (2011). *Nativi digitali*. Bruno Mondadori.

Fortunati, L., & … . (2022). Arts and crafts robots or LEGO® MINDSTORMS robots? A comparative study in educational robotics. *International Journal of Technology and Design Education*, *32*, 287–310.

Gardner, H., & Davis, K. (2013). *The App Generation: How Today's Youth Navigate Identity, Intimacy, and Imagination in a Digital World*. Yale University Press.

Geronimi, M. (1985). *Il bambino tra i Suoni: come e perché portarsi a scuola l'orecchio e la voce*. Ricordi.

Giletta, M., & .... (2021, July). A meta-analysis of longitudinal peer influence effects in childhood and adolescence. *Psychological Bulletin, 147*(7), 719–747.

Heitner, D. (2016). *Screenwise: Helping Kids Thrive (and Survive) in Their Digital World.* Bibliomotion. doi:10.4324/9781315213187

Hernandez-de-Menendez, M., & ... . (2020). Technologies for the future of learning: State of the art. *International Journal on Interactive Design and Manufacturing, 14*, 683–695.

Kuswandi, D. & Fadhl, M. (2022). The effects of gamification method and cognitive style on children's early reading ability. *Cogent Education,* Volume 9, 2022 - Issue 1.

Masril, M., ... (2019). The Effect of Lego Mindstorms as an Innovative Educational Tool to Develop Students' Creativity Skills for a Creative Society. *Journal of Physics: Conference Series*, Volume 1339, International Conference Computer Science and Engineering (IC2SE) 26–27 April 2019, Padang, Indonesia.

Munari, B. (1981). *Il laboratorio per bambini a Brera*. Zanichelli.

Penge, S. (1993). *Io bambino, tu computer*. Anicia.

Pollo, M. (2013). *Fondamenti di un'antropologia dell'educazione*. Franco Angeli.

Reid Chassiakos, Y. L., Radesky, J., Christakis, D., Moreno, M. A., Cross, C., Hill, D., Ameenuddin, N., Hutchinson, J., Levine, A., Boyd, R., Mendelson, R., & Swanson, W. S. (2016). Children and Adolescents and Digital Media. *Pediatrics, 138*(5), e20162593. doi:10.1542/peds.2016-2593 PMID:27940795

Shih, J.-L., Shih, B.-J., Shih, C.-C., Su, H.-Y., & Chuang, C.-W. (2010, November). The influence of collaboration styles to children's cognitive performance in digital problem-solving game "William Adventure": A comparative case study. *Computers & Education, 55*(3), 982–993. doi:10.1016/j.compedu.2010.04.009

Sina, E., Buck, C., Ahrens, W., Coumans, J. M. J., Eiben, G., Formisano, A., Lissner, L., Mazur, A., Michels, N., Molnar, D., Moreno, L. A., Pala, V., Pohlabeln, H., Reisch, L., Tornaritis, M., Veidebaum, T., & Hebestreit, A. (2023). Digital media exposure and cognitive functioning in European children and adolescents of the I.Family study. *Scientific Reports, 13*(1), 18855. doi:10.103841598-023-45944-0 PMID:37914849

Swider-Cios, E., Vermeij, A., & Sitskoorn, M. M. (2023). Young children and screen-based media: The impact on cognitive and socioemotional development and the importance of parental mediation. *Cognitive Development, 66*, 101319. doi:10.1016/j.cogdev.2023.101319

Twenge, J. M. (2017). iGen: Why Today's Super-Connected Kids Are Growing Up Less Rebellious, More Tolerant, Less Happy--and Completely Unprepared for Adulthood--and What That Means for the Rest of Us. New York: Atria.

Vinayastri,A. et al. (2021). Effects of Learning Media and Cognitive Style on Children 4-6 Years. *Middle European Scientific Bulletin* 13.

Zipory, O. (2018). Can Education Be Rid of Clichés? Philosophy of Education Society, Urbana, Illinois

Chapter 8
Body, Nature, Machines, a Feasible, Necessary Balance:
Real and Virtual From Market to Experience

ABSTRACT

For centuries and millennia, human experience has been living, natural, bodily, and only a minority, able to read and write, could think beyond. Visual culture, for all, was limited to painting, sculpture, architecture. Recently, within a few decades, radio, cinema, mass school, and the press came within everyone's reach, and television and internet across the Earth. Knowledge of the world for all humans is now mainly outside the lived experience, while our impact on the planet has become so strong that it endangers plant and animal species, the climate, and human survival itself. Examples show that balancing and reassembling the experience is not so desperate a venture. Virtual and real can easily meet and cooperate, though often we have to know the stories out of mainstream narratives, where actually people take part not only as spectators, but as active players in the planet in which they live.

1. INTRODUCTION

Emotion, consciousness, knowledge involve the human being in its entirety, the senses and the "digital", which cannot be considered separately. For the future, the possibility of enhancing natural bodies with technological extensions is a source of hope and fear and to replace too much the living experience with the virtual one could be a long shot.

As biodiversity is crucial for the balance of the planet, in the same way the safeguard of the diversity of thought and software, that is thought running technology, it seems a vital issue, in a society in which there is a tendency to confuse the library with the store, where instead of accumulating knowledge, products are simply replaced with other products. What has happened so far with author software, drawing programs, websites builders, indicates a dangerous tendency to standardization and impoverishment,

DOI: 10.4018/978-1-6684-8228-5.ch008

which risks tying the use of technology to the difficulties and laziness of the present, rather than projecting ourselves towards the future.

Is software a commodity, a service, or perhaps a collective and shared adventure that can take us much further than we imagine, not as simple consumers, but as protagonists?

2. BACK TO ROOTS OF HUMAN BEINGS, EMOTION, CONSCIOUSNESS

How does the brain generate the mental structures that make us to see images? How does it create this feeling of ourselves of which we have experience, when we think something, perceive something, imagine something? No, self-consciousness does not fall from the sky. (From the presentation to the French edition of the book of Damasio 1999, translation from French)

Emotion was probably set in evolution before the dawn of consciousness and surfaces in each of us as a result of inducers we often do not recognize consciously; on the other hand, feelings perform their ultimate and longer-lasting effects in the theater of the conscious mind ... just like emotion, consciousness is aimed at the organism's survival, and that, just like emotion, consciousness is rooted in the representation of the body. (Damasio, p. 293)

Our work investigates the epistemic status of experience and the living body in knowledge processes. It asserts that human experience contains a myriad richness and argues that a first-person epistemology and precise methods are needed to genuinely conduct experiential research. The stakes of such a proposal are not only epistemological but also nourish an ethical and societal goal. (Ollagnier-Beldame, 2020)

Knowledge and consciousness, human experience as a whole should be taken seriously into account, with all psychological and social implications, before using expressions such as "digital culture". Not knowing well what we are talking about, we run behind "innovations" that are often only market trends, we take for granted the existence of "digital natives", we are afraid that artificial intelligence can replace human one regardless of the choices of humans themselves, and the evanescence of thoughts and words can lead us to completely misleading conclusions. Especially in the Western cultures of the "first world", it seems almost that in a few decades we have left our bodies and we move, awkwardly and with a lot of stress, on new and in some ways exciting terrain, but that no longer welcome our roots of human beings, that before than digital citizens are probably still physical and animal, characterized by a high degree of consciousness and thinking ability. And leave them to run after clichés is not good for health, neither mental nor probably physical.

Even in past times, humans certainly did not live in a state of nature, but the perception of themselves in the world depended on the role occupied in society, on traditions, on religion. Only a little minority, belonging to the ruling classes, who made and told the history, was able to develop a cultural superstructure capable of partially replacing material existence. And yet the experience of the world of all, even of most of the members of the ruling classes, was well rooted in the material reality, which was difficult to ignore.

There were books, for the few who could read and write. There were rules, often very strict, for those who worked in the fields and factories and did not even imagine for themselves a possible different existence, facing every day hard work, poverty and hunger, the abuses of the powerful and the precepts of a religion that promised redemption from suffering, but in another life…

Probably none of us would make the change with those times, but many people come up with the idea that there was something more alive and truer in that life, which in the more advanced and elaborate societies has been lost.

Richard Louv speaks of Nature deficit disorder (Louv, 2008).

Today, with the acquired ease of access to information - guaranteed by the web - teens can get a very accurate knowledge on issues such as global warming, the ozone hole and environmental disruption in general, but they have lost that intimacy with the environment that allowed their experiential, pre-intellectual knowledge.

The child who walks in the stream learns something else from the child who reads its history in books: the richness of sensory experience is not substitutable by technical knowledge; however thorough and truthful they may be. Intimacy with the natural world also creates a healthy and private dimension for children, in a personal world that promotes discovery and wonder, a reality of its own, especially supporting individuals who grow up in violent families or little attentive to their needs. (Serafini, 2021, translated from Italian)

I was recently for twenty days for a multi-cultural project in Cuba, April 2023, in a country where the American cars of the 1950s or the carts pulled by horses that are still frequent on the streets give you the idea - as the locals sometimes tell you - of having taken the time machine. Things were very hard also

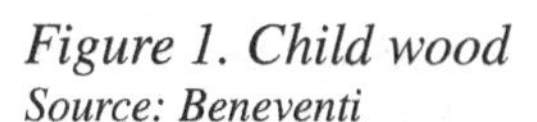

Figure 1. Child wood
Source: Beneventi

for the general bad economic situation and the fuel shortage, so that reaching the schools and the houses of culture was often an unpredictable adventure, with city buses, popular taxis, sometimes a truck, an electric tricycle, a tractor, and we had to cancel several events due to travel difficulties. People told you about the very hard of making a living, with the economy on its knees for the continuing American *bloqueo*, the pandemic, the further scarcity of resources for the war in Ukraine, inflation, and the historical difficulties of the government and bureaucracy.

But in all this there was - like a perception, not easy to understand and express - something necessary, alive, true. We simply were trying to do things, and people even in the poorest barrios answered us in a somehow sincere way. We were artists, and crazy, but maybe it had jumped a kind of cork on real life that habitually prevents us from touching things, and then we talk about them as from outside, and we feel that we are missing something... So, not better people or situations, but the feeling of just getting first to persons, more directly, without having to go so many times through that patina of artifice that seems to stand between us and the others, us and reality, in the everyday happenings of the opulent societies in crisis of the years 2020, where the set of human relationships, work, friendship, love, sex are lived mostly as a competition, where we do not meet others to feel good but to compare with them, and possibly collect likes! Not to say that is always necessarily so, for all of us, certainly not, but that often the moments we feel truer open like temporary windows on landscapes usually denied, for too many of us, in too many circumstances.

3. HUMAN INTENTIONS SHAPE TECHNOLOGY, AI SAYS!

Italy, May 2023, country place just outside the city, at the edge of a park that climbs up a mountain. It's a kind of political picnic, with a local formation supporting the election of the likely new mayor. Eating and drinking in company, breathing nature, the speech falls on artificial intelligence. The woman in front of me is scared. In her words and eyes, the expression of who sees looming on the horizon something alien and uncontrollable: "Who knows what they'll do to us?"

"They who?"

Can artificial intelligence go on for itself, apart from what humans decide to let it do?

A synthesis of Marshall McLuhan's typology of media, Carl Jung's theory of the Collective Unconscious, Teilhard de Chardin's Evolution, and Rudolf Steiner's Anthroposophy is used to explain the current crisis of Western Civilisation, as well as suggest possible responses. (Kazlev, 2022)

"Men have become the tools of their tools"; this rather strong affirmation of Thoreau (1854, p.54) dates almost two centuries ago ... Communication, work, friendship/intimate relationship formation, and even the concept of self have all been subject to change. Whether change is radical to the point of making men 'the tools of their tools', is however a debatable issue. In this context social media probably represents the best example showing how several basic human face-to-face activities have been transferred into the online world. (Melonashi, 2019)

Derrick de Kerckhove, introducing his reflection on AI, not by chance speaks of images, quoting the case of Boris Eldagsen, the photographer who refused Sony World Photography Award because his photo was actually a fake:

The event opened my eyes in a shocking way. For over 70 years, like most of my contemporaries, I had been accustomed to taking photography for granted as a reflection, representation and guarantee of the veracity of events and features. Of course, like other media scholars, I was aware of the many critical approaches to the "illusion of reality" by which people generally trust photography. But this creation of "reality" ex nihilo is something completely different. My confidence in photography has been shattered forever, adding to my doubts about my students' documents, the news I read online or in the press, the videos I watch, the music I listen to, and so on. (de Kerckhove 2023, translated from Italian)

In de Kerckhove's opinion, humanity is a crucial step, about to change the "operating system":

Language is the main operating system of every community ... Language produces meaning, algorithms produce decisions. To come to a decision, language requires deliberation and understanding, algorithms come to conclusions without understanding ... Whether spoken or written, language is not "thought" in itself, it is just a code. Like photography, writing is not "reality", but a partial representation of some aspects of it. Many people, however, mistake the GPT oracles for the expression of thought, just as they take photography for the representation of reality ... We all need, in the European Union, an intergovernmental conference on the risks presented by AI and algorithms to normal discourse and their relationship to conventional notions of what is "real".

There is a difference between fake news and news created ex-nihilo: the former are a mere distortion of evidence, based however on an existing context to which it refers, while the latter also create the context, as the award-winning photography does. The one is a matter of "editing", the other of "prompt engineering". (de Kerckhove 2023, translated from Italian)

The acute, prescient observation of Henry David Thoreau is a strong warning both for experts and ordinary people.

Figure 2. AI photo

We have seen that generally consumer citizens do not have an adequate technical preparation and therefore many hopes and fears about AI are, ultimately, based on science fiction stories; that the debate takes place especially on social networks and so the average level tends to fall, and that behind there are not indifferent commercial drives and interests.

We know also that digital systems, including the "intelligent" ones, for some reason sometimes may work not well. And it is not just a theoretical question, as entrusting control entirely to automatic systems can be problematic or even very dangerous or lethal. So, there may be unexpected computer blocks in London airports, causing annoying inconvenience to passengers, but also much more serious accidents, as those that happened for example to the Boeing 737 Max aircraft between 2018 and 2019, when two of these planes crashed in Indonesia and Ethiopia, the flight control software having activated an anti-stall system that the pilots could not disable, with hundreds of people dead.

Investigators in the Lion Air case highlighted how pilots battled to keep the plane pointing upwards as the system automatically forced the nose down. (Topham & Smith, 2019)

It's important that, as we introduce AI to avoid human error, we also keep the ability for human intelligence to correct machine errors. And here it comes to human choices.

So, the simple basic question is: «Can we talk about artificial intelligence and the possibility of it replacing human intelligence, without taking into account the intentions and choices of humans? »

I address it directly to the currently best-selling software of artificial intelligence, and this is the full transcript of the ChatGPT response:

Certainly, we can discuss artificial intelligence (AI) and its potential to replace human intelligence without considering human intentions and choices.

Artificial Intelligence is a field of computer science that focuses on creating machines capable of performing tasks that typically require human intelligence. AI has made significant advancements over the years, and there are various levels of AI, ranging from narrow or weak AI, which is designed for a specific task, to general or strong AI, which possesses human-like intelligence and capabilities across a wide range of tasks.

The idea of AI replacing human intelligence raises several important considerations:

1. Functional Replacement: AI can already outperform humans in specific tasks, such as playing complex games like chess or Go, analyzing vast amounts of data, or even driving vehicles. As AI continues to progress, it may replace human labor in various industries, leading to concerns about job displacement and societal impact.

2. Cognitive Abilities: General AI, also known as artificial general intelligence (AGI), is the theoretical level of AI capable of performing any intellectual task that a human can. If AGI were to be achieved, it could potentially perform tasks across multiple domains, including those that require creativity, problem-solving, and even emotional intelligence.

3. Limitations of AI: Despite significant progress, AI still has limitations. Current AI systems lack consciousness, emotions, and self-awareness, which are fundamental aspects of human intelligence. The ability to genuinely understand and empathize with complex human emotions and intentions is not yet within the scope of AI.

4. Ethical and Social Implications: Replacing human intelligence with AI raises ethical questions about the relationship between humans and machines. It raises concerns about dependency on AI systems and the potential for losing control over these systems if they become too powerful or autonomous.

5. Superintelligence: Speculations about the development of superintelligent AI, which surpasses human intelligence in every aspect, have led to debates about the potential risks and benefits. The concept of a superintelligent AI, without considering human intentions, has given rise to the "AI alignment problem" – ensuring that an AI's goals align with human values and do not pose harm.

6. Evolution of Society: The widespread adoption of AI could lead to profound societal changes, affecting education, labor markets, privacy, and more. The integration of AI into various aspects of life will require careful consideration of its implications on human society.

It is essential to consider human intentions and choices in discussions about AI's role in society. Humans play a crucial role in the development, deployment, and regulation of AI systems. The decisions made by individuals, organizations, and governments will ultimately shape the trajectory and impact of AI on humanity.

As AI technology advances, it is vital for society to have thoughtful and inclusive discussions about the ethical, legal, and societal implications to ensure that AI's development aligns with human values and benefits humanity as a whole. (ChatGPT answer, July 20, 2023)

Figure 3. AI dialogue

So, in the end, "It is essential to consider human intentions and choices ... in the development, deployment, and regulation of AI systems."

And then, please, let's talk about it for what it is, something that depends essentially on us!

In June 2023 Members of the European Parliament «gave the green light (499 yes, 28 no, 93 abstentions) to a legislative package to regulate the use of artificial intelligence.

It is the first legislation in the world that will set global standards for years to come. We will manage AI risks on the basis of privacy and respect for EU fundamental rights such as democracy and the rule of law. Thus said the President of Parliament Roberta Metsola during the press conference. (Valdambrini, 2023, translated from Italian).

In next years the legal and ethical aspects of applying AI to an ever-increasing number of human activities, in every field, will undoubtedly be one of the key problems to be tackled and resolved in our societies.

4. THE FATE OR CHOICE OF ENHANCED BODIES

Since the human race began, human invents technology: technology invents humans. The characteristics that make us human will continue to be manifest in our relationship with technology. Technology has been woven into the social and cultural fabric of different cultures. (Tripathi, 2017, p. 100)

The technologies we have been using for decades, such as PCs and phones, usually remain physically separate from the human body. We interact with them mainly through screens, but they do not completely absorb our vision and attention, except for our intentional act of focusing exclusively on what we see. Of course, if we use headphones, our sense of hearing can be shifted from the physical reality we live in, to that of the music we listen to, or the video game we are engaged in. The environment in which we move remains in any case that of the physical reality in which we find ourselves.

Things begin to change wearing a headset and other equipment for virtual reality. That normally occurs in very particular situation, apart our daily life.

But if we, as it happens to a large part of the population, need glasses for a defect of sight and choose to use *smartglasses* instead of normal ones

Focals connect to your phone via Bluetooth and have a small projector that beams data into the wearer's eyes. They can tell the wearer the weather or time, read text messages and even order an Uber. The glasses are also connected to Alexa, so if you can ask them for directions or information, a small speaker will tell you the answers. (Isaak 2018)

This is the new technologically enhanced human being – who is not an objective artefact (a technology) but a subjective artefact of the new technologically enhanced (perceptually, cognitively, and desire - and institutionally- oriented) human subject. The social/cultural changes that this brings about are usually neither determinate nor generally foreseeable; and, because of this, the changes will demand special oversight. This new technologically-enhanced human being opens up the social imagination of users to new worlds in which there is a redistribution of powers, such as powers to intrude into and manipulate the lives of others with or without their knowledge; powers to snoop, deceive, acquire resources secretly, defeat traditional rights and privileges as well as power to depose existing institutional authorities. (Tripathi, 2017, p. 102)

Some are fascinated by the perspective of an increasingly bionic man, perpetually connected thanks to chips implanted under the skin. For others this vision arouses fear and horror. Much depends, of course, on whether we are talking about a destiny that we all must adapt to, or a choice that some humans can make.

Clearly, until technology is something that we don't know, that we have to chase even if we don't understand, that we must use always and in any case, even if we do not see the need, it will be difficult to integrate it in a serene way in our everyday life, without triggering deep fears and motions of rejection.

The concept of technomorphism (first termed mechanomorphism) was mentioned initially in passing by Caporael (1986) as a "schema (albeit an elaboration of anthropomorphism) used by the scientific community, especially by researchers in artificial intelligence and cognitive science ... For example, in explaining how human memory works, it is common to describe the human memory system by using RAM as a symbol of working memory, whereas a computer hard drive can be considered a long-term memory structure. Thinking in technomorphic terms can help us understand a complex structure such as the brain in much simpler concrete and relatable ways. Because the construct of technonomorphism would not be present without the presence of technology, so next will be a discussion of how the world has changed in the wake of technology's presence. (Lum, 2021)

5. MACHINES ALONGSIDE AND NOT IN PLACE OF THE LIVED EXPERIENCE

Technology, creativity, education: fear or opportunities?

The root of the term creativity lies in the Latin verb creare, meaning to bring something forth, to produce something. For several centuries, this term was not applied to human activities. It was, rather, associated with the generative powers of gods and of nature. (Creativity: An Overview, in Marzano, 2022)

The digital revolution has transformed human social behavior, providing untold opportunities for people to become involved in collaborative activities. Accordingly, crowd-based applications offer a new way of collecting innovative ideas and solutions in many fields and from all types of people, not necessarily only professionals. (Social Creativity, in Marzano, 2022)

Irreverence, protest, insolence, derision, arrogance, mockery, discomfort, and disgust are often contemporary artists' basic ingredients to build their artistic productions. Technology can help them to express their originality hyperbolically. (The Arts, Creativity, and Digital Technologies, in Marzano, 2022)

The major innovations seem to emerge in the field of education. Digital technologies increasingly stimulate the interest of educators, offering extraordinary means of creating and experimenting with innovative forms of teaching-learning. (Creativity Research in the Digital Age: Current Trends, in Marzano, 2022)

A balance is possible, even if perhaps we have to look a little aside from the global market, apart from the spotlights of mainstream communication, among common people, free artists, silent builders of peace, the humble, the children, the people who take their time to watch the show and the stories of nature.

I meet a couple in a garden, aged, at the foot of a tree, looking at the leaves and at their phone, thinking. They tell me: "It seems to be a *Taxodium Distichum,* a bald cypress, the leaves, the cones, but here in the pictures we see its roots like knees, and this has not."

I'm not very expert, but I know that tree, like the other trees in that park, that I've been exploring several times with the kids.

So, I say: "It is a *Taxodium. Pneumatophores*, they form when the tree grows in water, to collect oxygen. This is in the ground, it doesn't need. If you go and see the others, by the pond, they do have knees."

PlantNet is one of the most useful and effective applications I have on my phone. It is not the only one of its kind, but it works well, it's completely free and, aimed at a community use, does not stress you with continuous advertising.

Simply taking a picture of the leaves, the blooms, the fruits, or seeds of a tree, it tells you what tree it can be, by percentage. If you have both leaves and blooms, obviously it is easier to identify the plant. You can also consider bark, but it is not such a good identifying element, because many trees have similar. It is also good for herbs, flowers and, using it often you learn a lot of things that, when you look back with your eyes, they see better. If one is sure of his identification and his photos are good, he can add them to the general online data base, so that they will help further identification by anyone in the world. With photos, localization is also added, so we also know where the plants are located.

In the case of a swamp cypress in an Italian city park, we know it is not an autochthonous plant, because it comes originally from the swamps of Florida or Guatemala. But evidently it grows well also in Europe. The one we were observing is small, young, maybe born spontaneously, or sown, or grafted when about twenty years ago they opened this new part of the park, from the tall, impressive, centenarian ones which live on the other side.

This is a very simple, ordinary scene, but how different from the stereotype of the humans lost in the screen of their phones and separated from the real world! And there's no need for a technology supplement from simple consultation of texts and photographs to compare with the real object: not an augmented reality that adds anything else to what we already see in front of the eyes and in the phone display, nor a reconstructed virtual reality, we don't know by whom, in which to dive into. There's the tree, there are the photographs I'm just taking, and the possibility through the web of linking that tree and those pictures

Figure 4. Plantnet

to the other pictures that people like me have taken in other parts of the world, to have news about that tree. There are probably some expert people who manage the application and periodically oversee the data base of pictures but, since the photos are practically evaluated by themselves when they receive a percentage of correspondence, it's difficult experience big mistakes.

For the app to work and be useful, you need not only to make your senses work, in this case your vision, but also your brain, which coordinates the experience data dynamically. Because the leaves are not always the same on trees, they can be just born, or on the verge of falling, and flowers, fruits, seeds have their times of growth and maturation, as well as being terribly different from one plant to another...

This kind of observations so inside nature, with instant feedback all across the world, were simply not possible before smartphones, as it was not possible, only by pointing the screen at the night sky, recognize in a few moments that star, at that moment, as only an experienced astronomer or a sailor would be able to do. Some star recognition apps are also too rich in extra information, sometimes it becomes complicated just that first look at the sky, but usually you can also communicate with the authors, the software developers, and you can send them suggestions to organize the menus better and separate, for example, from a graphic point of view the basic observation from additional information, or easily remove and replace certain overlays of mythological beings that maybe I do not need when I would simply know if that star is Sirius, or Vega, or Altair.

User experience is now becoming central to our understanding of the usability of technology. Today many interactive technology companies describe on their Web sites their commitment to experience based design. There is also a trend in HCI communities to foreground experience centered approaches to technology, a movement reflected in several recent articles offering theoretical statements about the sensual and emotional conditions of interaction with technology. (McCarthy and Wright, 2004)

User experience is becoming a key term in the world of interactive product design. The term itself lacks proper theoretical definition and is used in many different, even contradictory, ways ... To address this, a new elaboration called co-experience is presented. It builds on an existing approach but borrows from symbolic interactionism to create a more inclusive interactionist framework for thinking about user experiences. (Battarbee & Koskinen, 2004)

User experience is basically the sum or flow of feelings that the customer gets when using your device, webpage, or system. In many businesses, the user experience of the product is already the key battlefield. Forget about launching the newest technologies unless you have designed a great user experience around them.

Just look at the mobile phone industry. Was Apple the first company to apply touch screens to a smart phone? No. Touch screens existed in the mobile phone industry at least ten years before Apple launched the first iPhone. Bui Apple managed to create an excellent user experience for this old technology. Nokia, which used to be seen as the leader in user experience, failed for several years to create even an acceptable user experience for touch screen devices, and this is now reflected very much in the market situation. (Kraft, 2012)

People, the world, technology as a "natural" aid, an extension of the senses, helping you as when you have to find a way traveling by car. When one has learned – normally it's not so difficult - how to use it, few feel uncomfortable with a satellite navigator, and with some ease also learn not to listen to it, when it sometimes sends you for bends and vittles in the fields and you know that there is a straight road a little further...

Choosing not to run after technology according to the suggestions of the market or the trend of bureaucracy, but simply to use it when it meets our interests and needs, it may be not so weird an idea, and probably would immediately make our relationship with digital gadgets much more serene than attending courses, buying the latest model of mobile phone every year, or being caught in immersive Disneyland-like environments where someone will solve for us a lot of problems that we don't even have right now, as all the story of the metaverse seems to be.

Too easy? Yes indeed, and kids already do it, and when we succeed in doing it, suddenly everything begins to work.

We must shape technologies in accordance with human values and needs, instead of allowing technologies to shape humans. Our task is not only to rein in the downsides of information and communication technologies, but to encourage human-centered innovation. We call for a Digital Humanism that describes, analyzes, and, most importantly, influences the complex interplay of technology and humankind, for a better society and life, fully respecting universal human rights. (Vienna Manifesto on Digital Humanism, 2019)

Figure 5. Digital humanism

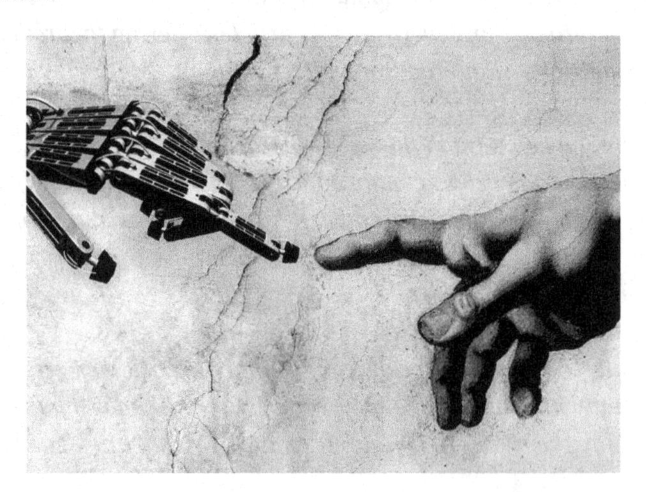

6. BIO AND SOFT DIVERSITY: THE LIBRARY AND THE STORE

Ecopsychologists argue that if we accept the ecological view that we are members of the biotic community, rather than mere exploiters, than we may learn to recognize the natural world as a social and psychological field, just as we do the human community. (Fisher, 2013)

Once I published a book whose title and subtitle were: *I bambini e l'ambiente: per una ecologia dell'educazione* (Children and the environment: for an ecology of education)

Educating to the environment is a bit like educating to be citizens, to civil coexistence not only with people, but also with the natural world, plants, animals, rivers, seas, mountains. Issue of particular importance today that the ability of man to transform and upset the planet in which we live has become enormous and is causing the effects of which we are not able to assess the exact scope.

To know the environment, or perhaps better perceive it. Not so much the technical expertise of experts in the various disciplines in their respective fields of intervention, how much the ability to feel ourselves as part of a whole, and therefore directly, deeply, personally involved. (Beneventi 2009, p. 20, translated from Italian)

Ecology is also, in the relationship between the human being and the environment - nature, things, society - seeking harmony rather that conflict, find in different situations the right balance point. (Beneventi 2009, p. 189)

We all know that one of the main indicators of the state of nature on our planet is the so-called biodiversity:

Biodiversity refers to the variety of living species on Earth, including plants, animals, bacteria, and fungi.

Scientists have estimated that there are around 8.7 million species of plants and animals in existence. However, only around 1.2 million species have been identified and described so far, most of which are insects.

Pollution, climate change, and population growth are all threats to biodiversity. These threats have caused an unprecedented rise in the rate of species extinction. Some scientists estimate that half of all species on Earth will be wiped out within the next century. (Biodiversity, National Geographic encyclopedic entry)

I would like to propose here, obviously not as a scientific category, to consider a possible analogy between biodiversity and "soft-diversity".

I believe that thinking by analogy, also because by its nature it lends itself to being elastic, not integralist and naturally open to suggestions and evolutions, it can be a good basis for a philosophy of everyday life that helps to understand and live the complexity of the present time, in truly inclusive ways that do not put people and ideas against one another.

Thus, just as the disappearance of plant and animal species impoverishes the environment, I believe it is reasonable to suppose that the disappearance of ideas and points of view within human societies can impoverish culture and civil coexistence. And software can be a powerful indicator, also quite easy to monitor.

Software, however, should not be understood only as programs and applications, but especially as documents: texts, images, videos, multimedia, and any other kind of data, which today are produced in huge quantities and that because of this fact itself are difficult to process, store, recover and use, and over which the vast mass of citizens of the information society has no control.

Moreover, as already mentioned in Chapter 4, the change that often occurs in the software used in the production and reading of different types of documents according to market mechanisms, together with the coexistence of different and sometimes incompatible encoding formats, can lead to situations in which digital documents can be completely unreadable within a few years.

Without going to see old literature publications in CD ROM of the 90s, or encyclopedias that had each their built-in software player among the files contained in the disk (and that still often allows us to access that material) only the differences between the different formats of the eBooks pose serious doubts about the real possibility of overcoming soon and easily paper books with their digital counterpart.

PDF is the most common ebook format in electronic scholarly publishing. While PDF does not allow for the greater functionality offered by ebook readers and other mobile devices, most readers and devices can accommodate it.

There are over twenty different types of ebook formats other than PDF. Some of the most widely used are listed below.

.AZW is Amazon's proprietary format for its Kindle devices, and only works on Kindles.

EPUB is an open standard ebook format that is supported by almost all e-readers and devices.

.PRC is the Mobipocket e-reader format which uses XHTML and Javascript.

.PDB is an ebook format for Palm OS devices that is frequently supported by other devices, as well.

E-Books are also published in familiar formats such as .txt, .doc, .docx, and .html. (eBooks: Formats & Devices, 2023)

Depending on the format and support, layout and appearance of electronic books can change dramatically.

The publications on paper - bulky, in some ways limited and by many periodically given for finished within a short time - have the great advantage of an "operating system" tested for many centuries, which is directly interfaced to the eyes of the reader, without the need for machines, electricity, decoders or anything else. The greatest limit is given by the support, which is not eternal, especially the paper used in recent decades, and therefore depends a lot on how they are kept. But if we go and see other media used during las century over time, vinyl and digital discs, analog audio and video cassettes, floppy disks, not to mention others less popular like laser discs, minidiscs, digital audiocassettes, maybe the paper is still the one that, to access content, poses fewer problems.

For each type of digital production, the number of formats in which it can be found encoded is actually huge, and this depends on several factors: efficiency, size, properties. There are compressed formats that are very good for traveling online and in social networks, others instead, aiming at the highest quality, contain a large amount of data and occupy a lot of space. The general user does not have to worry about these things and often, when for example he comes across images, on the screen of a laptop or smartphone, he does not notice the difference. There are also a lot of programs with which you can convert anything from one format to another.

Problems can arise when a format that has been popular stops being used and, for a number of reasons, you no longer find a way to read it. Then the images, the music, the texts that have been encoded in that format, they risk becoming inaccessible, and we to lose pieces of history.

Since it's a complex subject, let's just give two small examples, to make the idea.

Amiga computers were popular with creatives in the 1980s and 1990s. The file names did not need the so-called extensions (which in Windows are mandatory, even if sometimes hidden!), but in fact, for convenience and compatibility with other systems, to the most popular Amiga image format it was assigned the extension .iff, while for music produced with sequencers the standard format was .mod. Thousands of images and music were produced and spread in CDs and online, which at the time when the Amiga systems had run out on the market risked disappearing. Among the software available today, *Paint Sho Pro* for example reads the files .iff and *VLC* the .mod, but this happens quite by chance.

Files with the extension .fli and .flc (together named "FLIC" or also "FLH") did not run on a system defeated on the market, but on the absolute leader, MS dos, which would later evolve into Windows. They were the standard for the first, pioneering 3D animations that, devised by talented enthusiasts and published in thousands on CD ROMs, opened the way to those so largely used in contemporary film productions. It happens at some point that the Windows media player no longer reads those formats. Why? It seems quite absurd that the Microsoft system no longer recognizes the standard productions on Microsoft systems of few years before. But if you want to see those old animations, you must use *Quick Time*, which is Apple's. Now that also *Quick Time* is gone, how do I do if I happen to want to see the animations collected in an old CD ROM?

Figure 6. 3D Studio 1997

1997

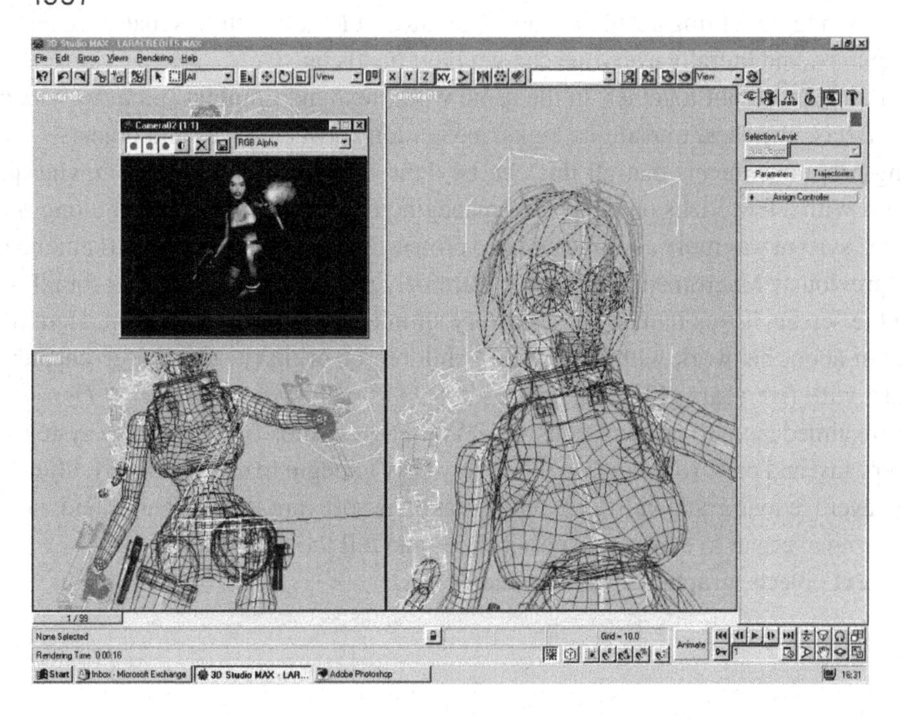

From a technical point of view, it takes nothing (or not so much, anyhow!) to make a new software read even old or rare formats. It is the idea behind *libraries* that the works of human genius are collected and made available, even if they are of interest to a few. While the idea behind the *store* is that the new merchandise replaces and makes the old one useless.

So, having mentioned the FLIC format, if we go browsing the Web for old screens of Autodesk *3D Studio*, a software that made the history of animation in the 90s, it's quite difficult to find them, as searches are addressed almost all to *3ds Max*, that is the new application that have replaced it.

In these digital times, a large part of cultural production does not follow the rules from the library, but from the store.

7. ONCE UPON A TIME… AND SOMEWHERE AROUND: MULTIMEDIA AUTHOR PROGRAMS

Again, examples here at the smallest terms, not to draw conclusions, but to introduce problems, where to have the map of so many problems, although hard to solve, it is probably more important than not going to see and deal with problems one by one. If "shortcuts" can make us less afraid, and we delude ourselves that we can do it, but when the other related and ignored problems come back, they'll make our lives more and more complicated, which is what is happening lately in the most diverse areas of human activities.

Multimedia and authoring software was probably, in my opinion, the most exciting adventure in the era of PCs. Why? Because, after the time of the first software almost only mathematical or for office, text and command based and difficult to manage, the time of the BASIC programming language with which it was easy for everyone to "code", but only for extremely simple tasks, the time of the first home processing of graphics and music, that allowed those who had artistic talent to do something great, here it was finally coming something absolutely new, that did not look like things that were done before even without computers, and literally everyone can get their hands on.

Multimedia means to put together, in the same work, text and graphics, pictures, video, sound and music, with effects, switches, transitions, links, navigation between pages and objects.

Authoring programs means that all this can be done by anybody, without knowing programming languages, just with a few clicks on the screen managing objects on the screen or along scores.

The "score" system was more complicated and professional – and the state of art among this software was Adobe (previously Macromedia) *Director*, extremely powerful but indeed not for all! – but moving "objects" in the screen, it was in many cases a very simple and intuitive operation. Here the author has already written about his work with objects and children of primary school (see chapter 3.07). With them, but also with five years old, he mainly used *Scala* (or its twin *Infochannel Designer*), a professional software aimed more to presentations and TV, used in studios first on Amiga systems and later on Windows, very fast and powerful, but also incredibly easy to begin to use. Normally, after 15 minutes of presentation, average four grade kids were able to take the software in their hands and, not individually but in small groups, began to explore its possibilities and tell the first stories.

There are text objects, graphic objects, sound objects:

Each type of object has its intrinsic properties (e.g. a text object can be changed with the keyboard on the page, while a sound object on the page is not visible, but of course you hear it!), and others that we must define (the color of a text, the volume of a voice, image input effect etc.)

On some objects you can apply special properties, and links to other objects, which allow what is called "navigation", that is the possibility to move through multimedia hypertexts, the web pages, interactive video game menus, etc. (Beneventi and Conati 2010, p.208, translated from Italian)

Here there is obviously no room to talk about the many author programs, easy or powerful, expensive, cheap, available during the 90's on different platforms. They could be the basis for the so-called multimedia publishing that, after the first interesting but often clumsy attempts, has practically ceased to exist before even being born. The works at those times were published on CD ROMs, and after the advent of Web 2 a certain production continued to develop online, where, however, the context of fast consultation and the progressive commercialization of the internet, has not favored its development and understanding. People went back to the consumption of mono media, books, music albums, movies, while those who wanted to continue doing things like with the author programs, had to fall back on software for presentations, as *Power Point*. Power Point does manage pages and objects, with their properties, transitions, links. But it was born to accompany human interventions in conferences, not to design video games!

If we look in nature, animals have worked out so many ways to fly: Birds, insects, bats, flapping and shaking wings, gliding, diving, standing in mid-air, and each of these ways works and evolves. Humans, beginning to use new machines they never had before, were beginning to develop new alphabets to tell new stories of different objects together, perhaps the dawn of a new communication, in the hand of everybody. But having entrusted everything to the market, out of the professional fields remained only a software for lecturers and all the others have stopped speaking the new alphabets...

Also online, the "choice" of normally producing works addressed to the stores more than to libraries, is causing a standardization of the web, to which from a cultural point of view it is difficult to find a sense. Web sites can be shops online, personal blogs, photo and art expositions, scientific, religious, government pages, works by children of schools, train timetables, weather reports, recipes, and other thousands of possibilities, covering all human activities, as information, expression, communication.

Instead of attending a general search to learn how to use this new universal medium, the website, available only since few years, in all possible declination, such as it normally happens with books, videos, photographs, so no one would ever dream of applying for example the same criteria of fashion photos to architecture photos, we often witness the curious application of general criteria to each website (SEO, fashion graphics, etc.), as well as the standard use of a software born obviously to make blogs, which, despite the different templates available, being in fact rather rigid, it makes too many sites today to look all alike in an impressive and annoying way.

Stores, not libraries, so that *WordPress* is driving now in the 2020s the global web communication in the same way as *Power Point* has driven at a certain point what remained of multimedia, according to a *Pensée unique* that denies soft diversity for the large mass of the citizens users.

The fact remains that, if the individuals or the groups go looking around, in the folds of online stores, in the catalogs of commercial and free software, in the myriad of industrial and amateur productions, they can still find all the possible alternatives, of thinking and software, programs and documents that don't just go with the current there, and they can use them. But it is not easy to still attend the library,

Figure 7. DeLuxePaint

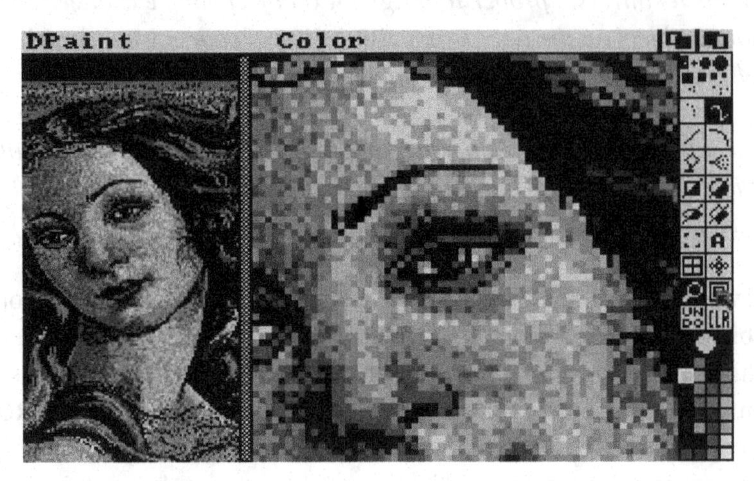

when the whole system, market, school, public opinion, inexorably almost always revolve around the store, where all people, to make things *simple*, buy and use the same products.

The author apologizes for this simplification but, in the end, we live in a world where, in front of infinite sets of available possibilities from the digital stuff, we are educated to use only few, possibly one, the most successful, the one everyone uses, and not by choice, but often by mere ignorance. We are told by the monastic school what are the textbooks on which we must study the lessons, instead of being ourselves the authors of our knowledge. (see chapter 5).

Paint programs were and are a true universe. During the 90s, trying things like *DeLuxePaint* or *Personal Paint* on Amiga, *Flying Colors* on Mac and Windows, and possible many other demo or free software one could find around, it simply could mean to understand what is *painting* using a computer, and how using computers can be an amazing non-stop looking for, until we find the right tool we like! But referring by default, as often it happened in schools, to a "sad and closed" program like Microsoft *Paint* (all software were updated every year, only *Paint* was always the same, along the years and the decades, and this probably was not by chance!) it meant just for children turning off that kind of research, at a certain point of which the light bulb lights up and one understands: "So, that's the way they do it!" (see chapter 3.08) They don't need to have the catalog of everything, but simply a software that invites them, if they take that tool and that color, to play with what happens, possibly together. From this point of view, even the very simple *Tuxpaint* is a "cheerful and open" software, and still some people wonder why Microsoft itself chose not to develop from its kids division a good piece of software as *Fine Artist*, out for Windows 3.1 in 1994, given then with Windows 95, but closed in 1997. Shame! Though they now, from 2016 give for free the new *Paint 3D* with the system, that's indeed a good quality leap from the previous painting software.

Let's remember it once more. Newborn children do not have an established study program, they "interface" to the whole world around without the problem that it is "too much" and, choosing what interests them, they learn a lot. When, within a few years, someone at school establishes what they need to learn, and selects things to make them "easier", then the problems begin (see chapter 7). And education in this sense does not aim to develop children's abilities, but rather to ensure adult control over them.

Writing about soft-diversity, and in general digital diversity, a hint may be done to the Nintendo *Wii* game console. That is, we are not talking about a product on the margin of the marked, but a leader, able to surpass in sales the most powerful and performing Sony *PlayStation* and Microsoft *Xbox*.

From the first Magnavox and Atari of the 70s, consoles had always been controlled with fingers, using increasingly elaborate joysticks and joypads, or dedicated accessories, such as pistols or rifles in shooting games, or steering wheels in driving ones. Hence the rather sad image of generations of children closed at home glued to screens and chairs, tending to obesity for too sedentary play but with very agile joints of the hands, even if sometimes sore from overtraining.

Out in 2006, «Wii changes everything around. The protagonist of the games becomes the whole body and, as they often interest a group and demand for more space, the device, more than in the children's room, is proposed to be kept in the living room and used by the whole family. So it happens that in sports games, thanks to a Bluetooth control that, held in hand, detects with great precision position and movements, the player moves as if he/she were actually holding a tennis racket, a sword, a baseball bat or a golf club, or pulling a bow or boxing, throwing a bowling ball or a Frisbee». (Beneventi, 2023)

One of the most successful software was *WiiFit*, based on the *Wii Balance Board*, an accessory on which the user can stay and perform a wide range of yoga and muscle exercises and various and fun balance games, guiding attention, and controlling the body, especially posture. The balance and the software worked, had a great success for the public and were also applied in physiotherapy and rehabilitation.

The purpose of this study is to investigate the effect of Nintendo Wii Fit exercise program to health-related physical fitness and quality of life among university students ... the Nintendo Wii Fit exercise program during 12 weeks may influence the body composition, health-related physical fitness, and QOL. (Hyun Joo, 2015)

But, as we have already seen, not always things that work well last on the market.

Today *Scala* Designer has become a very specialized and expensive signage software used for banks and airports, while the *Wii Balance Board* has not been resumed for the next Nintendo *Switch* console, which also incorporates many features of the *Wii* and remains market leader.

It is not easy to find permanently in stores what we have not put in libraries. Not only for the past, but for the future, towards which it would be important not to go completely blind:

Computers are one of mankind's most significant achievements, and the devices have enabled an era of change that is more rapid than any other time in history. Historical record is a vital, precious thing. We've kept records of just about everything since before written language. Cloud computing has no time for the past, though ... During the age of local software, they'll have tons of software that still works, either on an ancient piece of hardware or via emulation. If you wanted to see the first version of Microsoft Word, that's as easy as getting a copy of the software and installing it on the appropriate computer. What if you move forward a few years, though, and you want to take a look at the first version of Google Docs? You can't. It was entirely hosted on a Google server, and that server has been shut down. (Amadeo, 2014)

8. SOFTWARE: COMMODITY, SERVICE, OPEN TOOLS? OR THE INTANGIBLE FUTURE OF THE WORLD?

What is software technically, conceptually, commercially, socially?

Usually, the laymen dare not ask themselves such a question, which is thought to concern those who know more, experts, technicians. The fact is that this is not a technical issue. Software has been literally changing the world for several decades, and empires are being built on software with immense power over information, finance, and politics, all over the planet.

Perhaps only in intriguing television series, perhaps even in reality, those who hold the software could rule the world, and it's obvious how this affects every citizen on the earth. If only to understand if everything is established and decided elsewhere, without any possibility of action by ordinary people, or if each of us is in a position to have his say, participate, perhaps even decide.

Software is a new word, born in opposition to *hardware*, a term with which computers were once defined in a rather derogatory way, when it was clear that those jewels of refined technology, with all their processors, memories, cards, ultra integrated circuits, were in themselves unable to do anything. To work, computers need commands, sets of instructions, programs, which determine and even completely change the way the computers themselves work.

Software defines by analogy something intangible that would otherwise be difficult to call. That is a new word to say that the operation of a machine, for the first time in history, does not depend mainly on how the machine is made.

Traditionally, software has been considered to be a commodity. As a refresher, the term "commodity" refers to a basic good used in commerce that is interchangeable with other commodities of the same type. (van Zanten, 2017)

Software sold as a commodity, with a shrink wrap license, an idea pioneered by MicroSoft in 1975 with the release of Microsoft Basic. (Commodity Software, wiki.c2.com)

Low-Code, AI-driven development, GitHub's co-pilot: there is a long list of new inventions that are accelerating and simplifying software and application development.

What will happen to the traditional developer role, as new tools & technologies transform how software is built & deployed? Software developers: are they at risk of extinction? (Keller, 2022)

This most evolved outcome-based consumption model, where the initial financing is guaranteed and repaid by the sought economic value outcomes from the technology solution, can be called Consumption 4.0, where customers are not paying for consumption, but rather become collaborative partners with the technology provider, as both strive to achieve mutually beneficial goals. (Salem, 2020)

Programming will be obsolete. I believe the conventional idea of "writing a program" is headed for extinction, and indeed, for all but very specialized applications, most software, as we know it, will be replaced by AI systems that are trained rather than programmed. In situations where one needs a "simple" program (after all, not everything should require a model of hundreds of billions of parameters running on a cluster of GPUs), those programs will, themselves, be generated by an AI rather than coded by hand.

99% of people who are writing software have almost no clue how a CPU actually works, let alone the physics underlying transistor design. By extension, I believe the computer scientists of the future will be so far removed from the classic definitions of "software".

The new atomic unit of computation becomes not a processor, memory, and I/O system implementing a von Neumann machine, but rather a massive, pre-trained, highly adaptive AI model. This is a seismic shift in the way we think about computation—not as a predictable, static process, governed by instruction sets, type systems, and notions of decidability. AI-based computation has long since crossed the Rubicon of being amenable to static analysis and formal proof. We are rapidly moving toward a world where the fundamental building blocks of computation are temperamental, mysterious, adaptive agents. (Welsh, 2023)

You could imagine asking Alexa to make you an app to help organize your kitchen. AI would recognize the features, pick the correct patterns and in real time, over the air deliver an application to your mobile phone or maybe into your wearable mobile computer. (Ficklin, quoted in McKendrick, 2022)

What we should try to imagine more is an interaction with artificial intelligence that is not primarily related to our current models of individual consumption, but within processes of shared human intelligence that technology makes technically possible, but that our habits have so far stopped us from practicing.

So called *DevOps* in the software development and IT industry goes in this direction.

DevOps describes the adoption of iterative software development, automation, and programmable infrastructure deployment and maintenance. The term also covers culture changes, such as building trust and cohesion between developers and systems administrators and aligning technological projects to business requirements. DevOps can change the software delivery chain, services, job roles, IT tools and best practices.

DevOps is a methodology meant to improve work throughout the software development lifecycle. You can visualize a DevOps process as an infinite loop, comprising these steps: plan, code, build, test, release, deploy, operate, monitor and - through feedback - plan, which resets the loop. (Courtemanche, M. et al., 3023).

It sounds like the circle of life!

Martin Chikilian, a software developer formerly for IBM and Hewlett Packard with over a decade of experience employing DevOps principles, puts it in simple, concrete terms: "DevOps people are basically those who have found interest in both systems administration and software development and decided to combine their skills to create a unified, better approach to both."

DevOps is about translating complex manual processes involving error-prone human interaction into an instrumented approach that can be tested, measured, and easily scaled. For example, if a developer would like to create an environment that allows business users to provide feedback, he or she can initiate an automated process in which the developer can issue a command created by the DevOps team (rather

Figure 8. dev-ops or alternative + eventually

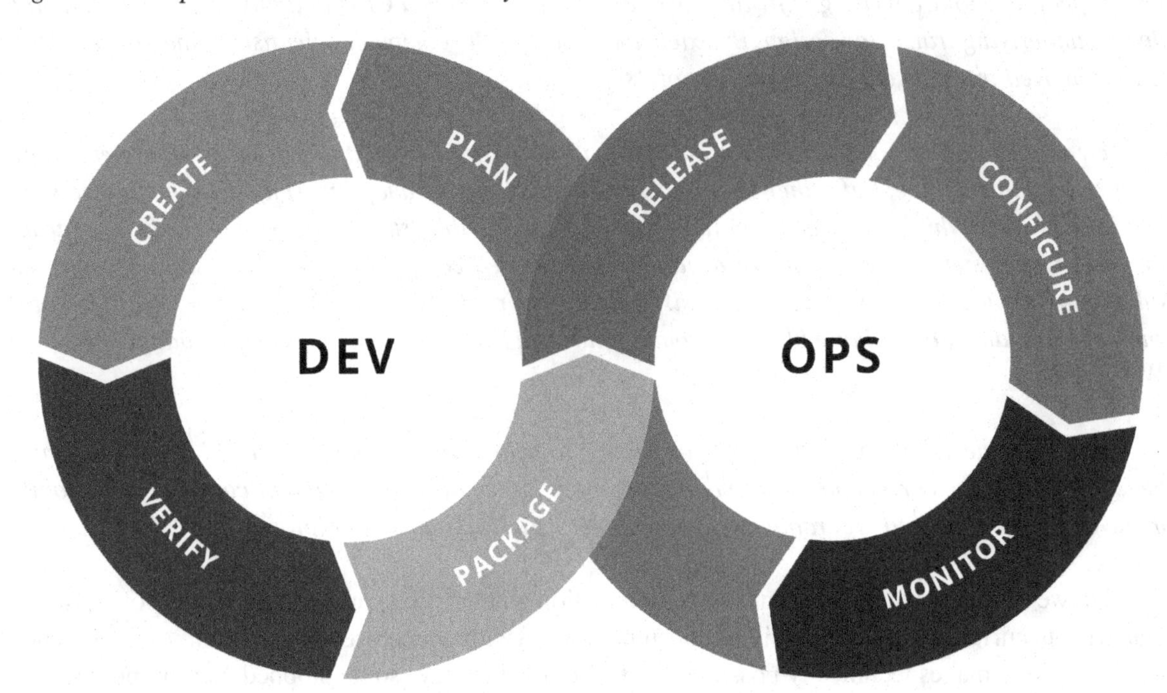

than handing off a piece of code to the infrastructure team), which performs the relevant task in a consistent and tested way, getting to the expected results quickly and enabling collaboration. (Oliveira, n.d.)

A successful "combination of cultural philosophies" applying DevOps methodologies is Amazon. Where other important questions to be faced in the practical application along all the process are the role and the rights of human workers.

REFERENCES

Amadeo, R. (2014, Jun 18). *Saving old software from extinction in the age of cloud computing*. Arstechnica.com.

Battarbee, K., & Koskinen, I. (2004). Co-experience: User experience as interaction. *International Journal of CoCreation in Design and the Arts, 1*, 2005.

Beneventi, P. (2009). *I bambini e l'Ambiente: per una Ecologia dell'Educazione*. Sonda.

Beneventi, P. (2023, Jan 18). Il successo di mercato, i videogiochi e il corpo. *Sapereambiente*.

Beneventi, P., & Conati, D. (2010). *Nuova Guida di Animazione Teatrale*. Sonda.

Biodiversity. (n.d.). *National Geographic*.

Courtemanche, M. (2023, Jan 22). *What is DevOps? The ultimate guide*. Academic Press.

Damasio, A. R. (1999). *The Feeling of what Happens: Body and Emotion in the Making of Consciousness*. Harcourt Brace.

de Kerckhove, D. (2023, May 11). Il linguaggio sfidato dagli algoritmi nell'era dell'IA generativa. *Media 2000*.

Deluxe Paint Series: A Visual Arts Program if Immense Flexibility. (2020, May 18). generationamiga.com.

eBooks: Formats & Devices. (2023). *Boston College Libraries*, web.

Failes, I. (2020, Jun 4). *A visual history of 3ds Max.* beforesandafters.com/

Fisher, A. (2013). *Radical ecopsychology: Psychology in the service of life*. SUNY Press.

Greg, W. (n.d.). *Aligning AI Through Compassionate Dialogue*. medium.com/@gregwnotsosharp

Grierson, J. (2023, Apr 17). Photographer admits prize-winning image was AI-generated. *The Guardian*.

Hyun Joo, M. (2015). Effect of Nintendo Wii Fit Exercise Program to Health-related Physical Fitness and Quality of Life among University Students. *Indian Journal of Science and Technology, 8*(8), 1-6.

Isaak, A. (2018, Oct 23). *These $1,000 smart glasses tell you the weather, read text messages and connect to Alexa.* Cnbc.com.

Kazlev, M. A. (2022). The Collective Unconscious and the Media Sphere: An Esoteric Analysis of the Disinformation Crisis Facing Western Civilisation. In *Handbook of Research on Global Media's Preternatural Influence on Global Technological Singularity, Culture, and Government*. IGI Global. doi:10.4018/978-1-7998-8884-0.ch004

Keller, D. (2022, Dec 5*). Software Developers: At Risk of Extinction?* [Infographic]. five.co/blog.

Kraft, C. (2012). *User Experience Innovation: User Centered Design that Works*. New York: APress.

Louv, R. (2008). *Last Child in the Woods, Saving our Children from Nature-Deficit Disorder*. Algonquin Books.

Lum, H. C. (2021). Exploring Technology Tendencies and Their Impact on Human-Human Interactions. In *Human Factors Issues and the Impact of Technology on Society*. IGI Global. doi:10.4018/978-1-7998-6453-0.ch010

Marzano, G. (2022). Creativity: An Overview; Social Creativity; The Arts, Creativity, and Digital Technologies; Creativity Research in the Digital Age: Current Trends. In *Sustaining Creativity and the Arts in the Digital Age*. IGI Global. doi:10.4018/978-1-7998-7840-7

McCarthy, J., & Wright, P. (2004). Technology as experience. *Interactions (New York, N.Y.), 11*(5), 42–43. doi:10.1145/1015530.1015549

McKendrick, J. (2022, Dec. 28). *It's the end of programming as we know it – again*. zdnet.com/topic/business.

Melonashi, E. (2019). Social Media and Identity: Understanding Identity Communication and Creation Through Social Media. In *Internet and Technology Addiction: Breakthroughs in Research and Practice*. IGI Global. doi:10.4018/978-1-5225-8900-6.ch001

Oliveira, A. (n.d.). *DevOps: What It Is and Why It Matters*. Toptal Insights. toptal.com/insights

Ollagnier-Beldame, M. (2020, December 2). A Body of Knowledge: The Role of Human Experience and the Living Body in Knowing. *Journal of Humanistic Psychology*. journals.sagepub.com

Pierluigi Riti, P. (2018, Jan 18). *Introduzione al Devops*. italiancoders.it.

PlantNet: l'app gratuita che riconosce le piante. (2021, May 22). ogigia.altervista.org/Portale/articoli/48-software

Salem, A. & Gadhi, S. (2020). *The Evolution of Technology Consumption*. techtrends.tech. Quantela.com.

Serafini, M. (2021). *Sostenere la sostenibilità* [Master Thesis]. Università Nicolà Cusano – telematica, Roma.

TechTarget. + ev. (2023, May 11). *Il linguaggio sfidato dagli algoritmi nell'era dell'IA generativa*. Media 2000.

Topham, G., & Smith, H. (2019, Mar 29). Investigators 'believe Ethiopian 737 Max's anti-stall system activated'. *The Guardian*.

Tripathi, A. K. (2017). Bodies and Technologies: Transformation of Human Experience. *Quadranti –. Rivista Internazionale di Filosofia Contemporanea*, *5*(1-2), 102.

Tucker, C. D. (2020, Apr. 23). *What is DevOps?* carldeantucker.com/blog/

Valdambrini, A. (2023, Jun 21). Intelligenza artificiale: la Ue alla ricerca del centro di gravità permanente. *Sapereambiente*.

Van Zanten, N. (2017, Oct 12). *Zoho One Review: Shifting Software from Commodity to Utility*. zbrains.net.

Vienna Manifesto on Digital Humanism. (2019). *The Digital Humanism Initiative*. caiml.dbai.tuwien.ac.at

Welsh, M. (2023, January). The End of Programming. *Communications of the ACM*, *66*(1), 34–35. doi:10.1145/3570220

ADDITIONAL READING

Allam, A. H. (2013). User Experience: Challenges and Opportunities. *Journal of Information Systems Research and Innovation*. seminar.utmspace.edu.my

Benyon, D. (2019). *Designing User Experience: A guide to HCI, UX and Interaction Design*. Pearson.

Bulterman, D & Hardman, L. (1995, Oct). *Multimedia Authoring Tools: State of the Art and Research Challenges*. researchgate.net/publication.

Goble, D. J., Cone, B. L., & Fling, B. W. (2014). Using the Wii Fit as a tool for balance assessment and neurorehabilitation: The first half decade of "Wii-search". *Journal of Neuroengineering and Rehabilitation*, *11*(1), 12. doi:10.1186/1743-0003-11-12 PMID:24507245

Gordon, E. C. (2023). *Human Enhancement and Well-Being: A Case for Optimism*. Routledge.

Hypermedia/Multimedia authoring systems as cognitive tools. (2001). *The Association for Educational Communications and Technology*. members.aect.or

Locatis, C., & Al-Nuaim, H. (1999). Interactive technology and authoring tools: A historical review and analysis. *Educational Technology Research and Development*, *47*(3), 63–75. doi:10.1007/BF02299634

Multimedia Authoring Software For The PC. (1995, Feb). soundonsound.com/people

he FLIC file format. (n.d). *compuphase.com*

Tripette, J. (2017). The contribution of Nintendo *Wii Fit* series in the field of health: a systematic review and meta-analysis. *National Center for Biotechnology Information*. ncbi.nlm.nih.gov/pmc/articles

Van Houtryve, T. (2023, Jul 15). VII Talk: Documentary Photography in the Era of Generative A.I. with Fred Ritchin. *tomasvh.com*.

Werthner, H. (2022). *Perspectives on Digital Humanism*. Springer. doi:10.1007/978-3-030-86144-5

Why human enhancement technology requires technological citizenship. (2018, Apr 13). *Rathenau Instituut*. rathenau.nl/en

Chapter 9
Inside and Outside Devices, the Software and the World:
Humans Can Search, Know, Invent

ABSTRACT

Google engine for searching, Gmail for mail, YouTube for videos, Meet for meetings. Discussing Whatsapp about Instagram and Facebook... People entrust their interactions with the world, social relationships, business, expression to a small bunch of global providers, look with hope and fear at artificial intelligence... Control is elsewhere anyway, technology familiar and alien. But if we look carefully through the online software stores for smartphones or go and see some computer magazines of the 1990s, we come across an incredible variety of programs, simple, complex, trivial, professional. Not rigid categories in which cowed consumers seek security and find themselves imprisoned, but a world of ideas, often realized, because software can be not only bought, but made, if not by all by many, even non-specialists. In many respects it's a return to craftsmanship, to people who, with the help of very advanced machines, make on their own things.

1. INTRODUCTION

In science fiction, big companies producing robots or global software are often at the center of events that put the earth at serious risk, almost like the invasions of aliens. But the same people who applaud and are moved when the heroes in films and novels save our freedom from huge powers, in the real world often rely blindly on a very small number of well-known brands. Artificial intelligence is making it even natural for many that machines write texts or edit videos on our behalf!

To learn how to use digital media well and not to "be used" by them, it may be good to have an idea of how many programs for personal computers and mobile phones exist and also something about their history, an amazing window on human creativity, not only from the industry, but above all from throngs of enthusiasts all across the world who have often introduced the most important innovations. Over the

DOI: 10.4018/978-1-6684-8228-5.ch009

Figure 1. Search-share
Source: Capala (2020)

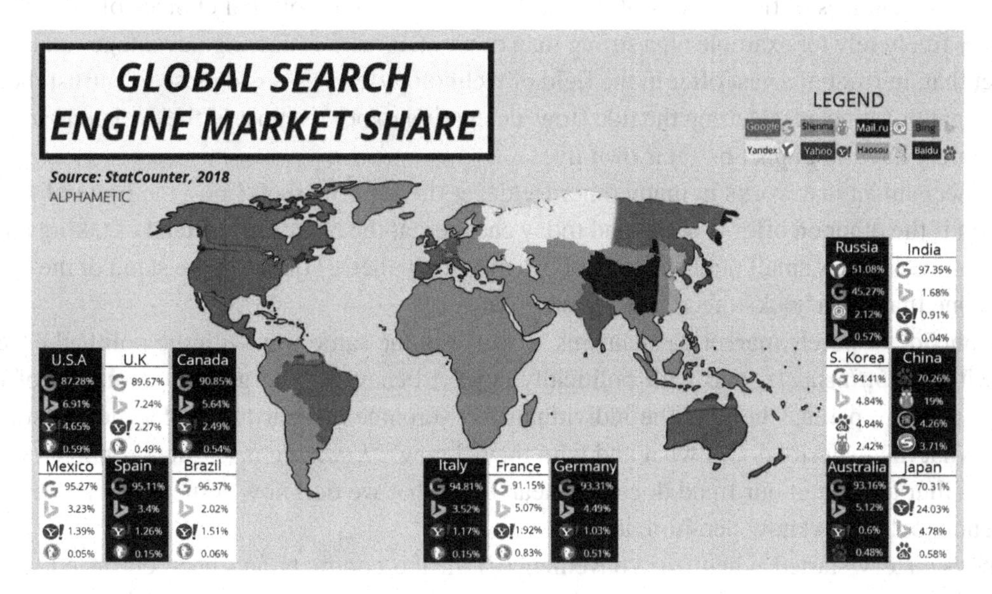

years, some possibilities of use have been refined, others lost because they did not work, others might have been caught if the public had been prepared to understand them.

There are millions of applications, and even just visit the online catalogs of today, or browse the magazines of a few decades ago, it allows us to know a world much larger, rich, and interesting than the one the most imagine, when they automatically connect in mind digital devices to a few stereotypical activities.

Being curious and trying, not only adapting, or following the instructions, it's the right attitude to learn to really use hardware and software, at different levels but in ways that improve and do not depress the quality of our lives.

2. IN THE GENEROUS HANDS OF THE BIG GLOBAL COMPANIES

Once every few minutes, my TV beams out a report about what's on my screen to Samsung, the company that made it. Chances are, your TV is watching you, too, through a few nosy pixels on the screen. (Fowler, 2019)

The film *I, Robot,* out in 2004 and based on the stories by Asimov, depicts a scenario in 2035 where a single large company, providing humanoid robots to the whole world, is basically able to dominate it. As in *The Invasion* (2007), remake of *Invasion of the Body Snatchers* of 1956, the division of the world between the good and the bad is not, in the end, so clear and absolute. In fact, the victory of the bad could bring a solution to some very big problems of mankind: no more wars, no destruction of the planet because of irrational behaviors. But this would mean giving up freedom, and the strong feelings that make human heartbeat, so the audience is happy when finally extraterrestrial or robotic solutions are defeated. Humans win, with all their weaknesses and the unwillingness to solve problems.

This is in fiction, in most stories. In the reality, freedom as so supreme a value does not seem to lead the actions and choices of the citizens of the earth, and not for the political choices of voters who in a democracy freely rely for example on a strong man or woman, with following advantages and risks. But it is a fact that, in front of a vast offer in the field of technology, most users choose to entrust themselves to a few gigantic companies, letting the tide flow, delegating to others most of the decisions and choices that ultimately have an impact on their own lives.

It's a mechanism that works in many other fields: at the supermarket, I buy the pasta of the known brand even if the other on offer is better and today cheaper; at the book fair, instead of taking advantage of the presence of many small publishers that I can meet only there, I queue at the stand of the big house, the same one that has a bookstore or even many in my city.

Even outside of purely market mechanisms, it works in the same way with the political or religious leader, with the *influencers*, and with politically correct behavior. The gregarious nature of humans challenges reason, perhaps helping the individuals to overcome insecurities under the reassuring umbrella of what the majority do, of what and who they "know". *Knowing* is in quotation marks, because having familiar a name in our mind does not mean at all that we do know someone or something. But we somehow believe to know her, him, it.

Asimovs's story started when (for convenience?) all the contracts had been entrusted to a single company. In the real world today, not a single company, but very few are in a position not so far from that "US Robotic" of the film.

But can I really entrust Google, Apple, Microsoft, Meta?

To some extent, of course I can, because they have a history of success, and they certainly know much about the products and services they offer. But that they are always automatically better and more reliable than others, it's another story. And some doubts could arise that perhaps relying too much on the same provider is not prudent, from different points of view.

First, too much power in hand may lead someone to take advantage of it. Sentences have been issued in many countries against web giants for misuse of the users' data. Moreover,

without a critical attitude on the part of users, they are more easily given what is convenient to the interests of companies rather than to their needs, and the quality of services declines

I don't want to build a theory on this, but the GPS that reveals my location, from my mid-high-end laptop with Windows 10 now updated to 11, for more than once and over several days, instead of the map of Brescia, Italy, where I live and where the computer was located, gave me back that of Hopetoun, Australia! Not that Hopetoun in Western Australia, near the ocean, to which DuckDuckGo search engine directs me immediately, but another one, north of Melbourne, which I can find thanks to a lake nearby, that I have seen widening backwards the map of the location where according to my computer I should be.

"Lake Coorong is a eutrophic lake located in the Wimmera region of western Victoria, Australia ... adjacent to the township of Hopetoun" (*Lake Coorong*, Wikipedia entry). That's my unknown second town!

And just while I'm writing these chapter, on the same unpredictable PC, the app *Meteo* yes it opens on my geographical area, but writings, fonts... What? I copy and paste that text into Google translate, asking for the language recognition. It's Hebrew!

רתוי תקיודמ תיזחת איה םיפסונ םינותנ לש תועמשמה.

תויזחתה תא רפשל תורזוע ךלש תויפצתה.

Translation into English: "More data means a more accurate forecast. Your observations help improve predictions."

In the options menu inside the weather app, I can correct the preference, evidently switched from Italy to Israel, very close in alphabetical order... But I'm sure I've never opened that menu before!

Another software, for translation, one day automatically sets the source language to Romanian. I am sure I am writing in Italian and have not made typos. It's possible that words look similar, so I correct manually: Italian! The software changes again to Romanian. I try with another sentence, then clear the text, and start from scratch... Romanian!

It only happened once, and then never again.

Just a hint here to my personal difficulties – evidently, I am much more "Boomer" than I thought - in synchronizing Windows contacts with Google, Outlook and the address book of my phone. But I found that it's all but automatic, it isn't!

By the way, nothing personal against Gmail service by Google, but I have a gut feeling, finding me so often in the condition of guessing the email address of colleagues and friends: "john.doe@gmail.com". Among millions of free possibilities, so many opt for the same provider, the same way of writing their name.... A general spontaneous standardization, but why?

This is of years ago:

Gmail, Google's free Web-based e-mail service, marked a new evolution in these procedures, scanning personal e-mail messages to deliver targeted advertisements. Google has an appetite for data, and their hundreds of millions of users deliver that every week ... One must back up and examine the potential privacy and intrusion risks associated with the technological conveniences being provided.

People flock to search engines without thinking twice. Google has become a part of everyday society and a verb in modern linguistics. When someone needs to find something online, they simply "Google" it. End-users enter names, addresses, phone numbers, interests, health ailments, questions, fantasies, and virtually anything imaginable into search boxes. Every search is logged and saved. Every user has a search engine "fingerprint trail." The data that search engines such as Google amount from logging search queries is astronomical, and the uses for such data are endless. (Pauxtis, 2009)

3. TECHNOLOGY, ECONOMICS, POLITICS, POWER

Google is a corporation whose main objective, from the point of view of the critical theory, is to generate profit and maximize its shareholders' wealth. As an organization and as a browser, Google is accompanied by some myths. One of the myths related to Google is about the possibility of finding answers to all questions free of charge. The myths about the organization may be strengthened as a result of providing and sharing tools that satisfy all needs of the users. The organization is able to sustain the myth of being indispensable and omnipotent. (Hapek, 2019)

Facebook changed its name to Meta in October 2021, announcing a new era of social interaction, enabled by the metaverse technology that appears poised to become the future center of gravity for online social interactions. (Kraus et al., 2022)

Facebook, buying booming platforms as *Instagram* in 2012 and *WhatsApp* in 2014 (for $19 billion, representing the company's largest acquisition at the time!) has become a global power able to compete with Google, Apple, Microsoft, in a field where it happens that new giants assert themselves through

Figure 2. Top tech giants
Source: Banerjee (2023)

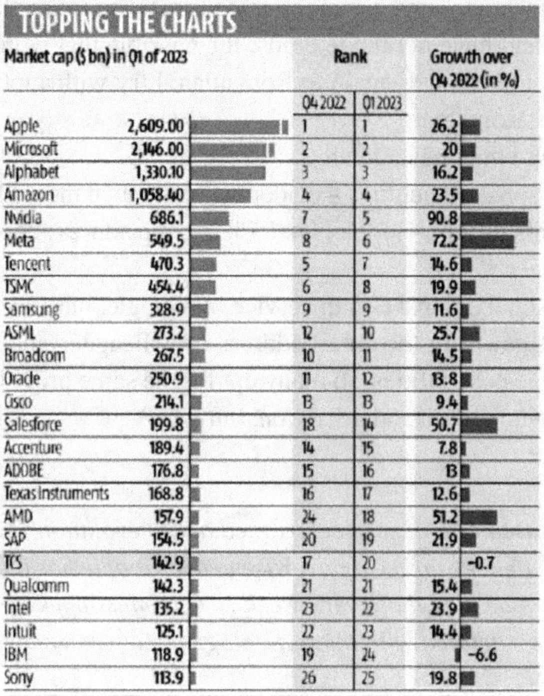

TOPPING THE CHARTS

Market cap ($ bn) in Q1 of 2023		Rank		Growth over Q4 2022 (in %)
		Q4 2022	Q1 2023	
Apple	2,609.00	1	1	26.2
Microsoft	2,146.00	2	2	20
Alphabet	1,330.10	3	3	16.2
Amazon	1,058.40	4	4	23.5
Nvidia	686.1	7	5	90.8
Meta	549.5	8	6	72.2
Tencent	470.3	5	7	14.6
TSMC	454.4	6	8	19.9
Samsung	328.9	9	9	11.6
ASML	273.2	12	10	25.7
Broadcom	267.5	10	11	14.5
Oracle	250.9	11	12	13.8
Cisco	214.1	13	13	9.4
Salesforce	199.8	18	14	50.7
Accenture	189.4	14	15	7.8
ADOBE	176.8	15	16	13
Texas Instruments	168.8	16	17	12.6
AMD	157.9	24	18	51.2
SAP	154.5	20	19	21.9
TCS	142.9	17	20	-0.7
Qualcomm	142.3	21	21	15.4
Intel	135.2	23	22	23.9
Intuit	125.1	22	23	14.4
IBM	118.9	19	24	-6.6
Sony	113.9	26	25	19.8

mergers and acquisitions - it's about seeing what is going to happen to *Twitter* over time after Elon Musk bought it in 2022 for 44 billion dollars and then renamed it as *X*! - or even develop in a few years almost from nothing, as *WhatsApp* itself or *TikTok*, or *Skype* at its time, when first it outclassed *Windows Messenger*, before Microsoft finally resolved the issue by buying *Skype* itself.

Talking about technological giants, it is not bad to remember other companies whose power is based on something much less ephemeral than the clicks of users, as everlasting IBM, Oracle, Cisco, as well as the hardware producers as Samsung, Huawey, Dell, Sony, Hitachi, Panasonic, Lenovo, HP, LG and so on, not to speak of processors, boards and cards manufactures, Intel, AMD, Nvidia, Asus, MSI, Gigabyte, and many others.

And here we can obviously get just a glimpse to the fact that the overestimation of software companies is coincident with the evolution phase of capitalism when the greatest wealth is realized without production (Lapavitsas, 2013; Ayres, 2014; Adrian, 2021).

These are "technical" discourses, such as the possibility, on the other side, of extending and generalizing forms of circular economy (Roy, 2020), or to practice a "happy degrowth" that does not involve a worsening, but rather an overall improvement of the living conditions of the inhabitants of the earth. These are choices that, though basically affecting the future itself, and the survival of mankind on the planet, they seem to have by the general public less appeal than how to get *likes* for photos of kittens on social networks.

There is also the question, addressed maybe more in political TV fictions than in reality, of «the rise of the platform economy into statelike dominance over the lives of entrepreneurs, users, and workers»

(Lehdonvirta, 2022), perhaps more powerful in some ways than major states or supranational entities like the US and the European Union.

Google trackers have been found on 75% of the top million websites. This means they're not only tracking what you search for, they're also tracking which websites you visit, and using all your data for ads that follow you around the Internet. Your personal data can also be subpoenaed by lawyers, including for civil cases like divorce. Google answered over 285,000 such data requests in 2022 alone!

More and more people are realizing the risk of relying on one company for so many personal services. If you're joining the ranks of people who've decided Google's data collection has become too invasive, here are some suggestions for replacements with minimal switching cost. Most are free, but even the paid apps and services are worth it — the cost of not switching is a cost to your personal privacy. The good news is that we have options! (How to Live Without Google, 2017)

Collecting data from users who are not only private, but also companies of all kinds, from the most frivolous to the most strategic, as well as government and military agencies, this makes the giants of the web global powers in every sense. And if they are based in competing countries, when international tensions grow, this makes them an object of the dispute between the political powers of the planet.

It's the latest step in a long-running feud between the West and China over data privacy issues, that besides TikTok has drawn in the likes of Hikvision, a manufacturer of IP surveillance cameras, and most famously, networking and comms giant Huawei, which found itself banned from the UK's core communications infrastructure in 2020. (Scroxton, 2023)

But the problem also arises at the level of countries, at a time when institutions such as the government, parliament and in general representative bodies risk being cut off, through which democratic countries should organize public life:

Digital platforms create new marketplaces and prosperity on the Internet ... but they are ruled by Silicon Valley despots with little or no accountability. Neither workers nor users can "vote with their feet" and find another platform because in most cases there isn't one. And yet using antitrust law and decentralization to rein in the big tech companies has proven difficult ... Pioneers who helped create—or resist—the new social order established by digital platform companies. The protagonists include the usual suspects—Amazon founder Jeff Bezos, Travis Kalanick of Uber, and Bitcoin's inventor Satoshi Nakamoto—as well as Kristy Milland, labor organizer of Amazon's Mechanical Turk, and GoFundMe, a crowdfunding platform that has emerged as an ersatz stand-in for the welfare state. Only if we understand digital platforms for what they are—institutions as powerful as the state—can we begin the work of democratizing them. (Lehdonvirta, 2022)

4. TEXTS AND PICTURES: THE WORK AND THE SHOP

Common language tends to synthesis, and proper names can be good to express in one word a more general concept. Speaking about software and what people can do with it on a computer, "Word" and

"Photoshop" are perfect names, even if their use to say more generically "writing or photo editing software" is likely to result in an unsolicited and free advertising for Microsoft and Adobe. It is also in the mentioned logic of the store rather than of the library (Chapter 8) so that writing a text or processing a photograph are in fact not associated with the work of a writer or a photographer, but to the consumption of a product. For convenience, brevity, conformity?

For more than 30 years, graphic word processors have all worked more or less the same way. Aside from the different fortunes, Lotus *Word Pro*, Corel *Word Perfect*, and all the dynasty *Star*, *Open* and *Libre Office* allow a writer to do in the end the same things in a very similar way as Word. I can like more – features in the 2023 releases I am using - how in *Word* texts are pasted from external sources, or how in *Libre Office* links are fast inserted with a crtl+K from the keyboard, but most users, even professional but not dealing with the ultimate paging and not compelled to maximum efficiency in their work, they probably do certain things by habit in one way, that could be done much better in another. But differences in *writing*, traditionally, do not depend much on the instrument.

In photo editing and graphics, instead, we know that every painter uses his/her techniques and stylistic approach, so that, in a non-digital environment, working with a brush or pencil, tempera or acrylic takes to different results. On a computer, using *Photoshop*, the most well-known commercial program, *Paint Shop Pro*, the cheap alternative, or GIMP, the main free one, it means to follow technical and thinking procedures sometimes very different. There are also other programs, free, or that one can try in demo versions for a fortnight or a month, or maybe less complete but available online, or on tablets, that can serve for general or special processing. Apart from specialized work situations, it isn't overall a correct approach to study and learn all that we could get from a single software, which we will probably never use completely, but it is better to have an idea as wide as possible of many different approaches, and to know, whatever software we decide to adopt as our main tool, that others exist, available, maybe more suitable for certain tasks, so that in the future we can use them directly, or have others working with us using them.

A sculpture can be made of marble, clay, bronze, wood, and for each we need different tools.

For education, a very useful function that was evident in old painting programs and now is to be searched a bit more into menus, is the setup of colors by moving sliders.

In RGB mode the sum of the three primary colors, red, green, and blue (additive color) gives white; in CMY mode the sum of the three complementary cyan, magenta and yellow (subtractive color) gives black. The typical division in 256 primary or complementary shades on the color panel gives the famous number 16.777.216 (256 to the third power) so many times mentioned years ago to emphasize the quality of screens (lately they begun to talk about billion colors!), which are not actually "visible" colors, but a simple mathematical result.

To change colors moving the sliders and see the mutual relationships can be interesting: no more confusion on *primary* colors as sometimes it happens in art and electronic books as, however we want to call them, any child can see that red + green = yellow; green + blue = cyan; red + blue = magenta. Those colors are not by chance, we have not to remember them by heart, but we can test in person what happens from the sum of them, or subtraction, which one is the negative of the other, and so on.

Dealing with colors, it is worth going to look for sliders, as well as for the "color wheel", and see what happens to play with them.

The author of this book works much on video editing, at a semi-professional level, for training and production, often with children. Along the years, he has used and tried many: Adobe *Premiere*, *Pinnacle Studio*, Corel *Video Studio*, *iMovie*, AIST *MovieXone*, Magix *Video Pro X*, *Hit Film Express* and

Figure 3. Home video editing
Source: Beneventi

Pro, *Vegas Edit* and *Pro*, *Final Cut*, *Da Vinci Resolve*. For personal search or requested for advice from schools, he also tested others, as well as programs running on tablets and phones. Among them there are expensive, cheap, for free, professional, for amateurs but with interesting features.

Apart from functionalities and personal taste, even from an entry level software today anyone can edit films with great precision, with titles and effects that thirty years ago were within reach only of the big film and television companies. Some are faster, others more precise and cleaner, others have something good for that particular task. If one can have more than one program, it makes no sense to use only one and leave completely the others. Like the craftsman who uses different tools in the various stages of a work.

And obviously it is not the case, except for particular emergencies or needs, to rely on software that assemble your videos "automatically". It's like asking someone else to talk, to think for us, or to have anyone of us replaced by an alien replica, as in the *Invasion of the Body Snatchers!*

AI video editing can also save influencers a lot of time when creating content. With all the features and capabilities AI offers, influencers can easily create high-quality content without spending hours in front of the camera or editing software ... AI video editing can help take some of the load off. (Noor, 2022)

In the article, we read about producing in this way "unique and engaging content"! That's to say that what we were interested in, what was important for us when we shot that video, is it decided by a *unique* artificial intelligence, which selects how "our" content is to be communicated to the others? Obviously, there can be situations in which a trip, race, concert, event, can be effectively summarized by a few random images, and then we can thank AI for helping to choose and putting together very quickly some effective ones. But if we think about a world where this becomes the *normal* way of editing videos, with a *unique* artificial intelligence possibly thinking for all the "creatives" of the planet... Big Brother didn't even imagine he could get that far!

5. AMAZING MUSIC BOXES

A friend of mine, musician, and good guitar player, uses a device whose software, following the chords and the rhythm of a guitar, produces by itself the bass line. It is artificial intelligence applied to musical composition and performance. I am a mediocre player but, crossing a clumsy approach of electric guitar with the bass notes as they came out from my fingers and ears and managing a music software on PC, in the end I produced a recording with something like a dialogue between the solo guitar and the bass not so bad!

In my phone, I have a synthesizer that I play with fingers, with wonder of friends, made by one who gives it for free, only asking musicians who use it during concerts to make him know. Simple, easy, normal, taking advantage of the sound capabilities of the devices, even the cheapest.

In the second half of the 80s, pop groups began to put a Macintosh on the stage, to manage their music, while personal computers were produced like Atari *ST* with inbuilt DSP (digital signal processor). The cheap 8-bit home machines of MSX computer family had their sound co-processor enhanced with external cards as the *Philips Music Module*, with which anyone, including the children of the kindergarten, could play in tune on an accompaniment, changing rhythms and instruments, inserting sounds and voices "sampled" from the outside and play and replay all together, directly on the computer keyboard or connecting a musical one. MIDI protocols were established to control keyboards and other instruments through a computer.

Today in digital musical keyboard even entry level and spending not so much more in impressive programmable workstations, anyone is enabled to produce any kind of music, without physically playing a note. Wonderful, or terrifying, depending on points of view.

Years ago, on computers it came the time of "sequencers", when a small but very active ranks of enthusiasts, all over the world, were moving to new forms of artistic creation:

Tracking is one of the oldest of the Amiga's music areas, simply because right from the machine's early days, programmers needed a convenient way of creating music for games and demos. One early utility that appeared was called SoundTracker, and within a few years of that, other similar programs had appeared. The only trouble was that, being essentially tools for programmers, these utilities used programmer-style conventions for creating music sequences. Song definitions were built around awkward-looking lists, showing the times and the pitches at which various samples should be played. Editing facilities were also very limited. (OctaMED v6 & Sound Studio, 1996)

The demoscene is a group of people, mainly coders, graphicians and musicians, who create digital art on a wide range of computer platforms both old and new. This website covers the demoscene on the Amiga platform ... Enjoy! (from the Amiga Demoscene Archive)

The new do-it-yourself practices, including sonic remixing and video mashups, are often explained as challenging existing structures of power ... The cultural industry's products are increasingly adopted and transformed into new forms of "remix culture" by individuals of various backgrounds, leading to practices and end-results that are manifestations of the democratizing potential of digital technology. (Brusila et al. 2021)

In general, to have even a little bit of experience of graphics, video and music processing, for understanding and use better technology, it's probably more useful for average people than attending in-depth training of office (if you don't work in an office!), as it simply means to set a connection between the media consumption of everyday life and the possibilities of somehow producing them, if we like. That's the great, still little understood novelty of the present time.

6. 3D PRINTING AND PROGRAMMABLE ROBOTS: ACTIVE TECHNOLOGY BEYOND FASHION

The flying shuttle, invented in 1733 by John Kay, a British weaver, allowed the production of wider pieces of cloth. Because its movement could be mechanised, the shuttle later became one of the innovations which paved the way for the Industrial Revolution. In 1913 Henry Ford brought motoring to the masses by making his Model T on a moving assembly line; but it was Ransom Olds, a decade earlier, who had come up with the idea of an assembly line to boost production of the Olds Curved Dash. Throughout the 1980s factory bosses scratched their heads over Taiichi Ohno's Toyota Production System and its curious methods, such as the just-in-time delivery of parts. Now it is the global benchmark for factory efficiency.

What, then, to make of the potential of Chuck Hull's invention in 1983 of "stereolithography"? Mr Hull is the co-founder of 3D Systems, one of a growing number of firms that produce what have become known as 3D printers. These machines allow a product to be designed on a computer screen and then "printed" as a solid object by building up successive layers of material. (3D printers will change manufacturing, 2017)

Fashionable technology is hardly truly innovative. Based on what we know well, what we have always done, it proposes a different, possibly automatic way of doing more or less the same things.

Interactive whiteboards and tablets in schools are welcome as technology, because they seem to replace the old blackboards and books. Cameras and editing software are less welcome, probably as they introduce a new idea, that students even very young can produce audiovisuals. 3D printers and robots, that open wide vistas never seen in the past, are used only by small avant-gardes, find space in magazines and fairs, but it is difficult that politicians, public opinion, and most teachers consider them at the center of the school's "digitization" process.

3D printing, also known as additive manufacturing, is empowering artists, designers and makers with affordable, easily accessible tools, not just for dreaming up masterpieces of craft and design but also for creating, exhibiting and monetizing them. It's a whole new kind of digital craftsmanship revolution. (Reichental, 2018).

3D printers available in primary schools and in factories are not exactly the same, obviously, but they are based on the same principles and even students can manufacture things, as well as they can shoot a movie as at Hollywood, without professional equipment and studios, using amatorial cameras and smartphones. Kids, literally *can do and play with the future.*

Figure 4. 3D
Source: Siu (2023)

3D printing has emerged in recent years as one of the most exciting breakthroughs the world has ever seen and one that is accessible to people of all ages ... Many educational institutions consider that purchasing 3D printers is not necessary at this time ... Students get more enthusiastic due to the technology since they have hands-on experience developing and experimenting at an early age. In the classroom, they may make items from scratch. Teachers will also find it simpler to finish the curriculum on time if they have a group of enthusiastic students rather than yawning ones. (Dhanesh, 2022)

I have a video, shot several years ago, of a beautiful example of the use of *Bee-Bots* by first-graders. They had done a theater on Pinocchio, they were wearing masks and, after putting masks on the robots as well, they had programmed their movement in a space in order to meet and interact with them. Another time, with older children, we planned the movement of a dog robot that lived an unlikely love story with a cricket robot!

Robots are in the end programmable toys that at some point do things themselves, based on our instructions. In a factory, as in children's play, it is science fiction that takes place in everyday life.

Drones are robots that fly, jump and swim. Their impact in education can be important and exciting.

Teaching with drones in education holds so many possibilities, from introducing kids to piloting or coding basics to exploring drone uses and careers. Whether in STEM programs, clubs, or CTE courses, children can explore practical STEAM concepts and gain hands-on experience. Though many elementary students have experience coding, it's often best to introduce drones to the STEM curriculum in middle school. By high school, though, many students—especially those in career and technical programs—are comfortable piloting. And, the good news is that educational drones are, by nature, easy to operate. (Applegate, 2023)

Figure 5. e + f
Source: Melissa (2023)

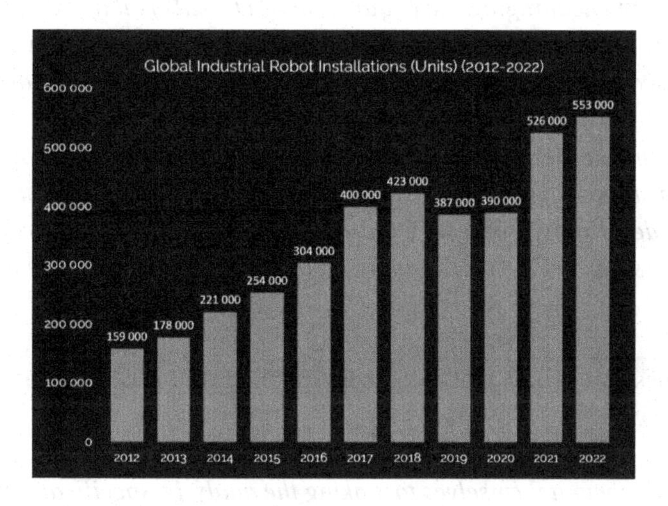

Meghan Salter, a public school teacher from Huntington, West Virginia (WV), has made it her mission to teach the children well, so they can lead the way in tomorrow's drone industry

... Her top three tips for teachers:

Be brave – Don't be afraid of technology. Students will love using drones in the classroom. Give it a chance (and also don't be afraid to fail!)

Network – Find organizations that support both STEM or STEAM education from other areas of the U.S. and globally, for both funding and course content.

Never stop learning – Drone technology changes rapidly, so keep up with it by getting the latest industry information through media outlets like DroneLife. (McNabb, 2021)

Like 3D printing, robots and drones require humans to be active, to imagine, to decide when, how and where to use them. Over the years, beyond the crises that cross the planet, the installation of industrial robots is constantly growing, a problem perhaps when they simply replace human labor or, always depending on the choices we make, an opportunity when they free it to other activities that cannot be carried out by machines.

A great challenge for humanity, for all of us, as it's probably up to everybody to rethink jobs and society, a task that the citizens of democracies cannot afford to delegate to anyone, in times when technology is on the way to "eliminate millions of current jobs — and create millions of new ones" (Urwin, 2023).

Other robots of any kind not only are used for a wide variety of jobs, but their design can also help us to observe, to better understand humans, animals, nature, how they work. There's a technology so to say of "action", that we could oppose to that of "consumption". And if we look at it, we can probably imagine a much better future for everyone.

Humanistic computing is still considered a 'niche' discipline, yet its breadth is pervasive. A prevailing misconception today when encouraging the acquisition of IT skills is that we only want to train technicians and programmers. Yet the real challenge lies in creating a new generation of versatile intellectuals ... "There is a twin misconception in the humanities, as the majority see the computer as a way of doing the same things more easily, thereby overlooking the contribution that information technology can make to redefining the humanities. Office tools are used, but they do not improve writing ... This is the very essence of humanistic computing, and what the humanities can (and must) gain from computing: acquiring the habit of describing problems with precision, and in so doing avoiding approximation". (Why tomorrow's professions will be increasingly scientific yet also more& humanistic, 2021, quote of Guido Milanese)

Humanism and ethics: two words that the general public is not used to associate with technological development.

Software engineers shall commit themselves to making the analysis, specification, design, development, testing and maintenance of software a beneficial and respected profession ... We seem to have been paying more attention to ethical conduct as a consequence of the increased availability of big data systems and infiltration of artificial intelligence (AI) into software-enabled system. (Ozkaya, 2019)

7. THE VARIOUS AND UNPREDICTABLE PANORAMAS OF THE SCREENS: MILLIONS OF SOFTWARE

Online stores are full of any kind of apps, for every kind of purpose. In quite recent years, good operating system for mobile as *Windows Phone* and *Symbian* were told to be losers on the market because of the lack of software compared to *Android*. On the Nokia store for *Symbian* there were "only" about 120.000 titles!

What we know about digital machines is mostly storytelling, AI and metaverse may frighten us because we hear about them, but we do not handle them directly, or only at the surface. Maybe it would be good, even for those who are not geeks and only know the canonical software that everyone uses, to go a bit exploring the variety of programs with which any of us can turn our PC or mobile phone in a device sometimes totally new and unpredictable.

According to Wikipedia, on the Android Play Store in 2017, there were available 3.500.000 applications! And from a survey in 2022, "The Abandoned Mobile Apps Report", in front of 1.300 apps refreshed in the latest 6 months in the stores for Apple and Android, there were more than1.5 million apps abandoned by their developers for at least two years. (Barbera, 2012). This "zombie software" can put a risk the devices, as I am promptly warned when, after changing phone, I try to install on the new one a couple of apps that I used regularly and that I realize that now are not even in the catalog anymore.

So, I go now on my tablet PC and - probably for different languages and markets on earth it's not always the same - I find that apps are divided into 37 categories, including games that are in turn divided into 17 lists, ordered starting from the most voted by the public.

Among games, not only for an alphabetical question, we find first the *Arcades*, whose quite curious name refers to their origin in bars or playrooms, even before the time of digital machines:

An arcade game or coin-op game is a coin-operated entertainment machine typically installed in public businesses such as restaurants, bars, and amusement arcades. Most arcade games are presented as primarily games of skill and include arcade video games, pinball machines, electro-mechanical games, redemption games or merchandisers ... Arcade video games were first introduced in the early 1970s, with Pong as the first commercially successful game. (Arcade Game, Wikipedia entry)

In May 2023, the first I find in the list, in full respect of tradition, is *Pinball Deluxe*!

In addition to Arcade, other lists of Games are Action, Adventure, Cards, Casino, Casual, Educational, General Culture, Music, Puzzles, Simulations, Races, Role, Sport, Strategy, Table, Words.

In the other 36 categories of apps there's literally the world: Business, Finance, Beauty, Art & Design, Home and Furnishings, Communication, Instruction, Meeting People, Medicine, Lifestyle, Music, Photography, Video, Maps & Navigators, Health & Fitness, Food & Drink, Sport, Children, Parents, etc.

For children as users there is a special list of apps "approved by teachers". I do not see written somewhere "animals", so I don't know where to find software for cats successful among the felines of my family, but I suppose it's enough writing "cats" or "cat games" in the search field. In a popular one, there are fish swimming in the screen and when the cat touches them with its paw they dive. Usually after a while the cat, which is a clever animal, tries to lift the tablet, to see if the fish have hidden under the device.

Many apps are for free, many have a "premium" version for sale, many have a lot of ads inside or do not work properly if one does not pay for additional services, but the way their authors propose them commercially - it can be huge software houses, but also solitary programmers - it is not our focus now. What we want to emphasize here is the huge amount of software available, able to make our device perform a literally infinite number of different functions. So, once again (*repetita iuvant*!) saying "use a smartphone" is a meaningless phrase.

For schools, the main concern is that students may be distracted in lesson time being connected to social networks and messaging apps. But strange situations can happen, when for example a photograph is needed for didactic, and the teacher says that students can't take it with a mobile because it is forbidden "to use phones"!

As often pointed up in these chapters, smartphones, as personal computers, are "infinite sets of possibilities depending on software" and, if some of these can be incompatible with school life, others can provide very good aids in many activities.

Mobile phones can be used to teach phonetics and pronunciation. Lessons, poems & lectures by eminent scholars stored in mobiles can easily be shown to the students time and again. Parents also can store good & useful lectures in any field in their mobile phones and can show those to their children ... The use of mobile technology is good for informal learning where learners can access information and learning materials from anywhere and at any time. It includes distance education and other open learning systems. (Sandhya-Swathi, 2017)

In general, to go and see the phone apps just starting from the point of view of possible school applications, and from those then broaden the gaze a little further, towards other uses, could be a good introduction to the variety of software. And curiosity the right attitude, as all of us know anyhow very little of a subject with a huge number of unexpected suggestions and solutions related to the most various aspects of human life.

Figure 6. Abandoned apps, 2022

8. FOLLOWING THE CURIOSITY: THE BEST TRAINING TO "DIGITAL"

Write, taking notes, exchanging texts with teammates, it could be the most "natural" task students are to perform at school, and not always powerful but complex and heavy programs like *Word* or *Libre Office* are the most suitable tools. Just look up in the productivity software list, read the features, download and try the interesting ones (we'll go to uninstall immediately what we don't like), and eventually choose the software that more fits the way we work, it increases our digital skills more than many refresher courses! It can be the look, the color of the "sheets", the way notes are sorted and can or cannot be imported and exported from and to other programs, the possibility to hand write on the screen, to dictate using the voice… We see what is available and we choose. A little, big step towards active digital citizenship.

Interestingly, while education experts are debating whether it is appropriate to still teach cursive writing in schools, software producers take this possibility clearly into account, knowing that many prefer to take notes by hand, writing in italics, which is often more convenient and faster (cursive comes from the Latin "cursus" = *running*) than using a keyboard or writing in block letters.

In the "Productivity" list, also every sort of calendars and agendas, scanners for printed texts, PDF, QR codes, managers for keeping in order digital archives in our devices and transfer large ones that cannot be attached to emails or compressed too much using social networks. But also, conceptual and mental maps which can give a visual order to our activities, vocal recorders, passwords managers, customer and membership cards collectors for smartphone, simple or scientific calculators, currency and measures converters, and much more. And in addition, of course, many voice assistants and programs of writing, reading, research, information based on artificial intelligence.

Starting from school, "Instruction" can be a good category to look up. There we find apps to learn languages, mathematics, music, memory software, the Rubik cube, the Holy Bible, the Koran, and simulation games for children in which real-life environments and situations are reconstructed and young users can experience them.

There is the school diary, the "portable" version of the software with which children do coding, the inevitable coloring books, but also powerful drawing software, geometry, origami, fractals, human body, nursery rhymes, and the programs for distance learning that became popular and indispensable during the complicated days of the pandemic, when schools in many countries remained closed during the lock-down. And hundreds, thousands of other applications of all kinds.

The categories in which to look are obviously not rigid, they are intertwined, but search, try, choose and discard is an essential attitude to begin to understand something about digital gadgets and apps. Usually, children and young people naturally tend to do so, many adults do not. But there is no need to rejuvenate, its' enough just start doing it!

Among the apps that are worth having on our phone, there are those - already mentioned in chapter 8 - that, through the sharing of photos taken by the users themselves, with the supervision of experts, can help us in the recognition of plants, insects, animals that we meet in real life, as well as those which, by pointing the phone to the night sky, help us to recognize stars and planets.

Since they do their job well, there is no need for teachers or courses. If they are decently made, people of all ages simply begin to use them and learn, as an effective interface with the real world.

Obviously, the phone, with its GPS and direction and moving sensors, is an excellent compass and, having often one provided with the device as basic software, simply typing "compass" in the virtual shop, we have access to an endless catalog, from which we can choose the one we like the most.

Choosing, the magic word that can really change the way so many people in the world today experience technology. And we don't have to be specialist or skilled in that field. We can really go with the compass, the clock, the music player that seems more beautiful and easier to us. Then, simply using them, next time we will be able to choose with a greater awareness.

If we go to a category like "Photography", there are apps to organize and watch pictures and videos and to take and edit them, with powerful filters and effects, allowing to warp images, change lights, shadows, and colors, remove backgrounds. Some are lite versions of PC software, including free releases of *Photoshop*, others are more suited to the characteristics of mobile phones and most popular social networks where people use to share their pictures. Usually, among the hundreds of possible operations available in a professional software, users can access here the most common and spectacular, possibly with a single click, and if the app is free, they have often to struggle with ads.

Kids have a great ability to find the right tools to give a personal impression to their presence on *Instagram* or *Tik Tok*, while probably many adults find unbearable even the idea of processing photographs on a 6-inch display. Different maybe if we have an iPad or a high-end Android tablet, because on the cheap ones the poor computing power often cancels the benefits of a slightly larger screen. A question of taste, of habit, but the possibilities are still enormous, with effects which, only a few years ago, were only possible at Hollywood!

To similar software it is possible to go also from "Art & Design" category, where it's easier to find sophisticated programs, maybe next to those of drawing and painting, allowing people to use fingers or pens on the screen as on paper or a canvas, in a very natural way.

In "House and Home" there are the apps of real estate agencies, but also programs that allow people to design or renovate a house, to arrange the furniture, in 2 or 3 D, on real or fictional data. One can find how to control TVs and other electronic devices at home, as heating, alarms, cameras, solar panels.

In "Business" category, we find tools for meeting people online, scheduling activities, managing customer archives and invoices, as well as reminders and planners, business card makers, e-signatures.

"Food & Drink" it's not only the list of every possible restaurant, pub, cafeteria and deliverer all across the planet, but also a huge collection of recipes, how to make bread at home, or beer.

"Medical" probably includes apps to connect to your doctor, but also visual anatomy, speech assistants for people who are speech impaired.

In "Music & Audio" one founds players for the music of the artists, locally or online, but also apps for singing karaoke, read texts while music is playing, tuning the guitar and other string instruments, have all the chords for ukulele or Venezuelan "cuatro", learning piano, play the already mentioned synthesizers, and we can also hit directly on the screen to play with our fingertips a battery that, by connecting the phone to an amplifier, it can sound as almost real!

Among the great choice in "Maps" and "Sports", more than the possibility of crossing the whole world by car without literally knowing where we are, fascinating is the chance of tracing, observing, reconstructing, programming on maps paths on foot or by bicycle, significantly deepening our actual knowledge of a territory. For those who talk of machines and software that dictate our behavior: it all depends on the choices we make!

Then, I do not know exactly in which kind of categories, but if we type or say "earthquake", we can have an instant information on the telluric movements in any part of the earth and be warned if it happens not far from where we are, or even directly see the seismic wave on the screen as in a seismograph. More in the quiet chores of every day, if we point the phone camera on the bar-code of a product, we are immediately told how we can dispose of the packaging in the separate waste collection.

Many things previously available only to specialists and at a high price, or that we had to look for in distant libraries or strange places, or even unthinkable, now they can be downloaded into mobile phones! And many more are coming. Do they work, can we trust in them? And can they help us to get better in the world we live in?

In the meanwhile, we begin to know that they are there, and we can try them. But without a "culture of curiosity", if we do not get into the habit of searching, seeing, and extricating ourselves in some way without stress among thousands of proposals and possibilities, we risk downloading and using only the apps of those around us who make the biggest voice. We risk making our mobile devices not the effective interface to the world they can be, but bizarre gadgets that take us away from ourselves and the others. And it is not a good way to live neither the digital, nor the real world.

When interacting with mobile technologies, users often experience strong emotional responses, which can result in the willingness to act without thinking ... entertaining apps heighten affective brand responses ... consumers might become brand vocals. Moreover, apps can trigger emotional connections between the consumer and the brand ... or self-app connection, arising from personalized consumption experiences that turn apps into digital manifestations of one's preferences, desires and needs. (Stocchi et al. 2021)

9. EXPLORED OR LOST ROUTES FROM THE PAST

The BASIC programs I wrote for the TRS-80 would run only on a TRS-80; later, when I got an Atari 400, I wrote programs that would only run on an Atari ... My programs were not elegant; oftentimes, they weren't even intelligible to anyone except for me and the TRS-80. But they were mine, and they let me tell the computer to do exactly what I wanted it to do. (McCracken, 2014)

In the years 80s and the first90s, before the spread of Internet, people who wanted to know about computers had magazines as the main reference, printed pages and with time more and more digital content, collected first in floppy disks and later in CD ROMs. To take a random look at those magazines, checking for further information from surviving online sources, it can be useful to go beyond the usual representation of the technological panorama as a continuous present, in which the novelties follow one another making simply useless and obsolete what there was before.

If we take publications about for say 1985, they are clearly addressed mainly to advances users. There are ads of hardware, computers, peripherals, accessories, monitors and printers, floppy readers, but many articles are on how to configure memories and cards, connect properly interfaces and expansions, understand how the systems deal with some internal operations. The era of IBM compatible PCs is still in its infancy and many different machines have their own system and their version, their "dialect" of BASIC, the easy programming language that comes above all with devices intended for the home market, while for the professional ones, people should learn at least some "DOS" commands.

As already written in Chapter 3, machines of a new generation are already out, but in the meanwhile, many BASIC *listings* are published, which one can copy, to use or even work on. They are times of sharing, and even of pure craftsmanship, if we think that it is a matter of typing pages of code, being careful not to miss a comma!

Between 1985 and 1986, on a magazine addressed to home computer users, we find software for IQ tests, monoscope for video signal, text-only adventures, Mandelbrot fractals, lunar eclipses, questionnaires with multiple answers, biorhythms, and even "AI for Commodore 64"! All in BASIC listings!

Home computers, less powerful and with less memory than PCs, having to run video games are normally superior for graphic and sound and above all much, much cheaper.

Commodore 64 mass memories are based by default on music cassettes, but it's also available a 5.25 floppy disk drive and users can even try emulated MS-Dos and GWBASIC (the BASIC for PCs). Its sound co-processor is quite advanced and, as well as allowing good sound effects in video games, it can be used as a music synthesizer. Sinclair Spectrum, born very small and with rubber keys no good for typing, is provided with new expanded and suitable keyboards. On MSX2, the first home computers with a dos system (on 3.5 diskettes), it's available a full running version of *WordStar*, that is and will be for years the reference word processor for writers and publishers, before the success of Microsoft Word.

It's a transitional period, with still black and white impact printers, and the first drawing programs on those old machines are operated with a joystick. But Macintosh release in 1984, as well as Atari ST and Amiga in 1985 are announcing that BASIC *listings* time is going to run out soon.

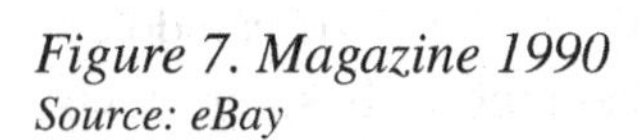

Figure 7. Magazine 1990
Source: eBay

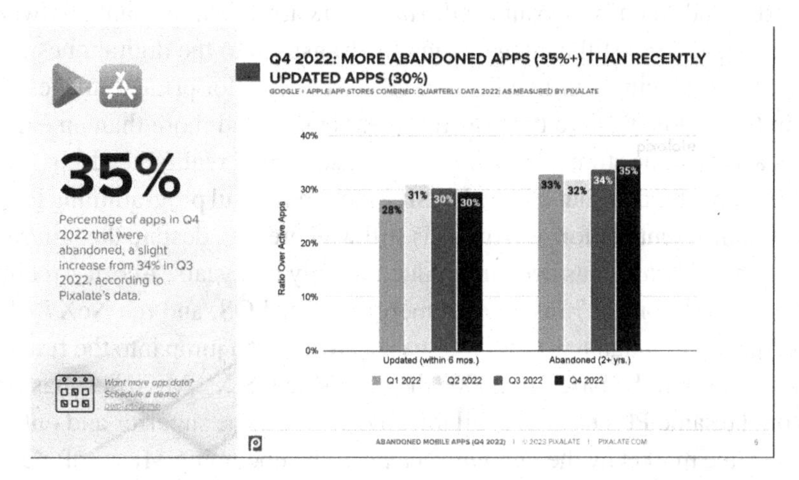

Ten years later - say for example in 1995 - easy and powerful office software is for everybody, writing, spreadsheets and data base, planners, notes, family money-management. Speech recognition software must still be "well trained", to get used to the voice and tone of just that human, but it can be a lot of fun, and there are already programs that translate, not very well, from one language to another.

Painting programs allow users to act as veritable painters, mixing colors on the canvas with shades and transparencies, using as brushes also parts of the images, dragging and spraying them, applying symmetries, perspectives and any sort of effects and working on details pixel by pixel; for software capable of handling animation, as *DeLuxePaint*, collections are available of readymade "animbrushes", as that zebra which, with a realistic effect that aroused hilarity and wonder, the author of this book made with few clicks galloped out of the mouth of a kindergarten child! Image processing software work more deeply on photographs, while good inkjet printers are available for mass market and average people can now print photographs, fliers, and booklets on their own. Morphing programs take cinema effects on PCs, allowing amazing animations from human faces to objects or animals. The so called "draw" programs, on the other hand, deal with vector images instead of bitmaps, which are not suitable for the fine reproduction of photographs, but which, based on mathematical models, can be enlarged, or reduced maintaining the same quality. Fractal generators are amazing adventures exploring and re-creating the "geometry of Nature".

Sound samplers and music sequencers have opened new perspectives in music, with or without a connection to MIDI keyboards. 3D modeling software suggests the creation of virtual environments, watching objects from any point of view and setting up materials, textures, paint, skins, shadows, smoke, and steam, or turns anyone into an airplane or car designer, with CAD like (Computer-Aided Design) procedures; with 3D scanners at affordable prices, even objects from the real world can be put into modeling projects. Other enchanting 3D programs are landscapes generators, that create worlds inspired to the real ones, mountains, valleys, rivers, woods and deserts, lakes and weather events, and allow to travel across them, watch animated daily and seasonal changes, from dawn to sunset with the morning fog, the sky and clouds, with the leaves on trees growing or falling in Autumn changing color, as well as the grass, and the snow advancing or retreating on the ground, also taking into account the altitude. For computers with TV compatible signal, as Amiga or MSX, titles makers, together with affordable genlocks for superimposing images, have broken into home and professional video productions, in some cases blending with the new emerging Hypertext and Multimedia software, with which one can do everything, but that immediately make a game to design "signage" for TV: weather reports, business news, election returns, sports and so on. Video and audio *digitizers* are also important hardware accessories in times when video and audio are still analogical and the transition to the digital ones has not yet begun. They are important for producing multimedia, as well as *scanners* for printed images or even films and *CD-writers*, that in the middle 90s are though still as expensive and more than an entire computer. On magazines, in fairs and in some stores, people can find also virtual reality headsets.

In the mid-1990s, more than the out of date BASIC, more powerful programming languages are given for the skilled users of different platforms. Amiga is still well present, despite the failure of Commodore, Atari survives, though the *Falcon* has been in production only two years, Acorn Archimedes is the first PC based on a RISC processor and runs an extremely advanced OS, and the NeXT of Steve Jobs - for some years out of Apple - although it is now over, has been almost a jump into the future (and on NeXT-STEP operating system it will be based in 2000s the new Mac OS X). Microsoft has finally updated to *Windows 95*, but on the same PCs *OS/2* is available, by IBM, maybe superior and out much earlier, but held back for years on the market by the *announcements* of the upcoming Microsoft new system release!

Some of these systems are designed to give the user, if he wishes, the opportunity to be him to organize software, data, and documents on his personal computer as precisely as possible, and software are popular to deal with files and directories, as well as with the setup of the graphic interface and the windows. In the Amiga community, for example, publishing screenshots of their "workbenches", users share at a glance their ideas on computer usage and their style of work.

Programming is also for children, with the spread of different versions of the language LOGO, conceived in 1967 by a little group lead by Seymour Papert, to control the movement of turtle robots moving on the floor and then brought to personal computers. It's powerful, neat, structured and, from the first very simple release for MS-Dos in the early 80s, it has developed on many systems, managing colors, sounds, movements and strikes. But kids, as already mentioned, can also "code" computer actions from the graphic environments of some author programs used for making multimedia.

From ads and reviews on magazines, we know that in those years multimedia publishing is in full swing, with productions of all kinds. The support is CD ROM, still produced industrially, waiting for the prices of the burners to collapse, so that they will be available on every PC a few years later.

Such multimedia productions are in fact trials of interactive works of science, physics, mathematics, didactic, geography, astronomy, literature, history, in times when internet is at its beginning and the web 1 does not allow videos and animations yet, but also what can be put into the limited space of a CD ROM is still little and quite poor. It's the first time in history that humans are imagining and publishing works like these, nobody really knows how to "write" and the public is not prepared to "read" them. But probably no one imagine that in a few years we simply will give up making them, returning to the traditional media, books and movies (and pretending that it's different if we read or watch them online!) and limiting digital home productions to sequence shots of speeches and ballets in front of a mobile phone, or exchange of ephemeral messages and pictures among millions of common and even illiterate people often unaware of what they do. And assuming that a possible evolution of those first multimedia are some websites, they are mostly intended only for a fast and distracted browsing, because people always in front of them have something else to do (and it would be nice to understand what!)

The first popular software for hypertexts had been probably HyperCard, for Macintosh, 1987, and the first program intended expressly as multimedia was *Amiga Vision*, out in 1990 with the first computer offered on the market as a multimedia machine, Amiga 3000. Some multimedia popular programs in 1995 are *ToolBook, Scala Multimedia, Macromedia Director, NeoBook, Illuminatus*. Remembering and quoting almost by heart, the author likes to mention his first piece of such a software, with an exchange of nice paper messages with their creators in Sweden. It seems there are no visible reference on it today online, but its name was *Image Vision*, with a very nice interface, born to run on Amiga and export works on PCs.

The basic idea that are people to tell machines what to do and not the contrary, it's still rather strong in 1995, and it appears great what even kids can do it, as editors, directors, using programs as the excellent *3D Movie Maker*, proposed by Microsoft with the launch of Windows 95 and withdrawn within a few years, or *KidsSim*:

Today, over 100 million people use them [personal computers] to write letters and reports, draw pictures, keep budgets, maintain address lists, access databases, experiment with financial models, play games, and so forth. Children as young as two years old can use a mouse and paint with programs like KidPix (a child's painting program, at one time the world's best selling application) or explore worlds like "The PlayRoom" (a child's adventure game). So computers are not inherently unusable. The key observation is that most of these applications are editors: with them, users produce an artifact by invoking a sequence of actions and examining their effects. (Smith et al., 1994)

Meanwhile, authoring software is also available to make games, that's always a great idea to address especially the young to go and see into a computer all that could be done with it.

The topic of video games and education has been covered countless times over the years, from many points of view. Here the opportunity to underscore that the experience can be particularly stimulating when, as in a multimedia, it relies on the possibility of establishing links between the engaging game at the computer and other elements of the culture of children and young people, like the possibility to consult books together and to write stories. The quote is personal about the author, just in those years:

The students of three Roman elementary schools ... lived an experience of sure interest, led by Paolo Beneventi, the writer from Brescia who animated their meetings with the computer. The peculiarity of the methodological path followed is to have used video games as a source from which to draw characters, objects, and environments for the stories to be invented on very intriguing topics: animals, the Middle Ages, the ancient Romans. (Maida, 1993, translated from Italian)

While interactive digital hypertexts, in different formats, are given alongside and gradually are going to completely replace the weighty printed manuals, sometimes hundreds of pages, which for several years have accompanied the production and distribution of the software.

10. TO DO (OR NOT TO DO) THINGS OURSELVES

This is an interesting presentation of a device to monitor people's health, written by Stefano Penge in his blog, a "special mask, light, comfortable, elegant", an example of how human creativity can be unleashed, starting also from difficult experiences, such as the pandemic Covid 19.

Sensors capture the sound emitted during breathing in real time and send it to the app. Here begins the magic of SmartBreath. A mathematical model correlates sound with the size of the oral and nasal cavity, with the diameter and shape of the opening of the mouth, the position of the tongue and throat, the force of inhalation and exhalation, the duration, the origin of air from the upper or lower part of the lungs, the position of the diaphragm ... So these data can be used to discriminate between healthy people and sick people ... The mask connects to the phone that recognizes it and registers the UUID (a unique ID) ... The app starts automatically when the breathing parameters deviate from those expected.

After a long, detailed, and persuasive description, including "the indication of the nearest gym, the presentation of the most suitable sportswear", the author concludes as follows:

I must clarify that at the moment this mask, the SmartBreath app and the RemoteBreathAssistant service do not exist, at least as far as I know. But you'll see they come. (Penge, 2023, translated from Italian).

REFERENCES

Abandoned Mobile Apps Report. (2022). pixalate.com.

Adrian, T. (2021, Sept 27). The Future of Finance and the Global Economy: Facing Global Forces, Shaping Global Solutions. *IMF Communications Department*. imf.org/en/News.

Amiga Demoscene Archive. (n.d.). ada.untergrund.net

Applegate, K. (2023, Aug 30). Best Drones For Education: From Building And Flying To Coding. *eduporium.com*/blog

Arcade Game. (n.d.). In *Wikipedia*.

Ayres, R. U. (2014). *The Bubble Economy: Is Sustainable Growth Possible?* The MIT Press. doi:10.7551/mitpress/9957.001.0001

Banerjee, M. (2023 Apr 26). *Top 25 tech firms' valuation grows $2.4 trillion in 2023, shows report.* business-standard.com.

Barbera. D. (2022, May 13). *App Store e Play Store sono pieni di app "abbandonate"*. wired.it/article

Brusila, J. (2021). Music, Digitalization, and Democracy. *Popular Music and Society*, *45*, 2022.

Capala, M. (2020 Mar 19). *Global Search Engine Market Share in the Top 15 GDP Nations (Updated for 2020).* alphametic.com.

Fowler, G. A. (2019, Sep 18). You watch TV. Your TV watches back. *The Washington Post.*

Hapek, M. E. (2019). Mythologization of New Media Organizations Illustrated With the Example of Google. In *Myth in Modern Media Management and Marketing*. IGI Global. doi:10.4018/978-1-5225-9100-9.ch004

How to Live Without Google: Alternatives That Protect Your Privacy. (2017, Sep 14). Spreadprivacy.com.

Kraus, S., Kanbach, D. K., Krysta, P. M., Steinhoff, M. M., & Tomini, N. (2022). Facebook and the creation of the Metaverse: Radical business model innovation or incremental transformation? *International Journal of Entrepreneurial Behaviour & Research*, *28*(9), 52–77. doi:10.1108/IJEBR-12-2021-0984

Lake Coorong. (n.d.). In *Wikipedia.*

Lapavitsas, C. (2013). The financialization of capitalism: 'Profiting without producing'. *Analysis of Urban Change, Theory, Action*, *17*(6).

Lehdonvirta, V. (2022). *Cloud Empires: How Digital Platforms Are Overtaking the State and How We Can Regain Control.* The MIT Press. doi:10.7551/mitpress/14219.001.0001

Maida, A. (1993, Mar 25). Storie da Videogiochi. *La Repubblica.*

McCracken, H. (2014, April 29). Fifty Years of BASIC, the Programming Language That Made Computers Personal. *Time.*

McNabb, M. (2021, Aug 02). Drones in Elementary Education: How the 2020 Cabell County's Teacher of the Year Makes it Work. *dronelife.com*.

Melissa, R. (2023, Oct). *IFR World Robotics 2023 Key Takeaways*. statzon.com/insights

Noor. (2022, March 31). *How to Automate Video Editing? Best Automated Video Editors*. Rav.ai.

OctaMED v6 & Sound Studio. (1996, Apr). Soundonsound.com.

Ozkaya, I. (2019, May-June). Ethics Is a Software Design Concern. *IEEE Software*, *36*(3), 4–8. doi:10.1109/MS.2019.2902592

Pauxtis, A. (2009). Google: Technological Convenience vs. Technological Intrusion. In *Online Consumer Protection: Theories of Human Relativism*. IGI Global. doi:10.4018/978-1-60566-012-7.ch001

Reichental, A. (2018, Jun 1). How 3D Printing Is Reviving Craftsmanship Across The Globe. *Forbes*.

Roy, M. (2020). *Sustainable Development Strategies: Engineering, Culture and Economics*. Elsevier.

Sandhya, T. & Swathi, P. (2017, Apr-Jun). Significance of Mobile Applications in Education System. *International Journal of Linguistics and Computational Applications, 4*(2).

Scroxton, A. (2023). *UK TikTok ban gives us all cause to consider social media security*. Computer-weekly.com.

Siu, K. (2023, Sep 22). *3D Printing for Kids*. teachyourkidscode.com

Smith, D. C. (1994, July). KIDSIM: Programming Agents Without a Programming Language. *Communication of Association Computer Machinery*, *37*(7).

Stocchi, Pourazad, N., Michaelidou, N., Tanusondjaja, A., & Harrigan, P. (2021). Marketing research on Mobile apps: Past, present and future. *Journal of the Academy of Marketing Science*, *50*(2), pages195–225. doi:10.100711747-021-00815-w PMID:34776554

Urwin, M. (2023, Sep 12). *AI Taking Over Jobs: What to Know About the Future of Jobs*. builtin.com.

Why tomorrow's professions will be increasingly scientific yet also more & humanistic. (2021, Apr 12). morningfuture.com.

ADDITIONAL READING

All Software Categories. (n.d.). technologyevaluation.com/c.

Asif, A., Lee, E., Caputo, M., Biglino, G., & Shearn, A. I. U. (2021). Role of 3D printing technology in paediatric teaching and training: A systematic review. *BMJ Paediatrics Open*, *5*(1), e001050. doi:10.1136/bmjpo-2021-001050 PMID:35290958

Bostrom, N., & Yudkowsky, E. (2011). The Ethics of Artificial Intelligence. In *Cambridge Handbook of Artificial Intelligence*. Cambridge University Press.

Eisenberg, M. (2012). *3D printing for children: What to build next?* sciencedirect.com.

Forward, A., & Lethbridge, T. (2008). A taxonomy of software types to facilitate search and evidence-based software engineering. *Proceedings of the 2008 Conference of the Center for Advanced Studies*. 10.1145/1463788.1463807

Georgiev, G. V., & Georgiev, D. D. (2018, July). Enhancing user creativity: Semantic measures for idea generation. *Knowledge-Based Systems*, *151*(1), 1–15. doi:10.1016/j.knosys.2018.03.016

Jobs of Tomorrow: Large Language Models and Jobs. (2023 Sep.). *World Economic Forum*.

Latouche, S. (2007). *Petit traité de la décroissance sereine*. Fayard.

Nørgård, J. S. (2013). Happy degrowth through more amateur economy. *Journal of Cleaner Production*, *38*, 61–70. doi:10.1016/j.jclepro.2011.12.006

Reyero, D. (2019). Humanists and techies: the future belongs to the "hybrid" professionals. *davidreyero.com*.

Russell, S. J., & Norvig, P. (2020). *Artificial Intelligence: A Modern Approach* (4th ed.). Prentice Hall.

Sarkar, A. (2017, May 3). Everything You Need To Know About Mobile App Ecosystem. *webskitters.com*/blog

Sharples, M., & Pérez y Pérez, R. (2022). *Story Machines: How Computers Have Become Creative Writers*. Routledge. doi:10.4324/9781003161431

Tobias, S. (2014). Multimedia Learning with Computer Games. In *The Cambridge Handbook of Multimedia Learning*. Cambridge University Press. doi:10.1017/CBO9781139547369.037

Understanding the Mobile App Development Ecosystem. (2023, May 4). *webiotic.com*.

Weiss, M., & Cattaneo, C. (2017). Degrowth – Taking Stock and Reviewing an Emerging Academic Paradigm. *Ecological Economics*, *137*, 220–230. doi:10.1016/j.ecolecon.2017.01.014 PMID:28674463

Chapter 10
Active Citizens in a New Communication Society:
WWW, Back to the Future! Examples to Aware Projects

ABSTRACT

Computers and the world wide web are for citizens to work first-hand and together, not only for a global market of buyers and sellers. But there is not still an "operating system" for civil society to run, not because of technology, but of people's choices: the greatest opportunity for democracy in history is likely be lost forever among increasing differences and contradictions and the risk of environmental catastrophe and war. To understand better the global world as a system, multidisciplinarity and communities can be alternatives to social networks towards a possible future of collaboration and peace, although it is difficult to see today how to overcome the individualistic and competitive old-industrial model. Not necessarily considering companies and citizens on opposing sides, an aware application of technology to life beyond the waste of the market, the lesson of open software and participation can allow the transition in society from single-use information to real, shared communication.

1. INTRODUCTION

Beyond the big difficulties of the present times, it is worth to go and see if it possible overcoming the general resignation to a technological development far from the control of people and civil society, in the hands of unknown and unapproachable powers, whose nature we know more from science fiction stories than from reality.

Works and studies about balancing human and robots' skills, an interdisciplinary approach to the complexity, the role of living communities, the open software movement, examples of digital applications out of the most known commercial trends in original fields and unconventional ways, this all can broaden the perspective, towards a sort of "operating system" in which the global humanity can apply the way technology develops to new social and economic models, rather than constrain that same de-

DOI: 10.4018/978-1-6684-8228-5.ch010

velopment within the previous old models, which is probably the reason why recurring crises prevent us from effectively addressing the problems of the planet.

In the end, the issue is not technical, but political and, as complex as it is, it concerns democracy, the participation and responsibility of the citizens, that is, all of us: many big difficulties, but also exciting opportunities.

2. AN OPERATING SYSTEM FOR HUMAN SOCIAL INTERACTIONS?

In human–robot collaborative assembly tasks, it is necessary to properly balance skills to maximize productivity. Human operators can contribute with their abilities in dexterous manipulation, reasoning and problem solving, but a bounded workload (cognitive, physical, and timing) should be assigned for the task. Collaborative robots can provide accurate, quick and precise physical work skills, but they have constrained cognitive interaction capacity and low dexterous ability. (Chacón, 2021)

In the process of continuous evolution of the emerging technologies, new fields of the theoretical practical knowledge are generated to develop unprecedented activities, with educational or working purposes, for instance. The novelty of those activities stands in direct relationship with an advance of the hardware and telecommunications, mainly in the emerging and information technology (IT). All of that a constant need of a software which adapts to the growing needs of the user in daily life. The main goal from the software is to facilitate an effective interaction with the new ICT (information and communication technologies) devices. (Cipolla-Ficarra, 2018)

There are so many kinds of tool, system, software, hardware, knowledge, thought, idea, principle, theory, and various kinds of human behaviors linked with Internet working by Information Technologies that have been facilitating human actions even in cases at Dense Interference Space (DIS). DIS is a place where so many people or information are/is gathered randomly unintentionally on a networking or at a physical place. (Sugiyama, 2019)

Studies are many, from different points of view, on the relationship between man - machine (hardware, software), on how work changes in widely automated contexts or in which most of the tasks are performed by artificial intelligence. Well!

But since computers would allow any woman or man and even children to be present first-hand in the information society and the World Wide Web could help the people of all the world to work together, for knowledge and life, we have in fact on one hand human activities increasingly fragmented, regulated and competing one another, and on the other only a global community of buyers and sellers, more than citizens. This does not help civil coexistence. And, as it seems that on the Internet the concern for catching unique visitors is much more considered than the opportunity humans are wasting to meet one another, even if it means peace or war, so, not because of "technology", but because people's choices the greatest opportunity for democracy in history is likely be lost forever.

We lack a sort of "operating system", able to supervise the civil society.

Maybe it is a hazard to apply the concept of "operating system" to human communities, but it can be worth thinking a little of it.

General system theory is a very suggestive science of wholeness, describing similarities of organization in subjects traditionally considered distant: animal organisms, macro and microcosms, machines, psychic, and social systems. Systems can be very simple or extremely complex and can be observed by humans from outside, existing in nature, in living beings, physics, astronomy, or directly "created" by them, as social systems, or the operative systems of digital devices too. These are very complex, are a novelty of last half century and have introduced new ways of thinking and doing that, referring to the operation of machines, must be extremely accurate and precise. Perhaps in some respects, they could provide useful insights to the management of social systems, which, conversely, have been formed along the history in a much more random way, conditioned by power relations and ideology, and whose operation, now with the globalization, seems increasingly difficult to control.

If knowing how instructions, commands and data run in circuits and electronic memories, is not a thing for everyone, how for example a software development team deals with problems, it can take interesting suggestions. When there are errors or malfunctions, the members of a team work to correct them, and they know that other corrections will always be made later, to introduce new features, face new errors. Where the word "error" is not a fault, but a normal situation that at some point somehow occurs. This should be a behavior that is part of the *change* induced by the massive entry of technology into our lives, the different and positive way to consider mistakes. As well as a *change* should be the familiarity to establish links between things, not only to browse the web, but to connect the pieces of life and experience that, in an increasingly complex society, we cannot continue to consider one by one.

In fact, in many work environments, as well as in social life, reporting a mistake continues to represent an "offense" for someone, and often the styles of work in schools, public administration, but also private companies, appear to remain firmly anchored in the past, rather than facing a possible future. While also new technologies are often superimposed in an artificial, somewhat authoritarian way, not being related to a wider system, whose mutual connections and "bugs" are not considered.

An operating system itself is above all a matter of logic, rather than electronics, and different starting points of view must converge ahead, towards a common goal. "Technical" points of view, linked to the different specializations and skills, methods and procedures of work linked to the professions, they should not conflict, and other unexpected elements can be inserted, that also are to be considered and corrected. So that, for example, if the greater theoretical efficiency of a new work process corresponds to discomfort for workers, it is not only a labor conflict, bosses against workers, but the overall efficiency of the system suffers. It it is a "bug" that can be understood in all its components and fixed, possibly together.

We should study and test deeply how working connections and relationships are established - we do not change culture from one day to another, just because we spend less time watching TV and more holding smartphones - and not only academically, but in people's life. And we should seriously try to understand why to all the new "facilities" we get, that free humans from many stressful and repetitive tasks, often it does not correspond a more relaxed lifestyle, but rather the opposite.

According to a survey by Associated Chambers of Commerce and Industry of India in 2015, increasingly demanding schedules and high stress levels in the private sector employees are leading to depression or general anxiety disorders and have wide range of effects like daytime fatigue, physical discomfort or low pain threshold leading to increased absenteeism and performance deterioration. The survey further points out that nearly 45% of the corporate employees in private sector sleep less than 6 hours a day, leading to severe sleep disorders. (Chhabra, 2022)

Many technological changes cause high levels of job insecurity because employees fear that they will be unable to cope with the changing environment. (Ghani et al., 2022)

The rapid development of mobile technology and smart devices, social media such as wikis, blogs, instant messaging (IM), and social networking sites (SNSs) have penetrated people's daily life ... Employees may become overloaded by accessing and mentally processing information related to both work and personal life during work hours ... Technostress is an emerging theoretical construct that has developed over less than two decades and has emerged from multiple streams of thinking, which do not allow a clear vision of its scope, references, and relevance. (Bondanini et al., 2020)

Noise factors pass through many jobs and activities, everywhere, not to mention the attempts - not new, because they always occur with the appearance of new technologies but magnified today by the extreme power of the current ones - to direct all digital innovation towards a huge increase in productivity and profit, including at the expense of the well-being of workers. While an effective use of technology in improving the quality of work could probably add satisfaction in carrying out activities, for the individuals and the groups, especially when technology itself is consciously managed by the workers.

3. A MULTIDISCIPLINARY APPROACH TO KNOWLEDGE IN THE GLOBAL INTERCONNECTED WORLD

Interdisciplinarity derives from a selection of ideas, approaches, theories, concepts, methods and comparisons from different fields or disciplines ... In no way does interdisciplinarity depend on the knowledge of entire disciplines or on global notions of the unity of knowledge. There is no single path to interdisciplinarity, no single model, no single standard for successful development (Graff, 2015). (Scanlon et al., 2019)

As the techniques and strategies for educational reform have spread rapidly throughout the world, teacher professional development practices have been borrowed across borders. It is important to study the global sharing of information on teacher professional development. (Al-Mahdi & Purinton, 2022)

It is essential to study these best practices and innovations that have been developed in remote teaching and learning to better understand the future of online education. (Research Anthology on Remote Teaching and Learning and the Future of Online Education, 2022)

Interdisciplinary orientation in teaching philosophy, political science, sociology, economic theories, psychology, pedagogy and teaching methods of a particular discipline in the context of interdisciplinarity offers some extra opportunities for the formation of the system of professional and pedagogical knowledge of the future teachers. (Vaskivska et al., 2017)

It is not only a matter of school and research, but also of economic and social strategies and policies and, in the end, to describe as much as possible what in our globalized world can be understood as a part of a system.

Figure 1. Multidisciplinary

Recurring political and economic crises in agriculture lie behind policymakers' demands for more interdisciplinary, problem-solving approaches. (Jansen, 2009)

Research projects which require developments in both computing science and the humanities can undertake novel research that would otherwise prove impossible ... interdisciplinary research and working practices can bridge computing or engineering science and more than one traditional aspect of humanities research. Individuals working in such interdisciplinary teams often find they are the 'Other' - working beyond a defined disciplinary cultural unit, with the need for the construction of roles and responsibilities that allow their skill sets to be admitted to a working team, rather than behaving, and treating each other, as if they come from foreign climes. (Terras, 2010)

Responsibility is the key. Too many times "technology" is indicated as an almost objective factor, independent of human will, as if the use of machines and software in this or that direction would not depend on precise human choices. When managing the digital power directly, in a society that has lost many of the old landmarks, anyone of us is more responsible in comparison to the past and we are to find new ways not only to use new means, but above all to manage relationships between people.

Combining computer science and social science in novel ways, we've been thinking a lot about how to create better systems for matching employers and employees that also give the workers voice and bar-

gaining power," Levi said. "What does it mean for a worker to have voice and power in an environment where unions have basically disappeared? What constitutes valuable skills?

The interdisciplinary center is an annual residential fellowship program ... in the fields of psychology, sociology, anthropology, political science and economics, as well as those researching social science questions in the humanities, law, medicine, engineering and other sciences. (Shashkevich, 2018)

However,

Domain specificity is an essential aspect of science that enables researchers to solve complex problems in a cognitively manageable way ... It constrains interdisciplinary research, is not yet fully understood, which attests to an important role for philosophers of science in the study of interdisciplinary science. (MacLeod, 2016)

Ethics has always been a main domain of philosophical study. Hypertextual discursive expression has never been considered as the technology that can revolutionise the way we interpret ethical events and actions ... Contemporary studies of philosophical hermeneutics are predominantly centred on the Gadamerian conception, giving due importance to the dialogue that should take place between what has been written in the past and the present situation of the interpreter ... This shall be done by entertaining the possibility of understanding and reshaping future hermeneutics within a different form of discursive expression - hypertextual writing. (Garcia, 2021)

AI is only one of many emerging technologies—from genome editing and 3D printing to a globally networked "Internet of Things"—shaping a future unparalleled in human history in its promise and its peril. Are we up to the challenge this future presents? If not, how can we get there? How can humans hope to live well in a world made increasingly more complex and unpredictable by emerging technologies. . . ? In essence my answer is this: we need to cultivate in ourselves, collectively, a special kind of moral character, one that expresses what I will call the technomoral virtues. (Vallor, 2016)

4. COMMUNITIES AS LIVING ALTERNATIVE TO SOCIAL NETWORKS

People stay much on social networks, but they do not live there. People live in communities. And understanding the future, it is not a question of technology, but of *philosophy*, that's to say, beyond the suggestions and academic discussions, the way all of us think about ourselves and the world. And we humans, although we are competing every day and many times conforming to distant external orders, a faith, a utopia, a technology, it is in our actual social relationships that we meet the others, feel fine or uneasy, love and hate, realize or waste our lives.

Connections can be not only intended as a nonstop link to ads and entertainment, or to channels where we comment from outside - that very frustrating, in the end - and complain about what wrong happens in the world. But the same everyday digital tools can be used to connect our thinking to our doing, and everyone can be an active actor, even if we have to invent new ways that are not in the culture of consumption in which we have grown up. We need to start again from the real world, from the factories, fields, offices, schools, cities in which we work and live, and learn to rethink them together, also including in a "working system" the outcasts, the last, who are forced to make a living in the increasingly numerous grey areas of our cities.

Even with the vast wealth and resources these cities generate, their most vulnerable populations live without adequate or affordable housing, safe water, healthy food, and other essentials. And yet, cities also often harbor the solutions to the inequalities they create ... Co-Cities outlines practices, laws, and policies that are presently fostering innovation in the provision of urban services, spurring collaborative economies as a driver of local sustainable development, and promoting inclusive and equitable regeneration of blighted urban areas. (Foster & Iaione, 2022)

It is not a matter - as many seem to think - of "defending" against an unstoppable rising tide, or returning nostalgically to a lost past, but of recovering the authentic spirit of a technological innovations that, in the absence of a mass culture able to welcome and develop them, are largely aborted but whose recovery, also on the pressure of economic, environmental and health emergencies, could bring enormous benefits to all the humanity. We must however really change, not just talk about change all the time, while we remain the same as before, increasingly frustrated, quarrelsome, and powerless, at the mercy of true or more often false narratives that divide us into fictitious factions and take away from us the possible strength and the joy of doing together.

Co-creation is everywhere: It's how the internet was built; it generated massive prehistoric rock carvings; it powered the development of vaccines for COVID-19 in record time. Co-creation offers alternatives to the idea of the solitary author privileged by top-down media. But co-creation is easy to miss, as individuals often take credit for—and profit from—collective forms of authorship, erasing whole cultures and narratives as they do so. (Cizek et al., 2022)

Misinformation has recently attracted considerable attention. Recent studies highlight the role of misinformation in shaping resistant-to-change misconceptions and conspiracy theories and giving rise to numerous environmental, societal, and global problems ... fake news outperformed real news on Facebook, favoring a candidate during the last three months preceding the 2016 United States election. Conspiracy thinking has also caused the politicization of climate science and consequently the increasing polarization of the public concerning critical environmental issues, such as global warming. These examples indicate that misinformation can damage our critical thinking abilities, thus incurring tremendous unnecessary costs on individuals and society and threatening democracy. (Shakeri & Hawamdeh, 2022)

The very nature of journalism will likely be received and interpreted within unique communities through innovative and inclusive ways ... As in-world journalists have sought to inform and engage unique communities within the context of their worlds, real and virtual, issues relevant to the mainstream have been played out in virtual culture. (Johnson & Punnett, 2022)

Technically, we would have the possibility of completely change the context in which journalist work, if we understand that all of us would have the means no longer only to argue idly about the news, but give them, verify, correct them, using social networks in a collaborative way, intervening from territories for a participatory and shared management of information. Technically, we need to process the right "software" for this kind of information to run, but the biggest problem is to start believing that

Figure 2. Online communities
Source: Uplift: Online Communities Against Sexual Violence (2017)

this can be done. Professional journalist could not depend only on their editorial staff, solid or precarious employment contract, or master, but become the terminals, hopefully intelligent, of a widespread information, in a world where also a part of the audience learns to not only publish photos of kittens.

This would be the real change made possible by current technology, and not to read the traditional newspaper or watch TV on mobile phones!

Some examples of this active way of exercising digital citizenship can be found in online communities.

The combination of low-cost access to increasingly powerful computing and networking capabilities combined with a deregulated internet has facilitated the rapid development of a new social phenomena, that of the online community. (Plant, 2004)

Online communities ... are independent groups of people who share common interests. Think of them as clubs: community members are drawn to a club to participate in an activity and to be a part of conversations surrounding that topic ... Independent communities are often on standalone apps or sites. (Bello, 2023)

Online communities are today a widespread phenomenon that takes a variety of forms. Free and open-source software is probably the most well-known case, where geographically dispersed individuals collectively develop new software and produce innovation ... In 1991 Linus Torvalds founded the Linux kernel, the heart of an operating system with the ability to have a real impact on Microsoft's market share ... From the original incorporation of some 10,000 lines of source code, by 2005 the community had developed more than 6,000,000 lines of code. (Dahlander et al., 2009)

For what is the purpose of this book, here are given only, piled up, a few examples that, knowing of their existence and observing them in perspective, could enter the public imagination as a possible outlet of technological transformation alternative to commercial stereotypes, to the digital bureaucracy, to the sectarian brawls in social networks. And perhaps, understanding that everything can depend on a small commitment of each of us, we could find the motivation to try to take back, without even too much effort, technology, and life.

Despite their recent emergence, WhatsApp neighbourhood crime prevention (WNCP) groups are an already pervasive phenomenon in the Netherlands. (Mols, 2021)

Technologies for older adults ... the communities may provide social support, contribute to self-preservation, and serve as an opportunity for self-discovery and growth. Because they offer both leisure activity and an expanded social network, it is suggested that active participation in the communities may contribute to the well-being of older adults. (Nimrod, 2010)

For organizations in the sharing economy, the online communities they host, where users interact with each other, are core to value creation. Little is known, however, about the organizational practices used to govern these online communities to encourage participation and to direct, coordinate, and control interactions strategically ... Scoping community boundaries encourage participation by demarcating the perimeters of interaction and defining the online community as a distinct social space; nudging social relations encourages participation by providing stimuli for interaction; and steering users exerts a form of social control over interactions. We discovered that organizations rely on both online and offline technologies to govern ... Our study highlights the dual role of organizations in the sharing economy as curators and guardians of online communities and displays the potential of sharing economy research to enhance knowledge about value creation, online communities, and organizational governance. (Reischauer & Mair, 2018)

Where human communication and development is possible, folklore is developed. With the rise of digital communications and media in past decades, humans have adopted a new form of folklore within this online landscape. Digital folklore has been developed into a culture that impacts the ways in which communities are formed, media is created, and communications are carried out. It is essential to track this growing phenomenon. (Papadakis & Kapaniaris, 2022)

5. POSSIBLE SEEDS OF FUTURE BEYOND THE MARKET

Traditional literacy is considered essential for citizens to be able to participate in productive activities in a dignified manner, but also it has a social, civil value, of freedom and democracy. A country is considered truly civilized when it guarantees a school for all and defeats illiteracy. And thinking that reading, writing and arithmetic can be applied only to some specific content established by some government, church or other power, it makes us think of a dictatorship.

Today, the new universal alphabets of the global world, the audiovisual and the "digital", are taught almost completely by the market, and when trends are indicated of the evolution of technology, the commercial point of view dominates the social and civil ones. In chapter 8 we had written about "the library and the store" and in other paragraphs we pointed out that for the web they are in practice accepted as general the rules that actually should refer to its commercial use.

This is not the only possible world. And as well in economy, as in culture, administration, health, science, and any other field of human activities, to use the new means substantially to try to optimize the old ways of doing, as often it happens, it can be counterproductive. To *change* doesn't just mean doing the same things in another way, but maybe begin to do different things.

Figure 3. Beyond market
Source: Bollier (2012)

As the world has adapted to the age of digital technology, present day business leaders are required to change with the times as well. Addressing and formatting their business practices to not only encompass digital technologies, but expand their capabilities, the leaders of today must be flexible and willing to familiarize themselves with all types of global business practices. (Smith & Cockburn, 2021)

In addition to productive applications and consumer market trends, other factors are pressing and driving our use of technology: pandemics, climate change, recurrent economic crises, migratory flows.

Information management in pandemic conditions involves accelerating the adoption of the digital transformation in manufacturing and service sectors that impact the economy. The risks of maintaining a dismissive view are already visible on the labor and economic side. (Argüelles et al., 2021)

The scholarly publishing industry is in its early days of the digital transformation, and blockchain and AI technology could play a major role in this. However, the industry has been resistant to change. These reasons include but are not limited to staying with legacy systems, cost of new platforms, changing cultures, and understanding and adopting new technologies. With proper research and information provided, the publishing industry can adopt these technologies for beneficial advancements and the generation of a bright future. (Gunter, 2021)

The present understanding of globalization is inextricably tied to the free market ideology for both proponents and opponents ... Globalization has many potential forms of which the neo-liberal recipe, applied up to now, is only one ... It would need to be production-centered and led; pro-growth and pro-development; with dynamic, locally differentiated markets, enhancing national and other identities and reaching towards optimum worldwide welfare. The immense wealth creating potential of this paradigm is capable of achieving such positive-sum goals under the appropriate enabling conditions ... Unleashing all the growth potential of each technological revolution in the deployment period requires overcoming the basic tensions inherited from the installation period ... Turning over the helm of the economy from financial to production capital ... Real economy over the paper economy at all levels: global, national and local ... in the direction of truly global welfare. (Perez, 2007)

A technological ecosystem is a metaphor to express a needed evolution of the traditional information systems ... that provides a set of services that each component separately does not offer and can evolve as a whole in a better way when its components do or when some components are dropped out or when new components are included. Moreover, the technological ecosystem is thought to offer a better user experience so that users are also part or components of the ecosystem ... The technological ecosystem metaphor comes from the Biology field, and it has been transferred into software development because it reflects so well the evolutionary nature of software. (García-Peñalvo, 2022)

Beyond metaphors, it is the unconventional applications of technologies that can point the way to possible significant innovations, for a possible new economy and society based not only on the market as we have known it so far. Those possibilities are manifested in a transversal way in the different sectors, as improvement of traditional production processes, or as invention of partially or completely new modes.

Although robots have pervaded many industrial sectors and domestic environments, the experiments in the food sectors are limited to pick-and-place operations and meat processing while we are assisting new attention in gastronomy. Given the great performances of the robots, there would be many other intriguing applications to explore which could usher the transition to precision food manufacturing ... The enhancement obtained through the gentle manipulation of foods, often delicate and fragile, such as fruit and vegetables are of uttermost importance not only for packaging industries and distributors but also for the harvesting and many food processing steps characterized by several human handling and mechanical operations which potentially may impart severe damages. (Derossi et al., 2023)

The hydroponics is a modern cultivation method without using soil as media but nutrient solution ... Without using the soil, the hydroponic promises some advantages compared to traditional agriculture methods such as in cleanness, space requirement, maintenance, and productivity ... Advanced computer technology could contribute in the agriculture sector in order to improve the food production in quality as well as in quantity. (Hermawan, 2022)

Today's technologies already allow us to use nonstandard building materials as found, or as made, and assemble them in as many nonstandard, intelligent, adaptive ways as needed: the microfactories of our imminent future will be automated artisan shops. (Carpo, 2023)

What if "democratizing" computer science went beyond the usual one-off workshop and empowered youth to create digital products for social impact. . . ? Stories of a diverse group of young people in Oakland, California, who combine journalism, data, design, and code to create media that makes a difference. (Lee & Soep, 2023)

During these uncertain and turbulent times, intelligent technologies including artificial neural networks (ANN) and machine learning (ML) have played an incredible role in being able to predict, analyze, and navigate unprecedented circumstances across a number of industries, ranging from healthcare to hospitality. (Segall & Niu, 2022)

6. ACROSS THE CONTRADICTIONS IN THE CENTER AND PERIPHERY OF THE DIGITAL PLANET

Here we are mentioning examples, not systematically, even randomly, where the combination of many and various quotations is to give an idea of the extreme complexity of the subject, existing problems and possible solutions, whose identification or research should involve a much larger part of the humanity than that now in fact engaged. That is, global problems require global and shared solutions, and the management of such a complex and branched social "operating system" cannot be delegated only to politics, economics, finance, as we know them, with the rest of the world that, when things go well, is limited every few years to draw a mark on a ballot. There are so many problems, but we also have the most powerful means of solving them in the history of humanity. Each of us has them in our hands!

At least that part of us who care about the future of the world could try to take part a little bit more than attending social networks, looking for and sharing a better information about actual problems, solutions, innovations.

The documentary on climate change *Before the Flood* (2016) by Fisher Stevens and Leonardo Di Caprio can be interesting in this respect. After a precise and almost desperate list of all the evils of the present world, which could lead us to the darkest despair, it comes to the possible solutions, some even completely unexpected, and proposed also by average people who try to use in a positive way the available technology and possibilities of communication. It's not about hoping that someone else, a superhero, a creator of metaverse saves the world, but maybe, by putting only a little extra effort - and possibly another organization, another "operating system" - we probably can do something ourselves.

For many basic, strategical for survival, and cultural challenging topics that can improve the quality of our lives, new technologies open a wide range of possible perspectives, driven both from big companies and local groups and operators, and sometimes a mixture between the two. The road is not already marked and can be good or bad depending on how we move along it.

Resolution tools can be used by global businesses to manage various types of crisis situations, such as natural disasters, information security issues, economic downturns, health crisis situations, and sustainability issues in education, among others. Further study and consideration of the uses of technology in the areas of crisis and change management and intra-company communication practice in the context of global business must be done to ensure successful and sustainable businesses. (Ali, 2022)

Digitalization has offered new ways to reach out to both members of the group and those outside it (citation Brusila, "Maximum"). Among indigenous peoples, the Internet has, for example, created cosmopolitanism, music revivals, activism, new ways of becoming recognized and ways to assert authorship over representation of alterity – thus offering a more accurate picture of themselves to the outside world (citation Hilder 7). The networks offered by digital media have allowed new forms of decentralized subcultural and transnational communities to emerge (citation Brusila, "'Impact'" 10).

The opportunities, but also threats, that the company's activities include are paradoxically summarized in the slogan "Sounds and stories that once remained local ... are now GLOBAL" (citation Spotify), which the company used when launching its new strategy in 2021. The local musicians now not only have the advantage, but also the disadvantage of competing with the biggest international stars and industries.

According to some theorists, convergences between older and new media have made it possible for the audience to engage in collectively creating "user-generated content," "participatory culture," or "convergence culture" (e.g. citation Jenkins). The renegotiations of the distinctions between producers and consumers have been summarized in concepts such as "presumption" (Ritzer and Jurgenson) and "produsage" (citation Bruns), emphasizing the restructuring of creative practices that previously were based on one-way communication. The technological and cultural changes also have consequences for institutions outside the core industry. For example, music learning is undergoing major changes that are often described by using the discourse of democracy as people study things on their own with the support of online materials online. (Brusila et al., 2021)

Languages, forms of communication, high and mass culture, tend to blend as never before, among themselves and with the social and civil life of nations.

Universality of certain components of audiovisual media (especially movies, both industry standard and independent productions) as a cause and possible instrument of international political communication ... usually neglected types of media such as advertisement, music videos and video games, as well as their rightful place in universal codes of media, which is established through articulated cases and status changes occurring within the relevant industries with the arrival of World Wide Web ... a logical transition from political movements, parties and wider examples to the context of singular political figures, musing on how using narrative techniques acquire in the media helps them to obtain statuses which are hardly related to professional capabilities and lie more in the fields of mythology ... presidential candidates through their appearances in movies, comics and music which keeps to be the case for every US President ever. (Yeromin, 2021)

From FinTech in the business realm to phygital churches in the realm of religion, innovation is applicable everywhere. It is essential that professionals study how to use these advancements to their advantage and also to examine their impact on society and its multitude of sectors. (Marchisio, 2022)

Field observations show that too few companies have the leadership capabilities to make digital transformation a success. A study in the finance industry reveals that 77% of firms deploying digital transformation solutions have not obtained the expected results. (Philippart, 2022)

Much depends on whether the use of technology is actually aimed at improving production and performances or maximizing profits. In the case of health, for example, great advantages in terms of the organization and efficiency of medical practices can be frustrated by policy choices only in favor of the privatization of the service.

A new generation of information technologies, such as the internet of things, cloud computing, big data, and artificial intelligence, have transformed the old medical system and improved the efficiency, conve-

nience, and personalization of healthcare. These changes are necessary to keep up with the requirements of individual people and the improvements in the efficiency of medical care, which largely enhances the experience of medical and health services. (Madaan et al., 2022)

At the end of November, a record 7.2 million patients in England were waiting for non-urgent medical treatment on the NHS, known as "elective" care. This spans diagnostic tests and scans, procedures such as hip and knee replacements, but also cardiac surgery, cancer treatment and neurosurgery ... To avoid joining a waiting list, more and more people are paying for their own private medical care or taking out health insurance. (Ziady, 2023)

The chapter investigates the adoption and use of YouTube to enhance teaching and learning of research methodology in Nigeria universities. (Omiunu et al., 2019)

The importance of narratives in education is evident by the new media rich environments, the online global educational models, which embrace worldwide presence, and the storytelling production process that has been democratized ... Transmedia storytelling can emerge within education as a product and as a practice in technology-supported environments. Jenkins (2006) described convergences in his book Convergence Culture: Where Old and New Media Collide ... the flow of content across multiple media platforms, the cooperation between multiple media industries, and the migratory behavior of media audiences who will go almost anywhere in search of the kinds of entertainment experiences they want' ... Jenkins' theory of convergence culture ... student-centered, technology-supported approaches to learning in the age of media convergence. (Kalogeras, 2019)

Technology in education is somehow misconceived by many scholars who think that it replaces conventional knowledge and its transmission ... technology in education requires a "handle with care" machine. Teachers must be able to use the "machines" and not to be used by them. (Kuboja, 2019)

E-governance is "...the use by government agencies of information technologies that can transform relationships with citizens, businesses, and other arms of government" (Steins, 2002: 18) ... E-government (or E-gov), refers to the use of IT, ICT, and other web-based telecommunication technologies to augment inter-organizational relations (Ronaghan, 2002) and enhance the "efficiency and effectiveness of service delivery in the public sector" (Fang, 2002). (Omar, 2020)

A smart city is an urban area that uses IoT technologies to collect data and manage resources ... solve the citizens' problems (e.g., energy consumption, transportation, recycling, intelligent security, etc.) in an efficient way ... Although the concept of a smart city is increasing and currently there exist many such cities in many developed countries, one of the key challenges faced by these cities is good governance ... Digital governance refers to the use of digital technology in government practices. (Humayun et al., 2020)

Smart Cities is a very important and controversial topic. Here it can be only mentioned, and it's not essentially about technology, but about politics. Also because of the inadequate awareness of citizens and many administrators, the technical proposals are likely to be understood only partially, while the attention of public opinion is above all centered on other basic and more traditional issues. Who knows

Figure 4. Smart cities
Source: Donada (n.d.)

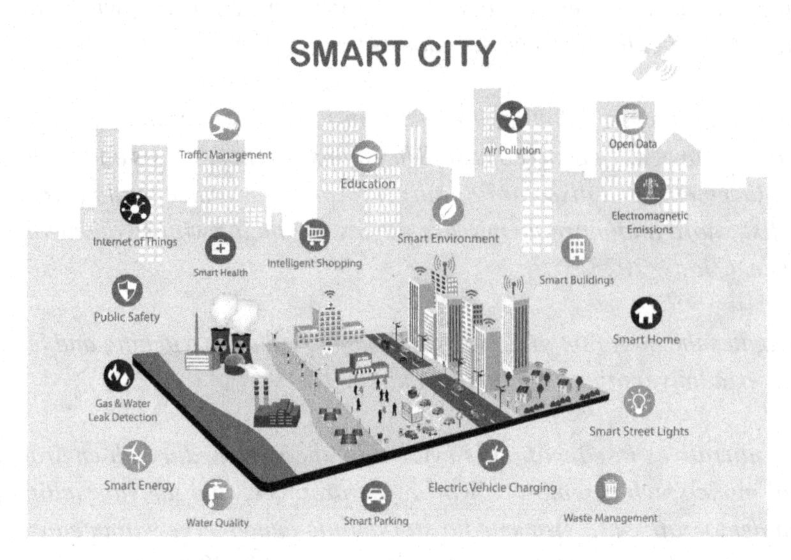

why the digitization of cities takes place in that direction and not in others? Who discusses it, who decides, who chooses?

7. USUAL MEANS FOR UNUSUAL PURPOSES

Using multimedia applications available in Mobile phones can result in the increasing retention rates, because people remember 20% of what they see, 40% of what they see and hear, but about 75% of what they see and hear and do simultaneously. Mobile phone has the potential to remove the barriers that are causing the problems of low rate of education in any country. It can be used as a tool to overcome the issues of cost, less number of teachers, and poor quality of education as well as to overcome time and distance barriers. (Sandhya & Swathi 2017)

This study shows that an increasing number of people around retirement age (55-65) in Zhengzhou are using smart phones and apps to reimagine the possibilities of post-work lifestyles. (Guo et al., 2019)

Management and technology experts Thomas Davenport and Steven Miller show that, contrary to widespread predictions, prescriptions, and denunciations, AI is not primarily a job destroyer. Rather, AI changes the way we work—by taking over some tasks but not entire jobs, freeing people to do other, more important and more challenging work. By offering detailed, real-world case studies of AI-augmented jobs in settings that range from finance to the factory floor, Davenport and Miller also show that AI in the workplace is not the stuff of futuristic speculation. It is happening now to many companies and workers. (Davenport & Miller, 2022)

Participation in the media involves not only making use of the media, but also being active in some way in the creation of content. During the era of mass media such opportunities were few and quite constricted.

Public service broadcasting, it could be argued, through its efforts to represent diverse voices and groups in society and with varying degrees of accountability built into the system, could be said to have been a major exception that facilitated (rather indirectly) participation in production. With the advent of the web and its affordances, participation in media has certainly been transformed. This is an important democratic step, and certainly the political can manifest itself in the media, within online networks focused on network issues. Still, we must bear in mind the distinctions in scale and impact between on the one side, small organisations, groups, and individuals, and on the other side, major corporate actors. The corporate colonisation of communicative space online and the growing domination of market logic on the web of course has implications for power relations online.

Participation via the media takes us into social domains beyond the media. Participation in these domains is facilitated by the media, but the focus of engagement lies with the contexts and issues that media connect us to. (Dahlgren, 2013)

The contemporary education system is disrupted by the plethora of emerging technologies, the aftermath of the COVID-19 pandemic, global financial woes, and the ever-present shifting of higher education structuration and needs. There is a necessity for a marker to capture this transition in order to teach future generations how to recover educational losses in crisis situations ... teaching and learning cases from Africa, the Americas, Asia, Australia, and Europe ... various innovative practices in education, covering crisis contexts, green education, and education technologies. (Chakravarti & Boukareva, 2022)

Innovation coming from a non-conventional approach to usual tasks can be very useful to shift the attitude of people from normally repeating given operations to slightly change their point of view according to a floating, liquid, never exactly equal to itself technological environment in which we are immersed. Remixing can be a suggestive key, as normally do children in their play, but not only.

When in times of touch screen everywhere, it was proposed a game for Nintendo DS based on the keyboard, it could be almost an educational revolution. At the end of the game, after pressing many keys here and there on the keyboard to chase the *Pokémons in* different ways, the child realized the he/she has learned to type with ten fingers! How many in the school noticed it? (Learn with Pokémon: Typing Adventure, 2011).

Many years before, a group from the university of Toronto already talked about "humanizing" a painting program, at the beginning of a research that today leads us to have mobile phones physically sensitive to a variety of gestures of our hand:

An interactive paint program has been built using multiple processes and message passing. The program has an anthropomorphic design, assigning independent processes to roles which might otherwise be considered in a human context. This design contrasts with traditional paint program implementations using sequential and interrupt driven procedures. (Beach et al. 1982)

Forty years later, interactive technologies are described at the university of Turin, where

People and machines establish a positive relationship to find solutions for social aspects and problems ... In these terms, digital systems and virtual and augmented reality technologies enable multi-dimensional

scenarios and additional levels of interdisciplinary collaboration to create a highly inclusive communication network and social framework. (Ugliotti & Osello 2022)

8. OPEN, FREE, NON-PROFIT ALTERNATIVES

We know that the open software movement is not a romantic and naive attempt to counter a dominant system based on copyright and competition, but an alternative that can be successful, as demonstrated by the prominent presence of the Linux operating system in the global network management.

Introducing the 2010 edition of *Free as in Freedom,* about "Richard Stallman and the Free Software Revolution", the author Sam Williams writes:

I'd probably have to call it the "iPad Effect" or maybe the "Kindle Effect" both in an attempt to keep up with the evolving brand names and to acknowledge parallel, tectonic shifts in the realm of daily journalism and electronic book publishing ... Being an effective reformer nowadays requires more than just titanic stamina and a willingness to cry out in the wilderness for a decade or more, it requires knowing how to articulate durable, scalable ideas, how to beat the system at its own game. (Sam Williams, 2010)

Stallman was a strict prophet of free software. Over time, even the purest had accepted the idea of a possible coexistence on the same machines of free and commercial software, even if in the meantime the market had expanded exponentially towards an undifferentiated and inexperienced public, in 2000 when the book was first published, in 2010 and even more in the years 2020. However, other than "to cry out in the wilderness", there are perhaps more reasons now that could push users and citizens towards a turnaround, and free software is still alive and active and could offer a viable alternative, though quite fragmented and "politically" half-hearted.

In fact, there are many moving around, proposing alternatives, especially in the direction of "degoogling" the user experience on the Web, now revolving mostly around Gmail, YouTube, the almost universally used search engine and the monopoly of Android. But other software can better protect privacy, avoid the systematic collection of data, and certainly not alone transform their users in an active citizenship movement.

Even online communities, if they do not have very precise concrete purposes, can hardly go far, in the absence of real and consolidated popular movements in civil society. And in the meantime, attempts are multiplying, "alternatives of alternatives" are being proposed, which anyhow keep alive the experimentation and research and serve to improve the tools that could be good for better times.

Community Builder is described as 'Social websites go far beyond Facebook look-alikes and CB has literally hundreds of built-in features and can be extended with extra (free or commercial) add-ons ... There are more than 50 alternatives to Community Builder for a variety of platforms, including Web-based, Android, Self-Hosted, Linux and iPhone apps ... are mainly Social Networks but may also be Microblogs or Group Chat Apps. (Community Builder Alternatives)

On the website of the *Foundation for Intentional Communities* we do not find speeches or proclamations, but only a list of the types of communities, and a world map where to find them. Ecovillages, Communes, Cohousing, Student Coops, Spiritual and Religious, Shared Housing:

Figure 5. Open source
Source: Bedadi (n.d.)

Are you forming an intentional community? It's free to list your project in our global Directory. (Explore Intentional Communities)

Looking to learn everything there is to know about creating, growing, and monetizing an online community? (Circle.so Alternatives, 2021)

In the list, The Best White Label Community Software, Tribe Alternatives, Facebook Group Alternatives, How to Build a Community Website with WordPress.

Working on the *Children's Virtual Museum of Small Animals* (see Chapter 7) I came online across for example the *Children & Nature Network*, that's a good virtual place where to find a lot of groups, activities, experience with kids in the natural world for many years, all around the world. I met in presence "The Organic Garden Dream", during an edition of the *Global Junior Challenge* in Rome, people who actually use the Web to share ideas and methods across all the world to grow vegetables.

Passion is lifted from the earth itself by the muddy hands of the young; it travels along grass-stained sleeves to the heart. If we are going to save environmentalism and the environment, we must also save an endangered indicator species: the child in nature. (Richard Louv, Children & Nature Network)

But even things that at first glance may seem technological wonders, out of our reach, they can in some cases be managed much more decentralized than you think.

Google Street View, in the end, is just a way of assembling photographs that anyone could do. Mapillary is a community whose members make their own street view, connected to free open maps that can be loaded on the phone and are no worse than those of Google, or Bing, Here or others that have more or less large commercial companies behind.

Capture imagery with any kind of camera to put places on the map through a collaborative street-level view of the world.

Update maps with details that are not visible from aerial images, using street-level imagery from anywhere you need it.

Open up data to help everyone make better decisions about cities and roads, mobility and navigation, and autonomous driving. (mapillary, web site)

Wikipedia is the most known and successful collaborative web enterprise. Though many people who consult it probably don't think about, it is something completely different from traditional centralized publications. Everyone can write on it, and if it poses problems similar to all other manifestations of democracy, in which the freedom of individuals often clashes with the powers present in society, Wikipedia remains the proof that today we can literally publish a collective world encyclopedia, without a central editorial staff, nor illustrious curators. It seems that, finally, it contains no more errors than a traditional encyclopedia, with the significant difference that, if we find a mistake, we can immediately correct it.

Wikipedia is the world's largest multilingual free-content encyclopaedia written by users collaboratively. It is interesting to investigate why individuals have willingness to spend their time and knowledge to engage in it. (Yang & Lai, 2009)

The perspectives, unthinkable until yesterday, that the collaborative enterprises open, exploiting the potentialities of the global network, are strongly hampered by the ideology of the competition pushed to the maximum in these latest years, in the challenges of the cooks on TV, in the continuous races to those who have more likes and followers on social networks increasingly directed to the affirmation of the individuals. Common people simply do not know that they can cooperate to the satisfaction of all, and as long as the old competitive system allows someone to get rich, there is the interest of those who now occupy positions of privilege to delay any possible change as much as possible. This is where politics comes in.

But the free software economy, where customers don't pay for the product, but for the service, where the wealth doesn't come from copyright, but from human work, it proposes a model that could put a stop to the spread of extreme inequalities that characterize the contemporary world, source of growing imbalances and social conflicts, and is taken very seriously even by the most advanced companies. It is not a simple challenge of opposite sides, and something is moving for years behind the shallow surface of traditional and social media.

Some commercial enterprises such as the Microsoft Corporation have viewed the open source movement as a threat to profitability, citing alleged intellectual property infringement violations. However, other commercial entities such as IBM, Oracle, Novell, and Apple computer have embraced open source technology to conduct business operations as well as satisfy customer needs. Public appeal for open source products has been strong enough for Microsoft, through a recent public statement, to disclose that the firm wishes to "build a bridge" with the open source community. (Hedgebeth, 2007)

9. NOT A CONCLUSION, FROM THE INFORMATION TO COMMUNICATION SOCIETY

Information can be a commodity that is consumed carelessly, with news that appear "automatically" on the mobile phone, between a chat and an advertisement. Information floods us, we do not control it, and the overdose of information causes us discomfort.

Communication implies a path at least bidirectional, or multidirectional, in which we also participate, and the "news" exchange, are enriched, and in the reciprocal comparison they can get closer to reality.

Trying to put together these "Considerations on Cyber Behavior and Mass Technology in Modern Society" has been a big gamble, a step – as we say in Italy - longer than the leg ("bite off more than one can chew", the online translator suggests), because every time you deal with a topic, another one presents itself, which in turn can be addressed from an infinite number of points of view. What are the current issues and which topics are worth focusing our attention on?

Observing what people publish and trying, on various subjects, to find collaborations to do or at least think together, my general impression is that yet asking the right question today is important. Complexity is probably scary, and it seems that very few people try to deal with it, mostly with the perception of being alone in the face of the problems of the whole world.

We find a lot of research on situations and behaviors that can be monitored perfectly and so explained, but marginal and whose knowledge do not help us to live better in society. It would be useful to try to reason together, to venture hypotheses, to go beyond the claim of scientific objectivity, towards a more general "philosophical" but actual understanding of reality. We often don't do it, and so in front of the really important facts of the world everyone is arranged as he can, and in the end our action is oriented by headlines, clichés, improvised and shallow slogans.

We describe the problems as if always others were to solve them and we are resigning ourselves to an increasingly low and elementary policy that, despite all the wonderful science of which we are proud and capable, now takes often place at almost absolute levels of ignorance. Not so bad, if it would not concern a planet poised on economic and environmental disaster and war.

I tried to put together a speech starting from our relationship with technology, from the point of view of those who do not resign and who, attempting to "save the world" try to do it possibly in fine, interesting, funny ways. Not surprisingly, I rely a lot on my work with children. I mean, I ask me why in some situations I feel good or bad and, even though I can't always produce "scientific" research, I'm starting to wonder, looking for possible answers! I analyze the elements of situations, my mood taking part in street theater in Latin America or in front of the bureaucratic machinery in Italy, that even with digital means continues more and more complicated and twisted.

Which means can open new perspectives, inside or outside of structured contexts, maps diffusion, possible connections? Who uses the different means, showing methods, intentions, improvements from the mutual comparison in the individual and collective use, in cooperation more than in competition, for actual projects and not only announcements, basing on how things work and not modulating everything on the Big Brother models? Why don't we find a way to organize at least part of ourselves, about information, putting together ideas and skills in few visible and well done publications, instead of dispersing them in thousands of individualistic and losing streams in social networks? Beyond the mirror of our own phones!

Figure 6. Project Defy org

Adapting to the existing, not taking initiatives to improve things, not correcting, but internalizing the bugs, and increasingly *externalizing* our lives... What does all this have to do with a society that claims to enhance efficiency and resource optimization?

A nook is a cost-effective, self-learning environment where the learners design & define education for themselves. It's a community space that fosters curiosity, social innovation, social entrepreneurship, design thinking process and creativity. A safe space where people from abject poverty, vulnerable communities, at-risk environments can come and create relevant life goals.

Nook Hub is a combination of a Nook and a growth office. These nodal points enable us to create teams in other geographies, to allow the concept to be locally customized and spread.

The first 2 Nook Hubs are in Rwanda and Zimbabwe. Third one at Matibi, Zimbabwe is in final stages of construction. (Abhijit Sinha, Project DEFY)

Years after our first and only meeting, I reconnected with Abhijit and I had a video call with him, while I was writing this book and working on the Children Museum of insects again and on another project on children producers of information (or promoters of the future of communication!).

It's great when technology, anytime, anywhere in the world, makes it possible for us to meet people.

REFERENCES

Al-Mahdi, O. (2022). *Global Perspectives on Teacher Performance Improvement*. IGI Global. doi:10.4018/978-1-7998-9278-6

Ali, M. (2022). *Future Role of Sustainable Innovative Technologies in Crisis Management*. IGI Global. doi:10.4018/978-1-7998-9815-3

Argüelles, A. J. (2021). Technological Spotlights of Digital Transformation: Uses and Implications Under COVID-19 Conditions. In *Information Technology Trends for a Global and Interdisciplinary Research Community*. IGI Global. doi:10.4018/978-1-7998-4156-2.ch002

Beach, R. J., Beatty, J. C., Booth, K. S., Plebon, D. A., & Fiume, E. L. (1982, July). The Message is the Medium: Multiprocess Structuring of an Interactive Paint Program. *Computer Graphics*, *16*(3), 277–287. doi:10.1145/965145.801292

Bedadi, M. (n.d.). *Open Source: A collaborative ecosystem.* digitalaoban.com/benefits-of-open-source-software

Bello, M. (2023, May 25). Online communities vs social networks: What's the difference? *Amity Social Club*. amity.co/blog.

Bollier, D., & Silke Helfrich, S. (2012). The Wealth of the Commons: A World Beyond Market & State. Amherst, MA: Levellers Press.

Bondanini, G., Giorgi, G., Ariza-Montes, A., Vega-Muñoz, A., & Andreucci-Annunziata, P. (2020, November). Technostress Dark Side of Technology. *International Journal of Environmental Research and Public Health*, *17*(21), 8013. doi:10.3390/ijerph17218013 PMID:33143270

Brusila, J. (2021). Music, Digitalization, and Democracy. *Popular Music and Society*, *45*, 2022.

Carpo, M. (2023). *Beyond Digital: Design and Automation at the End of Modernity*. The MIT Press. doi:10.7551/mitpress/13958.001.0001

Chacón, A., Ponsa, P., & Angulo, C. (2021). Cognitive Interaction Analysis in Human–Robot Collaboration Using an Assembly Task. *Electronics (Basel)*, *10*(11), 1317. doi:10.3390/electronics10111317

Chakravarti, S., & Boukareva, B. (2022). *Cases on Global Innovative Practices for Reforming Education*. IGI Global. doi:10.4018/978-1-7998-8310-4

Chhabra, B. (2022). Work Role Stress and Employee Outcomes: Mediating Role of Job Satisfaction. In *Research Anthology on Changing Dynamics of Diversity and Safety in the Workforce*. IGI Global. doi:10.4018/978-1-6684-2405-6.ch067

Cipolla-Ficarra, F. (2017). Optimizing Human-Computer Interaction with Emerging Technologies. Hershey, PA: IGI Global.

Circle.so Alternatives. (2021, Mar 22). *Online Community Builders*.

Cizek, K. (2022). *Collective Wisdom: Co-Creating Media for Equity and Justice*. The MIT Press. doi:10.7551/mitpress/13394.001.0001

Community Builder Alternatives. (n.d.). alternativeto.net/software

Dahlander, L. (2009). Online Communities and Open Innovation. *Industry and Innovation*, *15*(2).

Dahlgren, P. (2013). *The Political Web: Media, Participation and Alternative Democracy*. Palgrave Macmillan. doi:10.1057/9781137326386

Davenport, T. H., & Miller, S. M. (2022). *Working with AI: Real Stories of Human-Machine Collaboration*. The MIT Press. doi:10.7551/mitpress/14453.001.0001

Derossi, A., Di Palma, E., Moses, J. A., Santhoshkumar, P., Caporizzi, R., & Severini, C. (2023, November). Avenues for non-conventional robotics technology applications in the food industry. *Food Research International, 173*(Part 1), 113265. doi:10.1016/j.foodres.2023.113265 PMID:37803578

Donada, D. (n.d.). *Le Tecnologie delle Smart Cities restituiscono ogni anno 125 ore ai cittadini. recensionedigitale.it.*

Foster, S. R., & Iaione, C. (2022). *Co-Cities: Innovative Transitions toward Just and Self-Sustaining Communities*. The MIT Press. doi:10.7551/mitpress/11702.001.0001

Garcia, D. (2021). Visualising Ethics Through Hypertext. In *Human-Computer Interaction and Technology Integration in Modern Society*. IGI Global. doi:10.4018/978-1-7998-5849-2.ch006

García-Peñalvo, F. J. (2021). Information Technology Trends for a Global and Interdisciplinary Research Community. Hershey, PA: IGI Global. doi:10.4018/978-1-7998-4156-2

Ghani, B., Memon, K. R., Han, H., Ariza-Montes, A., & Arjona-Fuentes, J. M. (2022, October 20). Work stress, technological changes, and job insecurity in the retail organization context. *Frontiers in Psychology, 13*, 918065. doi:10.3389/fpsyg.2022.918065 PMID:36483719

Gunter, D. W. (2021). *Transforming Scholarly Publishing With Blockchain Technologies and AI*. IGI Global. doi:10.4018/978-1-7998-5589-7

Guo, C. (2019). Impacts of Mobile Use on Third Agers in China. In *Impacts of Mobile Use and Experience on Contemporary Society*. IGI Global. doi:10.4018/978-1-5225-7885-7.ch002

Hart, B. (n.d.). *Multidisciplinary approach.* slideplayer.com/slide/14705593, Ppt

Hermawan, H. (2022). A Development of Web Application for Hydroponic Monitoring Systems. *E3S Web of Conferences, 348.*

Humayun, M. (2020). Smart Cities and Digital Governance. In *Employing Recent Technologies for Improved Digital Governance*. IGI Global. doi:10.4018/978-1-7998-1851-9.ch005

Jansen, K. (2009). Implicit Sociology, Interdisciplinarity and Systems Theories in Agricultural Science. *Sociologia Ruralis*. onlinelibrary.wiley.com

Johnson, P., & Punnett, I. (2022). *Redefining Journalism in an Age of Technological Advancements, Changing Demographics, and Social Issues*. IGI Global. doi:10.4018/978-1-7998-3844-9

Kalogeras, S. (2019). The Practice of Transmedia Storytelling Edutainment in Media-Rich Learning Environments. In *Technology-Supported Teaching and Research Methods for Educators*. IGI Global. doi:10.4018/978-1-5225-5915-3.ch008

Kuboja, J. M. (2019). Ever Green Generation at the Dawn of the 21st Century: Is Technology a Deciding Factor on Learning Outcomes? In *Technology-Supported Teaching and Research Methods for Educators*. IGI Global. doi:10.4018/978-1-5225-5915-3.ch012

Learn with Pokémon: Typing Adventure. (n.d.). In *Wikipedia*.

Lee, C., & Soep, E. (2023). *Code for What?: Computer Science for Storytelling and Social Justice*. The MIT Press. doi:10.7551/mitpress/13695.001.0001

MacLeod, M. (2016). What makes interdisciplinarity difficult? Some consequences of domain specificity in interdisciplinary practice. *Synthese*, *195*, 697–720.

Madaan, R. (2022). *Smart Healthcare for Sustainable Urban Development*. IGI Global. doi:10.4018/978-1-6684-2508-4

Marchisio, E. (2022). *Analyzing Multidisciplinary Uses and Impact of Innovative Technologies*. IGI Global. doi:10.4018/978-1-6684-6015-3

Mols, A. (2021). Citizen Participation in Community Surveillance: Mapping the Dynamics of WhatsApp Neighbourhood Crime Prevention Practices. In *Human-Computer Interaction and Technology Integration in Modern Society*. IGI Global. doi:10.4018/978-1-7998-5849-2.ch007

Nimrod, G. (2010, June). Seniors' Online Communities: A Quantitative Content Analysis. *The Gerontologist*, *50*(3), 382–392. doi:10.1093/geront/gnp141 PMID:19917645

Omar, A. M. (2020). Digital Era Governance and Social Media: The Case of Information Department Brunei. In *Employing Recent Technologies for Improved Digital Governance*. IGI Global. doi:10.4018/978-1-7998-1851-9.ch002

Omiunu, O. G. (2019). Adoption and Use of YouTube to Enhance Teaching and Learning of Research Methodology at the Postgraduate Level in Nigeria Universities. In *Technology-Supported Teaching and Research Methods for Educators*. IGI Global. doi:10.4018/978-1-5225-5915-3.ch001

Papadakis, S., & Kapaniaris, A. (2022). *The Digital Folklore of Cyberculture and Digital Humanities*. IGI Global. doi:10.4018/978-1-6684-4461-0

Peres, C. (2007). Great Surges of development and alternative forms of globalization. *Technology Governance and Economic Dynamics*, 15.

Philippart, M. H. (2022). Success Factors to Deliver Organizational Digital Transformation: A Framework for Transformation Leadership. *Journal of Global Information Management*, *30*(8), 1–17. doi:10.4018/JGIM.304068

Plant, R. (2004, January). Online communities. *Technology in Society*, *26*(1), 51–65. doi:10.1016/j.techsoc.2003.10.005

Reischauer, G., & Mair, J. (2018). How Organizations Strategically Govern Online Communities: Lessons from the Sharing Economy. Academy of Management Discoveries, 4(3).

Research Anthology on Remote Teaching and Learning and the Future of Online Education. Description. (2022). IGI Global.

Sandhya, T. & Swathi, P. (2017, Jun). Significance of Mobile Applications in Education System. *International Journal of Linguistics and Computational Applications, 4*(2).

Scanlon, E., Anastopoulou, S., Conole, G., & Twiner, A. (2019). Interdisciplinary Working Methods: Reflections Based on Technology-Enhanced Learning. *Frontiers in Education, 4*, 134. doi:10.3389/feduc.2019.00134

Segall, R. S., & Niu, G. (2022). *Biomedical and Business Applications Using Artificial Neural Networks and Machine Learning*. IGI Global. doi:10.4018/978-1-7998-8455-2

Shakeri, S., & Hawamdeh, S. (2022). Combating Misinformation in the Open Access Era. In *Handbook of Research on the Global View of Open Access and Scholarly Communications*. IGI Global. doi:10.4018/978-1-7998-9805-4.ch011

Shashkevich, A. (2018, March 28). Research center at Stanford uses social science inquiry to tackle solutions to current problems. *Stanford News*. news.stanford.edu

Smith, P., & Cockburn, T. (2021). *Global Business Leadership Development for the Fourth Industrial Revolution*. IGI Global.

Stevens, F. (2016). *Before the Flood*. Film, documentary.

Sugiyama, S. (2019). Human Behavior and Another Kind in Consciousness: Emerging Research and Opportunities. Hershey, PA: IGI Global. doi:10.4018/978-1-5225-8217-5

Terras, M. (2012). Being the other: Interdisciplinary Work in Computational Science and The Humanities. In *Collaborative Research in the Digital Humanities*. Routledge.

Ugliotti, F. M., & Osello, A. (2022). *Handbook of Research on Implementing Digital Reality and Interactive Technologies to Achieve Society 5.0*. IGI Global. doi:10.4018/978-1-6684-4854-0

Uplift: Online Communities Against Sexual Violence. (2017). *How to write a great code of conduct: Your community deserves the best.* medium.com/uplift-online-communities-against-sexual-violence.

Vallor, S. (2016). *Technology and the Virtues: A Philosophical Guide to a Future Worth Wanting*. Oxford University Press. doi:10.1093/acprof:oso/9780190498511.001.0001

Vaskivska, H. (2017). Interdisciplinary links as a didactic basis of the future teacher's professional training. *Головна, Архіви, 10-11.*

Williams, S. (2010). *Free as in Freedom (2.0): Richard Stallman and the Free Software Revolution*. Free Software Foundation.

Yang, H. & Lai, C. (2009). Understanding knowledge-sharing behaviour. In *Wikipedia*.

Yeromin, M. B. (2020). *Universal Codes of Media in International Political Communications: Emerging Research and Opportunities*. IGI Global.

Ziady, H. (2023, Feb 6). Britain's NHS was once idolized. Now its worst-ever crisis is fueling a boom in private health care. *CNN Business*.

ADDITIONAL READING

Czaja, S.J. & Lee, C. C. (2007, Mar). The impact of aging on access to technology. *ACM SIGACCESS Accessibility and Computing*.

Halegoua, G. (2020). *Smart Cities*. The MIT Press. doi:10.7551/mitpress/11426.001.0001

Jenkins, H. (2006). *Convergence Culture: Where Old and New Media Collide*. New York University Press.

Marciano, C. (2015). *Smart City: Lo spazio sociale della convergenza*. Editrice Nuova Cultura.

Mattern, S. (2021). *A City Is Not a Computer: Other Urban Intelligences*. Princeton University Press.

Mora, L., & Bolici, R. (2016). *Progettare la smart city. Dalla ricerca teorica alla dimensione pratica*. Maggioli.

Morin, E. (1992). From the concept of system to the paradigm of complexity. *Journal of Social and Evolutionary Systems*, *15*(4), 371–385. doi:10.1016/1061-7361(92)90024-8

Papagiannidis, S., & Marikyan, D. (2020). Smart offices: A productivity and well-being perspective. *International Journal of Information Management*, *51*(April), 102027. doi:10.1016/j.ijinfomgt.2019.10.012

Shaikh, F., Afshan, G., Anwar, R. S., Abbas, Z., & Chana, K. A. (2023, June). Analyzing the impact of artificial intelligence on employee productivity: The mediating effect of knowledge sharing and well-being. *Asia Pacific Journal of Human Resources*, *61*(4), 29. doi:10.1111/1744-7941.12385

Stichweh, R. (1999). Systems Theory as an Alternative to Action Theory? The Rise of 'Communication' as a Theoretical Option. *Acta Sociologica*.

Townsend, A. M. (2013). *Smart Cities: Big Data, Civic Hackers, and the Quest for a New Utopia*. W.W. Norton.

Visvizi, A., & Troisi, O. (2022). *Managing Smart Cities: Sustainability and Resilience Through Effective Management*. Springer International Publishing. doi:10.1007/978-3-030-93585-6

Von Bertalanffy, L. (1972). – online 2017) The History and Status of General Systems Theory. *Academy of Management Journal*, *15*(4), 407–426. doi:10.2307/255139

Compilation of References

80-90s Computing: One guy and his life with old computers of all kinds. (2017, Jan 8). swarmik.tumblr.com

DOS. (n.d.). Wikipedia. https://en.wikipedia.org/wiki/86-DOS

A short history of the web. (n.d.). home.cern/science/computing/birth-web/short-history-web.

Abandoned Mobile Apps Report. (2022). pixalate.com.

Adrian, T. (2021, Sept 27). The Future of Finance and the Global Economy: Facing Global Forces, Shaping Global Solutions. *IMF Communications Department.* imf.org/en/News.

Agarwal, A. (2023, Jun 29). *The Future of Blogging: Are Blogs Still Relevant in 2023 And Beyond?* bloggerspassion.com.

Akmam, J., & Huq, N. (2019). Living Parallel-ly in Real and Virtual: Internet as an Extension of Self. In *Multigenerational Online Behavior and Media Use: Concepts, Methodologies, Tools, and Applications.* IGI Global. doi:10.4018/978-1-5225-7909-0.ch031

Algorithm. (n.d.). In *Wikipedia.*

Ali, M. (2022). *Future Role of Sustainable Innovative Technologies in Crisis Management.* IGI Global. doi:10.4018/978-1-7998-9815-3

Allgaier. (2018, Jul). MySpace. researchgate.net.

Al-Mahdi, O. (2022). *Global Perspectives on Teacher Performance Improvement.* IGI Global. doi:10.4018/978-1-7998-9278-6

Almomani, S. (2022). *Unesco Reports 244M Children will not start school this year.* worldforgottenchildren.org.

Amadeo, R. (2014, Jun 18). *Saving old software from extinction in the age of cloud computing.* Arstechnica.com.

Amez, S., & Baert, S. (2020). Smartphone use and academic performance: A literature review. *International Journal of Educational Research, 103,* 101618. doi:10.1016/j.ijer.2020.101618

Amiga Demoscene Archive. (n.d.). ada.untergrund.net

Anderson J. & Rainie, L. (2022, Jun 30). *The metaverse will not fully emerge in the way today's advocates hope.* Pew Research Center.

Anderson, J. & Rainie, L. (2022, Jun 30). pewresearch.org.

Anonymous. (n.d.). In *Wikipedia.*

Appel, M. (2019, Oct 16). Are Social Media Ruining Our Lives? A Review of Meta-Analytic Evidence. *Sage Journals, Review of General Psychology*.

Applegate, K. (2023, Aug 30). Best Drones For Education: From Building And Flying To Coding. *eduporium.com/*blog

Arcade Game. (n.d.). In *Wikipedia*.

Argüelles, A. J. (2021). Technological Spotlights of Digital Transformation: Uses and Implications Under COVID-19 Conditions. In *Information Technology Trends for a Global and Interdisciplinary Research Community*. IGI Global. doi:10.4018/978-1-7998-4156-2.ch002

Ashford, K. (2023, Feb 16). What Is Cryptocurrency? *Forbes Advisor*.

Assisi, C. (2018, Oct 20). Paul Allen the artist versus Bill Gates the entrepreneur. *Founding Fuel*.

Ayres, R. U. (2014). *The Bubble Economy: Is Sustainable Growth Possible?* The MIT Press. doi:10.7551/mitpress/9957.001.0001

Bali, M. (2016, Feb. 3). *Knowing the Difference Between Digital Skills and Digital Literacies, and Teaching Both*. International Literary Association. literacyworldwide.org/blog.

Banerjee, M. (2023 Apr 26). *Top 25 tech firms' valuation grows $2.4 trillion in 2023, shows report*. business-standard.com.

Baptiste, A. (2019, Dec 17). Digital Skills vs. Digital Literacy. *Medium*.

Barbera. D. (2022, May 13). *App Store e Play Store sono pieni di app "abbandonate"*. wired.it/article

Barone, R. (2023, Jan 8). *Yes, Video Games are Good...for Your Mind and Body*. idtech.com/blog

Battarbee, K., & Koskinen, I. (2004). Co-experience: User experience as interaction. *International Journal of CoCreation in Design and the Arts*, *1*, 2005.

Beach, R. J., Beatty, J. C., Booth, K. S., Plebon, D. A., & Fiume, E. L. (1982, July). The Message is the Medium: Multiprocess Structuring of an Interactive Paint Program. *Computer Graphics*, *16*(3), 277–287. doi:10.1145/965145.801292

Bedadi, M. (n.d.). *Open Source: A collaborative ecosystem*. digitalaoban.com/benefits-of-open-source-software

Bedingfield, W. (2019, Sep 19). *The rise and fall of Flash, the annoying plugin that shaped the modern web*. wired.co.uk

Bello, M. (2023, May 25). Online communities vs social networks: What's the difference? *Amity Social Club*. amity.co/blog.

Beneventi, P. & Conati, D. (n.d.). *Nuova Guida di Animazione Teatrale: A Scuola e nel Tempo Libero*. Sonda.

Beneventi, P. (2001). *La Patente - Il mio Computer è una Bicicletta e si Guida senza Patente!* paolobeneventi.it/Biblioteca

Beneventi, P. (2023, Jan 18). Il successo di mercato, i videogiochi e il corpo. *Sapereambiente*.

Beneventi, P. (1999). *Come usare il computer con bambini e ragazzi*. Sonda.

Beneventi, P. (2009). *I bambini e l'Ambiente: per una Ecologia dell'Educazione*. Sonda.

Beneventi, P. (2013). The Children's Virtual Museum of Small Animals: From the Schoolyard to the Internet. In *Handbook of Research on Didactic Strategies and Technologies for Education: Incorporating Advancements*. IGI Global. doi:10.4018/978-1-4666-2122-0.ch001

Beneventi, P. (2018). *Technology and the New Generation of Active Citizens*. IGI Global. doi:10.4018/978-1-5225-3770-0

Beneventi, P. (2022). Feb 23. In *Reame del Sospetto e della Paura*. Sapereambiente.

Beneventi, P. (2022, Feb 23). *Reame del Sospetto e della Paura. sapereambiente.it.*

Beneventi, P., & Conati, D. (2010). *Nuova Guida di Animazione Teatrale.* Sonda.

Bergland, C. (2020, October 2). Why Cursive Handwriting Is Good for Your Brain. *Psychology Today.*

Berners-Lee, T. (2012). History of the Web. *World Wide Web Foundation.* webfoundation.org.

Berners-Lee, T. (2019, March 12). 30 years on, what's next #ForTheWeb*? Web Foundation.*

Berners-Lee, T., & Fischetti, M. (2000). *Weaving the Web: The Original Design and Ultimate Destiny of the World Wide Web.* Harper.

Bill Gates Mugshot. (n.d.) Wikimedia. https://commons.wikimedia.org/wiki/File:Bill_Gates_mugshot.png

Binge-watching. (n.d.). Wikipedia. https://en.wikipedia.org/wiki/Binge-watching

Biodiversity. (n.d.). *National Geographic.*

Bisogna capirsi su cosa sia "l'intelligenza artificiale." (2023, May 10), *Il Post.*

Blankenship, R. J. (2021). *Deep Fakes, Fake News, and Misinformation in Online Teaching and Learning Technologies.* IGI Global. doi:10.4018/978-1-7998-6474-5

Blu-Ray media and devices market size & share analysis - growth trends & forecasts (2023 - 2028). (n.d.). mordorintelligence.com.

Bollas, C. (2018). *Meaning and Melancholia: Life in the Age of Bewilderment.* Routledge. doi:10.4324/9781351018500

Bollier, D., & Silke Helfrich, S. (2012). The Wealth of the Commons: A World Beyond Market & State. Amherst, MA: Levellers Press.

Bondanini, G., Giorgi, G., Ariza-Montes, A., Vega-Muñoz, A., & Andreucci-Annunziata, P. (2020, November). Technostress Dark Side of Technology. *International Journal of Environmental Research and Public Health, 17*(21), 8013. doi:10.3390/ijerph17218013 PMID:33143270

Bormetti, M. (2019). *Egophonia: Gli smartphone fra noi e la vita.* Hoepli.

Boursier, V., & Manna, V. (2019). Relational Body Identities: Body Image Control Through Self-Portraits – A Revision of the Body Image Control in Photos Questionnaire. In *Intimacy and Developing Personal Relationships in the Virtual World.* IGI Global. doi:10.4018/978-1-5225-4047-2.ch003

Bowens, J. A. (2022). Developing Digital Presence for the Online Learning Environment: A Focus on Digital AVC. In *Pedagogy, Presence, and Motivation in Online Education.* IGI Global. doi:10.4018/978-1-7998-8077-6.ch003

Bozoglan, B. (2019). *Multifaceted Approach to Digital Addiction and Its Treatment.* IGI Global. doi:10.4018/978-1-5225-8449-0

Brown, B. (2023, Sep 7). *How to Copy a DVD (Protected/Homemade) on a Mac with Best Quality.* macxdvd.com.

Brown, S. J. (2023). Social Media and Social Movements: Strengths, Challenges, and Implications for the Future. In *Research Anthology on Social Media's Influence on Government, Politics, and Social Movements.* IGI Global.

Brusila, J. (2021). Music, Digitalization, and Democracy. *Popular Music and Society, 45.*

Butler, S. (2022, Feb 25). *Why Don't Smartphones Have 4K Screens Yet?* Howtogeek.com.

Capala, M. (2020 Mar 19). *Global Search Engine Market Share in the Top 15 GDP Nations (Updated for 2020).* alphametic.com.

Carbonell, J. B. (1970, Dec). AI in CAI: An Artificial-Intelligence Approach to Computer-Assisted Instruction. *IEEE Transactions on Man-Machine Systems, MMS-11*(4).

Carpo, M. (2023). *Beyond Digital: Design and Automation at the End of Modernity.* The MIT Press. doi:10.7551/mitpress/13958.001.0001

Carvalho Relva, I. (2023). Cyberbullying: A Form of Peer Violence in the Digital Era. In *Handbook of Research on Bullying in Media and Beyond.* IGI Global.

Castleman, M. (2016, Nov 3). *Dueling Statistics: How Much of the Internet Is Porn?* psychologytoday.com/us/blog/all-about-sex.

Cathie. (2022, Oct 17). The Visionary And The Genius: The Story Of Steve Jobs And Steve Wozniak. *List Foundation.*

Certi, S & Toldi, F. (1986, Jan). AI: Un passato e un futuro. *Personal Computer,* 1.

Chacón, A., Ponsa, P., & Angulo, C. (2021). Cognitive Interaction Analysis in Human–Robot Collaboration Using an Assembly Task. *Electronics (Basel), 10*(11), 1317. doi:10.3390/electronics10111317

Chakravarti, S., & Boukareva, B. (2022). *Cases on Global Innovative Practices for Reforming Education.* IGI Global. doi:10.4018/978-1-7998-8310-4

ChatGPT sul Foglio: per 30 giorni piccoli testi scritti dall'IA sul nostro giornale. (2023, Mar 7). *Il Foglio.* ilfoglio.it/tecnologia/2023/03/07

Chatting with Friends Online. (n.d.). flylib.com/books/en/2.932.1.169/1/

Chen, B. X. (2010, Oct 11). Apple Registers Trademark for 'There's an App for That'. *Wired.*

Chen, B. X. (2023, Apr 19). The Future of Social Media Is a Lot Less Social, *New York Times.*

Chhabra, B. (2022). Work Role Stress and Employee Outcomes: Mediating Role of Job Satisfaction. In *Research Anthology on Changing Dynamics of Diversity and Safety in the Workforce.* IGI Global. doi:10.4018/978-1-6684-2405-6.ch067

Chikhi, I. (2021, May 27). *Financial Influencers and Social Media: The Role of Valuable and Trusted Content in Creating a New Form of Authenticity* [Student Theses]. Baruch College, City University of New York. academicworks.cuny.edu

Children and digital technologies: Trends and outcomes. (n.d.). *Education in the Digital Age: Healthy and Happy Children.* oecd-ilibrary.org/sites.

Chomsky, N. (2023, Mar 8). The False Promise of ChatGPT. *The New York Times.*

Choudhary, A. (2019). Cybersex. In *Intimacy and Developing Personal Relationships in the Virtual World.* IGI Global. doi:10.4018/978-1-5225-4047-2.ch011

Christensen, R. et al. (2019). Creating Technology Enriched Activities to Enhance Middle School Students' Interest in STEM. *EdMedia + Innovate Learning*, Jun 24

Cinefra, V. (2021). *Game Boy, artista trasforma la console in una vera opera d'arte.* spaziogames.it/notizie

Cipolla-Ficarra, F. (2017). Optimizing Human-Computer Interaction with Emerging Technologies. Hershey, PA: IGI Global.

Cipolletta, G. (2019). Ubiquitous Bodies: A "Metrobodily" Transition From Real to Virtual. In *Virtual and Augmented Reality in Mental Health Treatment*. IGI Global. doi:10.4018/978-1-5225-7168-1.ch001

Circle.so Alternatives. (2021, Mar 22). *Online Community Builders.*

Cizek, K. (2022). *Collective Wisdom: Co-Creating Media for Equity and Justice*. The MIT Press. doi:10.7551/mit-press/13394.001.0001

Clark, M. (2020). *Dealing with information overload.* accesswdun.com.

Clark, P.A. (2021, Nov. 15). The Metaverse Has Already Arrived. Here's What That Actually Means. *Time.*

Clayton, J. (2023, May 17). *Sam Altman: CEO of OpenAI calls for US to regulate artificial intelligence.* BBC News.

Click Wealth System Reviews - Real Make Money Online Program or Fake Profits Hype? (2023, Jul.). *News Direct Blog*. newsdirect.com/guest-content

Codecademy Team. (2020, Feb 14). *MySpace and the Coding Legacy it Left Behind.* codecademy.com/resources/blog/

Collins, M. E. (2017). *The New Narcissus in the Age of Reality Television*. Routledge. doi:10.4324/9781315463490

Community Builder Alternatives. (n.d.). alternativeto.net/software

Conscious Vibe. (2023, Apr 30). *Using Your Smartphones to Avoid Human Contact (the consequences).* theconscious-vibe.com.

Content Authenticity Initiative. (n.d.). *Authentic storytelling through digital content provenance.* contentauthenticity.org.

Conversational Artificial Intelligence (CAI). (n.d.). voiceflow.com.

Cook, D., in Shah, A. (2010, November 21). Children as Consumers. *Global Issues (Washington, D.C.).* globalissues.org/article/237

Cosa significa blog? (n.d.). wikibit.it/b/cosa-significa-blog-1997/

Cottone, N. (2022, Feb 18). Bonus psicologo: l'aiuto fino a 600 euro in dieci domande e risposte. *Il Sole 24ore.*

Courtemanche, M. (2023, Jan 22). *What is DevOps? The ultimate guide*. Academic Press.

Covarrubias-Moreno, O. M. (2023). *Artificial Intelligence and Systems Thinking in the Public Sector. In Handbook of Research on Applied Artificial Intelligence and Robotics for Government Processes*. IGI Global.

Crichton, M. (1997). *The Lost World.* Knopf.

Crichton, M. (2004). *State of Fear*. HarperCollins.

Crime TV Shows. (n.d.). netflix.com.

Crumbaugh, J. (2019). Common Mistakes in Delivering Cybersecurity Awareness. In *Cybersecurity Education for Awareness and Compliance*. IGI Global. doi:10.4018/978-1-5225-7847-5.ch002

Culley, K. E. (2021). *Mariners or Machines: Who's at the Helm? Shifting Roles and Responsibilities on Navy Warships. In Human Factors Issues and the Impact of Technology on Society*. IGI Global. doi:10.4018/978-1-7998-6453-0.ch009

Cyberbullying: What is it and how to stop it. (n.d.). *Unicef.* unicef.org/end-violence/how-to-stop-cyberbullying

D'Achille, P. (2021, Sep 24). Un asterisco sul genere. *Accademia della Crusca.* accademiadellacrusca.it/it/consulenza/

Dahlander, L. (2009). Online Communities and Open Innovation. *Industry and Innovation, 15*(2).

Dahlgren, P. (2013). *The Political Web: Media, Participation and Alternative Democracy.* Palgrave Macmillan. doi:10.1057/9781137326386

Dalkir, K., & Katz, R. (2020). *Navigating Fake News, Alternative Facts, and Misinformation in a Post-Truth World.* IGI Global. doi:10.4018/978-1-7998-2543-2

Damasio, A. R. (1999). *The Feeling of what Happens: Body and Emotion in the Making of Consciousness.* Harcourt Brace.

Davenport, T. H., & Miller, S. M. (2022). *Working with AI: Real Stories of Human-Machine Collaboration.* The MIT Press. doi:10.7551/mitpress/14453.001.0001

Davis Lazarus, B. (2005). Programmed Instruction Overview. In *Encyclopedia of Distance Learning.* IGI Global. doi:10.4018/978-1-59140-555-9.ch230

de Kerckhove, D. (2023, May 11). Il linguaggio sfidato dagli algoritmi nell'era dell'IA generativa. *Media 2000.*

Deep Blue (chess computer). (n.d.). *Wikipedia.*

Definizione Di Echo Chamber. (n.d). insidemarketing.it/glossario/

Deluxe Paint Series : A Visual Arts Program if Immense Flexibility. (2020, May 18). generationamiga.com.

Derossi, A., Di Palma, E., Moses, J. A., Santhoshkumar, P., Caporizzi, R., & Severini, C. (2023, November). Avenues for non-conventional robotics technology applications in the food industry. *Food Research International, 173*(Part 1), 113265. doi:10.1016/j.foodres.2023.113265 PMID:37803578

Desjarlais, M. (2020). Online Self-Disclosure: Opportunities for Enriching Existing Friendships. In *The Psychology and Dynamics Behind Social Media Interactions.* IGI Global.

Developing Digital Literacy Skills. (n.d). webwise.ie/teachers.

Devlin Barrett, D. (2019, May 24). Some federal prosecutors disagreed with decision to charge Assange under Espionage Act. *The Washington Post.*

Digital Education Lab. (2018, Dec. 18). *Che fine ha fatto Myspace, il primo Social di successo nel web?* digitaleducationlab.it/blog.

Digital Nation. (2019 Oct 18). Your Digital Footprint Matters. *Facebook.*

Dilci, T., & Eranıl, A. K. (2019). *Handbook of Research on Children's Consumption of Digital Media.* IGI Global.

Dixit, P. (2023, Jan. 31). *Why Are AI-Generated Hands So Messed Up?* buzzfeednews.com.

Donada, D. (n.d.). *Le Tecnologie delle Smart Cities restituiscono ogni anno 125 ore ai cittadini. recensionedigitale.it.*

Donald, B. (2016, Nov 22). Stanford researchers find students have trouble judging the credibility of information online. *Research Stories.*

Döring, N. (2017, Aug). *Online Sexual Activity Experiences Among College Students: A Four-Country Comparison.* pubmed.ncbi.nlm.nih.gov

Dubbels, B. R. (2018). *Exploring the Cognitive, Social, Cultural, and Psychological Aspects of Gaming and Simulations.* IGI Global.

Duffy, B. (2021). *The Generation Myth: Why When You're Born Matters Less Than You Think.* Basic Books.

Early Mapping. (2019). "Electronic Hive Minds" on the Web and Internet. In *Electronic Hive Minds on Social Media: Emerging Research and Opportunities*. IGI Global.

eBooks: Formats & Devices. (2023). *Boston College Libraries*, web.

El-Bably, A. Y. (2021). Combating the Exploitation of Children in Cyberspace: Technical Mechanisms to Protect Children from Sexual Content. In *Combating the Exploitation of Children in Cyberspace: Emerging Research and Opportunities*. IGI Global. doi:10.4018/978-1-7998-2360-5.ch003

Epstein, S. (2023, March 15). It's harder than ever to step away from our devices, which are so entwined in our lives. Is it fruitless to even try? *BBC*. bbc.com/worklife/article

Esposito, E. (2022). *Artificial Communication: How Algorithms Produce Social Intelligence*. The MIT Press. doi:10.7551/mitpress/14189.001.0001

Essex, D. (n.d.). *What is Web 3.0 (Web3)? Definition, guide and history.* techtarget.com.

Facebook. (n.d.). *Help Center*. Facebook.

Failes, I. (2020, Jun 4). *A visual history of 3ds Max.* beforesandafters.com/

Fatai, B. (2022, Feb. 9). *What VR looked like in the 90s - The Stone Age of VR.* linkedin.com.

Felaco, C. (2023). I Correct or Canceling You: Political Correctness and Cancel Culture on Social Media – The Case of Twitter Communication in Italy. In *Research Anthology on Social Media's Influence on Government, Politics, and Social Movements*. IGI Global.

Feldman, S. (2019, Jul 24). *Digital Advertisers Increasingly Target Kids.* statista.com.

Ferri, P. (2011). *I nativi digitali, una razza in via di evoluzione*. Cronache Editoriali.

Firth, J., Torous, J., Stubbs, B., Firth, J. A., Steiner, G. Z., Smith, L., Alvarez-Jimenez, M., Gleeson, J., Vancampfort, D., Armitage, C. J., & Sarris, J. (2019, June). The "online brain": How the Internet may be changing our cognition. *World Psychiatry; Official Journal of the World Psychiatric Association (WPA)*, *18*(2), 119–129. doi:10.1002/wps.20617 PMID:31059635

Fisher, A. (2013). *Radical ecopsychology: Psychology in the service of life.* SUNY Press.

Folena, U. (2023, Mar. 9). Soli, depressi, impasticcati: il malessere di una generazione. *L'Avvenire*.

Forbidden Planet. (n.d.a). *Britannica*.

Forbidden Planet. (n.d.b). *Wikipedia*.

Foster, S. R., & Iaione, C. (2022). *Co-Cities: Innovative Transitions toward Just and Self-Sustaining Communities*. The MIT Press. doi:10.7551/mitpress/11702.001.0001

Fowler, G. A. (2019, Sep 18). You watch TV. Your TV watches back. *The Washington Post.*

Frazetti, D. G. (2017). *Social and Scientific Aspects of The Hulk.* academia.edu.

Gallagher, W. (2023, Apr 17). *How Apple owes everything to its 1977 Apple II computer.* appleinsider.com/.

Ganguly, L. (2018, Feb 27). Global Television Formats and Their Impact on Production Cultures: The Remaking of Music Entertainment Television in India. *Sage Journals*, *20*(1).

Garcia, D. (2021). Visualising Ethics Through Hypertext. In *Human-Computer Interaction and Technology Integration in Modern Society*. IGI Global. doi:10.4018/978-1-7998-5849-2.ch006

García-Peñalvo, F. J. (2021). Information Technology Trends for a Global and Interdisciplinary Research Community. Hershey, PA: IGI Global. doi:10.4018/978-1-7998-4156-2

Gates, B. (2023, Mar. 28). *Here's what the age of AI means for the world, according to Bill Gates*. World Economic Forum. weforum.org/agenda

Gee, J. M. (2003, October). What video games have to teach us about learning and literacy. *Computers in Entertainment*, *1*(1), 20. doi:10.1145/950566.950595

Geetha, S. (2021). Augmented Reality Application: AR Learning Platform for Primary Education. In *Multimedia and Sensory Input for Augmented, Mixed, and Virtual Reality*. IGI Global. doi:10.4018/978-1-7998-4703-8.ch006

Germain, S. (2021). Echo chamber (K. McClintock, Trans.). In C. Gratton, E. Gagnon-St-Pierre, & E. Muszynski (Eds.), Shortcuts: A handy guide to cognitive biases (Vol. 4). Academic Press.

Ghani, B., Memon, K. R., Han, H., Ariza-Montes, A., & Arjona-Fuentes, J. M. (2022, October 20). Work stress, technological changes, and job insecurity in the retail organization context. *Frontiers in Psychology*, *13*, 918065. doi:10.3389/fpsyg.2022.918065 PMID:36483719

Ginès i Fabrellas, A. (2021, Feb 9). Do riders have the right to know the algorithm? *Do Better*.

Giordano, C. (2019, Dec). Magic Mirror on the Wall: Selfie-Related Behavior as Mediator of the Relationship Between Narcissism and Problematic Smartphone Use. *ResearchGate*.

Global Kids Tablet Market - Industry Trends and Forecast to 2028. (n.d.). databridgemarketresearch.com/reports

Godbole, A. (2017). *Five Steps to Survive Business in Digital Era*. wns.com/perspectives/

Gong, W., & Ooi, V. B. Y. (2008). Innovations and Motivations in Online Chat. In *Handbook of Research on Computer Mediated Communication*. IGI Global. doi:10.4018/978-1-59904-863-5.ch065

Gonzalez Rodriguez, J. L. (2020, August 24). When Technology Turns Into Wasted Time: How To Get Your Productivity Back At Work. *Forbes*.

Greg, W. (n.d.). *Aligning AI Through Compassionate Dialogue*. medium.com/@gregwnotsosharp

Grierson, J. (2023, Apr 17). Photographer admits prize-winning image was AI-generated. *The Guardian*.

Griffioen, N., Scholten, H., Lichtwarck-Aschoff, A., van Rooij, M., & Granic, I. (2021, July 20). Everyone does it—differently: A window into emerging adults' smartphone use. *Humanities & Social Sciences Communications*, *8*(1), 177. doi:10.105741599-021-00863-1

Guastavigna, M. & Penge, S. (2020). *Tecnologie per lo sviluppo umano: Dialogo tra Marco Guastavigna e Stefano Penge*. Creative Commons Licence BY – SA 4.0.

Guazzaroni, G. (2019). *Virtual and Augmented Reality in Mental Health Treatment*. IGI Global. doi:10.4018/978-1-5225-7168-1

Gunter, D. W. (2021). *Transforming Scholarly Publishing With Blockchain Technologies and AI*. IGI Global. doi:10.4018/978-1-7998-5589-7

Guo, E. (2022, Dec 19). *A Roomba recorded a woman on the toilet. How did screenshots end up on Facebook?* technologyreview.com.

Guo, C. (2019). Impacts of Mobile Use on Third Agers in China. In *Impacts of Mobile Use and Experience on Contemporary Society*. IGI Global. doi:10.4018/978-1-5225-7885-7.ch002

Hague, B. N., & Loader, B. D. (1999). *Digital Democracy: Discourse and Decision Making in the Information Age*. Routledge.

Hally, M. (2005). *Electronic Brains: Stories from the Dawn of the Computer Age*. Joseph Henry Press.

Hapek, M. E. (2019). Mythologization of New Media Organizations Illustrated With the Example of Google. In *Myth in Modern Media Management and Marketing*. IGI Global. doi:10.4018/978-1-5225-9100-9.ch004

Harp, K. (2021, Mar 31). *Teaching cursive writing helps improve brain development, should be required in schools*. Columbiamissourian.com.

Hart, B. (n.d.). *Multidisciplinary approach.* slideplayer.com/slide/14705593, Ppt

Havick, J. (2000, April). The impact of the Internet on a television-based society. *Technology in Society*, *22*(2), 273–287. doi:10.1016/S0160-791X(00)00008-7

Henricks, T. (2016, Apr 4). The Broken Self: Rethinking the Idea of Alienation. *Psychology Today, Spirituality.*

Hermawan, H. (2022). A Development of Web Application for Hydroponic Monitoring Systems. *E3S Web of Conferences, 348.*

Hern, A. (2019, Mar 18). Myspace loses all content uploaded before 2016. *The Guardian.*

Hernandez, I. (2022, Oct 21). *The Current State of Website Builders (Overview & Comparisons).* dreamhost.com.

Hernández-Santaolalla, V. (2023). The Social Media Politicians: Personalisation, Authenticity, and Memes. In *Research Anthology on Social Media's Influence on Government, Politics, and Social Movements*. IGI Global.

Himanen, P. (2001). *The Hacker Ethic and the Spirit of the Information Age*. Random House.

Hirshberg, P. (2014). First the Media, Then Us: How the Internet Changed the Fundamental Nature of the Communication and Its Relationship with the Audience. *Change, 19.*

Hirsh-Pasek, K. (2018). *The New Humanism: Technology should enhance, not replace, human interactions.* brookings.edu/articles.

Hogan, A. (2019). *How crime dramas influence perception of crime* [Undergraduate Honors Thesis]. Butler University. digitalcommons.butler.edu

Holgado-Ruiz, L. (2023). Activism in the Digital Age: Social Movements Analysis Using User-Generated Content in Social Media. In *Research Anthology on Social Media's Influence on Government, Politics, and Social Movements*. IGI Global.

Horvath J. & Cameron, R. (2015). *The New Shop Class: Getting Started with 3D Printing, Arduino, and Wearable Tech*. New York: APress.

How to cope with information overload as a marketer. (n.d.). etail-week-connect.com.

How to Live Without Google: Alternatives That Protect Your Privacy. (2017, Sep 14). Spreadprivacy.com.

Humayun, M. (2020). Smart Cities and Digital Governance. In *Employing Recent Technologies for Improved Digital Governance*. IGI Global. doi:10.4018/978-1-7998-1851-9.ch005

Hu, T.-H. (2022). *Digital Lethargy: Dispatches from an Age of Disconnection.* The MIT Press. doi:10.7551/mitpress/14336.001.0001

Hyun Joo, M. (2015). Effect of Nintendo Wii Fit Exercise Program to Health-related Physical Fitness and Quality of Life among University Students. *Indian Journal of Science and Technology, 8*(8), 1-6.

Illich, I. (1978). *Toward a History of Needs.* Pantheon Books.

Intel 8080 Microcomputer Systems Users Manual. (1975, Sep.). Intel.

International study reveals smartphone use around the world. (2021, May 17). *UCL Global.* ucl.ac.uk/global/news/

Isaak, A. (2018, Oct 23). *These $1,000 smart glasses tell you the weather, read text messages and connect to Alexa.* Cnbc.com.

Jamie Mahoney, J., & Buttrey, K. M. (2022). Using Gamification to Improve Literacy Skills. In *Handbook of Research on Acquiring 21st Century Literacy Skills Through Game-Based Learning.* IGI Global. doi:10.4018/978-1-7998-7271-9.ch015

Jamieson, J. N., & Capella, K. H. (2008). *Echo Chamber: Rush Limbaugh and the Conservative Media Establishment.* Oxford University Press.

Jansen, K. (2009). Implicit Sociology, Interdisciplinarity and Systems Theories in Agricultural Science. *Sociologia Ruralis.* onlinelibrary.wiley.com

Jarrahi, M. H. (2021, Jul 1). Algorithmic management in a work context. *Sage Journals.*

Johnson, P., & Punnett, I. (2022). *Redefining Journalism in an Age of Technological Advancements, Changing Demographics, and Social Issues.* IGI Global. doi:10.4018/978-1-7998-3844-9

Jones, S. (2008). *Whose Space is MySpace? A Content Analysis of MySpace Profiles.* researchgate.net.

Jorstad, L. (2021, Jun 8). Creating Catharsis: How to Write a Story That Works. *The Novel Smithy.*

Joseph, J. J. (2021). Facebook Depression or Facebook Contentment: The Relation Between Facebook Use and Well-Being. In *Research Anthology on Mental Health Stigma, Education, and Treatment.* IGI Global. doi:10.4018/978-1-7998-8544-3.ch061

Jowitt, T. (2023, Mar 15). *TikTok Mulls Split From Beijing-Based ByteDance – Report.* silicon.co.uk

Jungst, M. (2022). Effect of Technological Insecurity on Performance Through Emotional Exhaustion: A Moderated Mediation Approach. *International Journal of Technology and Human Interaction, 18*(1), 1–15. doi:10.4018/IJTHI.300282

Kalogeras, S. (2019). The Practice of Transmedia Storytelling Edutainment in Media-Rich Learning Environments. In *Technology-Supported Teaching and Research Methods for Educators.* IGI Global. doi:10.4018/978-1-5225-5915-3.ch008

Kazlev, M. A. (2022). The Collective Unconscious and the Media Sphere: An Esoteric Analysis of the Disinformation Crisis Facing Western Civilisation. In *Handbook of Research on Global Media's Preternatural Influence on Global Technological Singularity, Culture, and Government.* IGI Global. doi:10.4018/978-1-7998-8884-0.ch004

Keller, D. (2022, Dec 5). *Software Developers: At Risk of Extinction?* [Infographic]. five.co/blog.

Keogh, B. (2023). *The Videogame Industry Does Not Exist: Why We Should Think Beyond Commercial Game Production.* The MIT Press. doi:10.7551/mitpress/14513.001.0001

King List: Egyptian Chronology and Material Relating to Surviving Ancient King Lists. (n.d.). ancientegyptfoundation.org

Koelsch, E. (n.d.). Challenging the Overuse and Misuse of 'Digital Transformation'. *The National CIO Review.*

Koffman, E. B., & Blount, S. (1975). Artificial intelligence and automatic programming in CAI. *Artificial Intelligence, 6*(3), 215–234. doi:10.1016/0004-3702(75)90001-6

Köksalan, B., & ... . (2019). Media Consuming in Children: Child Development, Babyhood (0-2), Early Childhood, Interests. In *Handbook of Research on Children's Consumption of Digital Media*. IGI Global.

Kraft, C. (2012). *User Experience Innovation: User Centered Design that Works*. New York: APress.

Kraus, S., Kanbach, D. K., Krysta, P. M., Steinhoff, M. M., & Tomini, N. (2022). Facebook and the creation of the Metaverse: Radical business model innovation or incremental transformation? *International Journal of Entrepreneurial Behaviour & Research, 28*(9), 52–77. doi:10.1108/IJEBR-12-2021-0984

Kuboja, J. M. (2019). Ever Green Generation at the Dawn of the 21st Century: Is Technology a Deciding Factor on Learning Outcomes? In *Technology-Supported Teaching and Research Methods for Educators*. IGI Global. doi:10.4018/978-1-5225-5915-3.ch012

Kumar, S. (2021). The Deep Web and Children Cyber Exploitation: Criminal Activities and Methods – Challenges of Investigation: Solutions. In *Combating the Exploitation of Children in Cyberspace: Emerging Research and Opportunities*. IGI Global. doi:10.4018/978-1-7998-2360-5.ch002

L'era del disagio psicologico. (2023, Oct 9). *La Repubblica.*

Lake Coorong. (n.d.). In *Wikipedia.*

Lapavitsas, C. (2013). The financialization of capitalism: 'Profiting without producing'. *Analysis of Urban Change, Theory, Action, 17*(6).

Lariccia, G. (2010). *Informatica della Mente. Carignano (TO)*. Book-Jay.

Larsson, N. (2018, Apr 5). Putting pen to paper: the schools nurturing a love of the written word. *The Guardian.*

Laux, C. (2020, Sep 3). Why we no longer need superheroes. *BBC*. bbc.com/culture

Learn with Pokémon: Typing Adventure. (n.d.). In *Wikipedia.*

Lee Rood, M., & Schriner, J. (2022). The Internet Never Forgets: Image-Based Sexual Abuse and the Workplace. In *Research Anthology on Child and Domestic Abuse and Its Prevention*. IGI Global. doi:10.4018/978-1-6684-5598-2.ch032

Lee, C., & Soep, E. (2023). *Code for What?: Computer Science for Storytelling and Social Justice*. The MIT Press. doi:10.7551/mitpress/13695.001.0001

Lehdonvirta, V. (2022). *Cloud Empires: How Digital Platforms Are Overtaking the State and How We Can Regain Control*. The MIT Press. doi:10.7551/mitpress/14219.001.0001

Leprince-Ringuet, D. (2020, Feb. 24). AI: It's time to tame the algorithms and this is how we'll do it, says Europe. *ZDNet.*

Leprince-Ringuet, D. (2020, February 26). AI's big problem: Lazy humans just trust the algorithms too much. *ZdNet. Innovation.*

Leung, W. C., & Wan, A. (2022). My Little Joy in Life: Posting Food on Instagram. In *Research Anthology on Usage, Identity, and Impact of Social Media on Society and Culture*. IGI Global. doi:10.4018/978-1-6684-6307-9.ch057

Lightscribe. (n.d.). In *Wikipedia.*

Lijster, T., & Celikates, R. (2019). Beyond the Echo-chamber: An Interview with Hartmut Rosa on Resonance and Alienation. Krisis, Journal for Contemporary Philosophy, 39(1).

Linshi, J. (2015, February 12). Here's What Happens to Your Facebook Account After You Die. *Time.*

Liu, Y. (2003, June). Developing a Scale to Measure the Interactivity of Websites. *Journal of Advertising Research, 43*(2), 207–216. doi:10.2501/JAR-43-2-207-216

Lombardo, T. (2015). Dec). Science Fiction: The Evolutionary Mythology of the Future. *Journal of Futures Studies, 20*(2).

Losh, E. (2022). *Selfie Democracy: The New Digital Politics of Disruption and Insurrection.* The MIT Press. doi:10.7551/mitpress/14334.001.0001

Louv, R. (2008). *Last Child in the Woods, Saving our Children from Nature-Deficit Disorder.* Algonquin Books.

Lum, K. & Chowdhury, R. (2021, Feb 26). What is an "algorithm"? It depends whom you ask. *MIT Technology Review.*

Lum, H. C. (2021). Exploring Technology Tendencies and Their Impact on Human-Human Interactions. In *Human Factors Issues and the Impact of Technology on Society.* IGI Global. doi:10.4018/978-1-7998-6453-0.ch010

MacLeod, M. (2016). What makes interdisciplinarity difficult? Some consequences of domain specificity in interdisciplinary practice. *Synthese, 195*, 697–720.

Madaan, R. (2022). *Smart Healthcare for Sustainable Urban Development.* IGI Global. doi:10.4018/978-1-6684-2508-4

Maida, A. (1993, Mar 25). Storie da Videogiochi. *La Repubblica.*

Malick, J. (2016, Oct 30). Dario Fo's Politics of Subversive Laughter. *Wire, The Arts.*

Malicki-Sanchez, K. (2020). Out of Our Minds: Ontology and Embodied Media in a Post-Human Paradigm. In *Handbook of Research on the Global Impacts and Roles of Immersive Media.* IGI Global. doi:10.4018/978-1-7998-2433-6.ch002

Mancuso, S. (2017). *Plant Revolution.* Giunti.

Mao, A., & Raguram, A. (2009, October-December). Online infidelity: The new challenge to marriages. *Indian Journal of Psychiatry, 51*(4), 302–304. doi:10.4103/0019-5545.58299 PMID:20048458

Maragliano, R. (1996). *Esseri Multimediali: Immagini del Bambino di Fine Millennio.* La Nuova Italia.

Marani, G. (2016). *La calligrafia al tempo del digitale. Un convegno internazionale a Milano.* Artribune. artribune.com/editoria

Marchisio, E. (2022). *Analyzing Multidisciplinary Uses and Impact of Innovative Technologies.* IGI Global. doi:10.4018/978-1-6684-6015-3

Margulies, M. (2020, Sep 21). Kids Need Superheroes Now More Than Ever: If Captain America can defeat the Red Skull, a child can conquer her anxiety of a Zoom class. *The New York Times.*

Mariano, J. (2021, Feb 7). Too old for technology? Stereotype threat and technology use by older adults. *Behaviour & Information Technology, 41*(7).

Martin, J. (2023). Comics and Community: Exploring the Relationship Between Society, Education, and Citizenship. In *Exploring Comics and Graphic Novels in the Classroom.* IGI Global.

Marzano, G. (2022). Creativity: An Overview; Social Creativity; The Arts, Creativity, and Digital Technologies; Creativity Research in the Digital Age: Current Trends. In *Sustaining Creativity and the Arts in the Digital Age*. IGI Global. doi:10.4018/978-1-7998-7840-7

Massini, S. (2023, Jun 2). La Radice del male. *La Repubblica*.

Matthew 18:3. *Gospel*.

Maulana, I. (2019). Big Brothers Are Seducing You: Consumerism, Surveillance, and the Agency of Consumers. In *Handbook of Research on Consumption, Media, and Popular Culture in the Global Age*. IGI Global. doi:10.4018/978-1-5225-8491-9.ch004

May 9th Is Goku Day! Here's All the Information You Need!! (2021, May 9). Dragon Ball, official site.

Mazzucchelli, C. (2015). *E guardo il mondo da un display*. Delos Digital.

McCarthy, J., & Wright, P. (2004). Technology as experience. *Interactions (New York, N.Y.)*, *11*(5), 42–43. doi:10.1145/1015530.1015549

McCracken, H. (2014, April 29). Fifty Years of BASIC, the Programming Language That Made Computers Personal. *Time*.

McKendrick, J. (2022, Dec. 28). *It's the end of programming as we know it – again*. zdnet.com/topic/business.

McLuhan, M. (1964). *Understanding Media: The Extensions of Man*. McGraw Hill.

McLuhan, M., & Fiore, Q. (1967). *The Medium Is the Massage: An Inventory of Effects*. Random House.

McNabb, M. (2021, Aug 02). Drones in Elementary Education: How the 2020 Cabell County's Teacher of the Year Makes it Work. *dronelife.com*.

Media, Globalization, and Television. (2013, Dec). afghanpopculture.wordpress.com

Melissa, R. (2023, Oct). *IFR World Robotics 2023 Key Takeaways*. statzon.com/insights

Melonashi, E. (2019). Social Media and Identity: Understanding Identity Communication and Creation Through Social Media. In *Internet and Technology Addiction: Breakthroughs in Research and Practice*. IGI Global. doi:10.4018/978-1-5225-8900-6.ch001

Mihăeş, L. C. (2021). *Handbook of Research on Contemporary Storytelling Methods Across New Media and Disciplines*. IGI Global. doi:10.4018/978-1-7998-6605-3

Mikhaylova, G. M. S. (2014, Dec). *The "Anonymous" Movement: Hacktivism as an Emerging Form of Political Participation* [Master's thesis]. Texas State University.

Milivojević, T. & Ercegovac, I. (2014, Jan.). *Selfie or virtual mirror to new Narcissus*. ResearchGate.

Miller, D. (2021). *The Global Smartphone*. UCL Press. doi:10.2307/j.ctv1b0fvh1

Modern Technology as a Status Symbol. (2016, Aug 26). southuniversity.edu/news-and-blog

Mohan Kumar, L. (2022, Dec 24). Kletskassa': Know How This Dutch Supermarket's Slow-Moving Cash Counters Are Helping Combat Loneliness Among Elderly. *The Logical Indian Crew*.

Mols, A. (2021). Citizen Participation in Community Surveillance: Mapping the Dynamics of WhatsApp Neighbourhood Crime Prevention Practices. In *Human-Computer Interaction and Technology Integration in Modern Society*. IGI Global. doi:10.4018/978-1-7998-5849-2.ch007

Morrow, T. (2018, Mar 5). *12 Risks, Threats, & Vulnerabilities in Moving to the Cloud.* Software Engineering Institute, Carnegie Mellon University.

Munari, B. (1978). *Disegnare un Albero*. Zanichelli.

Munari, B. (1989). *Nei Disegni di una Foglia: Ambiente, lezione numero uno*. Comune di Milano – Cariplo.

Munger, K. (2023, May 22). Ban LLMs Using First-Person Pronouns. *Crooked Timber*.

Niemelä-Nyrhinen, N. (2007, August 7). Baby boom consumers and technology: Shooting down stereotypes. *Journal of Consumer Marketing*, *24*(5), 305–312. doi:10.1108/07363760710773120

Nimrod, G. (2010, June). Seniors' Online Communities: A Quantitative Content Analysis. *The Gerontologist*, *50*(3), 382–392. doi:10.1093/geront/gnp141 PMID:19917645

Noor. (2022, March 31). *How to Automate Video Editing? Best Automated Video Editors.* Rav.ai.

Nur Erdem, M. (2020). *Handbook of Research on Aestheticization of Violence, Horror, and Power*. IGI Global.

OctaMED v6 & Sound Studio. (1996, Apr). Soundonsound.com.

Oliveira, A. (n.d.). *DevOps: What It Is and Why It Matters*. Toptal Insights. toptal.com/insights

Oliveira, L. (2019). Sedated by the Screen: Social Use of Time in the Age of Mediated Acceleration. In *Managing screen time in an online society*. IGI Global. doi:10.4018/978-1-5225-8163-5.ch001

Ollagnier-Beldame, M. (2020, December 2). A Body of Knowledge: The Role of Human Experience and the Living Body in Knowing. *Journal of Humanistic Psychology*. journals.sagepub.com

Omar, A. M. (2020). Digital Era Governance and Social Media: The Case of Information Department Brunei. In *Employing Recent Technologies for Improved Digital Governance*. IGI Global. doi:10.4018/978-1-7998-1851-9.ch002

Omiunu, O. G. (2019). Adoption and Use of YouTube to Enhance Teaching and Learning of Research Methodology at the Postgraduate Level in Nigeria Universities. In *Technology-Supported Teaching and Research Methods for Educators*. IGI Global. doi:10.4018/978-1-5225-5915-3.ch001

Original Apple computer built by Steve Jobs and Steve Wozniak sells for $400k. (2021, Nov 10). moneycontrol.com/news/trends

Our democracy is only as good as the information that voters have. (2022). ippi.org.il

Ozkaya, I. (2019, May-June). Ethics Is a Software Design Concern. *IEEE Software*, *36*(3), 4–8. doi:10.1109/MS.2019.2902592

Packham, A. (2020, Sep 8). One in four students unable to access online learning during lockdown – survey. *The Guardian*.

Panettieri, J. (2023, Apr 27). *Huawei: Banned and Permitted In Which Countries? List and FAQ*. channele2e.com.

Papadakis, S., & Kapaniaris, A. (2022). *The Digital Folklore of Cyberculture and Digital Humanities*. IGI Global. doi:10.4018/978-1-6684-4461-0

Pauxtis, A. (2009). Google: Technological Convenience vs. Technological Intrusion. In *Online Consumer Protection: Theories of Human Relativism*. IGI Global. doi:10.4018/978-1-60566-012-7.ch001

Pearl, M. (2022, Dec 23). *TikTok admits to spying on U.S. users as effort to ban the app heats up*. mashable.com/article.

Penge, S. (2017). *Lingua, programmi e creatività: Coding con le materie umanistiche*. Anicia.

Peres, C. (2007). Great Surges of development and alternative forms of globalization. *Technology Governance and Economic Dynamics*, 15.

Personal Computer. (n.d.). Wikipedia. https://en.wikipedia.org/wiki/Personal_computer

Philippart, M. H. (2022). Success Factors to Deliver Organizational Digital Transformation: A Framework for Transformation Leadership. *Journal of Global Information Management, 30*(8), 1–17. doi:10.4018/JGIM.304068

Pierluigi Riti, P. (2018, Jan 18). *Introduzione al Devops.* italiancoders.it.

Pietilä, V. (1970). Alienation and Use of the Mass Media. *Acta Sociologica, 13*(4), 237-252.

Pittaro, M. (2020). Cyberbullying in Adolescence: Victimization and Adolescence. In *Developing Safer Online Environments for Children: Tools and Policies for Combatting Cyber Aggression.* IGI Global. doi:10.4018/978-1-7998-1684-3.ch006

PlantNet: l'app gratuita che riconosce le piante. (2021, May 22). ogigia.altervista.org/Portale/articoli/48-software

Plant, R. (2004, January). Online communities. *Technology in Society, 26*(1), 51–65. doi:10.1016/j.techsoc.2003.10.005

Popescu, F., & Scarlat, C. (2017). *Human Digital Immortality: Where Human Old Dreams and New Technologies Meet. In Research Paradigms and Contemporary Perspectives on Human-Technology Interaction.* IGI Global. doi:10.4018/978-1-5225-1868-6.ch012

Prensky, M. (2001, Oct). Digital Natives, Digital Immigrants. *On the Horizon, 9*(5).

Preston, R. (2023, Jun 8). *What Are Digital Skills? (And Why They're Important).* indeed.com/career-advice/career-development

Rabideau, C. (2019, March 24). *Website vs. Social Media: Which Is Better for Your Brand?* wordpress.com/go/digital-marketing.

Rawat, R. (2022). *Using Computational Intelligence for the Dark Web and Illicit Behavior Detection.* IGI Global. doi:10.4018/978-1-6684-6444-1

Raymond, E. S. (1999). *The Cathedral and the Bazaar.* O'Reilly. doi:10.100712130-999-1026-0

Recalcati, M. (2014). *L'ora di lezione. Per un'erotica dell'insegnamento.* Einaudi.

Reichental, A. (2018, Jun 1). How 3D Printing Is Reviving Craftsmanship Across The Globe. *Forbes.*

Reischauer, G., & Mair, J. (2018). How Organizations Strategically Govern Online Communities: Lessons from the Sharing Economy. Academy of Management Discoveries, 4(3).

Renieris, E. M. (2023). *Beyond Data: Reclaiming Human Rights at the Dawn of the Metaverse.* The MIT Press. doi:10.7551/mitpress/14119.001.0001

Research Anthology on Fake News, Political Warfare, and Combatting the Spread of Misinformation. (2021). IGI Global.

Research Anthology on Remote Teaching and Learning and the Future of Online Education. Description. (2022). IGI Global.

Roales, F. (2023, Mar 31). The Metaverse Gets the Hollywood Treatment. *Creative Insights.* creativeinsights.gettyimages.com

Robertson, A. & Peters, J. (2021, Oct 4). *What is the metaverse, and do I have to care?* theverge.com.

Rogers, B. (2023). *Data and Democracy at Work: Advanced Information Technologies, Labor Law, and the New Working Class*. The MIT Press. doi:10.7551/mitpress/11253.001.0001

Rosemberg, E. (2023, Feb 28). *What Happens When A Crypto Exchange Goes Bankrupt?* investopedia.com.

Rosen, J. (2017, August). Gender quotas for women in national politics: A comparative analysis across development thresholds. *Social Science Research, 66*, 82–101. doi:10.1016/j.ssresearch.2017.01.008 PMID:28705365

Ross Arguedas. (2022). *Echo chambers, filter bubbles, and polarisation: A literature review.* reutersinstitute.politics.ox.ac.uk

Rothwell, J. (2019, Jul 25). You Are What You Watch? The Social Effects of TV. *The New York Times.*

Roy, M. (2020). *Sustainable Development Strategies: Engineering, Culture and Economics.* Elsevier.

Sakurai, R. (2017). *Correcting aspect ratio distortion of natural images by convolutional neural network.* ieeexplore.ieee.org/document/7992894. 14th International Conference on Ubiquitous Robots and Ambient Intelligence (URAI)

Salaudeenm, M. A., & Onyech, N. (2020). Digital media vs mainstream media: Exploring the influences of media exposure and information preference as correlates of media credibility. *Cogent Arts & Humanities, 7*(1).

Salem, A. & Gadhi, S. (2020). *The Evolution of Technology Consumption.* techtrends.tech. Quantela.com.

Sandhya, T. & Swathi, P. (2017, Apr-Jun). Significance of Mobile Applications in Education System. *International Journal of Linguistics and Computational Applications, 4*(2).

Sandhya, T. & Swathi, P. (2017, Jun). Significance of Mobile Applications in Education System. *International Journal of Linguistics and Computational Applications, 4*(2).

Sandner, D. (2022). The Discomfort in Society or: The Shift of the Socio-structural Boundaries. In *Society and the Unconscious: Cultural Psychological Insights*. Springer. doi:10.1007/978-3-662-66175-8_13

Santos, I. N., & Azevedo, J. (2019). Running after time: temporality, technology, and power. In *Managing screen time in an online society*. IGI Global. doi:10.4018/978-1-5225-8163-5.ch002

Saptasagar, K. A. (2022). Effects of Digital Technology on Adolescents: Pros and Cons. In *Impact and Role of Digital Technologies in Adolescent Lives*. IGI Global. doi:10.4018/978-1-7998-8318-0.ch002

Satyendra. (2013 Dec 8). *Comparison between Hierarchical and Flat Organization Structures.* ispatguru.com

Scanlon, E., Anastopoulou, S., Conole, G., & Twiner, A. (2019). Interdisciplinary Working Methods: Reflections Based on Technology-Enhanced Learning. *Frontiers in Education, 4*, 134. doi:10.3389/feduc.2019.00134

Schou Andreassen, C. (2015). Online Social Network Site Addiction: A Comprehensive Review. *Current Addiction Reports, 2*(2), pages175–184. doi:10.100740429-015-0056-9

Scroxton, A. (2023). *UK TikTok ban gives us all cause to consider social media security.* Computerweekly.com.

Segall, R. S., & Niu, G. (2022). *Biomedical and Business Applications Using Artificial Neural Networks and Machine Learning*. IGI Global. doi:10.4018/978-1-7998-8455-2

Seifert, T., & Miara, I. (2019). The Effect of Social Networks on Relationships Outside the Network. In *Intimacy and Developing Personal Relationships in the Virtual World.* IGI Global. doi:10.4018/978-1-5225-4047-2.ch012

Şenel, S. (2021). Change of Good and Evil Concepts in Fantasy Genre. In *International Perspectives on Rethinking Evil in Film and Television.* IGI Global. doi:10.4018/978-1-7998-4778-6.ch003

Serafini, M. (2021). *Sostenere la sostenibilità* [Master Thesis]. Università Nicolà Cusano – telematica, Roma.

Shakeri, S., & Hawamdeh, S. (2022). Combating Misinformation in the Open Access Era. In *Handbook of Research on the Global View of Open Access and Scholarly Communications*. IGI Global. doi:10.4018/978-1-7998-9805-4.ch011

Shashkevich, A. (2018, March 28). Research center at Stanford uses social science inquiry to tackle solutions to current problems. *Stanford News*. news.stanford.edu

Shoam, A. (2022, Feb 22). *What Ever Happened to GeoCities?* Techspot.com.

Sinha, A. (2019). *Project Defy*. Academic Press.

Sitemap generator. (n.d.). lucidchart.com/pages/examples

Siu, K. (2023, Sep 22). *3D Printing for Kids*. teachyourkidscode.com

Small, G., & Vorgan, G. (2015). iBrain: Surviving the Technological Alteration of the Modern Mind. *Education Review*.

Smith, D. C. (1994, July). KIDSIM: Programming Agents Without a Programming Language. *Communication of Association Computer Machinery*, *37*(7).

Smith, P., & Cockburn, T. (2021). *Global Business Leadership Development for the Fourth Industrial Revolution*. IGI Global.

Snapes, L. (2023, Oct 26). The Beatles: 'final' song Now and Then to be released thanks to AI technology. *The Guardian*.

Soares, C., & Simão, E. (2019). Immersive Multimedia in Information Revolution. In *Trends, Experiences, and Perspectives in Immersive Multimedia and Augmented Reality*. IGI Global. doi:10.4018/978-1-5225-5696-1.ch009

Söderberg, J. (2022). *Resistance to the Current: The Dialectics of Hacking*. The MIT Press. doi:10.7551/mitpress/13466.001.0001

Sohn, S. Y., Rees, P., Wildridge, B., Kalk, N. J., & Carter, B. (2019). Prevalence of problematic smartphone usage and associated mental health outcomes amongst children and young people: A systematic review, meta-analysis and GRADE of the evidence. *BMC Psychiatry*, *19*(1), 356. doi:10.118612888-019-2350-x PMID:31779637

Souza, I. et al. (2018). A Systematic Review on the use of LEGO® Robotics in Education. *researchgate.net*/publication

Steeds, M., Clinch, S., & Jay, C. (2021, August-December). Device uses and device stereotypes. *Computers in Human Behavior Reports*, *4*, 100100. doi:10.1016/j.chbr.2021.100100

Stefanoni, F. (2019, Oct 24). Mattarella: «Covid e guerre, il mondo in tre anni cambiato in peggio. Evitare escalation in Medio Oriente». *Il Corriere della Sera*.

Stevens, F. (2016). *Before the Flood*. Film, documentary.

Stocchi, Pourazad, N., Michaelidou, N., Tanusondjaja, A., & Harrigan, P. (2021). Marketing research on Mobile apps: Past, present and future. *Journal of the Academy of Marketing Science*, *50*(2), pages195–225. doi:10.100711747-021-00815-w PMID:34776554

Stop Facebook Unverified Memorialized Accounts. (2022). Facebook.

Straubhaar, J. D. (2007). *World Television: From Global to Local*. The University of Texas. doi:10.4135/9781452204147

Sugiyama, S. (2019). Human Behavior and Another Kind in Consciousness: Emerging Research and Opportunities. Hershey, PA: IGI Global. doi:10.4018/978-1-5225-8217-5

Supremecreature. (2012, Oct 9). *The Hacker Ethic.* supremecreature.wordpress.com

Sweeney, P. (2015, February 26). How Globalisation And Technology Drive Insecurity. *Social Europe.*

Swords, J., Laing, M., & Cook, I. R. (2021). Platforms, sex work and their interconnectedness. *Sage Journals. Sexualities, 26*(3), 277–297. doi:10.1177/13634607211023013

TechTarget. + ev. (2023, May 11). *Il linguaggio sfidato dagli algoritmi nell'era dell'IA generativa.* Media 2000.

Terras, M. (2012). Being the other: Interdisciplinary Work in Computational Science and The Humanities. In *Collaborative Research in the Digital Humanities.* Routledge.

Testa, A. (2023, Feb 26). Che succede con l'intelligenza artificiale? *Nuovo e utile: teorie e pratiche della creatività.* nuovoeutile.it

Tezcan, U. T. (2019). Popular Culture and Peer Effects in Consumption: Survey of Economic Consequences. In *Handbook of Research on Consumption, Media, and Popular Culture in the Global Age.* IGI Global. doi:10.4018/978-1-5225-8491-9.ch002

The Globalization of Television. (2015). electricgargle.blogspot.com

The Instagram vs. TikTok Showdown Continues Plus 9 Other Updates. (2023, Apr 3). ohmydigitalagency.com.au

The Jetsons. (n.d.). *Wikipedia.* https://en.wikipedia.org/wiki/The_Jetsons

The Origins of The Italian Language. (n.d.). kwintessential.co.uk

The Philosophy of Computer Science. (2013-2021). *Stanford Encyclopedia of Philosophy.*

The State of TV and Video Advertising. (2022). *MediaRadar Blog.*

Till, B., Arendt, F., & Niederkrotenthaler, T. (2021, July 21). The Relationship Between Crime-Related Television Viewing and Perceptions of the Death Penalty: Results of a Large Cross-Sectional Survey Study. *Frontiers in Psychology, 12,* 715657. doi:10.3389/fpsyg.2021.715657 PMID:34367036

Timeline of events associated with Anonymous. (n.d.). In *Wikipedia.*

Time-sharing. (n.d.). Wikipedia. https://en.wikipedia.org/wiki/Time-sharing

Tindle, A. (2019, Aug 12). *The Steve Wozniak Guide to Building Better Software: Software development insights from the man who started the personal computing revolution.* medium.com.

Tomatis, J. (2019, Mar 19). Perché la cancellazione di MySpace è terrificante. *Giornale della musica.*

Topham, G., & Smith, H. (2019, Mar 29). Investigators 'believe Ethiopian 737 Max's anti-stall system activated'. *The Guardian.*

Torres, M. (2022, Oct 20). Do We Really Need To Cover Up Our Laptop Camera Lens For Privacy? *Huffpost.*

Triggs, R. (2017, March 18). *Do we really want an app for everything?* androidauthority.com.

Tripathi, A. K. (2017). Bodies and Technologies: Transformation of Human Experience. *Quadranti –. Rivista Internazionale di Filosofia Contemporanea, 5*(1-2), 102.

Trivedi, K. (2020, Aug 27). *Oedipus Rex Tragic Hero Comparison to Jon Snow of Game of Throne.* coursehero.com.

Tucci, L., & Needle, D. (2023, Sep 18). *What is the metaverse? An explanation and in-depth guide.* techtarget.com.

Tucker, C. D. (2020, Apr. 23). *What is DevOps?* carldeantucker.com/blog/

Turnacioglu, S. (2019). The State of Virtual and Augmented Reality Therapy for Autism Spectrum Disorder (ASD). In *Virtual and Augmented Reality in Mental Health Treatment.* IGI Global. doi:10.4018/978-1-5225-7168-1.ch008

Turner, R. (2020). *Microsoft Open-Sources GW-BASIC.* devblogs.microsoft.com/commandline

Ubaradka, A., Fathima, A., & Batra, S. (2023). Psychological Correlates of Perfectionistic Self-Presentation Among Social Media Users. *International Journal of Cyber Behavior, Psychology and Learning, 13*(1), 1–13. doi:10.4018/IJCBPL.324089

Ugliotti, F. M., & Osello, A. (2022). *Handbook of Research on Implementing Digital Reality and Interactive Technologies to Achieve Society 5.0.* IGI Global. doi:10.4018/978-1-6684-4854-0

Uplift: Online Communities Against Sexual Violence. (2017). *How to write a great code of conduct: Your community deserves the best.* medium.com/uplift-online-communities-against-sexual-violence.

Urwin, M. (2023, Sep 12). *AI Taking Over Jobs: What to Know About the Future of Jobs.* builtin.com.

Uzelli Yilmaz, D. (2020). Nursing Education in the Era of Virtual Reality. In *Virtual and Augmented Reality in Education, Art, and Museums.* IGI Global. doi:10.4018/978-1-7998-1796-3.ch003

Valdambrini, A. (2023, Jun 21). Intelligenza artificiale: la Ue alla ricerca del centro di gravità permanente. *Sapereambiente.*

Vallor, S. (2016). *Technology and the Virtues: A Philosophical Guide to a Future Worth Wanting.* Oxford University Press. doi:10.1093/acprof:oso/9780190498511.001.0001

Van Zanten, N. (2017, Oct 12). *Zoho One Review: Shifting Software from Commodity to Utility.* zbrains.net.

Vanni, G. (2022, Aug 1). Dark web: cos'è, che contenuti si trovano, perché è pericoloso. *HTML.it Magazine.* html.it/approfondimenti/.

Vaskivska, H. (2017). Interdisciplinary links as a didactic basis of the future teacher's professional training. *Головна, Архіви, 10-11.*

Vienna Manifesto on Digital Humanism. (2019). *The Digital Humanism Initiative.* caiml.dbai.tuwien.ac.at

Waisbord, S. (2004, Nov). McTV: Understanding the Global Popularity of Television Formats. *Sage Journals, 5*(4).

Wajcman, J. (2014). The Time–Pressure Paradox. In *Pressed for Time: The Acceleration of Life in Digital Capitalism.* The University of Chicago Press.

Walther, J. B., & Jang, J.-W. (2012). Communication Processes in Participatory Websites. *Journal of Computer-Mediated Communication, 18*(1), 2–15. doi:10.1111/j.1083-6101.2012.01592.x

Wegmann, E., Stodt, B., & Brand, M. (2015). Addictive use of social networking sites can be explained by the interaction of Internet use expectancies, Internet literacy, and psychopathological symptoms. *Journal of Behavioral Addictions, 4*(3), 155–162. doi:10.1556/2006.4.2015.021 PMID:26551905

Welsh, M. (2023, January). The End of Programming. *Communications of the ACM, 66*(1), 34–35. doi:10.1145/3570220

What is your favorite type of Hive Mind ? (n.d.). reddit.com/r/sciencefiction/

What to make of cryptocurrencies and blockchains. (2018, Aug 30). *The Economist.*

Wheeler, S. K. (2015, Apr 20). *The Relationships Between Television Viewing Behaviors, Attachment, Loneliness, Depression, and Psychological WellBeing* [Honors College Theses]. Georgia Southern University. digitalcommons.georgiasouthern.edu

Why tomorrow's professions will be increasingly scientific yet also more & humanistic. (2021, Apr 12). morningfuture.com.

Williams, S. (2010). *Free as in Freedom (2.0): Richard Stallman and the Free Software Revolution.* Free Software Foundation.

Wintermeyer, L. (2022, Aug 25). Web3 Will Make Or Break Social Media. *Forbes Digital Assets.*

Working with aspect ratio. (2023, Aug 23). helpx.adobe.com/il_he/premiere-pro

Wright, M. F. (2020). Negative Psychological Outcomes Associated With Emerging Adults' Cyber Aggression Involvement. In *Recent Advances in Digital Media Impacts on Identity, Sexuality, and Relationships.* IGI Global. doi:10.4018/978-1-7998-1063-6.ch001

Yang, H. & Lai, C. (2009). Understanding knowledge-sharing behaviour. In *Wikipedia.*

Yeromin, M. B. (2020). *Universal Codes of Media in International Political Communications: Emerging Research and Opportunities.* IGI Global.

Young, D. G. (2014, Sep 2). Theories and Effects of Political Humor: Discounting Cues, Gateways, and the Impact of Incongruities. In *The Oxford Handbook of Political Communication.* Oxford University Press.

Ziady, H. (2023, Feb 6). Britain's NHS was once idolized. Now its worst-ever crisis is fueling a boom in private health care. *CNN Business.*

Zoller Seitz, M. (2016, Aug 19). *War Dogs.* rogerebert.com

About the Author

Paolo Beneventi, from 1981 to 1985, takes part in the group of animazione / visual communication L'Alfabeto of Brescia, and later he goes on as a freelancer, deepening with children and young people projects coming from the rich vein of animazione teatrale, in a meaningful, cognitive and teaching way. He has been developing experiences of meeting books, the natural and human environment, as well as technological means of communication and networking. In collaboration with schools, libraries and agencies operating in the society, has created numerous products (books, videos, CD ROMs, web pages), closely correlated with the characteristics of truly multimedia experience of animazione * (body + image + text + sound + video). * animazione teatrale in Italy is something like "creative dramatics", but with a much more extended meaning. It was a big movement in the Seventies and many people goes on with it in advanced educational experiences.

Index

I

K

L

M

N

P

S

T

U

V

W

Y

Printed in the United States
by Baker & Taylor Publisher Services